Cloud-IoT Technologies in Society 5.0

Kamta Nath Mishra Ph.D. •
Subhash Chandra Pandey Ph.D.

Cloud-IoT Technologies in Society 5.0

 Springer

Kamta Nath Mishra Ph.D.
Department of Computer Science and
Engineering
Birla Institute of Technology
Jharkhand, India

Subhash Chandra Pandey Ph.D.
Department of Computer Science and
Engineering
Birla Institute of Technology
Jharkhand, India

ISBN 978-3-031-28713-8   ISBN 978-3-031-28711-4   (eBook)
https://doi.org/10.1007/978-3-031-28711-4

This Springer imprint is published by the registered company Springer Nature Switzerland AG
The registered company address is: Gewerbestrasse 11, 6330 Cham, Switzerland

*The author Dr. Kamta Nath Mishra dedicated this book to his mother **Late Dev Kali Devi,** his father **Shri Ram Nath Mishra,** and the **Almighty**.*

*The author Dr. Subhash Chandra Pandey dedicated this book to his mother **Late Prabhawati Pandey** and his father **Late Vindhya Basini Pandey**.*

List of Advisers/Recommenders

Prof. Anupam Agrawal, Professor & Head, Human-Computer Interaction Division, Indian Institute of Information Technology, Allahabad, India	**Prof. G. C. Nandi,** Professor & Dean, Indian Institute of Information Technology, Allahabad, India
Dr. Ramjee Prasad, Professor, Department of Computer Science, Albarga University, Denmark **Prof. Srinivas Singh,** Director, ABV-Indian Institute of Information Technology & Mgmnt, Gwalior, India	**Prof. (Dr.) G. Sahoo,** Professor, Department of Computer Science & Engg., Indian Institute of Technology -ISM Dhanbad, India **Prof. (Dr.) Sandip Dutta,** Professor, CSE, B.I.T. Mesra, India
Dr. P. K. Mahanti, Professor, Department of Statistics & Computing, University of New Brunswick, Canada	**Prof. R. K. Singh,** Professor of Computer Science & Dean, Indira Gandhi Technical University for Woman, Delhi, India
Dr. Naveen Garg, Professor, Department of Computer Science & Engg., Indian Institute of Technology, Delhi, India	**Prof. Arun Kumar Sharma,** Professor & Head, Department of Computer Science & Engg., Indira Gandhi Technical University for Woman, Delhi, India
Dr. Meena Jha, Course Coordinator- ICT School of Engineering and Technology, Central Queensland University, Australia	**Prof. (Dr.) Edries Abdehadi,** Head of Postgraduate Office, Department of Information Technology, University of Tripoli
Dr. Antonio J. Jara, CEO at HOPU (Smart Cities / Air Quality) Ceuti, Región de Murcia, Spain	**Prof. (Dr.) Alok Mishra,** Professor, Data Management & Software Engineering, Norwegian University of Science & Technology, Norway.
Dr. Dhananjay Singh, Professor of Computer Science, Hankuk (Korea) University of Foreign Studies, South Korea	**Prof. R. C. Jha,** Professor of Electrical Engg., Birla Institute of Technology, Mesra Ranchi, India
Prof. P. K. Jana, Professor, Department of Computer Sc. & Engg., Indian Institute of Technology (IIT-ISM), Dhanbad, India	**Prof. Vir Bahadur Singh,** Professor, Department of Computer & System Sciences, Jawaharlal Nehru University, Delhi, India
Dr. Antonio M. Alberti, Professor, INATEL - National Institute of Telecommunications, Brazil	**Prof. Vinay Sharma,** Professor of Production & Manufacturing Engg., B.I.T. Mesra, India

Prof. Sanjay Kumar Dwivedi, Professor & Head, Department of Computer Science, Bhim Rao Ambedkar University, (A Central University), Lucknow, India	**Dr. Amit Banerjee,** Scientist, Microelectronic Technologies & Devices, Department of Electrical and Computer Engineering, National University of Singapore
Prof. Rajiv Ranjan Tewari, Professor & Head of Department, Department of Computer Science, University of Allahabad, India	**Prof. (Dr.) Ajay Rana,** Director, Amity Institute of Information Technology, Amity University, Noida, India
Prof. Vandana Bhattacharya, Professor & Head, Department of Computer Science & Engg., Birla Institute of Technology, Mesra, Ranchi, India	**Prof. (Dr.) Rajeev Srivastava,** Professor, Department of Computer Science & Engg., Indian Institute of Technology – BHU, India
Prof. Supratim Biswas, Professor, Computer Sc., Engineering, Department of Computer Science & Engg, Birla Institute of Technology, Mesra, Ranchi, India	**Prof. (Dr.) Deepak Garg,** Professor & Dean, Department of Computer Science & Engg., Bennett University, Noida, India
Prof. (Dr.) Girish Sharma, Director & Professor of Computer Science, Bhai Parmanand Institute, Delhi Skill and Entrepreneurship University, Delhi, India	**Prof. Manish Gaur,** Professor, Department of Computer Science & Engg., Institute of Engineering & Technology, Lucknow, India
Prof. Uday Shanker, Professor & Dean, Department of Computer Science & Engg., MMM University of Technology, Gorakhpur, India	**Dr. Ved Prakash Mishra,** Associate Professor & Head, Department of Computer Science & Engg., Amity University, Dubai, UAE
Prof. U. C. Jaiswal, Professor, Department of Computer Science & Engg., MMM University of Technology, Gorakhpur, India	**Dr. Sanjay Kumar,** Associate Professor, Department of Electronics & Communication Engg., Birla Institute of Technology, Mesra, Ranchi, India
Dr. Peeyush Tewari, Associate Professor, Department of Applied Maths & Computing, Birla Institute of Technology, Mesra, India **Dr. Aruna Jain,** Director, B.I.T. Mesra – Deoghar Campus, India	**Dr. Rajesh Kr. Lal,** Associate Professor, Department of Electronics & Communication Engg., Birla Institute of Technology, India
Dr. Siddhartha Rautrai, Associate Professor, Department of Computer Science & Engg., Kalinga Institute of Industrial Technology, Bhubaneshwar, India	**Dr. Daya Shankar Singh,** Associate Professor, Department of Information Technology & Computer Applications, MMM University of Technology, Gorakhpur, India
Shri Munish Kumar, Scientist, Centre for Development of Advanced Computing (CDAC, Ministry of Communication & IT, Govt. of India), Noida **Shri Bhishm Tripathi,** Scientist, Defense Research Development Organization (DRDO) Laboratory, Bangaluru, India	**Shri Praveen Srivastava,** Scientist - F, Centre for Development of Advanced Computing (CDAC, Ministry of Communication & IT, Govt. of India), Noida **Shri Paras Nath Barwal,** Senior Director, Centre for Development of Advanced Computing (CDAC, Ministry of Communication & IT, Govt. of India), Noida

Preface

The Internet and cloud-IoT technologies are an essential part of any human society including rural societies, urban societies, smart city societies, and forthcoming societies (*Society 5.0*, a forthcoming society of Japan). Similarly, a research book on *Cloud-IoT Technologies in Society 5.0* is an essential part of any existing or forthcoming human societies. The cloud-IoT technologies are undergoing rapid change, as problems of human societies and human values are now prevalent in every arena of our day-to-day life. Now, it has become very difficult for us to make equilibrium between technologies and societies. At this stage of time, we are not able to decide that which one should have the highest priority: technology/society? Further, we are not able to make a balance between society and technology. We wrote this book as a text/research/reference book for getting in-depth knowledge in the areas of convergence of cloud-IoT technologies and Industry 4.0 with Society 5.0, machine-to-machine communication, machine-to-person communication, techno-psychological perspective of society 5.0, sentiment analysis of smart digital societies, multi-access edge computing for 5G networks, discovery and location reporting of multi-access edge enabled clients/servers, video surveillance of suspicious objects using UAV images, supervising communication services in smart societies, life quality enhancement in smart city societies, multiple disease infection predictions, and societal opinion mining in smart cities societies using cloud-IoT-integrated intelligent machine/deep learning technologies in the distributive environment. This book provides a lucid description of these concepts.

As prerequisites, we assume that the readers are familiar with the basics of intelligent computing techniques, cloud computing environments, the Internet of Things (IoT), machine learning, and Python language. The topics like the techno-psychological perspective of Society 5.0, and sentiment analysis of smart digital societies require a basic understanding of rural/urban societies and the general human psychologies. But, the readers can still understand the described approaches of psychological models of technophobia, societal data processing, sentiment data analysis, sentiment evaluation approaches, multi-access edge computing, video surveillance technologies, multiple disease predictions, and societal opinion mining algorithms without a thorough knowledge of prerequisites.

The concepts in this book are presented using intuitive descriptions. Important theoretical results are covered in this book, but formal proofs/source codes of these results are largely omitted. The references at the end of each chapter contain pointers to research papers in which results were first presented and proved, as well as references to recent material for further reading. In place of proofs, figures and examples are used in this book to suggest why we should expect the result in question to be true. The appendices (*Appendix I* to *Appendix XII*) presented at the end of the last chapter (Chap. 10) contain source codes of the described algorithms and tables whose outcomes have been included in the results and discussions sections of chapters.

The fundamental concepts, model designs, and algorithms covered in the book are often based on those used in both commercial and open-source digital environments. We aim to present the concepts, model designs, hardware designs, and algorithms in a general setting that is tied to the development of forthcoming societies (including *Society 5.0*). In this book, we present few examples that pertain to the most popular and the most innovative fuzzy logic-based mathematical model of social opinion mining (SOM), a linear algebra-based mathematical model of SOM), and effective machine learning tools for SOM. These tools, models, and algorithms can be efficiently used in the cloud-IoT-integrated distributive computing environment for getting opinions about rural, urban, and smart city societies.

The organization of the text and figures reflect our many years of teaching and research experience in the field of cloud-IoT technologies, intelligent machine learning, deep learning, multi-access distributive edge computing, and unmanned aerial vehicles (UAV)-based video surveillance technologies. We expect to receive comments and suggestions from readers of this book (First Edition) which will be included in the next edition.

Jharkhand, India   Kamta Nath Mishra
                                                                          Subhash Chandra Pandey

Reading Path

This book has been written keeping in mind that all the chapters should be complete in themselves. Various chapters have been written in such a way that the reader can read and understand any chapter individually he wants to read. An attempt has been made to see that there is no connectivity of any one chapter with another chapter or it is very less. This effort of the authors will be very useful for the readers and the reader can read and understand the topic of his need and interest in a short time. Authors believe so. Nevertheless, below is a suggested reading path for the convenience of the readers.

To read this book, it is suggestive the reader should first start from Chapter 1 because this chapter is intended to make a strong background on the role of Cloud-IoT technology and their impact on Industry 4.0 and Society 5.0. This chapter also renders the substantial technological development that created the paradigm shift in a different realm of global industrial systems, and these huge developments across the globe causing swift changes in the way manufacturing was being performed earlier. Moreover, Chap. 1 also displays the characteristics of Industry 4.0 and Society 5.0 and how cloud-IoT technology can assist in this pursuit and how the miscellaneous challenges to attain the global development can be tackled by the pragmatic use of cloud-IoT technologies. Even more, different inquisitive issues such as how technologies associated with the domain of information and communication, e.g., the Internet, big data analytics, and mobile phones, can substantially be utilized for social development across the world and consistent growth. The effects of machine learning approaches on social development and associated problems are also briefly discussed. This chapter also preludes deep insight into inter-relation and inter-twinning of Industry 4.0 and Society 5.0. Thus, it is highly advisable for all types of reader of this book to read Chap. 1 at first.

Chapter 2 deals with techno-psychological perspective of Society 5.0, so readers who are only interested in technological know-how of the cloud-IoT technologies can skip this chapter. However, if the reader wants to know the subject matter in depth, then they should read this chapter. Indeed, in order to enhance the usefulness of the book, this chapter has been adapted primarily for readers interested in psychology. Further, if the readers are interested to know the critical analysis of the aspects like how different modern technologies including information technology can influence people's behavior, opinion, and psychology, then they must go through this chapter. Furthermore, different positive and negative psychological consequences of society created because of the use of modern technologies are also delineated in this chapter, and it has been revealed that modern technologies generated psychological ambivalence in the society. Over and above, the psycho-dynamics of society are also illustrated with the help of two extremities, i.e., *technophilia* and technophobia as well as few psychological models is also included in this chapter.

Chapter 3 is equally useful for students of psychology, sociology, statistics, and computer engineering. Therefore, the authors recommend the readers to read this chapter. This chapter will be helpful in understanding the subject matter in a holistic manner. This chapter incorporates the use of deep machine learning technologies for analyzing the behavior and sentiment of smart digital societies. This chapter also entails the various challenges and application domains associated with the task of behavior and sentiment analysis. Finally, this chapter describes the deep learning method that has been emerged forth as a pragmatic ML method.

Chapter 4 is not written for students of psychology, sociology, and statistics. This chapter has been written keeping in mind the needs of the computer engineering students and research scholars. In this chapter, the authors have discussed the procedures, information flow necessities, and application layer architecture of multi-access edge computing for 5G networks to enable edge applications over 3GPP networks in the cloud-IoT-integrated distributive computing environment. Therefore, students of psychology, sociology, and statistics can skip this chapter.

Chapter 5 is also intended for the students and research scholars of the computer engineering domain. This chapter precisely discusses different pertinent issues of discovery and location reporting of multi-access edge-enabled clients and servers for 5G networks and has been tailored keeping in view the requirements of PG students and research scholars. Therefore, UG students and novice learner can skip this chapter.

Chapter 6 is also written for the students of computer engineering domain in general and particularly for those engaged in advanced research in the realm of enhancing the concert of m-health technologies in smart societies using cloud-IoT-based distributive networks. Therefore, students of engineering background not interested in this topic can skip this chapter.

In Chapter 7, the authors have described innovative and safe cloud-IoT-integrated computing and communication services which can further improve the recital of cloud-IoT-dependent communication systems. Further, this chapter describes the superior internetworked communication machinery based on web computing, Internet Protocol-Wireless Sensor Network (IP-WSN), and sprinkled scheme architectures for improving the efficiency of cloud-IoT-integrated distributive data/information communication and control systems. The cloud-IoT-integrated server is also illustrated for Intelligent Road Transport Communication Control and Management System (IRTCCMS). The insights given in this chapter are useful to further augment the safety of drivers and other traveling passengers. Therefore, the students not interested in this specific topic can skip this chapter. However, it is a must read for those students who want to develop a broader scenario of the subject.

Chapter 8 is useful for students of social sciences, government administrators working in Municipal Corporation, and computer engineering. This chapter is useful even for the UG level students.

Chapter 9 is useful for professionals working in the healthcare sector including doctors as well as computer engineers. This chapter will also play a vital role in knowledge enhancement of those students and researchers engaged in the research of multiple disease infection prediction in smart societies using intelligent machine learning techniques. Students of other domain can again skip this chapter.

Chapter 10 imparts deep insights and experimental results pertaining to societal opinion mining using machine intelligence. In this chapter, the authors presented a critical review and performance of different machine learning approaches for social opinion mining (SOM). Indeed, this chapter presents a beautiful amalgamation of different aspects related to SOM such as indispensable and inevitable concepts, implementation details, and efficiency to mine the opinion of society with the help of social media messages in the light of machine learning techniques. Therefore, students and researchers of psychology, social science, statistics, government administrators working in municipal corporation, and professionals working in the healthcare sector including doctors can skip this chapter. However, those who are engaged in the advanced research of societal opinion mining using machine intelligence must read this chapter thoroughly.

Content of This Book

The text is organized into ten major parts:

- **Convergence of Cloud-IoT, Industry 4.0 and Society 5.0**. Chapter 1 explains what are ^{cloud-IoT technologies, Industry 4.0, and Society 5.0}; in what way they are related to each other; and how can we converse cloud-IoT, Industry 4.0, and Society 5.0 for the welfare of smart societies using machine-to-machine communication and person-to-person communication. The presentation is motivational and explanatory. We have avoided a discussion of how things are done internally in this chapter. Therefore, it is suitable for individual readers or for students who want to learn what a Society 5.0 is and how cloud-IoT technologies can help societal developments in forthcoming years. The detailed description of advantages, goals, and challenges of Society 5.0 developments are described in this chapter without getting into the details of the internal algorithms.
- **A Glimpse of Techno-Psychological Perspective of Society 5.0**. Chapter 2 describes the various techno-psychological perspectives of Society 5.0 including the theoretical framework of social psychology, and how technology can influence social psychology? The psychological models of technophobia which are the heart of modern techno-psychological systems are described using various technology acceptance models. The pros and cons of techno-psychological effects in modern societies are also described in this chapter.
- **Behavior and Sentiment Analysis of Smart Digital Societies Using Deep Machine Learning Technologies**. Chapter 3 deals with challenges and applications of behavior and sentiment analysis of smart digital societies which includes personalized Gaussian process (PGP), logistic auto-regression (LAR), and behavior pattern search (BPS) models of deep learning technologies. To improve the efficiency of behavior and sentiment analysis algorithms, the societal data processing techniques are combined with deep learning-based sentiment data analysis and behavior evaluation approaches in this chapter.
- **Multi-Access Edge Computing for 5G Networks in Cloud-IoT Integrated Environment**. Chapter 4 describes various approaches and steps of multi-access edge computing (MEC) for 5G networks. We described the various require-

ments, key issues, and open issues of MEC for 5G networks. The hardware designs and architectures of enabling edge applications, request-response provisioning, service provisioning, and edge enabler clients/servers registration techniques for MEC for 5G networks used in cloud and IoT-based distributive computing environments are described and examined using various mandatory('M') and optional('O') conditions in this chapter.

- **Discovery and Location Reporting of Multi-access Edge Enabled Clients and Servers for 5G Networks**. Chapter 5 discusses the mechanisms and steps necessary for the discovery and location reporting of multi-access edge-enabled clients and servers for 5G networks. Further, the authors have described preconditions, processing steps, procedures, and implementation details required for providing edge application server/clients (EAS/EAC) discovery of MEC for 5G networks. The hardware/software designs of request-response, subscribe-notify, and detection of user equipment (UE) location from the 3GPP systems are described by the authors in this chapter. The result and discussion section of this chapter include the snapshots of the Linux interface and the working of the simulator in MEC 5G networks.
- **Enhancing the Concert of M-health Technologies in Smart Societies Using Cloud-IoT-Based Distributive Networks**. In Chapter 6, the authors have described for Enhancing the Concert of M-health Technologies in Smart Societies Using Cloud-IoT-Based Distributive Networks. Further, circumstantial evidence of this chapter suggests that innovations can further enhance the efficiency, quality, cost-effectiveness, and safety of e-healthcare delivery. It cannot be denied that as integrated multidisciplinary models of care incorporate e-health-related services into human resources, there is a growing curiosity among service providers about e-health information and the role of such information is becoming more and more decisive.
- **Supervision of Communication and Control Services in Societies of Smart Cities Using Sheltered Cloud-Based Confirmation and Access Techniques**. In Chapter 7, the authors have discussed verification and validation innards for evaluating the transmutation-based usefulness of cloud data/services in the cloud-IoT-integrated atmosphere. The described techniques of this chapter contain information on widespread threats to cloud-IoT-integrated services like IaaS (Information as a Service), PaaS (Platform as a Service), and SaaS (Software as a service) which should be provided to the cloud customers in the distributive computing environment. Further, the authors have described innovative and safe cloud-IoT-integrated computing and communication services which can additionally improve the recital of cloud-IoT-dependent communication systems. In this chapter, the architectures of superior internetworked communication machinery, Internet Protocol-Wireless Sensor Network (IP-WSN), and sprinkled schemes are designed which can be used for improving the efficiency of cloud-IoT-integrated distributive data/information communication and control systems. Finally, this chapter offers mechanisms for the safety of drivers and other passengers for several types of vehicles moving on roads/highways.
- **Life Quality Improvement in Smart City Societies Using Cloud–IoT and Deep Machine Learning (CIDML) Technologies**. Chapter 8 describes how we

can improve the life quality of smart city citizens using cloud-IoT technologies and deep machine learning approaches. Further, basic requirements, objectives, life quality improvement-related problems, and corresponding deep learning-based models to solve these life quality enhancement-related problems of smart city societies are described in this chapter. Furthermore, the described models of this chapter can solve traffic surveillance, accident detection, parking, waste management, and garbage collection-related problems of forthcoming societies 'Society 5.0' using intelligent machine learning techniques.

- **Multiple Disease Infection Prediction in Smart Societies Using Intelligent Machine Learning Techniques**. Chapter 9 describes intelligent machine learning (IML) based on multiple disease prediction and monitoring systems. The medical datasets used in this chapter are divided into test and train data sets and the machine learning algorithms are trained on the training data sets. The three supervised learning algorithms that have been described and implemented in this chapter for multiple disease infection prediction and monitoring are Decision Tree, Random Forest, and Naive Bayes algorithm. Out of the three algorithms, the Naive Bayes has produced the highest accuracy followed by Random Forest and Decision Tree. The SQLite database used in the described IML-based health-care diseases prediction/monitoring system of this chapter will allow the end-users (including patients) to register themselves in the system. A unique user ID is generated and the symptoms, as well as predicted diseases, are being recorded for each end-user/patient. In any specific case if the actual diagnosis of the disease is different from the predicted diseases of the system, then the user/patient can come back and record his actual disease in the system. In this chapter, the medical records of the patients are integrated with the medical datasets for increasing the transparency and efficiency of the described IML-based health-care diseases prediction/monitoring system.
- **Societal Opinion Mining Using Machine Intelligence**. Societal opinion mining is playing a vital role in the development of Society 5.0. Chapter 10 discusses theoretical backgrounds like source, object, and evaluation of societal opinion mining (SOM) and sentiment analysis (SA) technologies. In this chapter, the authors have presented two mathematical models of societal opinion mining, namely, Fuzzy Logic and Linear Algebra-based Mathematical Models. Further, the effective machine learning tools and their corresponding algorithms like clustering technique, Naïve Bayes classifier, artificial neural network (ANN), Firefly algorithm, Rough set classifiers, support vector machine classifier, decision tree classifier, ensemble classifier, random forest, and deep learning algorithms have been developed by the authors for social opinion mining. The experimental results and discussions section of this chapter uses SOM tools like societal features, linguistic patterns, and mining efficacy for evaluating the performance of various social opinion mining algorithms in the cloud-IoT-integrated distributive computing environment.

Kamta Nath Mishra
Subhash Chandra Pandey

Contents

About the Authors

Kamta Nath Mishra was born on August 15, 1973, in the Kushinagar district (Chandrauta Village) of Uttar Pradesh, INDIA. He received his Bachelor of Science (B.Sc., Maths) degree from the University of Gorakhpur, India, in 1992, and Master of Computer Application (MCA) degree from Madan Mohan Malviya Engineering College (Currently MMMUT), Gorakhpur, U. P., India in 1996. Dr. Mishra completed his M.Tech. (Software Systems) degree from Birla Institute of Technology and Science (BITS) Pilani, India in 2003 and Ph.D. (Engg.) from CSE department of B.I.T. Mesra – India, in May 2015.

Dr. Mishra has more than twenty-one years of teaching and research experience. Currently, he is working as a senior faculty member (Associate Professor) at Dept. of CS&E, Birla Institute of Technology, India since August **2009**; He has worked as a faculty member in the Department of Computer Science, Joint program of Michigan State University the USA and University of Sebha, LIBYA, from October **2006** to July **2009**. He was a senior lecturer at B.I.T. Mesra, (Noida Campus) from July **2004** to September **2006**. Dr. Mishra has worked as a senior project engineer from September **2003** to June **2004** and project engineer from September **2000** to August **2003**, in Centre for Development of Advanced Computing (CDAC), Ministry of Communication & IT, Govt. of India, Noida, Uttar Pradesh. Before joining CDAC, Dr. Mishra worked as a lecturer in the CS&E department at Krishna Institute of Engineering & Technology (KIET), Ghaziabad, India, from July **1998** to August **2000**. Dr. Mishra has published two authored research books (IGI Global USA, Springer), sixteen book chapters, and more than thirty-five research papers in journals and conferences of international repute. His research interest includes Biometric Systems, Image Processing, Analysis of Algorithms and Distributed Cloud Computing. Dr. Mishra is a professional member of IEEE Biometric Society USA, and **ACM, USA.**

Subhash Chandra Pandey completed his Ph.D. from Dr. APJ Abdul Kalam Technical University, Lucknow, India, and M.Tech in computer engineering from Motilal Nehru National Institute of Technology, Allahabad, UP, India. Presently, he is associated with the Birla Institute of Technology, India, as a Professor. He is a member of many professional bodies including "International Association of Engineers – Hong Kong", "Computer Science Teachers Association – USA" and "International Association of Artificial Intelligence and Law".

Dr. Pandey has also worked with the Ministry of Health, Saudi Arabia, and possesses deep insight into different technological issues related to the healthcare sector. He is regularly publishing research papers in reputed international journals and international conference proceedings. His research interests include the use of soft computing, evolutionary computing, bio-inspired computing, machine intelligence, and data mining in the domain of the medical sector. Moreover, he has published research papers in high-impact journals in the realm of "Philosophical aspects of machine cognition and IoT". Nowadays, Dr. Pandey is working in the domain of "Cloud Computing and IoT" and how these emerging technologies can pragmatically be used in the health-care sector.

Acronyms

2D	Two Dimensional
3D	Three Dimensional
5GC	5G Core Network
5GS	5G System
AC	Application Client
ACK	Acknowledgment
ACID	Application Client Identification
ACLs	Access Control Lists
ACP	Application Client Profile
AEP	Autonomous and Efficient Production
AF	Application Function
AGVs	Autonomous Land Vehicles
AI	Artificial Intelligence
AMA	American Medical Association
ANN	Artificial Neural Network
AS	Artificial System
ASAM	American Society of Addiction Medicine
ATM	Automated Teller Machine
AWS	Amazon Web Services
BD	Big Data
BFSI	Banking, Financial Services and Insurance
BMI	Body Mass Index
BPN	Back-Propagation Network
BPS	Behavior Pattern Search
BSF	Binding Support Function
BW	Black & White
API	Application Programme Interface
CAPIF	Common API Framework
CBOW	Continuous Bag-of-Words
CC	Cloud Computing
CD	Compact Disc

CDPs	Cisco Discovery Packets
CIDML	Cloud–IoT and Deep Machine Learning
CIT	Computer and Information Technology
CM	Conditional Mandatory
CNN	Convolutional Neural Network
CO	Conditional Optional
Covid-19	Coronal Virus-2019
CPS	Cyber-Physical Systems
CPUs	Central Processing Units
CRM	Customer Relation Management
CSP	Cloud Service Provider
CSV	Comma-Separated Value
CT	Control Technologies
DBN	Deep Belief Network
DDoS	Distributed Denial of Services
DFS	Detached Framework Structures
DL	Deep Learning
DML	Deep Machine Learning
DN	Data Network
DNN	Deep Neural Network
DNS	Domain Name Systems
DoS	Denial of Services
DSMMD	Diagnostic and Statistical Manual of Mental Disorders
DT	Decision Tree
EAS	Edge Application Server
EASD	Edge Application Server Discovery
EASID	Edge Application Server Identification
EC	Ensemble Classifier
ECS	Edge Configuration Server
ECT	Embedded Computing Technology
EChS	Evolved Charging Suite
EDN	Edge Data Network
EDNCS	Edge Data Network Configuration Service
EEC	Edge Enabler Client
EECID	Edge Enabler Client Identification
EES	Edge Enabler Server
EESID	Edge Enabler Server Identification
e.g.	For Example
EHE	Edge Hosting Environment
EIGRP	Enhanced Internal Gateway Routing Protocol
EPS	Evolved Packet System
ERP	Enterprise Resource Planning
FA	Firefly Algorithm
FFS	For Further Study
FMM	Flight Manager Module

FPIC	Fringe Portal Informing Convention
FPP	Factory and Production Planning
FPS	Frames Per Second
FQDN	Fully Qualified Domain Name
FR	Face Recognition
GB	Giga Bytes
GCS	Ground Control Station
GHz	Giga Hertz
GIS	Geographical Information System
GL	Genetic Learning
GPS	Global Positioning System
GPSI	Generic Public Subscription Identifier
GR	Gesture Recognition
GUI	Graphical User Interface
HMM	Hidden Markov Models
HMS	Hypervisor Management System
HTML	Hypertext Markup Language
IA	Internet Addiction
IAM	Identity and Access Management
IaaS	Information as a Service
IAD	Internet Addiction Disorder
IBM	International Business Machine
ICM	Internet Communication Machinery
ICMP	Internet Control Message Protocol
ICT	Information and Communication Technologies
ID	Identity
IEs	Information Elements
IGM	Interactive Graphical Map
IIC	Industrial Internet Consortium
IIoT	Industrial Internet of Things
IIRA	Industrial Internet Reference Architecture
IML	Intelligent Machine Learning
IoT	Internet of Things
IP	Internet Protocol
IP-WSN	Internet Protocol-Wireless Sensor Network
IQoS	Improved Quality of Services
IR	Industrial Revolution
IRP	Integration Reference Point
IRTCCMS	Intelligent Road Transport Communication Control and Management System
ITP	Important Transport Convention
ITS	Intelligent Transportation System
IwCT	Internetworked Communication Technology
KDD	Knowledge Discovery and Data Mining
k-NN	K-Nearest Neighbours

KPI	Key Performance Indicator
LADN	Local Area Data Network
LAR	Logistic Auto Regression
LBPH	Local Binary Pattern Histogram
LCC	Lower Camel Case
LCS	Location Services
LLC	Limited Liability Company
LMT	Logistic Model Tree
LPs	Linguistic Patterns
LR	Logistic Regression
LSTM	Long Short-Term Memory
LTE	Long-Term Evolution
M	Mandatory
M2M	Machine to Machine
M2P	Machine-to-Person Communication
MEC	Multi-access Edge Computing
MES	Manufacturing Execution Systems
MHz	Mega Hertz
ML	Machine Learning
MLP	Multilayer Perceptron
MNO	Mobile Network Operator
NB	Naïve Bayes
NBC	Naïve Bayes Classifier
NEF	Network Exposure Function
NGO	Non-Government Organization
NIST	National Institute of Standard and Technology
NLP	Natural Language Processing
NRF	Network Repository Function
O	Optional
OM	Opinion Mining
OS	Operating System
PaaS	Platform as a Service
PCA	Principal Component Analysis
PCAP	Packets from Packet Capture
PCF	Policy Control Function
PDLC	Product Development Life Cycle
PGP	Personalized Gaussian Process
POS	Part of Speech
OpenCV	Open Source Control Vision
OSAppId	Operating System Application Identity
OSId	Operating System Identity
PD	Product Development
PKI	Public Key Infrastructure
PLMN	Public Land Mobile Network
QoI	Quality of Information

QoS	Quality of Service
RAM	Random Access Memory
RAMI 4.0	Reference Architecture Management Industrial 4.0
RF	Random Forest
ReLU	Rectified Linear Unit
RNN	Recurrent Neural Network
RPP	Replication of Production Process
RS	Rough Set
RTAPS	Road Traffic Accident Preclusion Systems
SA	Sentiment Analysis
SaaS	Software as a Service
SAE	System Address Elucidation
SARS	Severe Acute Respiratory Syndrome
SCEF	Service Capability Exposure Function
SDK	Software Development Kit
SET	Science Engineering and Technology
SGP	Socialized Gaussian Process
SIM	Subscriber Identification Module
SLAR	Socialized Logistic Auto Regression
SLAs	Service Level Agreements
SLP	Single Layer Perceptron
SMM	Social Media Mining
SNMP	Simple Network Management Protocol
SOM	Social Opinion Mining
SPN	Sum-Product Network
SQL	Structured Query Language
SRTS	Smart Road Transportation System
SUT	Service Under Test
SVSII	Smart Video Surveillance and Intelligence Input
SVM	Support Vector Machine
TAM	Technology Acceptance Model
TBE-CNN	Trunk-Branch-Ensemble Convolutional Neural Network
TRA	Theory of Reasoned Action
TVs	Televisions
UAVs	Unmanned Aerial Vehicles
UCC	Upper Camel Case
UE	User Equipment
URI	Uniform Resource Identifier
USA	United States of America
VGA	Visual Graphics Adapter
VLANs	Virtual Local Area Networks
VM	Virtual Machine
VMs	Virtual Machines
VS	Video Surveillances
VSS	Video Surveillance Solutions

WDMS	Web Data Management and Security
WDSN	Wireless Distributive Sensor Networks
Wi-Fi	Wireless Fidelity
WKA	Well-Known Abbreviation
WiMAX	Worldwide Interoperability for Microwave Access
WSN	Wireless Sensor Network

Chapter 1
Convergence of Cloud-IoT, Industry 4.0 and Society 5.0

Abstract In preceding years, the substantial technological development has rendered the paradigm shift in a different realm of global industrial systems and these huge developments across the globe are causing swift changes in the way manufacturing was being performed earlier. Indeed, different production units are consistently becoming smarter and effective owing to the pragmatic use of advanced technologies such as cloud computing (CC) and IoT. In Germany, the conception of Industry 4.0 (I4.0) has delineated in 2011 and subsequently adopted and researched in many other developed countries. Further, Industry 4.0 draws attention toward the digitization of manufacturing processes and it requires the hybridization of various technologies. Precisely, the prime characteristic of Industry 4.0 is to generate a paradigm shift that entails inter-connected services of the prevailing network model. These interconnected services assimilate the operational technology and information technology. Moreover, Industry 4.0 tries to optimize the use of Information and Communication Technologies (ICT) in production phenomena so that modified goods can be produced which satisfies maximally the demanding needs of new consumers. This technological hybridization also creates an ecosystem of short, independent, and decentralized manufacturing. Furthermore, this innovative concept permits the generation of more supple manufacturing processes with the pursuit of connected systems and data sharing. Further, it is imperative to mention that big data (BD) and CC are indispensable technological components for substantially enhancing the potentiality of this approach. Over and above, the aim of Industry 4.0 is to implement the concepts of data processing and information technology so that the process complexity and long-term cost can be mitigated by connecting the entire individual network. The challenges faced in the pursuit of global development are effectively being tackled by the pragmatic use of cloud-IoT technologies. Different technologies associated with the domain of information and communication e.g., the Internet, big data analytics, and the use of mobile phones are substantially utilized for social development across the world and consistent growth is also being observed. In the coming future, Society 5.0 has to be incorporated by perceiving the hybridization of miscellaneous aspects and spirits of entrepreneurship, and innovation policy. However, in the future Society 5.0 will also render its different shortcomings besides high living standards. In this chapter, different critical issues of Industry 4.0 have been discussed. Its effect on societal development is also deeply analyzed. The effects of machine learning approaches and on social development and associated problems are also briefly discussed. This chapter also preludes deep insight into inter-relation and inter-twinning of Industry 4.0 and Society 5.0.

Keywords Machine learning · Cloud and IoT · Industry 4.0 · Societal impacts · Society 5.0

1.1 Introduction

From the ancient period, technologies are creating positive impacts in a pervasive manner for individuals, society, and the human race. Technology possesses the potential to transform the lives of living beings and society as well. Besides, technology can play a vital role to address many societal challenges together with rendering the host of opportunities. Indeed, the different industrial revolutions put forth various great movements. These movements can be treated as epoch-making events in the history of manufacturing. These are enumerated below [1].

1. The first phase of the Industrial Revolution (IR) → Steam Engine.
2. The second phase of IR → Electricity.
3. The third phase of IR → (a) The innovation of integrated microchips and (b) The use of information technology.

Each industrial revolution generated positive impetus and substantial changes within the purview of manufacturing and production processes. Even more, each industrial revolution also created some sort of social transformation. The first industrial revolution occurred around the nineteenth century and this revolution entirely changed the global scenario by transforming the heat energy of water and steam into mechanical energy and thus this revolution enables the manufacturing sector to yield more production with less effort of manpower. Similarly, the second industrial revolution commenced the uprising trends of mass production. Further, the third industrial revolution emerged in the twentieth century when information technology is implemented for production automation. However, across the globe, many people are struggling with numerous difficulties such as endemic poverty, education, communicable disease; climate changes, etc. These issues were largely considered insurmountable before the commencement of the fourth IR. The fourth IR is considered as a new revolution and not an extension of the third industrial revolution owing to its speed, scope, and its impact on the system. The term 'Industry 4.0 (I4.0)'or fourth IR is coined in Germany in 2011. This new concept is conceived in the government's high-tech strategy for 2020. The Reference Architecture Management Industrial 4.0 (RAMI 4.0) was developed in a project known as 'Platform Industries 4.0'. This project aimed to develop and implement Industry 4.0

as a strategy so that the new age of manufacturing by exploiting the advancement of technologies can become a reality [1]. Perhaps, the objective was to incorporate the latest advancement of human ingenuity in many domains, particularly in ICT. The prime objectives of this strategy were to include the following aspects in manufacturing phenomena such as:

- High-speed network
- Processing power
- Cloud computing (CC)
- Internet of thing
- Big data analytics
- Inclusions of other novel techniques

CC implicates the storage and access of data and programs over the Internet instead of the computer's hard drive and the cloud can be considered as the metaphor for the Internet. The era of the fourth IR (Industry 4.0) includes the aforementioned components for production processes. It also includes the concepts of Artificial Intelligence (AI). In [2], it is mentioned that inclusion of other novel techniques such as Cyber-Physical Systems (CPS) and augmented Reality renders Industry 4.0 as a new paradigm related to different industrial aspects and thus enable it for future development. The synergistic inclusions of these technologies in production processes of different manufacturing sectors emerged as Industry 4.0. Perhaps, the above-mentioned innovative technologies played a substantial role in the domain manufacturing sectors in a more precise and effective manner and it manifested an entirely different approach in comparison to the traditional manufacturing trend. Precisely, industry 4.0 entails information technology to facilitate the production processes associated with different manufacturing sectors. Further, the phenomenon of implementing CC and BD and associated challenges it encountered are two important aspects of I4.0. Moreover, the fourth IR generated a symbiotic co-existence and amalgamation of the following two streams:

- Operations Technology
- Information Technology

The incorporation of information and communications technologies (ICT) enabled manufacturing techniques to render contemporary reference architectures to facilitate their pragmatic implementation as well as consistent evolution [3].

Thus, the aim of industry 4.0 is to incorporate substantial changes in the existing production model so that optimized processes required for manufacturing, costs reduction, customization of products, customer-oriented services, and overall growth of industries can be witnesses [4]. Indeed, in Industry 4.0 the "ultra-connectivity" of miscellaneous systems required in the production process multiplies the data created from various sources with different formats in real-time. This requires the latest technologies and advanced algorithms for proper storage and analysis of the data. For these reasons, CC and BD are two important pragmatic technologies implemented and are considered as the basic requirements for Industry

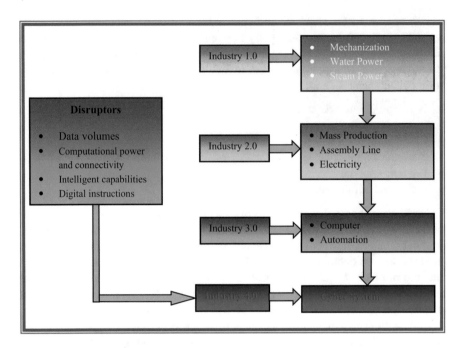

Fig. 1.1 Attributes of the different industrial revolution

4.0 because these two techniques provide pertinent and essential components [5]. The attributes of the different industrial revolutions are shown in Fig. 1.1.

Industry 4.0 is also putting forth huge advancements in different sectors and witnessed substantial changes. It has been observed that automation is required to tackle the gigantic chunk of data in the financial sector. Moreover, the approach of industry 4.0 permits the machine-to-machine (M2M) communication and also displays the intelligent use of customer's data for production processes and thus renders the 'customization of products. Following are the conspicuous attributions of industry 4.0.

- Machine to Machine Communication (M2M).
- Replication of Production Process (RPP)
- Autonomous and Efficient Production (AEP)
- Machine to Person Communication (M2P)

Industry 4.0 permits the M2P irrespective of their places and positions and also creates the efficacy to interact from several devices. Thus, industry 4.0 enables different associated entities to access and evaluate the data associated with goods and manufacturing processes in parallel due to optimized communication among them. It is explicit that these characteristics will create economic growth, opportunities for employment generation, and will also manifest an ecosystem amongst the suppliers and customers [6]. The concept of industry 4.0 is being witnessed in many countries

[7]. Perhaps, this is the reason that RAMI 4.0 has emerged at par with DIN SPEC 91345 (Germen industry 4.0 model) [8]. Moreover, Industrial Internet Consortium (IIC) has been established by many big companies in the USA. The objective of this consortium is to strategize, promote and implement the Industrial Internet so that inter-connection of several physical devices can take place. This reference architecture is known as 'Industrial Internet Reference Architecture (IIRA)' [9]. The IIRA and RAMI 4.0 are intended to digitize the production phenomena as well as to get them to imbibe 'artificial intelligence.

1.1.1   Smart Factory: The Metaphor of Industry 4.0

Smart or intelligent factories are treated as the metaphor of Industry 4.0. From this perspective, it is obvious that it entails the efficacy of processes improvement by rendering the phenomenon of self-optimization as well as autonomous decision-making in contrast to traditional manufacturing sectors. Thus, it is intuitive that smart factories are flamboyantly more intelligent in comparison to traditional factories. Moreover, smart factories are more flexible and dynamic contrary to traditional ones. Indeed, in smart factories, various manufacturing processes associated with the entire supply chain from logistics to life cycle management are organized differently. Over and above, every step of production is flawlessly connected. The main characteristics of smart factories are depicted in Fig. 1.2 and also enumerated below:

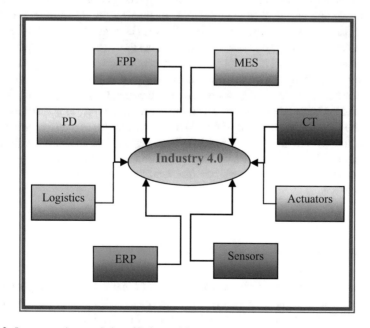

Fig. 1.2 Important characteristics of Industry 4.0

- Factory and Production Planning (FPP).
- Product Development (PD).
- Logistics.
- Enterprise Resource Planning (ERP).
- Manufacturing Execution Systems (MES).
- Control Technologies (CT).
- Wireless Sensor Network (WSN).
- Sensors.
- Actuators.

1.1.2   Indispensability of Industry 4.0

Perhaps, the huge developments across the globe are causing swift changes in manufacturing fashion. In the recent scenario of the manufacturing sector mainly there are two dissident schools of thought. These are: (1) Not desirous to invest in technological advancement and innovation (2) Keen to adopt new technologies and innovative means. Industry 4.0 is a global buzzword nowadays and particularly it was manifested in [10]. Presumably, it will substantially modify the way manufacturing is going on and thus will pragmatically enhance the efficacy of the entire manufacturing sector. It will also revolutionize the businesses framework of society. Indeed, the ever-increasing digital future emerging forth will create a new era for manufacturing which in turn will reform the entire spectrum of global businesses. Further, it is imperative and pertinent to mention that considering the incorporation of novel technical features and exploring how these features can transform the business processes to comply with expectations of modern business scenarios will play a vital role for manufacturers. Furthermore, industry reports reveal the fact that CC is a significant supporting component for the evolution of industry 4.0. Moreover, the commencement of industry 4.0 is substantially creating a symphony for IoT, automation, and robotics. Therefore, based on the latest research it has been observed by the experts that implementation of the cloud can greatly help in different manufacturing sectors as well as in the processes of banking and financial sectors. In [11], it is given that unlike other industrial revolutions or innovations observed before the industry 4.0 will cause huge impacts on our lives, the way of working, and the manner we connect.

1.1.3   Key Technology Factors of Industry 4.0

The phenomenon of linking any device with the Internet is a breakthrough in industrial development. This 'connecting with the devices' phenomenon can also be extended to the components of machines includes. Further, if it entails an on and off switch then it might become a part of the IoT.

Perhaps, Industry 4.0 draws attention toward the digitization of manufacturing processes and it requires the hybridization of various technologies. This technological hybridization creates an ecosystem of short, independent, and decentralized manufacturing. Further, I4.0 aims to implement the concepts of data processing and information technology so that the process complexity and long-term cost can be mitigated by connecting the entire individual network. Moreover, the approach of hybridizing the novel technologies also renders the enhanced efficiency and effectiveness of the majority of industrial operations. In [12], it is given that Industry 4.0 possesses the capability to transform the traditional production process. Moreover, it is entirely interconnected through the IoT [12]. Further, in [13] it is proposed that the approach of Industry 4.0 can manifest more supple production processes and will also display the optimized use of resources and reduced cost as well as effective communication between customers, industry, and suppliers.

Indeed, a hybridized technological approach associated with Industry 4.0 can reflect innovative products, processes, and business models [14]. In addition, the incorporation of subtle electronic components with increased capacity reduced cost, and the inclusion of sensors in products and machines shows tremendous growth in overall manufacturing efficiency. Moreover, simulation of the end product before the production phase becomes a reality in Industry 4.0 and thus renders more flexibility. Over and above, it permits the shared manufacturing irrespective of remote locations [15]. These phases are:

- The design phase.
- The product development life cycle (PDLC).
- The phase of logistics inclusion.
- The distribution phase.
- The delivery phase.
- The phase of after-sale.

Furthermore, technological enablers permit the incorporation of the product specifications requested by the consumer during the design phase and thus help the product customization. Similarly, the other Industry 4.0 key factors are:

1. It enhances the traceability of PDLC.
2. It shows the holistic hybridization of software applications.
3. It permits real-time access to information and thus helps in decision-making.
4. It allows autonomous decision-making without human intervention.
5. It renders transparency throughout the PDLC.
6. It can detect manufacturing errors and thus immediate remedial action can be taken.
7. It allows planning of the preventive maintenance,
8. Remote process monitoring is possible and thus avoids production loss due to equipment failure.

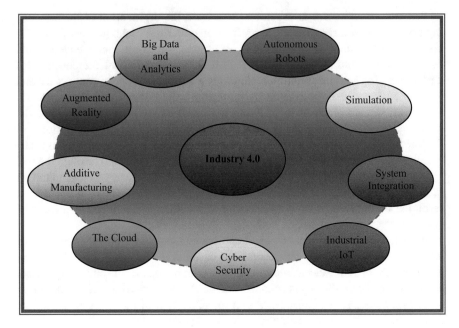

Fig. 1.3   The nine technologies transforming industrial production

  9. It allows the planning of manufacturing from different geographical locations.
10. Helpful in generating new business models.

However, Industry 4.0 has been driven by 4 disruptors. These are given below.

1. The huge growth in voluminous data.
2. Computational power and connectivity.
3. Analytics and business intelligence capabilities.
4. Digital instruction transfers to the physical world.

Figure 1.3 presents the main concepts and technologies associated with industry 4.0.

1.2   Role of CC in Advancement of Industry 4.0

Undoubtedly, CC can be treated as a new paradigm shift in the domain of information technology (IT). It has been visualized as the 5th utility service by many
researchers. It implicates that the services of IT will be consumed and paid similar
to water and electricity services. Further, cloud computing is visualized as a substantial constituent of industry 4.0. It is also considered a fundamental component
of CPS. It seems that CC in CPS of Industry 4.0 will commence a new impact of
global IT development by endowing the flexible expansion and centralized sharing
of various resources of computation [16]. Moreover, cloud computing will

subsequently enhance the efficacy of the product within the CPS. In addition, CPS and the causes of the machine's breakdown can be shared by a cloud platform with other geographically distant locations.

Perhaps, just beyond the technical sphere, it is a new business paradigm of selling IT services. The 'National Institute of Standard and Technology (NIST)' of the USA has given the lucid definition of CC:

> Cloud computing is a model for enabling convenient, on-demand network access to a shared pool of configurable computing resources (e.g., networks, servers, storage, applications, and services) that can be rapidly provisioned and released with minimal management effort or service provider interaction.

Further, in [17] the four prime characteristics of CC as enumerated below are given.

1. Assumption of unlimited computing resources.
2. Pay-for-use model.
3. Virtualized resources.

Furthermore, CC encompasses many advantages over traditional information technology services. These are given below [17]:

1. Reducing the cost especially for the small and medium enterprises.
2. Real-time and 24/7 access to IT resources.
3. Facilitate the innovation.
4. Paves the way for new classes of applications that were impossible earlier.

In [18], it is revealed that cloud platforms can pragmatically be used to hybridize the different domains of IT sectors such as mobile computing and IoT and thus can effectively help to perform the industrial automation systems through CC. However, some essential requirements still need to be properly analyzed and addressed for optimum use and adoption of CC. These pertinent issues are reduction in cost, issues of adaptability, hybridization of information, and relative capability. The decision of implementing CC also greatly depends on the perceived advantages and readiness of the organization. This decision is also influenced by competitive pressures and security concerns including the data loss and phishing being faced by the organization [19, 20].

Precisely, CC prevails to display the vital role for boosting the objectives of Industry 4.0 irrespective of the types of the industry by rendering the susceptible means to promote the business. Further, cloud computing has the potential to optimally use disruptive technologies such as robotics and AI.

1.2.1 Significance of CC in BFSI

Businesses across the globe are attempting to get the optimum advantages rendered by cloud technology. Further, the global market of CC is expected to grow exponentially in the coming years. The financial services industry is also considered embracing cloud technology. Perhaps, it is because the disruptive wave of digital transformation is obtaining a chunk of its capabilities from the cloud. It has been revealed from an extensive literature survey that 74% of businesses trust the use of a CC for achieving competitive advantages and 60% of decision-makers believe cloud computing is a worthy tool for unlocking the prospective of disruptive technologies [21]. Indeed, CC applications in the different sectors are growing at a fast pace of 150% whereas the growth rate of traditional software is only 11%. Further, it is assumed that probably in the coming years India will supersede the world in the use of hybrid cloud technology in a different sector. In 2018, the CC used in India was 13%. But, now it has been increased up to 43% in 2020. It is pertinent to mention that the banking segment had ever been inquisitive to adopt the cloud technique owing to its inherited features such as scalability, reduced cost, resilience, and ease of operations. In [22], the role of CC in the business sector is delineated.

Perhaps, the use of CC within the purview of Banking, financial services, and insurance (BFSI) sectors is relevant and versatile. However, its relevance is to be accepted before use [22]. Cloud technology is being implemented since 2017 in different payment interfaces in India.

1.2.2 Benefits and Applications of CC in BFSI

CC has proved its significance almost in every industrial sector around the globe. In particular, the financial sector will greatly be influenced and will obtain substantial benefits from it in the forthcoming future. It displays as an effective tool to fix the major drawbacks related to the following sub-domains of banking and financial sectors.

- Cost-effectiveness
- Reliability issue
- Issues related to flexibility

It helps the banking and financial sector to save the capital disbursement required for setting up the IT infrastructure and thus enables the banking and financial institutions to focus on their core banking functions. Further, the cloud infrastructure allows a higher degree of reliability by providing the choices of the private and hybrid cloud models. Securing the data while entertaining the speed and flexibility of the cloud is also becomes a reality banking and financial sectors. Moreover, the data can be encrypted as well as many other layers of security can also be implemented even in the case of public clouds. Over and above, the pay-as-you-use model of billing makes it more flexible. It renders a high grade of flexibility because banking and financial institutions can easily manage the increasing demand scenario and that too with disbursing extra investment. In addition, cloud-oriented applications render shifting from one application to another easy. The important applications of CC within the purview of BFSI are given below.

- Hosting
- Payment Gateway
- Enterprise Resource Planning ERP
- Customer Relation Management (CRM)

It is explicit that traditional IT system requires frequent maintenance and thus offering continuous service is cumbersome and difficult. In contrast, CC offers continuous service with secure transactions and an efficient customer experience. Indeed, CC can provide almost 100% continuous services. CC has already been implemented to transfer the payments and funds securely. The almost 100% continuous services offered by CC also render the increased security by avoiding any discrepancies. Further, ERP and CRM software are the most important features extended by CC. The Software as a Service (SaaS) is one of the highly demanding methods implemented for augmenting the scope of CC. It facilitates the vendor to control the application and it also extends better support. It is also indispensable from the users' viewpoint by rendering the remote access and easy installation.

From the above discussions, it is explicit that CC is substantially beneficial in the BFSI sector as well as in Industry 4.0. However, implementing this technology keeping in view various aspects related to security, regulations, compliance, etc. is of core importance. Moreover, CC services must be deployed by trusted and authenticated service providers. It is intuitive to mention that in the present days' cloud technology will go beyond the boundaries of reliability, scalability, and storage within Industry 4.0. Figure 1.4 illustrates the benefits and application of cloud computing in BFSI.

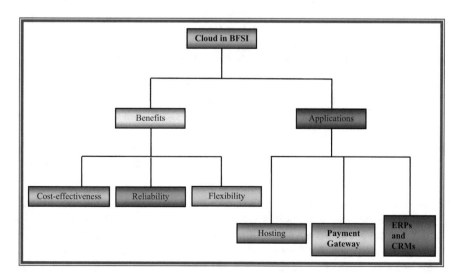

Fig. 1.4 Benefits and applications of cloud computing in banking, financial services, and insurance (BFSI)

1.3 Intelligent Machine/Deep Learning Approaches and Societal Developments

The major population of the world resides in developing countries and undoubtedly plethoras of research have been conducted by many researchers in different domains such as sociology, statistics, ecology, and economics. Machine learning is an active area of research and it has substantially been used by researchers for the pursuit of development research and practice. For example, supervised machine learning approaches have frequently been implemented for making a prudent decision in medical health and diagnostic domains with few resources. Similarly, deep learning techniques are implemented for the analysis purpose of satellite images and thus can be used as a novel economic indicator. However, many challenges need to be properly addressed before the implementation of machine learning techniques including deep learning. The challenges encountered with the use of these techniques in developing countries are because of many reasons such as:

- Availability of data is less as compared to developed countries.
- Computational capacity is lower as compared to developed countries.
- Internet accessibility is often considerably less than in developed countries.

In this sub-section, the possibilities of machine learning approaches for societal development of developing countries will be discussed and an attempt will be made to explore the burgeoning literature. Indeed, the term 'developing' is quite obscure and the author thinks that there is not a well-defined dichotomy between the 'developing' and 'developed' regions. However, the interested reader can refer to the material given in [23–25]. Machine learning approaches have thoroughly been applied for societal development. Different aspects of machine learning approaches such as big data and IT-related topics have been used for the pursuit of social development from a different perspective [26–29].

Precisely, the machine learning approaches for the societal development of developing countries entail five key characteristics. These are mentioned below.

1. Geographical constraints about applications and data [30].
2. Problems considered are mainly from the domain of vital advancement areas.
3. The solutions needed for the problem generally differ from the existing solution of the same problem in developed countries.
4. The accrued solution must incorporate such issues.
5. The accrued solutions must implement machine learning as an inevitable component of the projects.

It is explicit that the aforementioned first and second points are critical. Perhaps, it is because these points exclusively implicate that development issues of developing countries are only under consideration. Many issues about development are common between developed and developing countries. However, their solution approaches are entirely different. The third point emphasizes these differences. Often, it is also possible to have a unique problem domain in developing countries e.g., eradication of a particular disease. Contrary to this, seldom may the problem be occurred throughout the world, but its solution for developing countries can substantially be different than the developed countries e.g., the preventive care for non-communicable diseases. Therefore, it is intuitive to think that efficient solutions to a given problem in developed regions may not be effective in developing ones. The fifth point emphasizes the use of machine learning approaches for social development in developing regions. Indeed, the five points given above reveal the conditions of machine learning approaches for developing regions. However, it is pertinent to mention that machine learning approaches used for the societal development of developing countries do not necessarily include innovative statistical or machine learning techniques. Perhaps, in specific circumstances the societal developments may proceed with theoretical development and pragmatic implementations of existing techniques in an innovative and novel fashion may seem genuine for the social development of developing regions. That's why it seems correct to state that societal development does not require only machine learning methods. Instead, the combined approach of machine learning and development research is more worthy for this pursuit. Finally, it is observable that the significance of synchronizing works with societal goals of development reflects the difference between simply implementing machine learning to developed world datasets and machine learning for developing regions.

In [31], it is given that:

> intelligent society is a system that utilizes the potential of digital technology, digital instruments, and networks to improve the quality of human life.

Further, the deployment issues of CPS are discussed in [32]. In [33], different requirements of virtual artificial systems are given. These are given below and collectively abbreviated as ACP [33]:

- Artificial systems (AS).
- Computational experiments.
- Parallel execution.

Further, the main focus of Society 5.0 will be to focus on improving the efficacy to solve the miscellaneous problems related to society [31]. Figure 1.5 illustrates four key properties of machine learning approaches for developing regions.

1.4   Cloud-IoT and Societal Developments

The term 'Internet of Things' is coined in 1999 [34]. Perhaps, it was a paradigm shift in technological development and has substantially changed the way of performing things by entailing real-time information gain and also by enhancing the

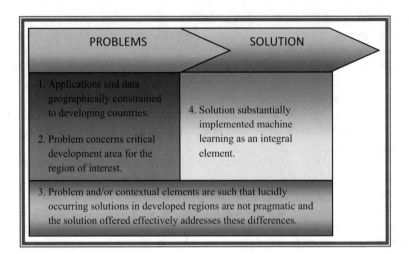

Fig. 1.5   Four key properties of machine learning approaches for developing regions

phenomenon of learning. Indeed, IoT is associated with the phenomenon of M2M and WSN while connectivity is concerned. It is also linked to BD while content outcomes are considered. The functioning of IoT is multi-fold. It incorporates the production and transmission of data between M2M and between M2P as well.

The challenges faced in the pursuit of global development are effectively being tackled by the pragmatic use of cloud-IoT technologies. Different technologies associated with the domain of information and communication e.g., the Internet, big data analytics, and the use of mobile phones are substantially utilized for social development across the world and consistent growth is also being observed. In [35], it is given that 157 new development projects based on these technologies have been started from 2014 to 2015. Further, 140 projects related to the realm of m-health have been launched in 2015 across the developing countries of the world. Moreover, it has also been observed that around 32 projects were started in 2015 related to big data analytics [36]. This is thus explicit that mobiles are a highly indispensable component for different societal development projects. In addition, devices required for the connectivity of sensors and M2M modules further play a crucial role in the purpose of societal development. The role of cloud-IoT is not merely to reform the functioning of financial and implementation aspects of industries but it is also viable different walks of societal development. The sensors connected with cloud-IoT systems may display a higher degree of human wellbeing in different important sectors such as:

- Healthcare sector.
- Water supply network.
- Agricultural sector.
- Natural resource management.
- Climate change.
- Energy sector.

However, there are many other sub-domains, not aforementioned required for the development of a society where cloud-IoT can substantially be used. It is also pertinent to mention that while deciding the suitability of a particular cloud-IoT framework for a given context, many compromises and trade-offs need substantial considerations and analysis. To witness observable development in society different attributions about technical trade-offs must thoroughly be analyzed. These attributions are:

- Performance analysis.
- Reliability criteria.
- Robustness of cloud IoT.
- The efficiency of proposed cloud-IoT.
- Power requirement.
- Data throughput.
- Overall cost analysis.

Different aspects of cloud-IoT for the pursuit of societal development are shown in Fig. 1.6. Further, the cultural scenario of society is also an important issue while discussing the role of cloud-IoT for the pursuit of societal development. Moreover, the emergence of big data techniques also paves the way for new opportunities associated with societal development. Indeed, it enhanced the growth in different streams required for societal advancement. The incorporation of big data techniques within the purview of the clout-IoT framework has generated effective learning

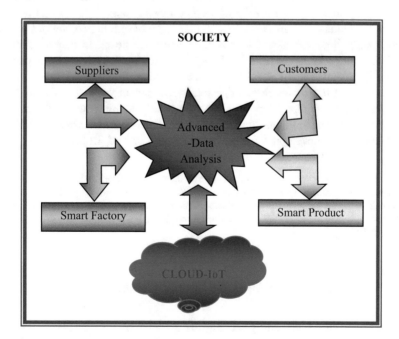

Fig. 1.6 Cloud-IoT and societal development

opportunities which in turn enhanced the efficacy of real-world processes. This hybridization is very much effective in different indispensable components of society as mentioned above as well as in several other application domains. Indeed, cloud-IoT displays the enhanced research work, policies for pubic governance, functioning of basic services, as well as the appraisal and monitoring of different sub-domains required for the pursuit of social development. However, it is also imperative and pertinent to reveal the fact that cloud-IoT also entails some specific regulatory implications regarding the issues of licensing, issues about spectrum, standards, and issues related to security and privacy, and more coordination is needed with the ICT and telecom regulatory bodies to get the increased benefits of the cloud-IoT system. It is because of the facts that these regulating bodies function with their peers to provide data protection and other emergency services. Further, the cloud-IoT framework can impart a substantial role in societal development if law and regulations regarding the data such as how the data can be accessed, how long data can be kept, and what constraints are imposed on the third party regarding the data accessing. Moreover, the impact of the cloud-IoT system on societal development depends on several other issues such as the chunk of information outputted from sensors. It may or may not be an open data type. The term 'open data type' implicates those data which may or may not be liberally accessible on the Internet. Similarly, the transmission of data may or may not cross the public Internet and it is also an issue of paramount importance while discussing the impact of cloud-IoT on societal development. Indeed, the machine-produced data like the sensors data and communication of these data are the pivotal elements to decide how efficient the cloud-IoT system will be for sake of societal development. The societal development of the cloud-IoT framework will be more pervasive if more countries are providing their policy framework and thus more factors can be taken into considerations which in turn make it viable to implement the cloud-IoT system across different sectors of societal development. Over and above, different stakeholders are involved in the cloud-IoT project required for societal development and their active participation in decision making renders the project pragmatic on the ground and thus promising opportunities for more streamlined policy making and implementation of cloud-IoT for the development of society can be observed. In [37], a super-smart society is characterized as:

> a society where the various needs of society are finely differentiated and met by providing the necessary products and services in the required amounts to the people who need them when they need them, and in which all people can receive high-quality services and live a comfortable, vigorous life that makes allowances for their differences such as age, sex, region, or language (p. 10).

1.4.1 Advantages of Cloud-IoT Based Societies

As mentioned in the preceding section, the domains of societal development are pervasive. In this sub-section, the important social applications of cloud-IoT are categorized.

- Smart home.
- Smart society.
- Smart environment.
- Smart Agriculture.
- Smart Health.

Smart living is the desire of every people, particularly those who reside in urban cities. Smart living implicates the remote connection and synchronization of wearable devices so that it could be possible to perform daily functioning flawlessly and easily. Therefore, the connectivity of household gadgets with the personal mobile phone is of the utmost importance so that various home appliances can be operated from remote places at any time. Further, society should also be automated with the cloud-IoT system so that different societal activities can easily be performed. Different issues like searching for a specific shopping mall in unknown cities, recognizing the competent authority to complain, and a lot of issues could be easily tackled and managed with the use of these technologies. Furthermore, an unpolluted environment is the fundamental characteristic of a smart society. Various precautionary measures for the pursuit of environmental cleanliness can effectively be implemented with the help of these technological endeavors. In addition, air pollution is also a matter of great concern and undoubtedly it causes health hazards for the society and this issue could also be manageable up to great extent with the help of cloud-IoT-based technologies. Moreover, a substantial quantity of water is being used as wastage and it is a big drawback for society.

Optimizing the actual need for water for irrigating the agricultural land is a serious problem for many countries for increasing the economy of the society in general and the farmer in particular. Perhaps, weather-assisted farming with cloud-IoT-based systems can play a tremendous role in enhancing the social economy up. Over and above, ICT-based alarming systems can be developed when scarcity or shortage of water is observed in agricultural land. Intuitively, a healthy society is a productive society and cloud-IoT technologies are also considered helpful for maintaining a healthy society. Different patient monitoring and health monitoring machines can be designed constructed with reduced cost using these technologies.

1.4.2 Challenges of Cloud-IoT for Societal Development

The present business scenario reflects cut-throat competition among companies in terms of cost, product quality, and delivery time [38]. Further, to meet the challenges of different sorts innovative ideas and strategies are being implemented in business sectors. Attempt to bring innovative products in a short period in the market is an effective way to reduce the completion around the world [39]. This competitive phenomenon in the industrial sector influences the process of societal development because dealing with competitiveness requires the design of a productive, efficient, and flexible product development cycle [38, 40]. The use of AI and machine intelligence techniques are frequently used nowadays to adapt to the changes of the fast product development cycle as well as to establish the synchronized connection between the machines, products, and processes [39]. Moreover, smart technology such as the CPS system which includes integration of cloud technologies with physical resources and skills of traditional computers can also be used in the business sector [40]. In [41], detailed characteristics of CPS are given. However, the use of these advanced technologies will certainly pose challenges from different fronts in society. In [41], it is mentioned that the companies will implement a global network of CPS systems to fulfill different business requirements and it will cause a central role in societal development. The hybridization of the CPS technique with different entities of industries such as production, logistics, and services will enable the traditional industrial functioning to evolve as Industry 4.0 and thus will contribute significantly to the economic growth of society [40]. Further, the dynamic production and product delivery will display better manageability of the product life cycle. However, it will cause challenges about digitization and automation of production processes. These challenges will also cause a paradigm shift and will provide new opportunities to industry and society as well [39, 42]. Furthermore, the centralized and huge production control of supply chain processes can be decentralized by the implementation of the cloud-IoT technique [43]. This will be a challenging task encountered by the researcher and scientists in the pursuit of social development. The implementation of cloud technologies will render different industrial processes more dynamic, effective in terms of changes, decentralization, optimality, and automation [42]. In [44], it is given that manufacturing units must learn first to walk before they could dream of flying. This can also be treated as the main challenge of social development.

1.4.3   Goals of Industry 4.0 in Society 5.0 Developments

It is inquisitive to visualize a future in which society is using highly advanced technologies. Perhaps, the hybridization of sensors, communication, and computation will converge in the coming future beyond the human perception, cognition, behavior, and physiological domain. However, achieving this phenomenal state will need an entirely different rethinking process at discrete levels. Some phenomenal changes witnessed in the coming future are listed below.

1. Physical infrastructure will not be treated merely as a physical entity. It will be considered as a service.
2. The very traditional service systems of today will emerge as cognitive cooperative systems.
3. The cyber-physical world will work in cooperation with the human world.

In [45–48], it is mentioned that outcome of Industry 4.0 will be the Society 5.0. It is also true that the central tenet of Industry 4.0 is to enhance the production whereas Society 5.0 will demand to engage the manpower in pursuit of innovation so that technology can be hybridized with the phenomenon of Industry 4.0 which in turn will increase the life quality and responsibility with sustainability as well. In [49], Japan's Society 5.0 is visualized as:

> "create new values by collaborating and cooperating with several different systems, and plans standardization of data formats, models, system architecture, etc. and development of necessary human resources... intelligence technologies and so on encourage Japan's competitiveness in "super smart society" (p. 264).

It is being perceived that Society 5.0 will be safe and comfortable for every individual in society. Moreover, Society 5.0 will be highly productive because of the use of advanced technology. In [50], the aims of Society 5.0 are delineated as:

> Every individual including elderly people and women can live safe and secured comfortable and healthy life and every individual can realize his/her desired lifestyle.... Improvement of productivity through digitization and reform of business models are promoted, and at the same time, the new economy and society will be realized by promoting innovation and globalization..... (p. 10).

However, Society 5.0 will also render many challenges. Perhaps, it is due to the paradigm shift in the business scenario. The new businesses and services will be globally expanded at a higher pace. Therefore, the challenges will be on a gigantic scale and different issues will be required to solve at the global spectrum. In [48], different challenges are given.

The goal of Industry 4.0 in Society 5.0 is substantially pervasive. In [50], the goals of Industry 4.0 in the development of Society 5.0 are enumerated as:

1. Strategies formulation and incorporation of government policy at the national and global level.
2. Development of regulations required for the implementation of advanced techniques developed.
3. Goal to establish the knowledge foundation.
4. Goal to actively engage all citizens in the emerging economy of Society 5.0.
5. Goal to hybridized advanced technologies and Society 5.0.

Indeed, the unprecedented outcome of Industry 4.0 will drastically change the life of Society 5.0 and thus the plethora of good and bad consequences will be witnessed. Perhaps, the implementation of cutting-edge technologies will also impart ethical, social, and legal changes in Society 5.0. As is given in [51]:

> The fundamental theory of Societies 5.0 research is parallel intelligence, which is a novel methodology that extends the traditional artificial intelligence theories to the emerging cyber-physical-social systems (CPSS)... parallel intelligence is particularly effective in dealing with "human-in-the-loop" type issues with both social complexity and engineering complexity... (p. 6)

1.5 Benevolent Contributions of Industry 4.0 to Society 5.0

As mentioned in the preceding section, Society 5.0 can be defined with the incorporation of parallel intelligence that includes the concepts of existing artificial intelligence to emerging CPS [52]. The main focus of Society 5.0 is to provide the benefits of technology and outcomes of innovations to human beings so that humanity can be boosted up. The revolution towards attaining Society 5.0 is commenced in Japan to revolutionize society [53]. In nutshell, the prime objective of Society 5.0 is to augment the life quality of human beings in society with the use of attributes provided as the outputs of Industry 4.0 [54]. The journey of Japan towards Society 5.0 is still in vogue with the implementation of new methodologies. However, the other countries of the world are also attempting to adapt to the challenges being imposed by Industry 4.0 [55].

It is explicit that in the current scenario the societal advancement is taking place with the help of research and innovations in science and technology. These scientific and technological innovations in general and particularly in the realm of computer science are significantly contributing to the advancement of society and business as well [32]. Now, different sociological and technological complex issues are being effectively tackled by using the efficacy of parallel intelligence. The implementation of parallel intelligence provides indispensable and pragmatic solutions for the problems of uncertain, diverse, and complex nature [52]. Mankind is indeed facing some challenges of global concerns such as pandemic disease, terrorism, and economic divergence [32]. Still, following the substantial development in different technological domains such as mechanization, electrification, IT, etc. the modern society is turning into a new era where we are witnessing unprecedented technological and innovative development. Moreover, this inter-connection will also display improved life quality of people and will render healthy economic growth [32]. It is obvious that in Society 5.0 the automation will play a central role and perhaps this central role of automation will lead to new developments in the domain of AI and will also render the plausible implementation for the sake of management and control of CPS systems [52].

1.5.1 The Future and Society 5.0

The future of Society 5.0 is quite vibrant. Different societal aspects such as employment, privacy, security, public administration, and industrial structure will observe severe alterations and digital information will reply to existing demands [56]. In the coming future, Society 5.0 has to be implemented by perceiving the hybridization of miscellaneous aspects and spirits of entrepreneurship, and innovation policy [54]. However, in the future Society 5.0 will also

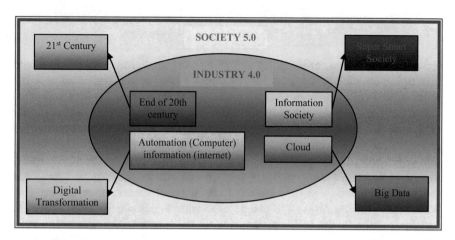

Fig. 1.7 Industry 4.0 and Society 5.0

render its different shortcomings besides high living standards. In [56], it is given that Society 5.0 will reflect some adverse effects on society such as unemployment, unethical division of wealth and information. Further, in the coming future, Society 5.0 will show the incorporation of different advanced technologies more pragmatically in different segments of human lives whereas Industry 4.0 will restrict the use of technological advancement within the industrial sector [57]. Thus, it will entirely depend on the perception of mankind to decide the direction people will like to proceed and it will certainly influence society [56]. The diversification of technologies for the pursuit of humanity like enhanced production, cost reduction, justified division of wealth, less emission of greenhouse gases, and different other issues related to society [58]. Figure 1.7 depicts the prime concerns associated with I4.0 and Society 5.0.

It is also intuitive that the continuous development in the IT sector will provide a plethora of opportunities to every entity of the society which will reflect research innovation, growth of individuals and society as a whole, and a high degree of human-machine interaction. However, as stated above this will also render miscellaneous issues and these issues will require due considerations to realize the benefits of Industry 4.0 in the development of Society 5.0. As is given in [46]:

> It promises to revolutionize society as we know it, and to improve our way of living and living in community, in our personal and professional life.

However, the future of Society 5.0 could only be pragmatic with the upcoming of innovative advanced research which will embrace the interdisciplinary social sciences, humanities, and engineering. Further, the convergence of different research endeavors will reconfigure the association of man, machine, and technologies that will render a sustainable, flamboyant, liveable society in which technology will play vital roles.

1.6 Conclusions

Industrial sectors are continuously observing massive digital transformation and thus trying to cater to the need for consistent evolution and also to resolve the requirements of a swiftly evolving society. The I4.0 is embracing new and innovative technological advancements. Further, the goal of Industry 4.0 is multifaceted such as cost reduction of the end product, energy-saving, enhancing the process efficiency of the production, swift response to customers, and augmentation in product quality, etc. Furthermore, Industry 4.0 renders the digital transformation to permit the constant evolution and consequently it addressed the challenges imposed by society. Indeed, in the present scenario, there are a gigantic and still growing network of people, machines, and products. This network is massively utilizing the facilities rendered by the internet. The innovative technologies about I4.0 could substantially be used for the pursuit of humanity. Moreover, the in-depth innovation and application of advanced technologies are attempting to impart societal benefits and also flourishing a new IR known as the Society 5.0 that concentrates on implementing the technologies for the pursuit of constant development and innovation of society. Society 5.0 also stimulates I4.0 to resolve different inconveniences about mankind and society and thus enhancing life quality of human beings. However, the hybridization of advanced technologies with society will be crucial and strenuous phenomenon because it requires consistent endeavor. It is intuitive that in near future different advanced technologies such as drone deliveries, AI, big data, autonomous vehicles, and robotics will pervasively be used for the benefit of humanity and the entire society.

References

1. Pereira AC, Romero F (2017) A review of the meanings and the implications of the industry 4.0 concept, Procedia manufacturing. Proc Manuf 13:1206–1214
2. Santos MY (2017) Int J Inf Manag. https://doi.org/10.1016/j.ijinfomgt.2017.07.012
3. Kearney AT (2017) Readiness for the future of production: country profiles. https://www.pearney.com/globalcities/2017
4. Schrecker S et al (2016) Industrial internet of things volume G4: security framework. Ind Internet Consort:1–173
5. Almada-Lobo F (2016) The industry 4.0 revolution and the future of manufacturing execution systems (MES). J Innov Manag 3(4):17
6. I. M. S. Board and F. I. for M. E. and A. IPA (2015) Factory of the future
7. Blanco R, Fontrodona J, Poveda C (2017) La industria 4.0: el estado de la cuestión. Econ Ind 406:151–164
8. Plattform Industrie 4.0 (2016) Digitization of Industrie – Platform Industrie 4.0. Plattf Ind 4.0 April:28
9. IIC (2016) The industrial internet of things, volume B01: business strategy and innovation framework. https://www.iiconsortium.org/bsif

10. http://www.euroblech.com/english/euroblech/community/sign/
11. Schwab K (2016) The fourth industrial revolution, Kindle edition. https://www.amazon.in/Fourth-Industrial-Revolution-Professor-Dr-Ing-ebook/dp/B01MSJM2TE
12. Schweichhart K (2016) Reference architectural model industrie 4.0 (RAMI 4.0): an introduction. Publikationen der Plattform Industrie 4.0 0(April)
13. Pfohl H-C, Yahsi B, Kuznaz T (2015) The impact of Industry 4.0 on the Supply Chain. Proc Hamburg Int Conf Logistics (HICL)-20 August:32–58
14. Reinhard G, Jesper V, Stefan S (2016) Industry 4.0: building the digital enterprise. Glob Ind 4.0 Surv:1–39
15. Gilchrist A (2016) Industry 4.0 the industrial internet of things, 2016th edn, Bangken/Nonthaburi
16. Yen CT, Liu YC, Lin CC, Kao CC, Wang WB, Hsu YR (2014) Advanced manufacturing solution to industry 4.0 trend through sensing network and cloud computing technologies. In: 2014 IEEE international conference on automation science and engineering (CASE), pp 1150–1152
17. Avram MG (2014) Advantages and challenges of adopting cloud computing from an Enterprise perspective. Proc Technol 12:529–534
18. Givehchi O, Trsek H, Jasperneite J (2013) Conference program. In: 2013 IEEE 18th conference on Emerging Technologies & Factory Automation (ETFA), pp 1–37. https://doi.org/10.1109/ETFA.6647936
19. Gangwar H, Date H, Ramaswamy R (2015) Understanding determinants of cloud computing adoption using an integrated TAM-TOE model. J Enterp Inf Manag 28(1):107–130
20. Dillon T, Wu C, Chang E (2010) Cloud computing: issues and challenges. In: 2010 24th IEEE international conference on advanced information networking and applications, pp 27–33
21. https://bfsi.eletsonline.com/how-cloud-computing-is-driving-the-industrial-revolution-4-0/
22. https://bfsi.eletsonline.com/has-bfsi-reached-cloud-nine/
23. Kothari U (2005) From colonial administration to development studies: a post-colonial critique of the history of development studies. In: A radical history of development studies: individuals, institutions and ideologies. Zed Books, London, pp 47–66
24. Myrdal G (1974) What is development? J Econ Issues 8(4):729–736
25. Sen A (1988) The concept of development. Handb Dev Econ 1(1988):9–26
26. Ali A, Qadir J, ur Rasool R, Sathiaseelan A, Zwitter A, Crowcroft J (2016) Big data for development: applications and techniques. Big Data Anal 1(1):2
27. Hilbert M (2016) Big data for development: a review of promises and challenges. Dev Policy Rev 34:1
28. Kshetri N (2014) The emerging role of big data in key development issues: opportunities, challenges, and concerns. Big Data Soc 1(2):2053951714564227
29. World Bank (2014) Big data in action for development. World Bank other operational studies 21325. The World Bank. http://EconPapers.repec.org/RePEc:wbk:wboper:21325
30. United Nations (2014) World economic situation and prospects 2014. Retrieved July 15, 2017, from http://www.un.org/en/development/desa/policy/wesp/wesp_current/wesp2014.pdf
31. Prasetyo YA, Arman AA (2017) Group management system design for supporting society 5.0 in smart society platform. In: International Conference on Information Technology Systems and Innovation (ICITSI), 2017
32. Yoshihiro Shiroishi KU (2018) Society 5.0: for human security and well-being. IEEE Comput Soc
33. Shibata M, Ohtsuka Y, Okamoto K, Takahashi M (2017) Toward an efficient search method to capture future MOT curriculum based on the society 5.0. In: PICMET '17: technology management for interconnected world
34. Ashton K (1999) That 'internet of things' thing, in the real world things matter more than ideas. RFID J

35. Keynote presentation by Dr. Carolyn Woo of Catholic Relief Services. http://schd.ws/ hosted_files/crsict4dconference2015a/84/2015%20ICT4D%20Conference%20Welcome%20 Presentation%20Final.pdf
36. Big Data for a More Resilient Future", World Bank Group/2015 Spring Meetings, Big Data for Development, Summary of Projects. https://www.worldbank.org/en/events/2015/03/31/ big-data-for-a-more-resilient-future
37. Harayama Y (2017) Society 5.0: aiming for a new human-centered Society. Collaborative Creation through Global R&D open innovation for creating the future: volume 66 number 6 August 2017. Hitachi Review. pp 8–13. Hitachi Review vol 66, no 6. http://www.hitachi.com/ rev/archive/2017/r2017_06/pdf/p08-13_TRENDS.pdf
38. Dombrowski U, Richter T, Krenkel P (2017) Interdependencies of Industrie 4.0 & lean produc-tion systems – a use cases analysis. In: 27th international conference on flexible automation and intelligent manufacturing, FAIM2017, pp 1061–1068
39. Hecklau F, Galeitzke M, Flachs S, Kohl H (2016) Holistic approach for human resource management in industry 4.0. In: 6th CLF – 6th CIRP conference on learning factories. Elsevier, pp 1–6
40. Lee J, Bagheri B, Kao H-A (2015) A cyber-physical systems architecture for industry 4.0-based manufacturing systems, vol 3. Elsevier, pp 18–23
41. Hermann M, Pentek T, Otto B (2015) Design principles for Industrie 4.0 scenarios: a literature review. Technische Universität Dortmund
42. Lu Y (2017) Industry 4.0: a survey on technologies, applications and open research issues. J Ind Inf Integr
43. Almada-Lobo F (2015) The industry 4.0 revolution and the future of manufacturing execution systems (MES). J Innov Manag 3:16–21
44. Ruttimann BG, Stockli MT (2016) Lean and industry 4.0 – twins, partners, or contenders? A due clarification regarding the supposed clash of two production systems. J Serv Sci Manag 09:485–500
45. Prasetyo YA, Arman AA (2017) Group management system design for supporting society 5.0 in smart society platform. In: 2017 International conference on information technology systems and innovation (ICITSI). https://doi.org/10.1109/icitsi.2017.8267977
46. Costa JM (2018) Sociedade 5.0: a mudança que aí vem. 13/04/2018. https://hrportugal.pt/ sociedade-5-0-a-mudanca-que-ai-vem/
47. i-SCOOP (2018) From Industry 4.0 to Society 5.0: the big societal transformation plan of Japan. https://www.i-scoop.eu/industry-4-0-society-5-0/
48. Serpanos D (2018) The cyber-physical systems revolution. Computer 51I(3):70–73
49. Hayashi H, Sasajima H, Takayanagi Y, Kanamaru H (2017) International standardization for a smarter society in the field of measurement, control, and automation. In: 2017 56th annual conference of the Society of Instrument and Control Engineers of Japan (SICE). https://doi. org/10.23919/sice.2017.8105723
50. Keidanren (Japan Business Federation) (2016) Toward realization of the new economy and society. Reform of the economy and society by the deepening of "Society 5.0". http://www. keidanren.or.jp/en/policy/2016/029_outline.pdf
51. Wang F-Y, Yuan Y, Wang X, Qin R (2018) Societies 5.0: a new paradigm for computa-tional social systems research. IEEE Trans Comput Soc Sys 5(1). https://doi.org/10.1109/ TCSS.2018.2797598
52. Wang F-Y, Yuan Y, Wang X, Qin R (2018) Societies 5.0: a new paradigm for Computational social systems research. IEEE Trans Comput Soc Syst 5:2–8
53. Costa JM (2018, February 1) Dinheiro Vivo. Available: https://www.dinheirovivo.pt/opiniao/ sociedade-5-0-o-futuro-pelo-presente
54. Ferreira CM, Serpa S (2018) Society 5.0 and social development: contributions to a discussion, vol 5. Sciedu Press, pp 26–31

55. Francisco J (2017, August 7) Revista Cargo. Available: https://revistacargo.pt/japao-avanca-sociedade-5-0-drones-camioes-autonomos
56. Nakanishi H (2019, January 9) World Economic Forum. Available: https://www.weforum.org/agenda/2019/01/modern-society-has-reached-its-limits-society-5-0-will-liberate-us
57. Skobelev PO, Borovik SY (2017) On the way from industry 4.0 to industry 5.0: from digital manufacturing to a digital society. Int Sci J "Industry 4.0":307–311
58. Oliveira H (2019, January 17) VER – Valores, Ética e Responsabilidade. Available: http://www.ver.pt/a-sociedade-5-0-e-a-co-criacao-do-futuro/

Chapter 2
A Glimpse of Techno-Psychological Perspective of Society 5.0

Abstract Industry 4.0 (I-4.0) entail the use of very advanced technologies and plays a vital role in the pursuit of augmenting the quality of life of the individuals in the society and the society as a whole. Further, the technologies invented and developed by technology 4.0 are also used for solving the complex problems of Society 5.0 (S-5.0) and thus renders benefits to mankind. S-5.0 has peculiar attention which encompasses the sentient being at pivotal of modernization while technological revolution and the automation of industrial processes are being motivated by I-4.0. The S-5.0 is visualized as a society in which a happier, satisfied, and fulfilled paradigm will be reflected and thus the society will be more productive. Moreover, S-5.0 also displays an increased degree of interconnection between people and computers and the use of the Internet and information technology exists prominently. The scope of this chapter is to determine if different modern technologies including information technology can influence people's behavior, opinion, and psychology or not. Further, this chapter also analyzes the impact of modern technologies on the overall arena of societal psychology. Furthermore, different positive and negative psychological consequences of society created because of the use of modern technologies are also delineated in this chapter and it has been revealed that modern technologies generated psychological ambivalence in the society. Perhaps, it is because modern technology is responsible for creating ease and comfort in society and simultaneously it creates negative impacts of catastrophic degree. Over and above, the psycho-dynamics of society are illustrated with the help of two extremities. These are the 'technophilia' and 'technophobia. Some psychological models are also included in this chapter.

Keywords Social psychology (SP) · Social behavior (SB) · Technology4.0 · Society 5.0 (S-5) · Psychological models

2.1   Introduction

> The same technology that simplifies life by providing more functions in each device also complicates life by making the device harder to learn, harder to use. This is the paradox of technology. [1]

Nowadays technology is pervasive and its use is widely available and is also consistently promoted throughout society. This is around us and is involved in each everyday action and different entities around us. Indeed, in the recent past, we observed gigantic growth in different technical domains, and in the past decades, technology has noted an exponential advancement. Indeed, Industry 4.0 has been revolutionized the entire production processes of the industry with associated operational efficiency. Many business models, products, and services have also been conceptualized within the purview of Industry 4.0. It renders real-time production, planning, and dynamic optimization a reality contrary to traditional forecasting. Consequently, Industry 4.0 commences the emergence of Society5.0 in Japan. Industry 4.0 also created Intelligent systems which are considered beneficial for society rather than as foes.

The outbreak of different state-of-art technologies including computer and information technology (CIT) rendered miscellaneous psychological effects on society. It is true that as the advancement of technologies takes place more it seems to have control over sentient life. Perhaps, it is because the modern state-of-art technologies create in the same measure, comfort, and disasters. Undoubtedly, technology renders life easier but it also reflects many associated problems for the society of living beings. Everyone can observe that normal social behavior is being mitigated gradually owing to more and more encroachment of technology in the life of living beings.

Yet, the existing societies visualized the significance of intelligent emerging technologies as a form of new knowledge and believe these technologies as essential tools to solve many intricate problems. The word 'technology' comprises of two sub-parts and can be defined as:

> The methods and tools that a society has developed to facilitate the solution of its practical problems and to provide the necessary needs for the community.

It is also intuitive that the application of science, engineering, and technology (SET) in society also enhances the perils, terrorization, and offenses and undoubtedly reflects negativity and also creates a sense of confinement on the use of technology in different purview [2]. Humans are a social creature and it is also the fact that in present societal scenario the mutual relationships of human beings is substantially governed by SET. For example, social media has mitigated the sense of distance but it also encompasses numerous negative consequences which severely and adversely influence the human relationship in family and society as well. In contrast, modern technologies are also visualized as the essential requirement of life and are also considered as the indicator of the community's cultural awareness. Moreover, in the modern era, technologies also incorporate a prominent role because technologies have crept in all walks of sentient beings and are imparting miscellaneous services, improving the standard of living, and augmenting virtual connectivity across the globe. Further, the use of the Internet and communication mediated with advanced computation has also rendered incredible advancement in society and created drastic changes in societal scenarios about the means of communication. Internet technology has also influenced many society related tasks like the way professional conducts the customers as well as the large scale survey conduction [3]. Due to the emergence of Internet technology, conventional paper-based surveys have substantially reduced, whereas online surveys have popularly become the favorite means. But, it is inquisitive to ponder many associated questions such as: which approach is more effective? What are the merits and demerits of each approach? Will the replacement of one approach with the other be realizable? Many researchers worked in these perspectives and attempted to investigate how these approaches display the behavior in different sectors. In [4–6], it has been mentioned that the succinct use of the Internet proposes a novel way to collect the data and to perform the survey. However, the online survey witnessed hybrid consequences in comparison to conventional hard questionnaires (paper questionnaires). The Internet-based survey rendered easiness in accumulating the reply from a wide variety of people, from geographically and demographically diverse areas [7]. The lower costs, the fewer data entry errors, the faster transmission, and reception are some other points that some researchers found as pros in this category [8, 9]. According to the response rates, local paper surveys seem to be shorter. It has also been observed during the literature survey that in earlier research papers, researchers had attempted to define related groups of factors to evaluate methods performing surveys.

The central belief of SET in the different purview of human activity has been created different philosophical aspects such as philosophy of SET, sociological aspects of knowledge as well as the historical phenomena of science and technology. The literature survey revealed the fact that in the recent past the emergence of succinct inter-disciplinary subjects about studies of science and technology took place. Further, such inter-disciplinary subjects attempted the systematic and strategic investigation to find the dynamic relationship among the science, technology, and the life of human beings. It is observed that researchers have also been attempted to analyze the psychological phenomenon of the individual as well as a social psychological phenomenon created because of the proliferation of science and technology in society. However, research in this realm is still marginal. Perhaps, this marginality is because of three reasons as enumerated below.

1. Psychology has not been treated as an important attribute within the domain of science and technology.
2. The realm of psychology has not seriously been represented as an element of SET.
3. The psychological research associated with SET has witnessed the very little impact on the discipline of psychology itself.

However, the critical analysis of psychological science has created a sub-discipline within the wide domain of psychology which entails: (a) Theoretical psychology (b) Critical psychology, and (c) Feminist psychology. It is also revealed from the literature survey that the required interfacing between these endeavors within the studies of science and technology is not optimally covered. Even today, psychology is considered a subject of rigorous investigation in natural sciences.

While studying the psychological consequence of individuals in particular and society in general, there are two extremities on the socio-psychological thread. These are:

- Technophilia i.e., affection to technologies and
- Technophobia i.e., rejection of technologies.

These two extremities generate several important issues about the societal and psychological thrust of modern technologies. These two extreme positions have also created impetus presumably will create substantial debatable aspects about advantages and dangers by the development of technologies. These two extremities reflect the association between SET and the sentient being. But more specifically, these two reflect the relationship between technology and society. In this chapter, emphasis is given on the psychological implications of society owing to the emergence of modern, novel, and innovative technologies.

Indeed, the preceding attempts could not create a cusp for developing the psychology of SET in general and more particularly in the larger community of studies about SET. Perhaps, this is because the preceding attempts have comprised the tendency to have a firm promise to a non-reflexive epistemology and this non-reflexive epistemology does not permit for varying approaches such as historical, critical, constructionist, qualitative, and theoretical approaches. Contrary to this paradigm, the approaches of studies of SET are inter and multi-disciplinary. Moreover, the approaches of studies and researches of SET deeply interrogate and investigate the scientific limits onto the modernity of western epistemology [10]. Undoubtedly, significant historical work about cognitive approaches of SET and associated methodologies considerably enabled to churn out the micro-level of specialties in the domain of machine cognition in the early 1980s [11, 12]. Further, these findings helped a lot in the domain of psychological science [13, 14]. Furthermore, different qualitative methods also helped in the creation of the empirical philosophy of SET [15]. However, these endeavors could not render psychology a science [16].

Presumably, psychological contributions to SET, or the studies of psychological attributes of SET need a substantial concern. Thus, it seems that because of the swiftness of spreading of modern technology and its uses associated with false and negative thrust an increased concern is required. Perhaps, this phenomenon exists owing to the deficiency of efficient supervision, and thus a sector of society rendered themselves against the applications of SET in society. It is also worthy to mention that teaching and learning is a prevailing domain of society and the implementation of technologies in universities, colleges, and schools can greatly enhance the effectiveness of the teaching-learning process [17].

In this chapter, an attempt has been made to discuss briefly the psychological contributions and perspective of SET. Moreover, this chapter will display the adverse effects of SET on society and will provide insights to enhance people's wakefulness to use modern technologies in an optimum way. Certainly, modern technologies play a vital role in an individual's life and prospects. Therefore, the authors believe that the positive influences of technologies on individuals and society as well will increase by illustrating the negative influences of technologies on society.

2.2 Literature Review

For long researchers were interested to examine the roles of SET within the contextual purview of society and history. In the 1960s, questions were raised by historians regarding technological determinism. Technological determinism is the doctrine that can entail the passivity of the general public associated with the natural development of science and technology. It has also been observed through the literature survey that almost at the same time contextual approaches to the history of medicine commenced by the historians. In [18], the structure of the scientific revolution is published. This publication discussed the concept of changes in intellectual paradigm concerning changes in scientific theories. After this publication, programs were founded in different reputed universities of the world that brought together philosophers and historians of science to work in an ensemble manner. Further, in mid of the 1960s, the combined social movements of faculties and students in many reputed universities of the world rendered a variety of interdisciplinary domains of studies. These interdisciplinary domains of studies addressed miscellaneous relevant topics that were previously been ignored by the conventional curriculum such as the development of programs about hybridization of 'science, technology, and society. This program is comprised of different streams such as history, sociology, and political science. Different scholars of this program designed the undergraduate-level curricula to investigate and explore different issues related to science and technology. It is pertinent to mention that the scholars of this program were keenly working to create substantial changes unlike the attitude of so-called 'ivory tower' researchers. Moreover, the working paradigms of the researchers of this program were and are also different from the scholars of science, scholars working on the historical and philosophical perspective of SET. For example, feminist scholars of this program addressed themselves not as the member of the domain of science and technology.

The studies of SET and policies related to public administration came forward in the1970s. The concerns behind these studies are numerous. But, the main concern was a sense that the domain of science and technology was expanding in a manner that was considered not suitable with the interest of the larger public. Indeed, the domain of science and technology as well as the societal movement were also attempting to improve the living standard of those who would make the SET of the coming future, but this stream adopted a distinct way. Further, this different approach was used for the training purposes of students and professionals and thus enabled them to become connoisseurs in the SET policy.

It has been witnessed that some programs emphasized quantitative techniques, and many such programs were ultimately imbibed into systems engineering. It has also been observed that others programs focused more on sociological aspects as well as on qualitative phenomena. Such programs were implemented by scholars in the domain of SET and different societal sectors. Furthermore, between the decades of seventy and eighty of the twentieth century different prominent universities of the United States, United Kingdom, and Europe tried to implement these programs and thus formed new and interdisciplinary programs such as hybridized the studies of science with history and philosophy. The hybridization of different streams resulted in unique identities owing to variations in the attributes hybridized together. Moreover, unique identities were also developed because of variations in the geographical locations of different universities. For example, the studies of the SET program of the University of Virginia encompassed scholars from a variety of domains. However, the teaching responsibility of the program was carried out within an engineering institution where ethics was taught to undergraduate engineering students by the faculty having a strong interest in engineering ethics.

A plethora of research has been conducted in different countries as found in a literature survey that investigated the negative impact and misuse of modern state-of-art technologies on society across the globe. In [19], attempts have been made to analyze the advantages and disadvantages of Internet technology and it has been observed that the majority of participants were desirous for using the Internet. Further, the majority of the participants were also keen to use Internet technology for communication, searching for information, and the purpose of entertainment. It has also been revealed in this study that Internet technology is also associated with certain negative aspects such as a cause of the cultural invasion. Moreover, participants reported that frequent use of Internet technology also creates problems related to society, ethics, and health.

In [20], research was organized to examine the role of media in the domain of information technology (IT) and its adverse influence on family relationships. This study also concentrated on the adverse effect generated due to the consequence of media and IT on society. In this study, it has been concluded that the media and IT reduces the family-oriented value system and it can be considered as a substantial negative impact on society. Further, this study recommends the upbringing of young and adults as per the requirement of the moral system which supports their identity. In [21], the study was also conducted to observe the effects of text messaging and social media on teenagers. In this study, forty people have participated from the age group of eleven to thirteen years. The study revealed the fact that indeed the friendship created without the help of technology and friendship created with the help of social media are almost two distinct phenomena and there exists only a limited overlapping between these two. The study also concluded that instant online messaging cannot replace the need for social support for people suffering from isolation.

Further, in [2], a study was performed to examine the role of new and innovative technologies such as the Internet to analyze and identify the negative implications of cell phones and pertinent Bluetooth technology and it has been found that there are substantial dichotomies in the usage pattern of Internet technology and cell phone among antisocial and non-antisocial young [2].

In [22], further studies have been carried out among the students of Jordanian society to identify the impacts of the use of the Internet on different social relations. In this study, 325 male and female students were randomly selected to form the sample of the study. It has also been analyzed that the students use the Internet mostly within the campus and even maximum use of the Internet was for scientific research. Moreover, it was found that the use of the Internet was also influenced by several other factors which encompass societal mutual relations and other qualitative variables. These are:

- Gender
- Age
- Types of college
- Academic level
- Monthly income etc.

In [22], different statistical values are given for these variables. In [23], it is stated that the impact of Internet-based social networking substantially influences the values and morality of young people in Saudi Arabia and there is a need to create a well-defined procedure to augment the degree of morality and to determine the moral order of the country. It is believed that such a mechanism is necessary for the young people of Arab and Muslim religions to the adoption of a high degree of moral and religious values. Furthermore, emphasis was also given on the mechanism that can explain how the youth of Saudi Arabia managed the virtual time provided by the Internet-based social media and on the mechanism that can monitor the opinion and attitudes of young people which could generate and spreads immoral behavior in Saudi Arabia and other Islamic countries.

In [24], a study was conducted regarding the pros and cons of modern technologies. The outcome of this study revealed the adverse effect of modern technologies on the health of the individual. This study worked out the different negative impacts of excessive use of the Internet like decaying of self-control, overlooking of personal status, decaying of adequate communication, and loss of relationship in the social environment. The outcome of this study asserted that Internet addiction even being a bad habit is increasing among people, particularly in the case of university students.

Indeed, there is a lot of research investigating and exploring the negative impact and misuse of modern state-of-art technologies within the social framework. It is the authors' opinion that by analyzing and exploring the adverse effect of modern technologies, their positive impacts on the individual and the society as well can effectively be observed. Moreover, it is an important area of research because modern state-of-art technologies play a pivotal role in an individual's life and social life, as well as numerous future possibilities, which is also associated with this issue.

2.3　Theoretical Framework of Social Psychology

Nowadays, SP is considered as basic science and similar to different other sciences categorized in distinct phases. The SP stemmed from ancient Greek philosophy commenced around 600 BC [25]. The philosopher Aristotle hypothesized the body as the function of the mind and stated that the bodily processes are responsible for the activity of the mind which subsequently reflects behaviors. Even more, he supported mental capabilities and said that environmental effects exerted on the body are responsible for the creation of mental actions. The sensory organs sense the environmental effects and subsequently, these effects are carried to the heart, and thus the thought and reasoning processes start. Indeed, the realm of SP possesses multifold purposes and its objective is not merely an analysis of human beings and their association with other individuals of society like general psychology rather its scope is wider and it paves the way to study the social aspects of human personality. Perhaps, two aspects of human personality should be considered to understand things in a better way. These are the individual aspect of human beings and the social aspect of a human being. However, practically it is a hard issue to distinguish between these two aspects. Indeed, this differentiation can only exist in terms of relativity because the action of a human being what he does in isolation and away from society is also influenced by his social environment [26]. Undoubtedly, SP is an important subject and it must be deeply researched while technology is exponentially expanding.

From the above discussion, it is obvious that SP is the realm in which we study the behavior of individuals and the theories about behavior and deviance. Following theories are of paramount importance in this pursuit.

- The Contagion Theory.
- The Emergent Norms Theory.
- Looking Glass Self.
- Durkheim's Anomie Theory.
- Inter-actionist Theory.

These theories are diagrammatically depicted in Fig. 2.1. Contagion theory is a theory of collective behavior and it was given in [27]. This theory delineates the hypnotic impact of the crowd on individuals. We can say that according to this theory crowd governs the individual's behavior and the individuals' viewpoint would greatly be mitigated. In [28], it is stated that an in-crowd individual mimics the action of the crowd and follows the same [28].

In [29], the 'emergent norms theory' was proposed. According to this theory, the individual's behavior is incorrectly portrayed by the contagion theorist. This theory suggests that individuals display varying behavior in crowed. Some individuals are passive supporters of the crowd whereas some individuals are dominated by the crowd. Even some individuals are just the onlookers and do not follow the crowd. Therefore, the behavior cannot be simultaneous [28].

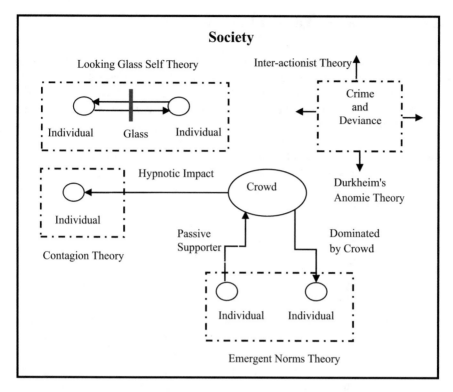

Fig. 2.1 The different theoretical frameworks of SP

In [30], the theory of Looking Glass Self' was proposed. According to this theory, human personality possesses a peculiar characteristic. Individual's personality possesses the tendency of adjustment of conduct in accord to the conduct of others towards him. This theory states that one individual manifests the thoughts of other persons and calibrates his self-feelings according to comments of others [28]. This is the reason that it is named as looking glass self.

Durkheim's Anomie theory visualizes crime, offense, and deviance as a social fact. Further, as per this theory, deviance is indispensable for society because it can incorporate novel and innovative ideas and challenges. These changes bring further different socio-cultural changes in the later discourse of the time. Moreover, these changes also distinguish superior and inferior behavior existing in society [31]. Furthermore, the inter-actionist theory also argues that deviance is a constructive phenomenon for society. This theory rejects the concept of inherent deviance and thus also rejects the deviance tag [31].

2.4   How Does Technology Influences SP?

Some person adopts most or all the technologies with a positive attitude and visualizes the technologies as the means to improve the living conditions and to combat the social problem [32]. At the same time, it is also true that because of the explosion of modern and innovative technologies almost in every walk of human life, fear is also manifested in many people. This fear often causes different symptoms in individuals such as ignoring the technology as well as some organic symptoms like sweating and palpitations while using the technology or just thinking about the technology. It has been visualized that approximately one-third of the entire population is affected by this phenomenon. In [33], a dramatic assertion regarding the SP is proposed as given below.

> social psychology's guiding paradigm – the study of the relationship between psychological states and social behavior – has run its course (p. 205).

The assertion given in [33] uses the inference that:

> Social psychology should no longer be concerned with classification systems that 'describe dynamic mental processes that cannot be directly seen, touched, or measured'

Perhaps, the motive behind these changing elucidations is that the behavior cannot be argued as an apparent real phenomenon. Further, behavior cannot be gauged and categorized impartially. Therefore, the elucidations are vulnerable to debate and substitution [33]. It is also pertinent to mention that current society is substantially computer or machine-oriented and therefore it is highly required that social psychologists must analyze the present society keeping in view the influence of technologies [33].

Indeed, some people have the feeling of 'technophobia or 'computer phobia'. This causes the emergence of illogical dreads and anxieties and creates a tendency of the behavior to avoid the use of technology. Techno-phobia generates mental resistance to new technology. This term is incorporated to depict people refrain to utilize computers while they have a chance to use them or when it is mandatory to use. It is pertinent to mention that techno-phobia does not implicate fear of retrenchment from a job due to intervention of technology or fear from the radiation emitted by a computer screen. Instead, it is the effective stimulus and pessimistic attitude about technologies. It has also been observed that there is no relation between techno-phobia with age. This psychological phenomenon can influence young and elderly populations alike and subsequent researches manifest that this psychological are far from being improved. Perhaps, two psychological phenomena are important to discuss and analyze the social-psychological paradigm created because of the use of technology. The characteristics of these two are opposite. These two have already been mentioned in the introduction section. However, to maintain the continuity in the text these two are again mentioned below:

- Techno-phobia
- Technophilia

Technophilia generally refers to the enthusiasm created owing to the use of technology, more specifically due to the use of new technologies. Now, these two aspects will be discussed in more detail in the forthcoming sub-sections.

2.4.1 Technophilia

In [33], it is suggested that SP is exclusively associated with illustration SB reflected in repercussion of purposive alteration in technologies. More than fifty years back, Edwin Holt, the behavior scientist of Harvard proposed a similar claim regarding consciousness and human behavior. It is mentioned in [34] that

> Contents of consciousness are simply a set of specific responses to the objects in the environment that control a person's behavior.

Further, previous findings related to human behavior suggest a substantial inert function for living beings in influencing their future as humans merely are influenced by, but humans do not affect the environment [35]. The same claim is also made in [33] and it is asserted that SP should limit itself to investigate how human beings are influenced by modern SET. However, this is a ridiculous approach on SB because it is surely not the scenario that human beings are simply imprudent to responses created because of the environmental stimuli as well as technology. However, it is given in [34] that human beings are also evenly proactive and fundamental persuading entities onto the environment.

The term 'technophilia is primarily used in sociology to examine the mutual interaction between individuals and society and was coined in the 1960s. This term implicates simple adaptation for alteration in society created by novelties of modern technologies and emphasizes how intense futuristic positive feelings can be created by the use of technology. However, there is a certain drawback of this phenomenon. Often, it restricts pragmatic evaluation of the technological impact on the environment and society because of the extreme craze for technology. But, authors found in the literature that human society does not entail the efficacy to refuse to accept the influences of technology. It is evidentiary that so many technologies are being in use because of the expression of personal narcissism and technophiles take pleasure in using technology and egocentric benefits are their center of attention [36].

It is revealed from the literature survey that in the eighteenth century it was hypothesized that improvement in techniques is of the utmost importance for the development and expansion of industrialized societies so that efficient and effective useful products can be manufactured for the comfort of consumers. Precisely, it can be stated that societies of this manifestation are primarily technophiles in characteristic. Thus, there is no doubt that technophilia is likely to set norms in most modern societies and is linked with the occurrence of 'normality' of SP [36].

In the subsequent sub-section, the authors will describe Internet addiction and related pathological issues.

2.4.1.1 Internet Addiction (IA) or IA Disorder (IAD)

The phenomenon of technological addiction implicates excessive and obsessive binding of people with the technology they possess and is frequently considered as the negative linking of technophilia. Many people are addicted to the use of the Internet. This term was firstly used in [37] and subsequently taken as the specialized terminology. IA or IAD manifests the tendency of compulsive use of the Internet. In [38], Internet addiction is direct expression of 'addiction without drugs'. Presently, IAD is comprised in the diagnostic and statistical manual of mental disorders (DSMMD)'. But, 'American Medical Association (AMA)' and the 'American Society of Addiction Medicine (ASAM)' are not agreed to include IA in this manual [39].

In 1995, clinical psychologist Mark Griffiths had been interested in research on gambling, computer use, and use of various machines or technology by humans and published his article titled 'technology addiction' [40]. Further, in 1996, he published on 'Internet addiction' [41]. Contrary to these researchers, I. Goldberg considered IA as a sign unlike to disorder. Further, to illustrate the IA, he visualized its similarity with gambling. I. Goldberg stated that the addictive behavior reflects the socio-affectionate infantile behavior in the individual's inefficacy to develop a true and concrete psychosocial characteristic:

> Internet addiction can cause the denial or the avoidance of other current issues of life… all mental disorders related to the use of computer equipment, harmful to the human individual.

There is another type of disorder often related to ID. This is known as 'communication addiction disorder' which reflects the behavioral disorder of constantly communicates with others, even when there is no need or pragmatic explanation for the same. It is a type of IAD in which an individual becomes addicted to the social network whether is real or virtual elements of the Internet like social media. Often, these activities create intra-psychic disagreement and remorse [42].

2.4.2 Technophobia

As mentioned above, the characteristics of technophobia are the reverse of technophilia. Some people feel fear, dislike, and uneasiness towards using complicated technical devices and modern SET and complex SET equipment particularly computers because of technophobia. The expression technophobia is associated with cyber-phobia and is concisely depicted as an unreasonable dread or anxiety created as the fringe consequences because of the use of modern SETs. The depiction of technophobia consists of two attributes:

- Dread was created as a repercussion owing to SET advancement.
- Dread was created from the use of SET devices.

Technophobia is an exaggerated and unjustified fear. That's why the majority of researchers pondered that it always has a pathological character. However, some quantum of fears may be rightly justified such as fear of radiation exposure. Indeed, it is also true that technical progress can sometimes be harmful to the balanced ecosystem. Often, it is conceptualized that technology is detrimental to the environment and ethics. The technology of biometrics and video surveillance is considered a serious threat to an individual's freedom and thus attempting to create a progressive social control which in turn may degenerate into a new structure of despotism. The technophobic negative side of technology was depicted in some literary works and movies also such as in the literary work 'Frankenstein' and in the movies like 'Metropolis' and 'Modern Times'.

In [43], three dominant types of technophobes are identified as given below.

- Uncomfortable users.
- Cognitive computer phobia.
- Anxious computer phobia.

The degree of anxiousness is much less in 'uncomfortable users' due to lack of sufficient information regarding the efficient utilization of computers while the second category of technophobes i.e. cognitive computer phobia look serene and controlled externally but they feel negative cognition and anxiety from inside. Moreover, the people of the third category that is 'anxious computer-phobia' display typical characteristics during the use of computers such as palpitations of the heart and sweating on the palms, etc. Observing the symptoms of these three categories, it can be inferred that the technophobes cannot completely ignore the root cause of their anxiety. Further, it is intuitive to ponder that an elevated degree of anxiety can generate the tendency of ignoring the use of technologies or at least can render the reduced performance. This is the particular outcome of technophobia in comparison to other phobias. It is worthy to mention that with the increased complicacy of modern technologies the numbers of technophobes are also increasing. In [36], a research outcome is given which was based on the students of different countries and is published in 'Computers in Human Behavior in the early 90 s. This research shows the following data of technophobia (1) USA -29% (2) Japan- 58% (3) India-82% (4) Mexico-53%. Further study was also conducted in 2000 and it has been observed almost 85–90% of newly recruited employees may feel uneasiness about new technologies and they reflected the symptoms of technophobes to some extent. Some researchers also observed that aged people have less anxiety in comparison to younger.

In [44], it was visualized that social psychologists are working extensively but they are obsessed with social power and control. Further, in [33], a new and important insight into social psychology was proposed which aimed to show how the skill-effort demand of technology is linked with the psychological processes. In [33], a ghost town was hypothesized in which the author visualized:

a 'paradigm that has run its course; a discipline that deals with 'processes that cannot be directly seen, touched, or measured...these 'ghosts' have such names as dissonance, inequity, expectations, attributions, cognitive schema....there are no empirical procedures used to verify their independent existence (p. 207)

One explanation appears as good as another; certainly, we cannot prove anybody wrong (p. 208)

social psychology has neither the methodology nor the conceptual tools to examine how behavior is influenced by more than one, two, or, at most, three variables at a time. (p. 207)

It is also objected in [33] that:

The consensus [among social psychologists] that it is more important to study how people perceive and react to events than to study the events themselves. (p. 207)

Indeed, technophobia is usually related to computers but it can be because of any technical device. A research was conducted as given in [45] and it has been observed that when a camera was installed in the classroom the anxiety of students was increased and consequently their vocabulary acquisition substantially decreased. The term 'technophobia' has been defined in multiple ways. However, its definition seems to render more and more complexities with technological advancement. One important definition of this term is given in [46] which constitute the following attributes.

- It is a form of mental obstruction that arises when discuss or ponder about computers.
- It renders dread or anxiety towards the computer.
- It creates antagonistic or violent feelings for computers.

Therefore, in [36], three attributes of this term are given. These are: behavioral, emotional, and attitudinal. Moreover, in [47], different attributes of this term are given as:

- It creates anxiety about the present or future interaction with computers or allied technologies.
- It creates a negative global impact related to computers, associated operations, and its impact on society.
- It creates peculiar adverse cognitions while interacting with computers/pondering about future interaction.

Further, several questionnaires have been designed regarding the anxiety and manifested attitudes towards computers based on postulates given in [46] to identify the potential characteristics of such people. Several scales were also created to measure the anxiety created because of the attributes mentioned above. One such scale is discussed in [48]. It is also mentioned in [36] that different theories also revealed the fact that anxiety and attitude towards the computer are included in the phenomenon of technophobia and both the factor is anxiety and negative attitudes are recognized as the basic factors to ameliorate the symptoms of technophobia. In [36], it is mentioned that;

The researchers also revealed the fact that anxiety will be more when it is like a personality trait rather than a transient mental state and the researchers revealed that anxiety towards computer is higher when it is like a personality trait rather than a transient mental state. The degree of neuroticism correlates positively with anxiety toward the computer, while the introversion-extraversion dimension of personality, does not show any relevance.

There are miscellaneous pertinent questions regarding technophobia like what remedial actions should be taken against technophobia and whether it is a problematic feature or not. Indeed, all such questions depend on the perception of the legitimacy of technophobia itself. In [49], it is given that if technophobia is visualized as a state that must and can be conquered, then, the technophobe must take pathological assistance. However, if technophobia is identified as a rightful and coherent outcome of the obligatory modern SETs then the scenario will be different.

2.5 Psychological Models of Technophobia

Researchers have also been attempted to find the aspects which may create an impact on the performance. In [50], many such aspects have been assessed from different participants related to the following attributes.

- Computer anxiety
- Cognitive approach
- Locus of control
- Self-efficacy

These factors are shown in Fig. 2.2. In this study different participants participated to perform the searching of information from a database with the help of a computer. Provision had been made to complete the task via two approaches: (1) by visual observation of the database. (2) Structuring the query [51, 52]. Further, participants were allowed to apply both strategies and it has been revealed after multiple regression that self-efficacy plays a substantial role in content prediction while the structuring was of the highest level.

In this study, it had been observed that participants, whose confidence level was high, were supported by questions to get the data in tables. In contrast, less confident participants searched the data in every line in a sequential manner to find the information required.

Further, the experimental factors mentioned earlier were given due consideration for the analysis of the next stage so that the level of self-efficacy can be predicted. It was found that the degree of anxiety was an important parameter for the prediction of self-efficacy. However, in principle, at least theoretically, the relation is reversed. Over and above, the cognitive approach was also observed as a prime factor to predict self-efficacy and the more analytical participants obtained an increased score of self-efficacy.

In this study, different psychological tests conducted to assess the cognitive style were performed by the computer and thus the degree of empathy of participants for use of computers also influenced the study and thus attributes of personality traits

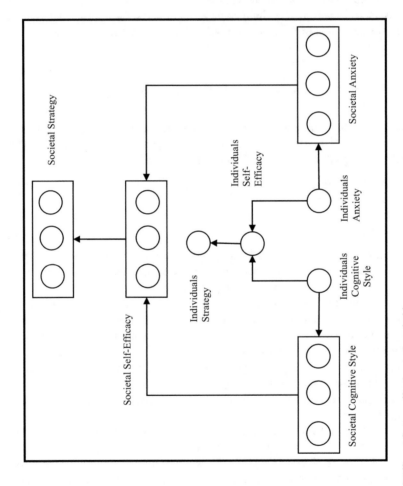

Fig. 2.2 Inter-linking of different factors affecting technophobia

linked with technology acceptance were included for analysis [53] while partici-
pant's attitude was not considered in this analysis. In [53, 54], technology acceptance models were proposed to include those psychological factors which persuade
the acceptance of computers by individuals. It is formulated in the technology
acceptance model introduced in [53] that how to decide the effect of external parameters on an individual's inner belief, attitudes, and aims. This formulation took the
help of the theory of reasoned action (TRA) given in [55]. The TRA suggests that
the behavioral intention is a gauge of an individual's intention to accomplish a peculiar behavior and attitude and thus represents the individual's feelings about behavior performance [55]. The TRA is diagrammatically illustrated in Fig. 2.3.

The technical acceptance model introduced in [53] combined these two concepts
with two attributes as given below.

- Perceived Usefulness
- Perceived Ease of Use

The first attribute is the subjective likelihood of the prospective users. These are the
users trying to enhance their performance with the help of a task-oriented application system. The second attribute indicates the degree to which the prospective user
thinks that there is no substantial role of the target system [54]. It is also pertinent to

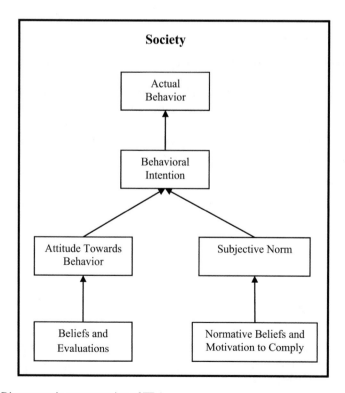

Fig. 2.3 Diagrammatic representation of TRA

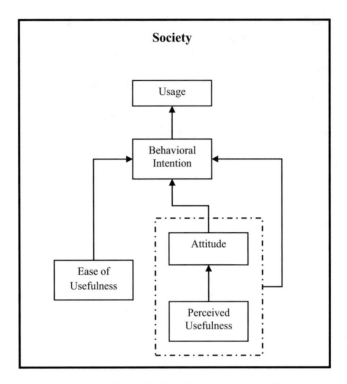

Fig. 2.4 Technology Acceptance Model (TAM) with inter-linking of different components

mention here that both the attributes are discrete factors from the perspective of psychology and statistics. Often, some entities are perceived as useful but it is also observed that their use is difficult. Vice versa is also correct.

In Fig. 2.4, given below, four components used to predict the usage of computer is illustrated. These four components are:

1. Behavior Intention
2. The attitude of the User
3. Perceived Usefulness
4. Ease of Usefulness

In this model, attempts have been made to predict the use of computers based on behavior intention reflected by the combination of attitude and perceived usefulness. This model also incorporates the determination of attitudes based on components 3 and 4 given above. This model also delineates that ease of use also considerably influences the perceived usefulness. Further, in [54], it is stated that multiple regression can greatly help in finding the relative weights. It is also given in [54] that if the perception of self-efficacy is influenced by experience and anxiety then the self-efficacy can be obtained by the extended technology acceptance model as is illustrated in Fig. 2.5 given below.

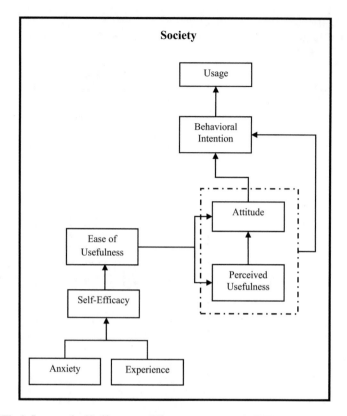

Fig. 2.5 The influence of self-efficacy on different components in TAM

Indeed, there is mutual linking between components 3 and 4, and attitudes, and this linking is shown in the figure given below. In [56], three subscales of attitude assessment are identified. These are:

- Entertainment
- Utility and
- Ease of use

Using these three subscales, the technology acceptance model as derived by the theory of reasoned action, further turned into a new model and established a new inter-relationship. This is shown in Fig. 2.6.

However, there is no consensus about the directionality of some of these relationships, and is still debatable. For example in [57], it has been stated that self-efficacy is decided by component 4. Further in [58], it is given that self-efficacy can be decided with the help of perceived usefulness. Therefore, in [59], a new theoretical model was proposed using multiple regressions. However, the actual model was not compatible with the theoretical model in terms of accuracy. This model is given below in Fig. 2.7.

Fig. 2.6 Diagrammatic illustration of Brosnan's model of technology acceptance

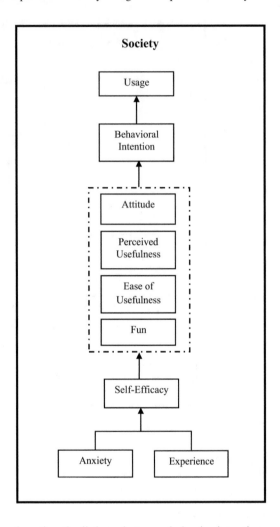

In [60], it is stated that by corroborating the linkage between behavior intention, actual behavior, and intention to use a computer, effective use can be predicted. It is also important to mention that component 3 given above is useful to envisage the intention to use a computer. Moreover, if SET is not supposed to facilitate a task then the people will feel some sort of technological burden. Perhaps, four components enumerated above are also liable to decide the usefulness of technology. In [61], it has been observed that the prior experience of computer entails a substantial correlation of better perception and usefulness of computer as suggested by the model given in Fig. 2.3. In [62], it is given that computer anxiety encompasses an indirect influence on the acceptance of technology and this indirect influence is caused through the perceived usefulness. It was also inferred in [62] that self-efficacy is a good analyzer of anxiety but anxiety is not a predictor of self-efficacy.

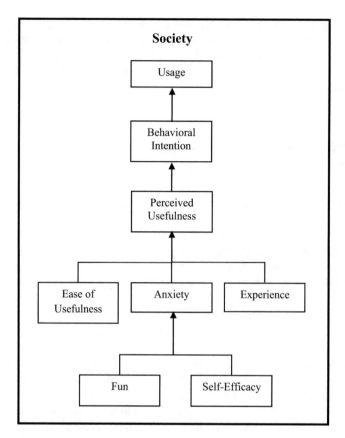

Fig. 2.7 The latest theoretical model of technophobia

The model shown in Fig. 2.7 manifests the way different variables are assimilated to analyze the condition human beings may or may not utilize computers and this model is not a certain model of technophobia. It may be possible that distinct variables behave prominently and their mutual relationship may vary depending upon the context of computer interaction. However, some researchers also argued that there is no correlation between attitude and behavior. In [63], it is argued that certain features of user attitudes are not even properly understood. Further in [64], a distinction between attitudes and opinion is made. In [36], it is suggested that augmented familiarity with computers merely leads to an enhancement of opinions about technology and does not affect attitudes. Therefore, an improved opinion about computers is of paramount importance to mitigate the scale of technophobia. Moreover, in [60], attempts have been made to differentiate the attitudes from component 3 given above. However, it would not be genuine to think that familiarity with technology and component 3 can form a view.

Indeed, perception of the usefulness of computers enables more concentration on the task and therefore reduces the negative influences of technophobia and technophobia is a diverse occurrence that can be managed by recognizing the basic factors enveloped in this phenomenon. It should also be noted that the individual attributes of technophobia render only a single facet of the model and its other factors are components 3 and 4, and the context which implicates factors related to the organization.

2.6 Pros and Cons of Techno-Psychological Effects in Modern Societies

It is a general view that a computer is a complex device. In [1], it is argued that the future computers will be 'invisible' and we will be bound to use computers often against our will. Nowadays, we can observe this phenomenon everywhere like the use of computers in modern cars, in microwave ovens, washing machines, compact disc (CD) players, games, and numerous other gadgets. It seems that the transformation of all modern technologies in an invisible plan is taking place and undoubtedly this is the turning point. However, it is intuitive to think that until the technology will turn 'invisible', it will have developed huge anxiety in the majority of people. Its extreme form known as technophobia has already been discussed in the preceding section.

In the present scenario, modern state-of-art technologies are the cornerstone of human social life. Even, the significant and fast development of technologies is rendering ease in social communication. However, there are several drawbacks of ever-growing technologies such as creating instability in different sectors of life frame. Further, it is also ridiculous to decide the impact created because of the use of technologies. It is also inquisitive to think that the existence of a novel and enhanced spectrum of behaviors and ethics affected the mutual interactions in society. Indeed, the exponentially growing technology incurred many negative impacts on the health and behavior of individuals and society. Some such impacts are given below.

- Configuration of individual's beliefs.
- Social separation.
- De-strengthening of affinity within the family.
- De-strengthening of social ties.
- Apathy
- Loss of aspiration to perform discrete activities.
- Time wastage in non-useful objects.
- Increased rate of violence.
- High crime rate.

The modern-day youth often has the desire not to interact directly with other individuals or groups and often abstains to establish social relationships. For such people, technology offers a great leap of help as a resilient substitute for social visits, the mutual transmission of feelings and experiences. Electronic media further created impetus in changing the perspective of young people towards different modern technologies. Indeed, satellite technology played a vital role in ideology transformation from one reason to another reason across the globe. Thus, the feelings of need, experience, and independence are also blindly imitated and disseminated in the youth community across the nation. Perhaps, the psychological instincts prohibited are tempted the most. It is also intuitive that the majority of youth want to take their own decision without the interference of family and society further augmented this ideological transformation. It has also been observed that the majority of the people who feel comfortable in social isolation are often Internet-addicted because such people spend a substantial chunk of time with these technologies. Moreover, the communicative process of such people is confined to written discourse in which no sensory feelings are involved.

Some other disadvantages often associated with the spreading of modern technologies are the dissemination of false, non-verified information and swift proliferation of lies in society with the use of these modern technologies are the considerable drawbacks faced by the society. Instant propagation of sarcasm related to divinity, religion, false belief is often observed owing to modern SETs in different versions like voice, image, and video. These are susceptible to cause jeopardy effect to the young community. These can also have the cascading effect of numerous psychological, health-related issues and can direct to isolation. Cultural amalgamation can also put society at stake and can generate negativity which might germinate many weird conventions in the pretext of modernity and internationalism. As a consequence, these phenomena have substantial impacts on individual's personalities that make them abstain from reading books and obtaining the information through printed paper.

Different studies, researches, and investigations revealed the fact that there are dissident groups about the impact of techno-psychology on society. The viewpoints of people associated with positivism and negativism of modern technologies contradict. Certain people emphasize the use of technologies to cater to the need of modern life as already mentioned in the preceding section. In contrast, another group of people visualizes advanced state-of-art SETs as a serious threat and believes this will certainly exert an astringent blow to family and societal structure like increased cases of divorce. People of this group also demand to restrict the use of technologies so that they can protect their children to be entered into the weird sphere of delusions and suppositions and thus can maintain the affinities of society and family affinities [10]. It is also the religious viewpoint of a certain group of individuals who visualizes the advanced SETs as the outrage of Satan. Moreover, such people ponder that technologies are responsible for weakening the values and lack of ethics. In contrast, some other groups of people consider it as a constructive means and advantageous for the individual as well as society.

In addition, family budget, achievements of the children, individual's life within the family are also severely influenced by modern technologies. Nowadays, it is common to have many televisions (TVs), mobile phones, and computers in a family while all members of the family are living together in one home and thus imposed financial burden. However, from a psychological perspective, this is adversely affecting societal and health-related issues like easy access to violent images creates a serious negative effect on children's minds. This also leads to a sense of fear, anger, discomfort, revolting, and aggression tendency in children. Undoubtedly, there is an explicit retreat of children in academic achievement due to excessive use of modern technologies.

In this changing scenario, it is the ethical duty of the parents to establish a healthy affinity within the family especially with children, and keep them away from excessive use of the Internet, mobile, and other modern technologies. To fulfill the psychological needs of family members, particularly of the children, there must be sufficient mutual constructive conversation on the daily basis among the family members and must create an environment of freedom of expression and discussion within the family. It will also be a good practice to encourage the family members, especially children to utilize their leisure time in useful training courses. Over and above, it is the responsibility of parents to supervise their children in the best possible way and make them explicitly clear the pros and cons of modern technologies so that they can use these technologies without intolerance or severity and can hold the sense of responsibility and internal control.

Indeed, the 'digital revolution' is considered the second industrial revolution (IR). This revolution manifests that modern technology particularly information technology plays a substantial role in the education system and the work activities of society. In the current scenario, the technological skills of the incumbent are also assessed for employment at the organizational level. Therefore, the chances of employment for technophobes are supposed to reduce in the coming future. The lack of technophobia is a currently essential requirement for various jobs in modern society [65].

In the current social scenario, the use of computers is as much important as literacy. Therefore, the exponential growth of technology will give it the importance equal to reading and writing skills, and thus the educational system of the society will increase the quantum of technophobia. Studies have revealed the fact that even the teacher of computer science is also suffering from technophobia.

Moreover, incoming future educational software will be abundantly used in various teaching institutions. There are also positive impacts of this phenomenon. The educational software will render the teaching lucid and interesting for the students and the teaching-learning process will be more effective and value-oriented. Research suggests that if parents are suffering from technophobia, they must hide it in the presence of children.

It is intuitive to think that the techno-psychological effect will create a need for a program for the reduction of technophobia in abundance in society. Such reduction programs will use situational etiology-based mental techniques instead of individual etiology. Individual etiology is associated with the personality traits of the individual suffering from technophobia.

Even today, many companies are offering support to technophobes and employees suffering from anxiety due to excessive use of computers. This practice will become more common in society in the recent future.

2.7 Conclusions

SP is basic science and many approaches have been proposed in the literature for modeling the SP. It is also a fact that social psychology is consistently influenced by the exponential growth of technology. Indeed, the digital transformation of industries is taking place at a fast pace to meet the demands of persistent evolution and the challenges inflicted by society. Indeed, there is a massive and constantly increasing network of man, machines, and materials by the huge application of the Internet. Undoubtedly, the novel SETs of Industry4.0 are being used for the sake of humanity but technologies are also negatively impacting society. Many countries are thinking and attempting systematically to enhance the overall standard of life in society. It has already been mentioned in Chap. 1 that applications of technologies for societal benefits have emerged an IR whose outcome is S-5.0. Indeed, S-5.0 will concentrate on the use of technologies for consistent advancement and innovation inspired by Industry 4.0. Thus, S-5.0 will entail different technologies to resolve the various problems of mankind like aging, natural disasters, security, improved quality of life, and social inequality.

Further, technophobia is also a legitimate response to technology. Various factors included in the manifestation of technophobia seem to be of paramount importance than ever. Further, this phenomenon has become more evident due to its scientific and systematic approach. Different researches revealed the fact that nearly fifty percent population of different categories are suffering from technophobia. Therefore, anxiety towards technology especially for computers must not be underestimated. It is seen that modern technologies in general and computers, in particular, have caused anxiety in approximately 50% of the population. Thus, technophobia can be treated as a serious issue for society5.0, and undoubtedly the symptoms displayed by it can be considered to be created because of inadequacies in the designing process of the technologies.

Conclusively, modern technologies including computers offer substantial ease and comfort to individuals and society as well. However, it is also responsible for causing many negative impacts on the individuals and society such as on the feelings, attitudes, values, opinions.

References

1. Norman D (1990) The Design of everyday things. Doubleday Currency, New York
2. Al Aga I (2009) The misuse of the internet and mobile technology and their role in juvenile delinquency in the GCC, Ph.D., DIRASAT: Naif Arab University for Security Sciences, College of Graduate Studies, Department of Social Sciences
3. Couper MP (2005) Technology trends in survey data collection. Soc Sci Comput Rev 23:486–501. https://doi.org/10.1177/0894439305278972
4. Looij-Jansen PMV, Wilde EJ (2008) Comparison of web-based versus paper-and-pencil self-administered questionnaire: effects on health indicators in Dutch adolescents. Health Res Educ Trust 43:1708–1721. https://doi.org/10.1111/j.1475-6773.2008.00860.x

 5. Poggio J, Glasnapp DR, Yang X, Poggio AJ (2005) A comparative evaluation of score results from computerized and paper & pencil mathematics testing in a large-scale state assessment program. J Technol Learn Assess 3:1–30
 6. Ebert JF, Huibers L, Christensen B, Christensen MB (2018) Paper- or web-based questionnaire invitations as a method for data collection: cross-sectional comparative study of differences in response rate, completeness of data, and financial cost. J Med Internet Res 20(1):e24. https://doi.org/10.2196/jmir.8353, RL: http://www.jmir.org/2018/1/e24/; PMID:29362206
 7. Reips U-D (2002) Standards for internet-based experimenting. Exp Psychol 49:243–256. https://doi.org/10.1026//16183169.49.4.243
 8. McDonald H, Adam S (2003) A comparison of online and postal data collection methods in marketing research. Mark Intell Plan 21:85–95. https://doi.org/10.1108/02634500310465399
 9. Cobanoglu C, Warde B, Moreo PJ (2001) A comparison of mail, fax, and web-based survey methods. Int J Mark Res 43:441–455
10. Latour B (1993b) We have never been modern. Harvard University Press, Cambridge
11. Nersessian NJ (1984) Faraday to Einstein: constructing meaning in scientific theories. Martius Nijhoff/Kluwer, Dordrecht
12. Tweney RD (1989) A framework for the cognitive psychology of science. In: Gholson B, Shadish WR Jr, Neimeyer RA, Houts AC (eds) Psychology of science: contributions to metascience. Cambridge University Press, New York, pp 342–366
13. Dreier O (2016) Conduct of everyday life: implications for critical psychology. In: Schraube E, Højholt C (eds) Psychology and the conduct of everyday life. Routledge, London, pp 15–33
14. Giere RN (ed) (1992) Cognitive models of science, vol 15. University of Minnesota Press, Minneapolis
15. Wagenknecht S, Nersessian NJ, Andersen H (eds) (2015) Empirical philosophy of science: introducing qualitative methods into philosophy of science. Springer International, Cham, pp 13–35
16. Feist GJ, Gorman ME (1998) The psychology of science: review and integration of a nascent discipline. Rev Gen Psychol 2(1):3–47
17. Al Hawsawi A. Impediments to the use of educational technologies in teaching mentally retarded students as perceived by teachers of Education in Riyadh. The first scientific conference, Department of Mental Health, the College of Education, Benha University
18. Kuhn TS (1962) The structure of scientific revolutions, University of Chicago
19. Khulaifi M (2002) The impact of the Internet in the community: a field study. Alam Al Koteb 22(5 and 6):469–502
20. Lailah A (2009) The role of mass media and information technology in the family disruption: monitoring the movement of the reaction from the center to the margin. In: Scientific conference: media, and challenges of the times. Cairo University, Faculty of Information, p 23
21. Bryant A, Sanders J, Mal W (2006) Instant image text and adolescents social networks. J Comput Commun Mediat 4
22. Al-Majali F (2007) The use of the internet and its impact on social relations among university students, An Empirical Study. lighthouse 13(7)
23. Rabab R, Al-Gammal (2013) The impact of the use of social networks to form a pattern of the ethical value system for Saudi youth, An Empirical Study, Department of Media, Faculty of Arts & Humanities, King Abdulaziz University
24. Al Yousef S (2006) Modern technologies advantages and disadvantages of a study of the negative effects on the health of the individual. The Book of the nation-Qatar, no 112, twenty-sixth year, the first edition
25. Vatsyayan (1993) Social psychology, 12th edn. Kedar Nath Ram Nath publications, Meerut, p 3, 5
26. UNDP (2009) Human development report: overcome barriers: human mobility and development. UNDP, Geneva
27. Bon GL (1960) The crowd: a study of the popular mind. Viking Press, New York. (Original work published 1895)

28. Tagga A (2012) An introduction to sociology. Abdul Hameed Tagga and sons Nadeem Younis printing press, Lahore, pp 347–348
29. Turner RH, Killian LM (1972) Collective behavior, 2nd edn. Prentice-Hall, Englewood Cliffs
30. Charles Horton Cooley (2002) Concept of the looking Glass self. Nathan Rousseau, Self, Symbols & Society. Rowman & Littlefield
31. Giddins A (2009) Sociology, 6th edn. Polity Press, Cambridge, pp 941–942, 945
32. Amichai-Hamburger Y (2009) Technology and psychological Well-being. Cambridge University Press, Cambridge, NY/Melbourne
33. Kipnis D (1997) Ghosts, taxonomies, and social psychology. Am Psychol 52:205–211
34. Collier G, Minton HL, Reynolds G (1991) Currents of thought in American social psychology. Oxford University Press, New York
35. Watson JB (1913) Psychology as the behaviorist views it. Psychol Rev 20:158–177
36. Osiceanua M-E (2014) Psychological implications of modern technologies: "technophobia" versus "technophilia". The 6th international conference edu world 2014 "Education facing contemporary world issues", 7th–9th November
37. Young KS (1996) Internet addiction: the emergence of a new clinical disorder. CyberPsychol Behav 1(3):237–244
38. Fenichel O (1945) Drug addiction. In: The psychoanalytic theory of neurosis. W. W. Norton, New York, pp 375–386
39. Price HO (ed) (2011) Internet addiction. Nova Science Publishers, New York
40. Griffiths MD (1995) Technological addictions. Clin Psychol Forum 76:14–19
41. Griffiths MD (1996) Internet addiction: an issue for clinical psychology? Clin Psychol Forum 97:32–36
42. Bucy E, Newhagen J (2004) Media access. Social and psychological dimensions of new technology use. LEA, London
43. Rosen LD, Sears DC, Weil MM (1993) Treating technophobia: a longitudinal evaluation of the computer phobia reduction program. Comput Hum Behav 9:27–50
44. Kipnis D (1994) Accounting for the use of behavior technologies in social psychology. Am Psychol 49:165–172
45. MacIntyre PD, Gardner RC (1994) The subtle effects of language anxiety on cognitive processing in the second language. Lang Learn 44:283–305. https://doi.org/10.1111/j.1467-1770.1994.tb01103.x
46. Jay T (1981) Computerphobia – what to do about it? Educ Technol 21:47–48
47. Rosen LD, Weil MM (1990) Computers, classroom instruction, and the computer-phobic university student. Coll Microcomput 8:275–283
48. Heinssen RK Jr, Glass CR, Knight LA (1987) Assessing computer anxiety: development and validation of the computer anxiety rating scale. Comput Hum Behav 3(1):49–59
49. Gorayska B, Mey JL (1996) Of minds and men. In: Gorayska B, Mey J (eds) Cognitive technology: in search of humane interface. Advances in psychology, vol 113. Elsevier/North-Holland, Amsterdam, pp 1–24
50. Brosnan T (1994) Using spreadsheets to develop an understanding of science. In: Mellar H, Bliss J, Ogborn J, Boohan R, Tomsett R (eds) Learning with artificial worlds: computer-based modeling in the curriculum. Falmer Press, London, pp 76–84. ISBN 0-7507-0312-1 (cased) ISBN 0-7507-0313-X (paper)
51. Witkin HA, Moore C, Goodenough D, Cox P (1977a) Field dependent and field independent cognitive styles and their educational implications. Rev Educ Res 47:1–64
52. McKenney JL, Keen PGW (1974) How managers work. Harv Bus Rev:79–90
53. Davis FD (1986) A technology acceptance model for empirically testing new end-user information systems: theory and results. Sloan School of Management, Massachusetts Institute of Technology, Cambridge, MA
54. Davis FD (1989) Perceived usefulness, perceived ease of use, and user acceptance of information technology. MIS Q 13(3):319–340

55. Fishbein M, Ajzen I (1975) Belief, attitude, intention, and behavior: an introduction to theory and research. Addison-Wesley Pub. Co., Reading/Don Mills
56. Todman J, Dick G (1993) Primary children and teachers' attitudes to computers. Comput Educ 20(2):199–203
57. Henry J, Stone R (1995) Computer self-efficacy and outcome expectancy: the effects on the end user's job satisfaction. Psychology. ACM Sigcpr. Comput Pers. https://doi.org/10.1145/219716.219722
58. Hill T, Smith ND, Mann MF (1987) Role of efficacy expectations in predicting the decision to use advanced technologies. J Appl Psychol 72:307–314
59. Brosnan MJ (1998) Technophobia. The psychological impact of information technology. Routledge, London/New York
60. Davis FD, Bagozzi RP, Warshaw PR (1989) User acceptance of computer technology: a comparison of two theoretical models. Manag Sci 35(8):982–1003. https://doi.org/10.1287/mnsc.35.8.982
61. Byrd D, Koohang A (1989) A professional development question: is computer experience associated with subjects' attitudes toward the perceived usefulness of computers? J Res Comp Educ 21:401–410
62. Igbaria M (1994) An experimentation of the factors contributing to microcomputer technology acceptance. Account Manag Inf Technol 4(4):205–224
63. Burton E, Swanson. (1982) Measuring user attitudes in MIS research: a review. Omega 10(2):157–165
64. Mahmood MA, Medewitz JN (1989) Assessing the effect of computer literacy on subjects' attitudes, values, and opinions toward information technology: an exploratory longitudinal investigation using the linear structural relations (LISREL) model. J Comput Based Ins 16(l):20–28
65. Chmiel N (1998) Jobs, technology and people. Psychology Press

Chapter 3
Behavior and Sentiment Analysis of Smart Digital Societies Using Deep Machine Learning Technologies

Abstract Prediction of behavior and sentiment cues plays a pervasive role in smart digital society including the domains of healthcare and social behavior and sentiment research. The social behavior and sentiment analysis can be performed from the individuals' offline or online mutual communications and interactions. The corpus of these communications and interactions is considered important for visualizing the behavior and sentiment of a smart digital society. This chapter delineates how these features could be implemented or subsequently fused with other pertinent behavioral, sentimental, and physiological traits to enable different machine learning (ML) techniques to perform the classification problem. This chapter also entails the various challenges and application domains associated with the task of behavior and sentiment analysis. Perhaps, the accuracy of prediction along with the efficacy to imbibe the role of individuals' behavior and sentiment determinants and to render the explicit explanations to the behavior and sentiment predicted are also indispensable. This is because these aspects can enhance the trust, liability, and reliability of the system. However, the majority of behavior and sentiment analysis approaches do not reflect the logical inferences and explanations for the pursuit of behavior and sentiment prediction. Finally, this chapter describes the deep learning method that has been emerged forth as a pragmatic ML method. Deep learning (DL) possesses the characteristic of enhancing learning related to the data and outputted the superior quality of results. Different DL-based methods have been implemented in different problem domains successfully and researchers also implanted deep learning techniques within the purview of behavior and sentiment prediction. This chapter also incorporates the implementation details of deep learning-based approaches for this purpose.

Keywords Smart digital society · Behavior and sentiment analysis · Deep neural network (DNN) · Convolution neural network (CNN) · Recurrent neural network (RNN) · Long short-term memory (LSTM)

3.1 Introduction

As a consequence of the upward enhancement of the cities' population across the globe, cities emerged forth as one of the apex architecture of human society [1]. Indeed, a plethora of resources, miscellaneous essential services, and opportunities are rendered by the cities. In [2, 3], it has been given that smart cities are offering these amenities with extended potential and coming forth as a new paradigm. Smart cities entail deployment of the architecture of sensors and thus attempt to provide new, innovative, and uninterrupted services round the clock to citizens as well as policymakers. Even more, the deployment of sensor-based architecture permits the quick processing of a huge chunk of data and thus displays the improved decision-making phenomenon, renders the entire environment of the cities more intelligent, and consequently offers the services to citizens in a more intelligent fashion. In [4], it is stated that this intelligent environment of smart cities is very suitable for habitation, which includes citizens aged from 60 to 69 and assists in a great manner to control and manage the different illnesses about old age. Perhaps, smart cities help a lot to detect illness and diseases in an early stage and impart ambient supported life [5].

Intuitively, the modeling of human behavior and sentiments requires a mechanism of prediction so that the future behavior and sentiments of individuals can be predicted. This predictive mechanism needs the observed behavioral and sentimental features of the individuals and societal hierarchical network as inputs and produces the score of prediction in the form of outputs. The higher score outputted by this mechanism reveals the behavior and sentiments of individuals more likely to the predicted behavior and sentiments. Further, it is explicit that the application domain of the prediction of human behavior and sentiments is considerably versatile. Its application domains encompass different sectors and realms such as the medical sector, political sector, business, and financial sectors including e-commerce, the realm of psychology, as well as in personal life, etc. [6]. However, the behavior and sentiments prediction mechanism has certain associated shortcomings like the majority of predictive models used for this purpose do not reflect the explanations for the predicted behavior and sentiments whereas it is also intuitive that it is of paramount importance to display the explanation observed behind the prediction, in the majority of applications such as in affective computing, biological and medicinal computing, in the realm of psychology and sociology, e-commerce, social media, etc. [6, 7].

In this chapter, an attempt has been made to reveal the different research-oriented problems and their solution approaches model human behavior and sentiments so that it can be predicted with reasonable explanations and thus can suitably be implemented in different application domains in general and particularly in the healthcare sector. Even more, the proposed prediction model can also be used to intervene in the social network to provide medical assistance to overweight and obese people. In [8], it is suggested that various diseases caused due to obesity like diabetes, cardiovascular diseases, cancer, etc. can be prevented or mitigated through regular exercise. Many predictive intervening systems that display explanation have been constructed and developed for smart cities to motivate and engage people to perform exercises regularly. Undoubtedly, the Internet is considered as the precursor of such systems to identify and display important health-related information [9]. In [10], it is given that perhaps these observations are deeply rooted in the realm of social science and psychology and the realm of social science and psychology.

Further, social influences are within a social network are dichotomized as implicit and explicit, and thus is arduous to model the social influences that exist in social networks [11]. It is pertinent to mention that obvious influences of society depend on user's behavior and sentiments and is a derivative of direct relationship in a medical social network. However, this derivation of the user's behavior and the sentiment is inadequate to entirely recognize the social influences. In contrast, implicit influences of society are the cumulative phenomenon of confined elicited information about users' activities in society, varying circumstances of society, and derived influences obtained from unaccustomed users [11]. Indeed, an individual's self-motivation also plays a vital role in behavior and sentiment prediction as an individual's self-motivation establishes concomitant relations between an individual's historic and current attributes. It is also intuitive that the influence of environmental events on the behavior and sentiments of the users can be observed in the existing linking of offline events with the users' attributes. It is also a fact that explanation-oriented modeling of human behavior and sentiment for the pursuit of health-related social networks entails associated advantages such as it enhances the trust in the process of intervention and thus aims to resolve the conspicuous and truthful problems. Therefore, such systems are considered useful to maintain and augment the users' health and consequently enhance the adaptability of the systems. But, as of date, the explanation-oriented human behavior and sentiment prediction intervention system is still widely in the stage of underdevelopment. An attempt has also been made by the researchers to develop and model an innovative explanation-oriented social restricted Boltzmann machine (SRBM) to predict human behaviors and sentiments. In addition to insightful explanations, the SRBM renders accurate predictions of human behaviors and sentiments. Even more, the SRBM model comprises of temporal dependencies of the individual user on the social communities as well as on the personal representative and in this way attempts to renders the quantification of implicit social influences. The individual's implicit social influences can be treated as the function of aggregation of the precedent of the health-related social network whereas the individual's self-inspiration can be considered as a function of aggregation of an individual's historical representation. However, it is the authors' candid view that hybridizing the hidden and clear influences of society into a linear adaptive bias can enable the model with the explanation of social influences. The SRBM model includes different environmental events like competitions, meet-ups, and social games. These included events of the model are considered as the observed variables and help in assisting the predictive behaviors and sentiments of users and thus this model statistically estimates the human behaviors and sentiments naturally by implementing different advanced interpretable classifiers [12–16].

Web2.0 has also created a substantial role in the development of smart cities because it enables us to create blogs, forums, and online social networks where citizens can discuss and express their views about a topic. Citizens may for example express their views about political issues, can debate on current social and other issues, etc. Taking advantage of such information about the user's solution to the functioning of the majority of applications including the recommender system is vital in different purviews like analyzing the surveys conducted by different institutions and organizations as well as in deciding the campaigning strategies of various political parties. Even more analyzing public views help government agencies in a long way because it delineates the activities of the citizen as well as the behavior and sentiments of citizens which in turn are affected by the viewpoints of others. It is also true that in the realm of behavior and sentiment prediction, the inferences churned out from the user behaviors and sentiments are indispensably useful for making up the paucity of explicit user feedback on a given service. Apart from machine learning, other novel state-of-art techniques like the techniques based on similarity criterion of results can also be used for this pursuit [17]. It is an obvious fact that sources of data for the systems of behaviors and sentiments analysis are obtained online from social media and this chunk of data is consistently hiked by the users and therefore these data are treated as the big data provided different other pertinent issues like efficient data storage, data access, data processing are dealt efficiently as well as the reliability of results obtained [18].

Perhaps, the pursuit of developing automatic behavior and sentiment analysis is an emerging research domain. However, behaviors and sentiments analysis has a broad range of applications as stated above but it is explicitly not a well-defined task because it encompasses the processing of natural languages that have many associated challenges. Recent advancements in the domain of behavior and sentiment analysis encountering inherent theoretical and technical challenges and these challenges are obstructing the classification accuracy in polarity detection [19, 20]. In [20], the relationship between these challenges and the structural details of behavior and sentiments including their thrust on the result's accuracy has been discussed. It has also been revealed in [20] that accuracy is of paramount importance in the studies of behavior and sentiment analysis and it is propounded that accuracy is influenced by some challenges like:

- Dealing with negation or domain dependence.
- The source of data for behavior and sentiment analysis.

The author would like to recall the pre-stated fact that social media is the main avenue for collecting data for behavior and sentiment analysis. In this context, it has been suggested in [18] that it would not be a good practice to concentrate the attention only on structural details and interrelations of data, but it is a lifelong learning phenomenon to cope with the following parameters:

- Data presentation.
- Data analysis.
- Inference from the data.

- Visualization of the data.
- Search and navigate through the data.
- Decision-making in complicated networks.

An extensive literature survey revealed the fact that so many efficient models have been proposed to deal with the ever-advancing complexity of big data and maintaining the viability and diversity of the behavior and sentiment prediction of the model for varying range of applications as well. These models have also been used for discrete applications such as:

- Financial forecasting [21, 22]
- Marketing strategies [23]
- Medicine analysis [24, 25]
- Other areas [26–28]

Different challenges and application domains of behavior and sentiment analysis are illustrated diagrammatically in Fig. 3.1. However, few researchers also focused their attention to implement the different approaches of deep learning so that they can render the pragmatic evidence of the model's performance [21, 29–31]. These researches implemented different neural network techniques like CNN and RNN and it observed that when these techniques have been validated for the representation of a single technique with one dataset of a specific domain then these neural networks render the augmented overall accuracy [30–32]. In [32], it is derived that CNN and RNN methods can avoid the drawbacks of brief text within the purview of deep learning models. Further, in [26], it is mentioned that LSTM performs efficiently when implemented on miscellaneous text concepts. In [29], the impetus of data quality on the performance behavior and sentiment prediction has been discussed and three criteria have been considered for this purpose. These are:

- Informative resilience.
- Readability.
- Subjectivity to elicit the review quality of the online product.

Moreover, this research reflected two parameters that influence the degree of accuracy of behavior and sentiment analysis. These parameters are (1) readability and (2) length of the reviews. It has also been observed that an enhanced degree of readability and brief text datasets produced the enhanced quality of behavior and sentiment prediction. However, the varying scenario of data's size or domain renders the proposed approach dubious. Moreover, the literature survey reveals the fact that the majority of research work attempts to incorporate the reliability metrics, and the evaluation criteria are worked out based on small datasets number. Over and above, these researches were based on the research gap observed by lucid comparison of behavior and sentiment analysis of different approaches proposed in the literature with an experimental work that evaluates and validates the performance of models based on deep learning approach and associated techniques taking different datasets about varying topics.

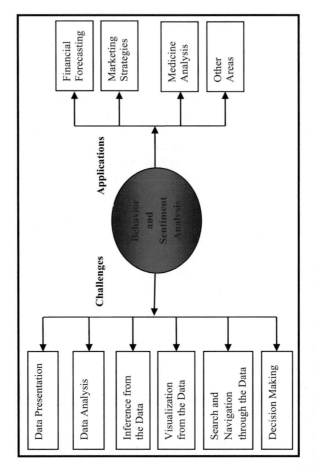

Fig. 3.1 Challenges and applications of behavior and sentiment analysis

In this chapter, the author would also attempt to discuss if it is feasible to implement the approaches that perform extraordinarily for datasets of multiple types and sizes. This chapter will also propose a model by hybridizing three criteria. These are the F-score, model's overall accuracy, as well as processing time. Even more, this chapter will also present an overview of various approaches and thus will benevolently pave the way to researchers to develop an even better model. However, in recent past, several deep learning-based types of research have been conducted for the pursuit of behavior and sentiment analyses, comprising of various attributes and performance and it is difficult to accumulate all the works in one chapter but the author will wittingly try to comprise of main research finding in this direction. Section 3.2 presents a brief background of behavior and sentiment analysis.

3.2 Theoretical Background

Sensor-based monitoring and vision-based monitoring are the two most frequently used monitoring approaches for automatic behavior and sentiment evaluation. In [33], the vision-based approaches of automatic behavior and sentiment evaluation are thoroughly reviewed. In [34], it is given that sensor-based approaches for automatic behavior and sentiment evaluation are frequently used for evaluating human behaviors and sentiments while dealing with an intelligent environment. Perhaps, it is because vision-based strategies strive to create privacy concerns among the users [35]. The sensor-based approaches of monitoring the behaviors and sentiments comprise the emerging state-of-art sensor network technologies. The sensor-based approaches generate the sensor data. These sensor data are chiefly of the type of time series dataset. Different attributes of this time series data are mainly state change or various parameter values. These parameter values are primly processed through the following methods:

(a) Data fusion.
(b) Probabilistic methods
(c) Statistical methods
(d) Formal knowledge technologies for activity recognition.

Further, it has been revealed from the literature survey that the sensor-based approach for the monitoring purpose of behavior and sentiment entails two pragmatic approaches. These two approaches are given below:

(a) Data-driven approach
(b) Knowledge-driven approach

The data-driven approach mainly implements the technique of data mining and ML to learn the behavior and sentiment models and often supervised learning strategies are used for the data-driven approach. Indeed, in data-driven approach different supervised learning techniques are implemented to learn behavior and sentiment from the accumulated sensor data. The supervised learning techniques used in data-driven approaches require labeled big datasets of different activities to train the different classifiers used. From an extensive literature survey, it has been observed that the supervised learning techniques implemented in the data-driven approach are considerably broad and versatile. Some techniques widely used for this pursuit are:

(a) Naive Bayes classifiers [36]
(b) Hidden Markov models (HMM) [37]
(c) Dynamic Bayesian networks [38]
(d) Support vector machines [39] and
(e) Online (or incremental) classifiers [40].

It has been observed in the literature survey that in the recent past the social behavior and sentiment have been studied from a different perspective. In [52], user interactions in Facebook have been analyzed. In [53], an activity recommendation system is proposed. Further, models have been proposed for the prediction of the user's activity level [54, 55]. The model proposed in [55] attempted to predict the problem of 'chum prediction' i.e. users having a propensity of lowering their activity levels. This helps a lot to service providers to analyze and find the reason behind so that strategy can be worked out to hold such users in different applications like online social games [56], and QA forum [57], etc.

In contrast, the knowledge-driven approaches attempted to implement the existing domain knowledge so that the requirement of labeled datasets to train the model could be avoided. In [41], it has been attempted to defeat the problem of manually labeling activity datasets and researchers tried to extract the activity clusters by implementing the techniques of unsupervised learning. Researchers tried to use the clusters thus obtained from the unsupervised learning strategies to train a boosted HMM that can identify many activities. In [42], a logic-based strategy is implemented for activity identification, and this logic functions on the ground of the preceding knowledge extracted from the realm.

The literature survey also revealed the fact that ontology-based approaches have also been used for behavior and sentiment prediction. These approaches permit explicit presentation of activities and thus are algorithmically independent. Therefore, ontology-based approaches render portability, interoperability, and reusability [43–45].

Users' behavior and sentiment prediction in an intelligent environment is an indispensable task. Indeed, the users' conduct is described by the users' activities and these descriptions assist to identify the users' behavior and sentiment in an intelligent environment. Perhaps, modeling of users' behaviors and sentiments requires an abstraction layer on top of the recognized activities. It is also intuitive that a good behavior and sentiment model should delineate how conspicuously activities are being performed by the users and what activities display their routine living characteristics. This is very useful in anticipating the requirements of the users to identify the shifting in behavior and sentiment and can be used to resolve different health-related issues. In [46], an algorithm has been constructed to identify the mobilization patterns of the users and their device usage. This algorithm entails the techniques of sequence matching, compression, as well as Markov models [47] and thus permitted the intelligent environment for adapting the users' needs. Furthermore, some researchers have also implemented prediction methods to identify the activities of the users in the smart environment [39]. In [48], the necessities and importance of predictions in an intelligent environment have been delineated and it is mentioned in [49] that prediction in an intelligent environment is also useful to control the artificial illumination with the use of neuro-fuzzy systems, to control the various climatic parameters based on users' behavior [50]. A deep-rooted insight about the prediction of users' behavior and sentiment in the domain of comfort management in an intelligent environment is given in [51]. Behavior can be categorized into two domains. One is intra-activity behavior that defines how the activities are being performed by the users and another one is the inter-activity behavior that delineates the actions and activity sequences comprising of the users' daily routine. In addition, inter-activity models are predominantly used to predict the inter-activity behavior and sentiment and this phenomenon incorporates the sequencing of actions for this purpose because it permits the subtle illustration of the users' conduct during the time of abstracting the model from specific sensor technology. Two human behavior and sentiments prediction methods are proposed in [54]. These are the personalized approach and socialized approach. It is pertinent to mention that the personalized approach takes advantage of users' past behavior and sentiment record to predict the future behavior and sentiment whereas socialize approach attempted to use users' past behavior and sentiment records as well as the users' friend past behavior and sentiment records for future prediction of behavior and sentiment. More specifically, five models are described in [54]. These are:

(a) Socialized Gaussian Process (SGP) model
(b) Socialized Logistic Auto Regression (SLAR) model
(c) Personalized Gaussian Process (PGP) model
(d) Logistic Auto Regression (LAR) model
(e) Behavior Pattern Search (BPS) model

However, these models also have some demerits such as:

1. Demerit of not having the ability to take multiple users features such as body mass index (BMI), messages, and physical activities.
2. Demerit of not having the ability to effectively extract the social correlations and social influences such as SLAR, and LAR.

In [106], a WTFW model is proposed in which user-to-user links are explained. However, this model does not explain human behavior.

In this chapter, attempts have been made to address different challenging issues mentioned above. Over and above, different aspects required are to predict with the understanding of the objectives of individual behavior and sentient determinants as well as to give explanations for predicted behaviors and sentiments are also incorporated. Section 3.3 describes different issues related to the information processing of smart digital society using deep ML techniques.

3.3   Information Processing of Smart Digital Societies Using Deep Machine Learning Techniques

It is explicit that a huge amount of data will be generated by different devices installed in smart cities. These data are accumulated from various domains like traffic, medical domain, business sector, etc. It is also a reality that the rate of data generation ranges from device to device. It is also a fact that irrespective of data generation rate, chances are always there to have useful information loss. Therefore, it is difficult and challenging to process the data created from different sources at varying rates [59, 60]. In [61], an approach for processing the Big Data is proposed and this method is used for distinguishing the correlation between the temperature and traffic data. Further, a framework for synergizing the big data and Industrial Internet of Things (IIoT) is proposed in [62].

Another feature of huge data generated by the devices installed in smart cities is that these data are dynamic. For example, the data generated by autonomous cars will be dynamic because the sensor outputs will be changed concerning locations and times. It is pertinent to mention that the quality of gathered data is important and in the context of smart cities where data is gathered from different heterogeneous sources, the quality of collected data will be questionable. In [63], it is delineated that the information quality gained from each data source depends on four factors. These are:

1. Measurement error.
2. Precision was performed in data collection.
3. Noise is created in the environment from the devices.
4. Discrete observation and measurements.

To gain better Quality of Information (QoI), it is of paramount importance to mine higher levels of data abstraction and provides pragmatic and actionable information to other services. In the case of smart data, the QoI depends on two factors. These are the applications of data, and the characteristics of data. However, there exist different approaches for improving the quality of information such as:

- To enhance the data accuracy.
- To select the trustworthy sources
- Hybridizing the data collected from heterogeneous sources with as much precision and accuracy as possible.
- By observing enhanced frequency and sample density.
- Improved precision of the observations and measurements.
- Attempt to reduce the environmental noise.
- Annotation of semantic data.

Figure 3.2 illustrates different characteristics of data about IoT and smart cities. Perhaps, it is because the data generated by smart devices are raw and thus entail low-level abstraction. Therefore, the semantic models are implemented to impart its quality, original attributes, and the description of data interpretable [64]. In [65], it

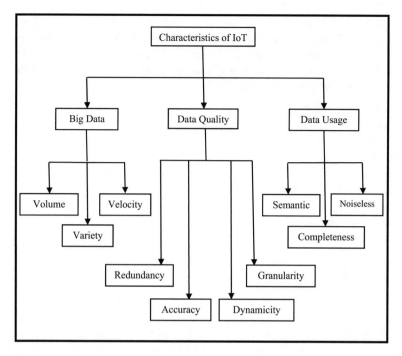

Fig. 3.2 Characteristics of IoT and smart city data

Table 3.1 Smart data in smart dada characteristics in smart cities

S. No.	Use cases of smart city	Data types	Location of data processing	References
1	Traffic	Steam/massive	Edge	[59, 66]
2	Health	Steam/massive	Edge/cloud	[67]
3	Environment	Steam/massive	Cloud	[68]
4	Weather prediction	Stream	Edge	[69]
5	Citizen	Stream	Cloud	[70, 71]
6	Agriculture	Stream	Edge/cloud	[72]
7	Home	Massive/ historical	Cloud	[73]
8	Air controlling	Massive/ historical	Cloud	[60]
9	Monitoring of public place	Historical data	Cloud	[74]
10	Activity control of individual	Stream/historical	Edge/cloud	[75, 76]

is given that semantic annotation is advantageous in interpretable and knowledge-based information fusion. Different characteristics of smart data about smart cities are briefly depicted in Table 3.1.

Figure 3.3 shows the sample data collection process from Twitter. Further, in smart cities, social media also plays a vital role in different activities and is also a source of data accumulation. Indeed, the data gathered from social media is of paramount importance in a different area of interest about smart cities. Some of the data types mined are enumerated below.

1. Demographic data.
2. Spatio-temporal data.
3. Multimedia data.
4. Textual content.
5. Community data.
6. Social relationship data.
7. Personal data.
8. Social interactions data.

3.3.1 Social Data Processing

Social behavior biometric is a complex phenomenon and undoubtedly is a challenging task because it requires the identification of consistent idiosyncratic features. In [30], it has been given that social behavior biometric can be tackled using three types of analysis. It is also true that the identification of frequency-based features from social data requires statistical techniques. These statistical techniques need different components of social media such as comments, tweets, tags, abbreviations, replies, blogs, etc. for a certain period. Figure 3.4 represents the flow diagram for the process of biometric enrolment and authentication. The features obtained from the social behavior biometric are used to match user profiles.

The frequency-based features thus obtained are further used to construct the social network. This social network is constructed based on similarity measures and correlations observed among the features. Moreover, the information extracted from these features is used to generate the different number of social networks needed for further identification of features and consequently fortify the strength of connectivity using the weighted feature matrix. This concept is illustrated in Fig. 3.5 [107]. This approach also permits for other functioning like reducing the dimension, selection of the algorithm for classification, and aggregating the decision-making process. The weighted social network thus constructed is implemented to accomplish the task of individuals' social profile matching. Furthermore, the individuals' social profile matching can subsequently be used in the security system of multi-model biometric.

A model for sentiment and behavior analysis is proposed in [58]. This model includes visual as well as textual contents of social networks. This innovative strategy incorporates the functioning of a deep neural network like De-noising and skips gram. The cornerstone of this model is Continuous Bag-Of-Words (CBOW). This model includes two components of CBOW with logistic regression and is called

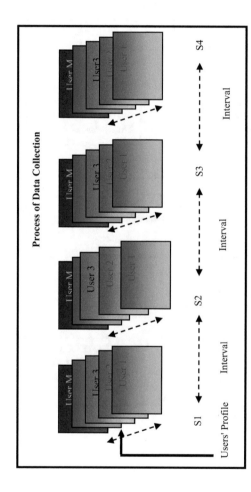

Fig. 3.3 Sample data collection process from Twitter

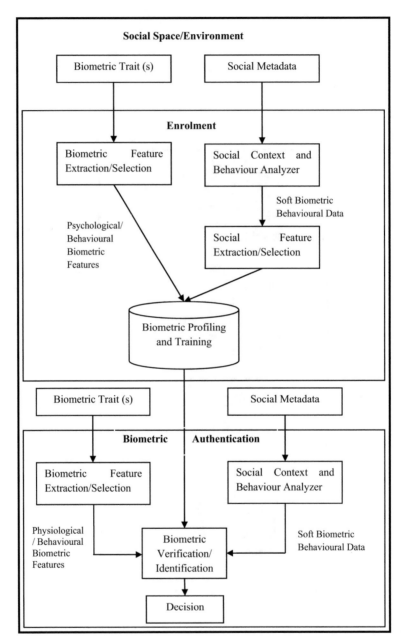

Fig. 3.4 Diagrammatic representation of enrolment and authentication system using hybridization of social, behavioral, and psychological data

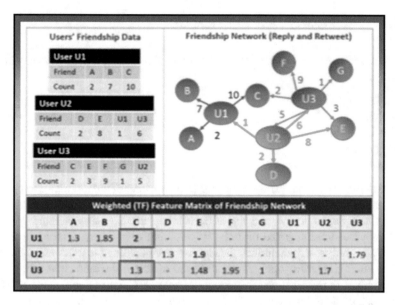

Fig. 3.5 Illustration of friendship network social connection algorithm using weighted feature matrix [107]

CBOW-LR to tackle the textual contents and is expanded as the CBOW-DA-LR. In addition, the polarization of information related to visual and textual materials is used for classification in this model. The model proposed in [58] is also evaluated for four datasets and it is observed that the proposed model performs superior in comparison to CBOWS+SVM and completely supervised probabilistic language model. However, the extended completely supervised probabilistic language model performs better than the proposed model. It is also relevant to mention that large datasets are suitable for feature learning and skip grams. Different aspects of information management for a smart digital society are given in Sect. 3.4.

3.4   Information Management of Smart Digital Societies Using Operative Processing Techniques

Information management of a smart digital society is also an important aspect to discuss. In this section, the author will discuss different aspects of information management about smart digital societies. This section is divided into two sub-sections for this purpose. These are:

- Data flow in smart cities.
- Information management in smart cities.

3.4.1   The Flow of Data in Smart City

There are many essential ingredients in the evolutionary process of smart cities. These are:

- Holistic rapid growth.
- Volume
- Quality of life.
- Frequency
- Consistency and accuracy of data flow in different domains of city activity.

It is also important that the decision and policymakers of smart cities can observe and see all the data received from different sources for integration. In [77], it is given that in Santander, a smart city of Barcelona, different data generated from different sources are integrated on one platform, and even more, different users can access and analyze this combined data as per their needs and requirements. Further, in this smart city reality applications are used to access the municipal data to provide numbers of information related to traffic and weather to citizens at many points like parks, gardens, beaches, etc. in the city. Furthermore, in [78], it is given that the smart London city dashboard also displays similar information as well as the status of public transport, air pollution, weather, traffic cameras, and news updates. In [79], it is stated that in some cities of Brazil data from 30 agencies including surveillance are captured and further algorithms and analytic techniques process the data in real-time. It is explicit that adaptation of these systems motivates the data providers to render their data publically available and also to persuade the citizens and others concerned to use the data. Moreover, it is also a fact that with the enhancement of the smartness of the city, the increased analysis of this data can be performed and consequently let the data providers recognize the most viable and useful information and the existing gaps in the entire phenomenon. As the author has already stated above the plethora of information is received by the networks of sensors distributed and installed around different nooks and corners of the city, and more availability of such information is possible with the extension of this sensor network. The consistency and accuracy of information received from the sensors can further be improved if the sensors are primed to gather the data constantly and frequently. For example, the sensor installed on every vehicle can provide data about different geographic locations, speeds, local and global traffic conditions and thus enable the traffic controller to monitor and control the congestion and can also subsequently send the updated information to other drivers for easing out the existing congestion. However, in [80–84], it is mentioned that there should not be the involvement of public authority in the phenomenon of providing this information rather this should be on a crowd-sourced basis. Figure 3.6 displays a transport ecosystem for a smart city.

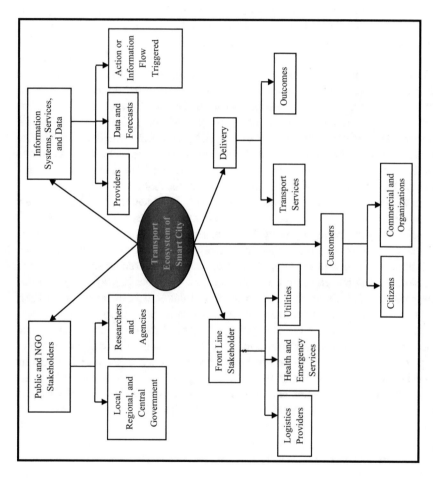

Fig. 3.6 Transport ecosystem of smart city

3.4.2 Information Management for Smart Cities

It is also obvious that the need for planning tools will arise before the planning agencies and government describe their planning strategies and future planning map of progress so that they can assess and evaluate the progress of projects related to smart cities. It is also important that the participants of private sectors should also be competent to assess the commercial opportunities. In Fig. 3.7, a model is proposed for the information management of the smart city. This model entails the model given in [85] about product and service. In Fig. 3.7, it is delineated that how improved management of information influences the progress of smart cities.

It is suggestive that at each stage in all these models there should be a simplification of characteristics and characteristics should not be considered as the absolute criteria. However, in [86], it is given that experience of other domains renders the value of such an approach, in terms of providing a sense of present development as well as to visualize the glimpse of targets remain. Moreover, individual assets and components of an ecosystem are also examined by these models and thus displaying the phase of a specific smart city reached. Even more, these models also enable to identify the changes required in the information management system to further smarten the city. These models find the domains of the requirements of new datasets and how the data should be gathered, stored, and implemented. However, different issues related to outcomes such as its development, sponsorship controls by city authority or by the third party or by the commercial members of the ecosystems are debatable topics. In [87], it is mentioned that raising the question of what is the business model of the city or the public transport authority can render sufficient help to fix the confusion related to different issues of the outcome. In [88], it is given that many business models run for transportation in London e.g., underground rail service provider, buses contract manager, taxis regulator, maintainer of the road network, road quality auditor, etc. It is perhaps needed of the time because in modern times private sectors are taking an important role in the innovative phenomenon of different platforms in a bid to facilitate many private users irrespective of consumers or businesses [89]. However, in [90–93], it is argued that there is no need for the monopoly of city authorities regarding the smartening of cities. In [88, 89], it is mentioned that an open and sharing approach together with a competitive environment among a different wide spectrum of information management services providers can be an optimum approach. However, the city authorities may have the key role of regulation and set of standard norms. Particularly, it seems indispensable to set up open APIs [94].

Further, different pertinent issues of data analysis and evaluation are given in Sect. 3.5. Section 3.5 also entails the implementation details of deep ML techniques for behavior and sentiment analysis.

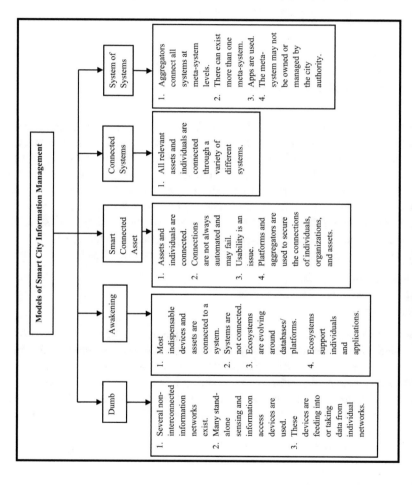

Fig. 3.7 Different models and their characteristics for information management of the smart city

3.5 Smart Digital Society's Data Analysis and Evaluation Approaches

Data analysis and its evaluation are of the utmost importance in a smart digital society. Perhaps, the issues of data analysis and its evaluation also play a vital role in the task of behavior and sentiments prediction. In this section, the author will discuss different pertinent issues related to data analysis and its evaluation particularly in the realm of behavior and sentiment prediction.

3.5.1 Framework of Behavior/Sentiment Data Analysis and Evaluation Approaches

As is already stated in the preceding section, behavior and sentiment analysis is the phenomenon of finding out information about an entity. It is also obvious that the information extracted is subsequently used to identify the subjectivities of that entity automatically. The intention behind this data analysis is to determine behavior and sentiment concepts as positive, negative, or neutral from users' generated textual data. Indeed, the behavior and sentiment prediction can be performed on three levels of mining. These are Feature level, sentence level, and document level.

In [95], it is mentioned that there are three ways to deal with the quest of behavior and sentiment prediction. These three approaches are given below.

- Lexicon-based approaches
- Machine-learning-based approaches
- Hybrid approaches.

Lexicon-based approaches were the first to be implemented for behavior and sentiment prediction. Later on, lexically based techniques are categorized into two domains. These are based on: (1) dictionary and (2) corpus [96]. In the first approach, behavior and sentiment prediction is accomplished with the help of considering a dictionary of terms like Senti-Word-Net and Word-Net. In contrast, in a corpus-based approach, any such use of a dictionary does not require. The corpus-based approach entails different statistical tools to analyze the contents of compiled documents. The corpus-based techniques often use the following algorithms for this purpose.

- K-nearest neighbors (k-NN) [97].
- Conditional random field [98]
- Hidden Markov models (HMM) [99], etc.

Further, ML-based approaches frequently suggested in literature can be dichotomized into two categories [100]. These are:

1. Traditional models
2. Deep learning models

Traditional models include classical ML methods like Naïve Bayes classifier [101], maximum entropy classifier [102, 103], or SVM [104]. Furthermore, in traditional models different lexical features, adjectives, adverbs as well as parts of speech are given as inputs. However, the accuracy of these models is greatly influenced by features selected as inputs. Whereas, the models based on deep learning render superior accuracy than the traditional models. Different deep learning techniques widely used for behavior and sentiment prediction are CNN, DNN, and RNN. These techniques deal with the issue of behavior and sentiment analysis at different levels such as (1) document level (2) sentence level (3) aspect level. Details insight about deep learning will be given in forthcoming sub-sections.

In [105], a hybrid model is proposed that entails the integration of lexicon-and-ML-based techniques. It is also pertinent to mention that behavior and sentiment lexicons generally perform a vital role within the purview of the majority of these approaches. The taxonomy of deep-learning-based techniques for behavior and sentiment analysis is depicted in Fig. 3.8.

The cleaning of textual training data is essential while performing the task of behavior and sentiment analysis irrespective of traditional and deep-learning approaches. It is because textual data generally contains different anomalies. These are useless features because they do not contain any useful information for behavior and sentiment prediction and thus must be removed with the help of available libraries like Beautiful Soup. Once the cleaning of textual data has been done, it is segregated into individual words. Further, these segregated words are converted into the basic form using the method of lemmatization. Next, the words in their base form are transformed into numerical vectors. Different techniques are available to perform this task like word embedding, term frequency-inverse document frequency (TF-IDF). In [108], it is given that Word embedding is a method to model the language and to learn the features and in this embedding technique, each word is mapped to a real values vector. This mapping is performed in such a fashion that words with similar implications render similar vector representations. Further, value learning can be achieved with the help of neural networks.

3.5.2 Implementation Details of DL Based Sentiment Data Analysis Approaches

In [109], tests are conducted using a GeForce GTX2070 GPU card. Keras (https://keras.io), as well as Tensorflow (https://www.tensorflow.org/) libraries, are also used. Further, in this implementation DNN, CNN, and RNN models are used to demonstrate the experiment. In this test different datasets are used as shown in Table 3.2. This table also includes the performance of these algorithms for the task of feature extraction with the implementation of word embedding and TF-IDF. In this experimentation, different parameter values are taken as echoes = 5, batch-size = 4096, and in k-fold cross validation k is taken equal to ten. Different metrics

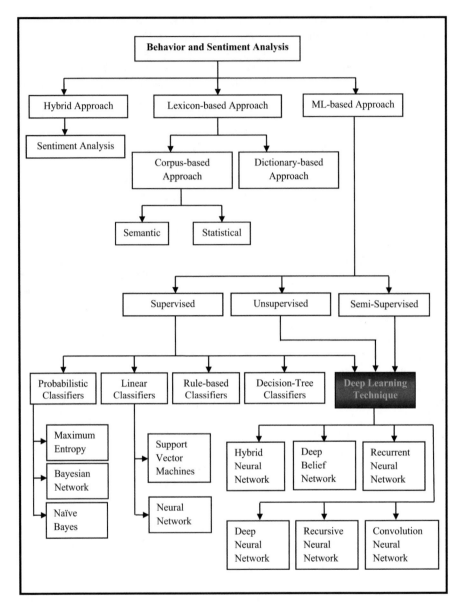

Fig. 3.8 Taxonomy of behavior and sentiment analysis methods [41, 95]

like accuracy, the area under the curve, and F-score are computed to evaluate the performance of the models. In this experimentation, recall and precision are also calculated because F-score is derived from these two parameters. In this experimentation, the Sentiment 140 dataset is processed first and the contents of this dataset are labeled positive or negative.

Table 3.2 Accuracies obtained by different algorithms for different datasets [109]

	TF-IDF			Word embedding		
Datasets	DNN	CNN	RNN	DNN	CNN	RNN
Sentiment 140	0.7649	0.7668	0.5695	0.7881	0.8006	0.8281
Tweets airline	0.8593	0.8545	0.8280	0.8979	0.9037	0.9045
Tweets SemEval	0.8367	0.8137	0.5485	0.8367	0.8431	0.8517
IMDB movie reviews (1)	0.8523	0.8230	0.5639	0.8457	0.8607	0.8705
IMDB movie reviews (2)	0.8551	0.8062	0.5872	0.8025	0.8262	0.8668
Corenell movie reviews	0.7043	0.6786	0.5078	0.7022	0.7136	0.7669
Book reviews	0.7587	0.7274	0.5169	0.7456	0.7663	0.7334
Music reviews	0.7685	0.6920	0.5170	0.7080	0.7445	0.7310

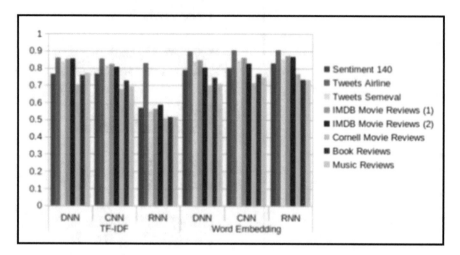

Fig. 3.9 Accuracy of different DL models using TF-IDF and word embedding [109]

Moreover, in this experiment, the performance of the models is analyzed considering different subsets constructed with different percentages of the data taken initially. This %age ranges from 10% to 100%. Comparison of accuracy for different datasets comprising of two concepts i.e. positive and negative are shown in Table 3.2 [109]. Figure 3.9 shows the graphical representation of the accuracy of different DL methods using TF-IDF and word embedding [109].

3.5.3   Implementation Details of DL Based Behavior Evaluation Approaches

In [110], a probabilistic technique is developed for behavior prediction. In this model, a deep neural network architecture is implemented as shown in Fig. 3.10. The architecture given in [110] is developed using RNN and LSTM [111]. In this

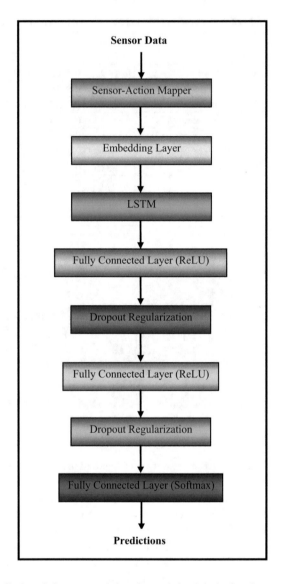

Fig. 3.10 Long short-term memory (LSTM) network for behavior modeling [110]

implementation of behavior prediction, it is assumed that the activity label of action is solely dependent on actions already registered earlier. The memory of LSTM is managed recurrently so that the problems related to sequential dependencies can be modeled. In this implemented architecture, the LSTM is divided into three different components. These are (1) input component (2) sequence modeling component (3) predictive component. The implementation steps of this model can be enumerated as:

(a) The input component receives the primitive sensor data and subsequently maps these data to corresponding earlier defined equivalent actions [112].

(b) Further, these actions are then inputted to the trainable embedding layer. This layer renders the model more informative for the inputted actions.

(c) The weights of the layer are initiated with the values obtained by the algorithm such as Word2Vec.

(d) This layer elicits the corresponding action IDs and converts them with semantics into embeddings.

(e) Now, the action embeddings got in the input component are processed by the subsequent layer i.e. sequence modeling component.

(f) Further, the processing takes place in the LSTM layer that comprises 512 network units.

(g) Finally, the processing takes place in the predictive component. The predictive component implements the sequence models generated by the LSTMs for prediction.

(h) After this, the processing is carried out in rectified linear unit (ReLU). Each of these layers comprises 1024 network units.

(i) Further, dropout regularization with a value of 0.8 is used. It prevents the complex co-adaptations of the fully connected layers. This prevention exists by avoiding random neuron selection during the training process. The dropout regularization also prevents overfitting.

(j) Finally, a third fully connected layer is implemented for obtaining the subsequent action predictions. This layer uses the soft-max activation function.

Detailed implementation of behavior prediction using a deep learning-based approach is given in [110]. Finally, concluding remarks are given in Sect. 3.6.

3.6 Conclusions

Perhaps, the development of automatic behavior and sentiment predictor is the need of time because it is pervasive and of the utmost importance. However, the task of behavior and sentiment analysis is still obscure because it requires performing the task of natural language processing. Explicitly, this is a complicated task associated with a different number of challenges. Researchers have been attempted to strive hard to tackle different problems and to find their solutions related to automated predictions of behavior and sentiment so that the behavior and sentiment of smart digital societies can be envisioned. Even more, researchers also attempted to develop the automated behavior and sentiment predictor whose final prediction can logically and reasonably be explained so that it can be used in different applications consistency and satisfaction including intervention in the social network. Further, the automated behavior and sentiment predictor of the smart digital societies will have to deal with a gigantic chunk of data generated and accumulated from different devices at the different locations of the smart cities. These data are accumulated from various domains like traffic, medical domain, business sector, etc. However, the data generation rates vary from device to device. In addition, chances are always there to have information loss while performing the task of data accumulation. Besides data accumulation, information management of smart digital societies is an important issue that has been discussed in this chapter with substantial insights. Furthermore, the planning agencies and the government authorities will also need different planning tools to describe and measure their planning strategies and the planning itineraries of the recent future so that the evaluation and assessment of the smart city project could become a reality. It is also worthy to mention that extracted information as mentioned above can subsequently be implemented to identify the subjectivities of different entities in an automatic manner. Moreover, the objective behind the analysis of accumulated data is to compute the level of behavior and sentiment as positive, negative, or neutral from user' generated textual data. Indeed, the automated behavior and sentiment analysis can be demonstrated on three levels of mining such as feature, sentence, and document level and deep learning-based techniques can successfully be used at all these three levels.

References

1. United Nations (2014) World Urbanization Prospects: The 2014 Revision, Highlights; Department of Economic and Social Affairs, Population Division, United Nations, New York
2. Caragliu A, Del Bo C, Nijkamp P (2011) Smart cities in Europe. J Urban Technol 18:65–82
3. Shapiro JM (2006) Smart cities: quality of life, productivity, and the growth effects of human capital. Rev Econ Stat 88:324–335
4. Forman DE, Berman AD, McCabe CH, Baim DS, Wei JY (1992) PTCA in the elderly: the "young-old" versus the "old-old". J Am Geriatr Soc 40:19–22
5. Rashidi P, Mihailidis A (2013) A survey on ambient-assisted living tools for older adults. IEEE J Biomed Health Inform 17:579–590
6. Siegel E (2013) Predictive analytics—the power to predict who will click, buy, lie or die. Wiley, Hoboken
7. Freitas AA (2014) Comprehensible classification models: a position paper. SIGKDD Explor Newslett 15(1):1–10
8. Pate R, Pratt M, Blair S et al (1995) Physical activity and public health: a recommendation from the centers for disease control and prevention and the American college of sports medicine. JAMA 273(5):402–407
9. Marshall A, Eakin E, Leslie E, Owen N (2005) Exploring the feasibility and acceptability of using internet technology to promote physical activity within a defined community. Health Promot J Aust 16:82–84
10. Bandura A (1989) Human agency in social cognitive theory. Am Psychol 44(9):1175–1184
11. Christakis N (2010) The hidden influence of social networks. In: TED2010. http://www.ted.com/talks/nicholas_christakis_the_hidden_influence_of_social_networks
12. Bien J, Tibshirani R (2011) Prototype selection for interpretable classification. Ann Appl Stat 5(4):2403–2424
13. Breiman L, Friedman JH, Olshen RA, Stone CJ (1984) Classification and regression trees. Wadsworth International Group, Wadsworth
14. Fung G, Sandilya S, Rao RB (2005) Rule extraction from linear support vector machines. In: KDD'05, pp 32–40
15. Meinshausen N (2010) Node harvest. Ann Appl Stat 4(4):2049–2072
16. Van Assche A, Blockeel H (2007) Seeing the forest through the trees: learning a comprehensible model from an ensemble. In: ECML'07, vol 4701, pp 418–429

17. Pouli V, Kafetzoglou S, Tsiropoulou EE, Dimitriou A, Papavassiliou S (2015) Personalizedmultimediacontent retrieval through relevance feedback techniques for enhanced user experience. In: Proceedings of the 2015 13th International Conference on Telecommunications (ConTEL), Graz, Austria, pp 1–8

18. Thai MT, Wu W, Xiong H (2016) Big data in complex and social networks. CRC Press, Boca Raton

19. Cambria E, Das D, Bandyopadhyay S, Feraco A (2017) A practical guide to sentiment analysis. Springer, Berlin, Germany

20. Hussein DME-DM (2018) A survey on sentiment analysis challenges. J King Saud Univ Eng Sci 30:330–338

21. Sohangir S, Wang D, Pomeranets A, Khoshgoftaar TM (2018) Big data: deep learning for financial sentiment analysis. J Big Data 5:3

22. Jangid H, Singhal S, Shah RR, Zimmermann R (2018, April 23–27) Aspect-based financial sentiment analysis using deep learning. In: Proceedings of the companion of the web conference 2018 on the web conference, Lyon, pp 1961–1966

23. Keenan MJS (2018) Advanced positioning, flow, and sentiment analysis in commodity markets. Wiley, Hoboken

24. Satapathy R, Cambria E, Hussain A (2017) Sentiment analysis in the bio-medical domain. Springer, Berlin, Germany

25. Rajput A (2020) Natural language processing, sentiment analysis, and clinical analytics. In: Innovation in health informatics. Elsevier, Amsterdam, pp 79–97

26. Qian J, Niu Z, Shi C (2018, February 26–28) Sentiment analysis model on weather-related tweets with deep neural network. In: Proceedings of the 2018 10th international conference on machine learning and computing, Macau, pp 31–35

27. Pham D-H, Le A-C (2018) Learning multiple layers of knowledge representation for aspect-based sentiment analysis. Data Knowl Eng 114:26–39

28. Preethi G, Krishna PV, Obaidat MS, Saritha V, Yenduri S (2017, July 21–23) Application of deep learning to sentiment analysis for recommender system on the cloud. In: Proceedings of the 2017International Conference on Computer, Information and Telecommunication Systems (CITS), Dalian, pp 93–97

29. Li L, Goh T-T, Jin D (2018) How textual quality of online reviews affect classification performance: a case of deep learning sentiment analysis. Neural Comput Appl 32:1–29. [CrossRef]

30. Alharbi ASM, de Doncker E (2019) Twitter sentiment analysis with a deep neural network: an enhanced approach using user behavioral information. Cogn Syst Res 54:50–61. [CrossRef]

31. Abid F, Alam M, Yasir M, Li CJ (2019) Sentiment analysis through recurrent variants latterly on convolution neural network of twitter. Future Gener. Comput Syst 95:292–308. [CrossRef]

32. Hassan A, Mahmood A (2017, April 24–26) Deep learning approach for sentiment analysis of short texts. In: Proceedings of the Third International Conference on Control, Automation and Robotics (ICCAR), Nagoya, pp 705–710

33. Weinland D, Ronfard R, Boyer E (2011) A survey of vision-based methods for action representation, segmentation, and recognition. Comput Vis Image Underst 115:224–241

34. Chen L, Hoey J, Nugent CD, Cook DJ, Yu Z (2012) Sensor-based activity recognition. IEEE Trans Syst Man Cybern Part C (Appl Rev) 42:790–808

35. Yilmaz A, Javed O, Shah M (2006) Object tracking: a survey. ACM Comput Surv (CSUR) 38:13. https://doi.org/10.1145/1177352.1177355

36. Bao L, Intille SS (2004, April 21–23) Activity recognition from user-annotated acceleration data. In: Proceedings of the international conference on pervasive computing, Linz and Vienna. Springer: Berlin/Heidelberg, pp 1–17

37. Van Kasteren T, Noulas A, Englebienne G, Kröse B (2008, September 21–24) Accurate activity recognition in a home setting. In: Proceedings of the 10th international conference on ubiquitous computing. Seoul, ACM, New York, pp 1–9

38. Oliver N, Garg A, Horvitz E (2004) Layered representations for learning and inferring office activity from multiple sensory channels. Comput Vis Image Underst 96:163–180

39. Fatima I, Fahim M, Lee YK, Lee S (2013) A unified framework for activity recognition-based behavior analysis and action prediction in smart homes. Sensors 13:2682–2699
40. Ordóñez FJ, Iglesias JA, DeToledo P, Ledezma A, Sanchis A (2013) Onlineactivityrecognitionusingevolving classifiers. Expert Syst Appl 40:1248–1255
41. Rashidi P, Cook DJ (2013) COM: a method for mining and monitoring human activity patterns in home-based health monitoring systems. ACM Trans Intell Syst Technol 4:64–20. https://doi.org/10.1145/2508037.2508045
42. Chen L, Nugent CD, Mulvenna M, Finlay D, Hong X, Poland M (2008) A logical framework for behavior reasoning and assistance in a smart home. Int J Assist Robot Mechatron 9:20–34
43. Riboni D, Bettini C (2011) COSAR: hybrid reasoning for context-aware activity recognition. Pers Ubiquitous Comput 15:271–289
44. Chen L, Nugent CD, Wang H (2012) A knowledge-driven approach to activity recognition in smart homes. IEEE Trans Knowl Data Eng 24:961–974
45. Aloulou H, Mokhtari M, Tiberghien T, Biswas J, Yap P (2014) An adaptable and flexible framework for the assistive living of cognitively impaired people. IEEE J Biomed Health Inform 18:353–360
46. Das SK, Cook DJ, Battacharya A, Heierman EO, Lin TY (2002) The role of prediction algorithms in the MavHome smart home architecture. IEEE Wirel Commun 9:77–84
47. Cook DJ, Youngblood M, Heierman EO, Gopalratnam K, Rao S, Litvin A, Khawaja F (2003, March 26) MavHome: an agent-based smart home. In: Proceedings of the First IEEE international conference on pervasive computing and communications (PerCom 2003), Fort Worth; IEEE: Piscataway, pp 521–524
48. Cook DJ, Das SK (2007) How smart are our environments? An updated look at the state of the art. Pervasive Mobile Comput 3:53–73
49. Kurian CP, Kuriachan S, Bhat J, Aithal RS (2005) An adaptive neuro-fuzzy model for the prediction and control of light in integrated lighting schemes. Light Res Technol 37:343–351
50. Morel N, Bauer M, El-Khoury M, Krauss J (2001) Neurobat, a predictive and adaptive heating control system using artificial neural networks. Int J Sol Energy 21:161–201
51. Dounis AI, Caraiscos C (2009) Advanced control systems engineering for energy and comfort management in a building environment—a review. Renew Sust Energ Rev 13:1246–1261
52. Viswanath B, Mislove A, Cha M, Gummadi K (2009) On the evolution of user interaction in Facebook. In: WOSN'09, pp 37–42
53. Lerman K, Intagorn S, Kang JK, Ghosh R (2012) Using proximity to predict activity in social networks. In: WWW'12 Companion, pp 555–556
54. Shen Y, Jin R, Dou D, Chowdhury N, Sun J, Piniewski B, Kil D (2012) Socialized Gaussian process model for human behavior prediction in a health social network. In: ICDM'12, pp 1110–1115
55. Zhu Y, Zhong E, Pan S, Wang X, Zhou M, Yang Q (2013) Predicting user activity level in social networks. In: CIKM'13, pp 159–168
56. Kawale J, Pal A, Srivastava J (2009) Churn prediction in mmorpgs: a social influence based approach. In: CSE'09, pp 423–428
57. Yang J, Wei X, Ackerman M, Adamic L (2010) Activity lifespan: an analysis of user survival patterns in online knowledge-sharing communities. In: ICWSM'10
58. Baecchi C, Uricchio T, Bertini M, Del Bimbo A (2016) A multimodal feature learning approach for sentiment analysis of social network multimedia. Multimed Tools Appl 75(5):2507–2525
59. Qin Y, Sheng QZ, Falkner NJ, Dustdar S, Wang H, Vasilakos AV (2016) When things matter: a survey on data-centric internet of things. J Netw Comput Appl 64:137–153
60. Costa C, Santos MY (2015) Improving cities sustainability through the use of data mining in a context of big city data. In: 2015 international conference of data mining and knowledge engineering, vol 1, IAENG, pp 320–325

61. Jara AJ, Genoud D, Bocchi Y (2014) Big data in smart cities: from poisson to human dynamics. In: Advanced Information Networking and Applications Workshops (WAINA), 28th international conference on, IEEE, pp 785–790
62. Wang H, Osen OL, Li G, Li W, Dai H-N, Zeng W (2015) Big data and industrial internet of things for the maritime industry in northwestern Norway. In: TENCON 2015–2015 IEEE region 10 conference, IEEE, pp 1–5
63. Barnaghi P, Bermudez-Edo M, Tonjes R (2015) Challenges for quality of data in smart cities. J Data Inf Q 6(2–3):6
64. Puiu D, Barnaghi P, Tonjes R, Kumper D, Ali MI, Mileo A, Parreira JX, Fischer M, Kolozali S, Farajidavar N et al (2016) Citypulse: large scale data analytics framework for smart cities. IEEE Access 4:1086–1108
65. Sheth A, Henson C, Sahoo SS (2008) Semantic sensor web. IEEE Internet Comput 12(4):78–83
66. Kafi MA, Challal Y, Djenouri D, Doudou M, Bouabdallah A, Badache N (2013) A study of wireless sensor networks for urban traffic monitoring: applications and architectures. Procedia Comput Sci 19:617–626
67. Toshniwal D et al (2013) Clustering techniques for streaming data-a survey. In: Advance Computing Conference (IACC). IEEE 3rd International, IEEE, pp 951–956
68. Jakkula V, Cook D (2010) Outlier detection in a smart environment structured power datasets. In: Sixth international conference on Intelligent Environments (IE), IEEE, pp 29–33
69. Ni P, Zhang C, Ji Y (2014) A hybrid method for short-term sensor data forecasting in the internet of things. In: 2014 11th international conference on Fuzzy Systems and Knowledge Discovery (FSKD)
70. Ma X, Wu Y-J, Wang Y, Chen F, Liu J (2013) Mining smart card data for transit riders' travel patterns. Transp Res Part C Emerg Technol 36:1–12
71. Derguech W, Bruke E, Curry E (2014) An autonomic approach to real-time predictive analytics using open data and internet of things. In: Ubiquitous intelligence and computing, 2014 IEEE 11th international conference on and IEEE 11th international conferecne on and autonomic and trusted computing, and IEEE 14th internationl conferecne on scalable computing and communications and its associated workshops (UTC-ATC-ScalCom), IEEE, pp 204–211
72. Han W, Gu Y, Zhang Y, Zheng L (2014) Data-driven quantitative trust model for the internet of agricultural things, in the internet of things (IoT). Int Conf IEEE 2014:31–36
73. Souza AM, Amazonas JR (2015) An outlier detect algorithm using big data processing and internet of things architecture. Procedia Comput Sci 52:1010–1015
74. Monekosso DN, Remagnino P (2013) Data reconciliation in a smart home sensor network. Expert Syst Appl 40(8):3248–3255
75. Shukla M, Kosta Y, Chauhan P (2015), Analysis and evaluation of outlier detection algorithms in data streams. In: International conference on computer, communication, and control (IC4), IEEE, pp 1–8
76. Shilton A, Rajasegarar S, Leckie C, Palaniswami M (2015) Dp1svm: A dynamic planar one-class support vector machine for the internet of things environment. In: International conference on Recent Advances in Internet of Things (RIoT), IEEE, pp 1–6
77. Barcelona Ciutat Digital (2018) Barcelona ciutat digital https://ajuntament.barcelona.cat/digital/ca. Accessed 26 June 2018
78. City Dashboard (2018) Citydashboardorg. http://citydashboard.org/london/. Accessed 26 June 2018
79. COR (2018) Centrodeoperaçõesrio. http://cor.talentstecnologia.cloud/. Accessed 26 June 2018
80. Amin-Naseri M, Chakraborty P, Sharma A, Gilbert SB, Hong M (2018) Evaluating the reliability, coverage, and added value of crowdsourced traffic incident reports from Waze. IA State University
81. Batty M, Axhausen K, Giannotti F, Pozdnoukhov A, Bazzani A, Wachowicz M, Ouzounis G, Portugali Y (2012) Smart cities of the future. Eur Phys J Spec Top 214(1):481–518

82. Jin J, Gubbi J, Marusic S, Palaniswami M (2014) An information framework for creating a smart city through internet of things. IEEE Internet Things J 1(2):112–121
83. Farkas K, Feher G, Benczur A, Sidlo C (2015) Crowds ending based public transport information service in smart cities. IEEE Commun Mag 53(8):158–165
84. Zook M (2017) Crowd-sourcing the smart city: using big geosocial media metrics in urban governance. Big Data Soci 4(1):1–13
85. Porter ME, Hepplemann J (2014) How smart, connected products are transforming competition. Harv Bus Rev 92(11):64–88
86. Parnell B, Stone M, Aravopoulou E (2018) How leaders manage their business models using information. Bottom Line. https://doi.org/10.1108/BL-04-2018-0017
87. Stott R, Stone M, Fae J (2016) Business models in the business to business and business to consumer worlds–what can each world learn from the other. J Bus Ind Mark 31(8):943–954
88. Stone M, Aravopoulou E (2018) Improving journeys by opening data: the case of transport for London (TfL). Bottom Line 31(1):2–15
89. Wright LT, Robin R, Stone M, Aravopoulou E (2018) Adoption of big data technology for innovation in B2B marketing. J Bus-Bus Mark
90. De Vries H, Bekkers V, Tummers L (2016) Innovation in the public sector: a systematic review and future research agenda. Public Adm 94(1):146–166
91. Arundel A, Casali L, Hollanders H (2015) How European public-sector agencies innovate: the use of bottom-up, policy-dependent and knowledge-scanning innovation methods. Res Policy 44(7):1271–1282
92. Balfour D, Demircioglu M (2017) Reinventing the wheel? Public sector innovation in the age of governance. Public Adm Rev 77(5):800–805
93. Torfing J (2018) Collaborative innovation in the public sector: the argument. Public Manag Rev 21:1–11. https://doi.org/10.1080/14719037.2018.1430248
94. Namiot D, Sneps-Sneppe M (2014) On software standards for smart cities: API or DPI. In: Proceedings of the ITU kaleidoscope academic conference: living in a converged world Impossible without standards? pp 169–174
95. Bhavitha B, Rodrigues AP, Chiplunkar NN (2017, March 10–11) Comparative study of machine learning techniques in sentimental analysis. In: Proceedings of the 2017 International Conference on Inventive Communication and Computational Technologies (ICICCT), Coimbatore, pp 216–221
96. Salas-Zárate MP, Medina-Moreira J, Lagos-Ortiz K, Luna-Aveiga H, Rodriguez-Garcia MA, Valencia-García RJC (2017) Sentiment analysis on tweets about diabetes: an aspect-level approach. Comput Math Methods Med 2017:1–9
97. Huq MR, Ali A, Rahman A (2017) Sentiment analysis on twitter data using KNN and SVM. IJACSA. Int J Adv Comput Sci Appl 8:19–25
98. Pinto D, McCallum A, Wei X, Croft WB (2003) Tableextractionusingconditionalrandomfields. In: Proceedings of the 26th annual international ACM SIGIR conference on research and development in information retrieval, Toronto, pp 235–242
99. Soni S, Sharaff A (2015, Mrach 6) Sentiment analysis of customer reviews based on hidden Markov model. In: Proceedings of the 2015 International Conference on Advanced Research in Computer Science Engineering & Technology (ICARCSET 2015), Unnao, pp 1–5
100. Zhang X, Zheng X (2016, July 10) Comparison of text sentiment analysis based on machine learning. In: Proceedings of the 2016 15th International Symposium on Parallel and Distributed Computing (ISPDC), Fuzhou, pp 230–233
101. Malik V, Kumar A (2018) Communication. Sentiment analysis of twitter data using naive Bayes algorithm. Int J Recent Innov Trends Comput Commun 6:120–125
102. Mehra N, Khandelwal S, Patel P (2002) Sentiment identification using maximum entropy analysis of movie reviews. Stanford University, Stanford
103. Wu H, Li J, Xie J (2017) Maximum entropy-based sentiment analysis of online product reviews in Chinese. In: Automotive, mechanical and electrical engineering. CRC Press, Boca Raton, pp 559–562

104. Firmino Alves AL, Baptista CDS, Firmino AA, Oliveira MGD, Paiva ACD (2014, November 18–21) A Comparison of SVM versus naive Bayes techniques for sentiment analysis in tweets: a case study with the 2013 FIFA confederations cup. In: Proceedings of the 20th Brazilian symposiumon multimedia and the web, João Pessoa, pp 123–130

105. Pandey AC, Rajpoot DS, Saraswat M (2017) Twitter sentiment analysis using the hybrid cuckoo search method. Inf Process Manag 53:764–779. [CrossRef]

106. Barbieri N, Bonchi F, Manco F (2014) Who to follow and why: link prediction with explanations In KDD'14, pp 1266–1275

107. Gavrilova, ML (2018, June 11–14) Machine learning for social behavior understanding, CGI 2018, Bintan Island, ACM. https://doi.org/10.1145/3208159.3208187

108. Mikolov T, Sutskever I, Chen K, Corrado GS, Dean J (2013) Distributed representations of words and phrases and their compositionality. In: Proceedings of the advances in neural information processing systems, Lake Tahoe, pp 3111–3119

109. Dang NC, Moreno-García MC, De la Prieta F (2020) Sentiment analysis based on deep learning: a comparative study. Electronics 9:483. https://doi.org/10.3390/electronics9030483

110. Almeida A, Azkune G (2018) Predicting human behavior with a recurrent neural network. Appl Sci 8:305. https://doi.org/10.3390/app8020305

111. Hochreiter S, Schmidhuber J (1997) Long short-term memory. Neural Comput 9:1735–1780

112. Azkune G, Almeida A, López-de-Ipiña L, Chen L (2015) Extending knowledge-driven activity models through data-driven learning techniques. Expert Syst Appl 42:3115–3128

Chapter 4
Multi-Access Edge Computing for 5G Networks in Cloud-IoT Integrated Environment

Abstract The Multi-access Edge Computing (MEC) features of 5G networks provide information technology (IT) services to the end-users including clients and servers using cloud-computing capabilities at the edge level of the distributive networking systems. The creation of the MEC environment provides high bandwidth and ultra-low latency in real-time access of radio frequencies and wireless network information which can be used by various users of cloud-IoT technologies of our forthcoming modern societies including *Society 5.0*. In this chapter, the authors have discussed the procedures, information flow necessities, and application layer architecture of multi-access edge computing for 5G networks to enable edge applications over 3GPP networks in the cloud-IoT integrated distributive computing environment. The described algorithms and approaches of this chapter include application-layer architecture of edge applications in 5G networking environment. The detailed technical specifications and information flow steps of the edge enabler client, edge configuration server, edge application server, uniform resource identifier, edge enabler server, and edge enabler clients are also provided by the authors.

Keywords 5G networks · Cloud-IoT technologies · Edge application server · Edge configuration server · Edge enabler client · Edge enabler server · Multi-access edge computing · Uniform resource identifier

4.1 Introduction

The edge computing is a type of network architecture that enables cloud-IoT computing capabilities and service-related environments, which are deployed close to the user equipment (UE). The edge computing promises numerous benefits to the users like lower latency, reduced backhaul traffic, higher bandwidth, and opportunities for new services in a cloud-IoT environment. This technical specification provides application layer architecture and related procedures for enabling EAs over 3GPP networks [1].

K. N. Mishra, S. C. Pandey, *Cloud-IoT Technologies in Society 5.0*,
https://doi.org/10.1007/978-3-031-28711-4_4

The Multi-access Edge Computing (MEC) provides the capabilities of cloud-computing and an IT (information technology) service environment at the edge of the network to the content developers and application developers. This MEC environment is providing high bandwidth and ultra-low latency in real-time access to radio network information which can be leveraged by various users of cloud-IoT technologies of our modern society [2].

The MEC may provide eco-friendly and value chain-based communication networks. Further, the operators can open their edges of RANs (Radio Access Networks) to the certified third parties, and these third parties may be allowed to deploy innovative applications and services for mobile subscribers, enterprises, and vertical segments in a flexibly and rapid manner. An important strategic significance of MEC is that the MEC is naturally developed in the development of mobile base stations and telecommunication networking systems. Further, the MEC will be able to permit new vertical and horizontal business segments and services for enterprise customers and consumers. Some of the basic level applications of MEC are Internet-of-Things (IoT), video analytics, augmented reality, data caching, and optimized local content distribution [3].

The MEC permits software applications to spout into local content and provide real-time information about the network conditions of local-access networks. Mobile core networks are alleviated of further congestion by deploying a variety of services and caching content at the network edge and can proficiently serve local purposes. The industry standardization and deployment of MEC platforms will act as enablers for innovative revenue-generating streams to the vendors, operators, and third parties [4].

4.2   Theoretical Foundations and Related Work Descriptions

For the discussions, the terms and expressions given in 3GPP TR 21.905 [1] are applied in this chapter. The terms which have already been defined and described in this chapter will get priority [1]. The *application software is resident* in the cloud and it performs the server function. It is described in 3GPP TS 23.501 [1] that n order to achieve an efficient service delivery through the minimized load and end-to-end latency on the transport network the edge computing enables operators and other third party services to be hosted close to the UE's access point of attachment. The edge computing service provider (ECSP) is a mobile network Operator or a third party service provider who offers edge computing services [1, 2, 4, 5]. The edge data network (EDN) is a local data network that may support the architecture to enable the edge applications. The edge hosting environment (EHE) provides support and a computing environment for EASE (edge application server's execution). For the present document, the following symbol format will be used by the authors:

Symbol format (EW) symbol   Explanation

The Tables 4.1 and 4.2 are representing the abbreviations and the corresponding descriptions that have been used in this chapter. The abbreviations are defined in Tables 4.1 and 4.2 will get preference.

The sub-clauses of *the high-level features clause* will describe high-level features of the application architecture for enabling EAs. If the need exists then this clause can be merged with the 'Architectural principles and requirements' clause before the approval of the 3GPP TS 23.501. The architectural requirements, edge configuration data requirements, EEC registration requirements, EAS registration requirements, EAS discovery requirements, capability exposure to edge application servers security requirements, subscription service requirements, traffic management requirements, lifecycle management requirements, and edge application KPIs related requirements for Multi-Access Edge Computing for 5G Networks in Cloud-IoT Integrated Environment will be as follow [6, 7]:

Table 4.1 Abbreviations table and corresponding descriptions

	Abbreviation	Description
1.	5GC	5G core network
2.	5GS	5G system
3.	AC/ACs	Application client/application clients
4.	AF	Application function
5.	ACID	Application client identification
6.	CM	Conditional mandatory
7.	ALA	Application layer architecture
8.	CO	Conditional optional
9.	DN	Data network
10.	EAs	Edge applications
11.	EAS	Edge application server
12.	EASID	Edge application server identification
13.	ECS	Edge configuration server
14.	EEC	Edge enabler client
15.	EDNCS	Edge data network configuration server
16.	EECID	Edge enabler client identification
17.	EENCS	Edge enabler network configuration server
18.	EES	Edge enabler server
19.	EESID	Edge enabler server identification

Table 4.2 The abbreviations and the corresponding descriptions

	Abbreviation	Description
1.	EHE	Edge hosting environment
2.	EPS	Evolved packet system
3.	IRP	Integration reference point
4.	KPIs	Key performance indicators
5.	LCC	Lower camel case
6.	M	Mandatory
7.	MEC	Multi-access edge computing
8.	MNO	Mobile network operator
9.	NEF	Network exposure function
10.	O	Optional
11.	OSAppId	Operating system application identity
12.	OSId	Operating system identity
13.	PLMN	Public land mobile network
14.	SCEF	Service capability exposure function
15.	SSID	Service set identifier
16.	UCC	Upper camel case
17.	UE	User equipment
18.	URI	Uniform resource identifier
19.	WKA	Well known abbreviation

Architectural Requirement 1: (The ALA will support the deployment of Edge Application Server(s) and AC(s) [AR-5.2.1.2-a].

Architectural Requirement 2: The ALA may hold up various operational models in concurrence with an operator's 3GPP network using [AR-5.2.1.2-b].

Architectural Requirement 3: The ALA may be companionable with the 3GPP network system using [AR-5.2.1.2-c].

Edge Configuration Data Requirement 1: The ALA has the capability to provide mechanisms for supplying the Edge Enabler Server(s) using [AR-5.2.2.2-a].

Edge Enabler Client Registration Requirement 1: The ALA will provide mechanisms for an EEC to register onto the EES using [AR-5.2.3.2-a].

Edge Enabler Client Registration Requirement 2: The ALA will provide mechanisms for an EEC to de-register from the EES using [AR-5.2.3.2-b].

Edge Enabler Client Registration Requirement 3: The ALA will provide abnormal termination detection to EES using [AR-5.2.3.2-c].

Edge Application Server registration Requirement 1: The ALA will provide mechanisms for an EAS to register to the EES using [AR-5.2.3.3-a].

Edge Application Server registration Requirement 2: The ALA shall support EAS exposing availability using [AR-5.2.3.3-b], which varies with time, and location, etc.

Edge Application Server registration Requirement 3: The ALA will provide a mechanism so that the Edge Application Servers are uniquely identifiable using [AR-5.2.3.3-c].

Edge Application Server registration Requirement 4: The ALA will provide deregistration from EES for an EAS using [AR-5.2.3.3-d].

Edge Application Server registration Requirement 5: The ALA will provide abnormal termination of EAS for the EES using [AR-5.2.3.3-e].

Edge Application Server discovery Requirement 1: The ALA will provide mechanisms for an EEC to discover available Edge Application Servers using [AR-5.2.4.2-a].

Edge Application Server discovery Requirement 2: The ALA will provide configuration information of the Edge Application Servers to the EEC using [AR-5.2.4.2-b], to enable communication between ACs and the Edge Application Servers.

Capability Exposure to Edge Application Servers Requirement: The ALA will support the exposure of 3GPP network's capabilities to the EAS using [AR-5.2.5.2-a].

Security Related Requirement 1: The ALA will provide the edge computing service between the UE and the functional entities using [AR-5.2.6.2-e].

Security Related Requirement 2: The ALA will support authentication, and mutual authorization checks between servers and clients or vice versa using [AR-5.2.6.2-f].

Security Related Requirement 3: The ALA will support Edge Application Servers to obtain user's authorization using [AR-5.2.6.2-g] for accessing to user's sensitive information e.g. user's location. As for as resolving security-related problems is concerned, the security requirements are in the scope of SA3.

Subscription Service Requirement 1: The ALA will provide mechanisms to notify an EEC about relevant changes in the availability of Edge Application Servers using [AR-5.2.7.2-a].

Subscription Service Requirement 2: The ALA will provide mechanisms to notify an EAS about relevant changes to elements in the edge application architecture using [AR-5.2.7.2-b].

Lifecycle management Requirements: The ALA will support interactions with a lifecycle management system using [A.5.2.9.2-a].

Edge Application KPIs Related Requirement 1: The Edge Application Server will be able to publish its or application-level requirements or KPIs using [AR-5.2.10.2-a].

Edge Application KPIs Related Requirement 2: The Edge Application Server will be able to update its application-level requirements or KPIs using [AR-5.2.10.2-b].

4.3   The Described Algorithms and Methodology

4.3.1   Key Issues and the Corresponding Open Issues

Following are the 14 key issues and the corresponding open issues related to the implementation of multi-access edge computing for 5G networks in the cloud-IoT integrated distributive environment [8, 9, 10]:

Key Issue 1: Service Provisioning and Configuration
For availing edge computing services deployed in the EDN (Edge Data Network), user equipment (UE) must be connected EDN. Here, the critical thing is whether the AC can find an Edge Application Server.

Open Issues Related to Key Issue 1

- Whether some configuration information is needed by the UE to connect with the EDN or not? If yes, what are the configuration parameters?
- How the configuration information, if required, is securely provided to the UE?
- In the case that multiple Edge Application Servers are available in multiple Edge Data Networks, what application information is needed to determine the best suitable Edge Data Network?

Key Issue 2: EDN Discovery and Registration
The employment of EDN may or may not be accessible at all the locations of the network due to certain operational constraints., The user equipment (UE) needs to determine the availability of an EDN at the UE's location before attempting to avail edge computing services for certain applications.

Open Issues Related to Key Issue 2

- Whether and how a UE determines the availability of an EDN at the UE's location?
- Whether and how a UE determines the availability of an EES at the UE's location?
- Whether and how the UE registers to the EES before availing Edge Computing services?
- Whether and how the UE de-registers from the EES?
- Whether and how the EES detects an abnormal termination of the UE registration?
- If there are changes in the availability of the EDN, whether and how the UE is notified?
- If there are any changes in the accessibility of the EES, whether and how the UE is notified?

Key Issue 3: Enable the EAS (Edge Application Server) on the EHS (Edge Hosting Environment)
Many application providers may use the EDN to provide their applications as EAS (edge application servers). To activate such EAS on the EHS (edge hosting

environment), the application providers will be required to provide EAS-related information to the EES (Edge Enabler Server). The EAS-related information may include the constraints on the accessibility of the EAS to the specific time of operation or geographical area.

Open Issues Related to Key Issue 3

- How the EASs are registered on the EES? How the EES identifies the registered Edge Application Servers?
- Whether and how do the Edge Application Servers provide availability information such as certain geographical areas, time of operation, etc. to the EES?
- What are the parameters required for EAS's enablement on the EES?
- How do the Edge Application Servers de-register from the EES?
- How the EES can allocate EDN messages efficiently to a set of subscribed EASs?
- Whether and how the EES detects an abnormal termination of the EAS registration?

Key Issue 4: Edge Application Server Discovery
Due to certain operational constraints, the deployment of EAS may or may not be homogeneous throughout the Edge Data Networks. The UE needs to determine the availability of the EAS from the EES before attempting to avail services from an Edge Application Servers for certain applications. The meaning of availability of the EAS includes both the EAS running on the Edge Hosting Environment and the Edge Application Server, which can be instantiated on the Edge Hosting Environment.

Open Issues Related to Key Issue 4

- Whether and how to discover the EASs available on the EHE within the Edge Data Network?
- How to check authorization to discover the Edge Application Servers?

Key Issue 5: Capability Exposure to Edge Application Server
The 3GPP network capability exposure function (i.e. SCEF, NEF) provides northbound restful APIs which can be utilized by third party applications (see 3GPP TS 29122 [5] and 3GPP TS 29.522 [11, 12] for information regarding available northbound APIs). For a third party EAS to access such northbound APIs exposed by SCEF/NEF, the third party application developer would need to onboard onto the MNO's platform (e.g., CAPIF) and accept MNO's SLA terms and conditions. On the other hand, it would be beneficial if the third party Edge Application Servers in the EDN can utilize service API(s) exposed by the EES, which may rely on the SCEF/NEF northbound APIs. Some of the service API(s) that are exposed by the EES may facilitate communication between AC(s) and Edge Application Server(s).

For example, in the smart factory system of society 5.0, EAS may have the demand to obtain location information of industrial robotics to activate corresponding actions or operations based on location. This kind of location-based service requires the EAS to be authorized to obtain the location information of the UE through the EES.

Open Issues Related to Key Issue 5

- Whether there is a need for new service API(s) provided by the EES to the Edge Application Server, and how to support it?
- How do Edge Application Servers discover available service API(s) within the Edge Data Network?
- How CAPIF, as specified in 3GPP TS 23.222 [4], can be utilized, and is there a requirement of enhancing the functionalities of CAPIF?
- Whether there is a need to support the exposure of service API provided by the EAS to the other EAS within the Edge Data Network, and how to support it?
- Whether there is a need to support the exposure of service API provided by the EAS to the other EAS of the different Data Network, and how to support it?
- How does the EES re-expose service API(s) to the EAS (if the service API(s) is depending on the SCEF/NEF northbound API(s))
- How to uniquely identify the UE between the EAS and the EES for utilizing capability exposure API(s) which may rely on the SCEF/NEF northbound API(s)?
- Whether and how the location information of the UE can be exposed to the EAS from the EES.
- How the EAS API(s) can be used to provide EASs' with information about the capabilities of EECs that may host the Edge Application Server's AC(s).
- How EES service API(s) facilitate communication between AC(s) and EAS(s).

Key Issue 6: Edge Computing Service Authorization
To support Edge Computing Service authorization, the following key issues related to edge computing service authorization need to be studied:

- How to enable the MNO to authorize the usage of Edge Computing Service by UE?
- How to authorize the UE to use Edge Computing Service by non-MNOs, if required in specific deployments?
- How to enable the EEC to authenticate with the EDNCS?

Key Issue 7: Flexible Deployment
To support flexible deployment for Edge Computing, the following key issues need to be studied.

- How to support the multiple Edge Computing Service Providers per PLMN operator network?
- How to identify Edge Data Network, in the case of multiple Edge Data Networks within a single PLMN where one EDN is defined as a subarea (e.g. list of TAs or cells) in the PLMN coverage?

Key Issue 8: EDN Selection
The user equipment (UE) may have access to more than one EDN including Edge Application Servers due to e.g. dual registration with 3GPP access and non-3GPP access. An EEC in the UE needs to discover not only available Edge Application Server(s) but first select the optimal EDN if more than one is available.

Open Issues Related to Key Issue 8

- How to assist the UE to select the optimal Edge Data Network? (Note: This key issue is related to key issues #2 and #4.)

Key Issue 9: Preserving Service Continuity

Whenever UE handoffs to a new location then in that situation the EAS (edge application servers) will have better suitability for serving the ACs (ACs) in the user equipment (UE). While replacing the *serving edge application Server* (SEAS) with the *target edge application server* (TEAS), we need to provide a path for ACs to continue their service in the user equipment. Furthermore, similar service continuity requirements exist for the cases in which the Edge Application Servers are transferred from the EDN to Servers in the cloud and vice versa. Such transitions may occur as a result of a mobility event, or even as a result of other non-mobility events such as load balancing.

This key issue proposes to study *"upper layer enablers"* for service continuity that are within the scope of the application architecture for Edge Application Servers (e.g. mechanisms for traffic redirection).

Open Issues Related to Key Issue 9

- How to detect the need to reroute traffic from the serving EAS instance to the target EAS?
- How to enable the required switch in the connection between the AC and the EAS while preserving service continuity?
- How to transfer any required context between Edge Application Servers within the Edge Data Network?
- How to transfer any required context from the serving EAS to the target EAS (or Server) regardless of their location: In the same Edge Data Network, in a different EDN or in the Cloud?

Key Issue 10: Dynamic Availability

Availability of EDN and the EASs can change dynamically due to multiple reasons, such as a change in deployments, mobility of the UE, etc. These types of changes must be given to the UE to fine-tune the provided services.

Open Issues Related to Key Issue 10

- How to keep the UE updated with information about Edge Data Network?
- How to keep the UE updated with information about Edge Application Servers?

Key Issue 11: User Consent/Authorization for Network Capability Exposure to EASs'

User's consent is an important aspect while dealing with sensitive information about the user or the devices of the user. With the capabilities of the Edge Application Servers to request invocation of 3GPP network capability exposure APIs, such as location APIs, to obtain information about the user and the devices of the user, it is of utmost importance to capture the consent of the user.

The user needs to be in full control of which applications are allowed to request and obtain what information about the user and the devices belonging to the user and how frequently. Such approvals by the end-users ensure that only the legitimate applications, trusted by the user, can obtain and make use of the information and services involving the user or user's sensitive information. While capturing and using user consent is important, it is also important to ensure only authorized users are allowed to grant or modify consent.

Open Issues Related to Key Issue 11

- How to obtain the user's consent to allow an Edge Application Server's service or information request?
- How to ensure that only an authorized user can grant or modify the consent?

Key Issue 12: Lifecycle Management
To ensure efficient deployment of third-party applications in the Edge Data Network, the application provider should be able to invoke requests about the lifecycle of applications. These include on-boarding, instantiation, upgrade, scaling, and termination of user applications deployed as Edge Application Servers in the Edge Data Network. The Edge Computing Service Provider should process the requests and authorize them when appropriate based on e.g. its policies, resource availability, etc.

Further, it should be possible for an Edge Computing Service Provider to manage the lifecycle of the EES and EDNCS to deploy edge ecosystems dynamically. This should include the capability to manage the performance and fault of both entities. These actions may be the result of requests from the application provider.

Open Issues Related to Key Issue 12

- A mechanism for the application providers to request lifecycle operations (e.g. instantiation, termination, scaling) for their EESs.
- A mechanism for edge computing service providers to manage the lifecycle (e.g. instantiation, termination, scaling), performance assurance, and fault supervision of Edge Enabler Servers.
- A mechanism for edge computing service providers to manage the lifecycle (e.g. instantiation, termination, scaling), performance assurance, and fault supervision of EDNCSs.

Key Issue 13: Provision of QoS Information for the EAS
Edge Application Servers of the same type may have different requirements in terms of QoS (e.g., guaranteed bit rate, maximum bit rate, priority). For instance, certain video streaming applications may be expected to provide higher QoS than other video streaming applications.

Open Issues Related to Key Issue 13

- Whether the information related to QoS (e.g., QoS parameters) can be exposed to the Edge Application Server? If yes, how to do it?
- Whether to differentiate the QoS requirements for the same type of Edge Application Servers? If yes, how to do it?

- Whether to define certain policy rules (e.g. QoS modification is forbidden) for certain Edge Application Servers? If yes, how to do it?

Key Issue 14: Exposure of AC KPIs

During service provisioning and EDN discovery, the AC must be able to find an EAS in such a manner that the range of required AC KPIs (e.g. latency, compute resources) is satisfied.

Application Client KPIs may be included in the application package that is initially *on boarded,* and subsequently instantiated in the EDN if they are present.

Open Issues Related to Key Issue 14

- What are the specific applications KPIs?
- Whether and how the determination of the availability of a suitable EDN is based on a range of AC KPIs?
- Whether and how the determination of the availability of a suitable EES is based on a range of AC KPIs?
- What is the range of AC KPIs (e.g. latency, compute resources) needed for a UE to connect with the best suitable EDN (e.g., with EAS available that satisfies the KPIs)?
- How to assist the UE to select the optimal EDN when the serving EDN can no longer meet the performance required by one or more of the AC KPIs?

4.3.2 Architecture of Enabling Edge Applications

The ALA for enabling EAs in Multi-Access Edge Computing for 5G Network is presented in Fig. 4.1 [12, 13].

In Fig. 4.1, the EDN consists of the Edge Application Server(s) and the Edge Enabler Server. The ECS provides configurations related to Edge Data Network. The functional entities of application layer architecture are Edge Enable Server, Edge Enable Client (s), Edge Configuration Server(s), AC, Edge Application Server(s), the Reference Edge Points (EDGE-1 to EDGE-8), and Application Data Traffic.

4.3.2.1 Edge Enabler Server (EES)

The EES provides supporting functions needed for EASs and EEC. The functionalities of EES are as follow:

- Provide configuration information to enable the exchange of Application Data Traffic with the EAS;
- Providing information related to the EASs to the EEC; and
- Support the functioning of Application Programme Interface invoker and the Application Programme Interface exposing function as specified in 3GPP TS 23.222 [6].

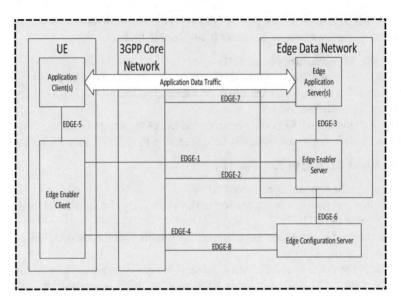

Fig. 4.1 Architecture for enabling edge applications

4.3.2.2   Edge Enabler Client

The EEC provides supporting functions required for AC(s) which includes the discovery of Edge Application Servers available in the Edge Data Network.

4.3.2.3   Edge Configuration Server (ECS)

The ECS provides supporting functions needed for the EEC to connect with an EES.

4.3.2.4   Application Client

The AC is the application resident in the UE performing the client function.

4.3.2.5   Edge Application Server (EAS)

The EAS is the application server resident in the Edge Data Network, and it performs the server functions. The AC connects to the EAS for availing the application services.

The EAS may consume the 3GPP Core Network capabilities in the following three different ways: such as:

(i) It may directly invoke 3GPP Core Network functions if it is an entity trusted by the 3GPP Core Network;

(ii) It may invoke 3GPP Core Network capabilities through the EES; and
(iii) It may invoke the 3GPP Core Network capability exposure functions.

4.3.2.6 The Edge Reference Points (EDGE-1 to EDGE-8)

The edge reference points used for multi-access edge computing in cloud-IoT integrated distributive 5G networks are EDGE-1, EDGE-2, EDGE-3, EDGE-4, EDGE-5, EDGE-6, EDGE-7, and EDGE-8.

The *EDGE-1* reference point enables interactions between the EES and the Edge Enabler Client. Further, it can support the following things to the clients and servers:

- Registration and de-registration of the EEC to the EES;
- Retrieval and provisioning of EAS configuration information; and
- Discovery of Edge Application Servers available in the Edge Data Network.

The reference point *EDGE-2* enables interactions between the EES and the 3GPP Core Network. Further, it provides access to 3GPP Core Network functions and APIs for retrieval of network capability information, e.g. via SCEF and NEF APIs as defined in 3GPP TS 23.501 [2], 3GPP TS 23.502 [3], 3GPP TS 29.522 [4], 3GPP TS 29.122 [5], and with the EES acting as a trusted AF in 5GC (see 3GPP TS 23.501 [2] clause 5.13). Furthermore, it may be noted that the EDGE-2 reference point reuses 3GPP reference points or interfaces of EPS or 5GS considering different deployment models.

The reference point *EDGE-3* enables the interaction between the EES and the Edge Application Servers. It can support the following things:

- Registration of Edge Application Servers with availability information (e.g. time constraints, location constraints);
- De-registration of Edge Application Servers from the EES.
- Provides access to the location information. Further, it may be noted that the optimized distribution of events across the EDGE-3 interface is the responsibility of CT groups.

The *EDGE-4* provides interactions between the ECS and the EEC. It provides the provision of Edge configuration information to the EEC. The *EDGE-5* provides interactions between the AC(s) and the EEC. The *EDGE-6* provides interactions between the ECS and the EES which may support the registration process of EES. The *EDGE-7* reference point enables interactions between the EAS and the 3GPP Core Network. It supports access to 3GPP Core Network functions and APIs for retrieval of network capability information, e.g. via SCEF and NEF APIs as defined in 3GPP TS 23.501 [2], 3GPP TS 23.502 [3], 3GPP TS 29.522 [4], 3GPP TS 29.122 [5], and with the EAS acting as a trusted AF in 5GC (see 3GPP TS 23.501 [2] clause 5.13). It may be noted that the *EDGE-7* reference point reuses 3GPP reference points or interfaces of EPS or 5GS considering different deployment models. The *EDGE-8* reference point enables interactions between the ECS and the 3GPP Core Network.

4.3.2.7   The Cardinality Rules, Clauses, and Commonly Used Values

Various cardinality rules may be applicable for application client (AC), edge enabler client (EEC), ECS, edge hosting environment (EHE), edge enabler server (EES), edge and application server (EAS) in cloud-IoT integrated multi-access 5G networks.

Cardinality rules apply for ACs: Zero or more ACs may be located in one user equipment.

Cardinality Rules for Edge Enabler Client (EEC): An EEC may communicate with one or more ECSs.

Cardinality Rule for Edge Configuration Server (ECS): An ECS may communicate with one or more EESs.

Cardinality Rule for Edge Hosting Environment (EHE): The representation and cardinality of EHE (number of EES and relationship with EASs) in DN is FFS.

Cardinality Rules for Edge Enabler Server (EES): Whether an EES may register with one or more ECSs is to be decided. Whether EASs in a DN may register with one or more EESs is to be decided

Cardinality Rule Edge Application Server (EAS): An EAS can communicate with one EES.

The commonly used values are identified by the clause list identities and these are used in the technical specification of cloud-IoT integrated multi-access 5G networks are Edge Enabler Client ID (EECID), EESID, EASID, Application Client ID (ACID), User Equipment ID (UEID), and User Equipment Location (UEL).

The User equipment ID can uniquely identify a particular UE within a PLMN domain. Following identity is an example that can be used:

GPSI, as defined in 3GPP TS 23.501 [02].

The user equipment location identifies where the UE is present. Following are the example values that we can use in 5G networks:

(a) For UEs that are connected via the 3GPP connection – Cell Identity, as defined in 3GPP TS 23.003 [11]; or

(b) Another possibility for UEs that are connected via the 3GPP connection – TAI (Tracking Area Identity), as defined in 3GPP TS 23.003 [11].

4.3.3   Procedures and Information Flows for Service, Requests, and Response Provisioning

The Common Information Elements (CIE) describes commonly used information elements. The ACP includes information about AC used to determine services and service characteristics required. The Table 4.3 provides the AC profile for cloud-IoT integrated multi-access 5G networks. The Application Client Service (ACS) KPIs

Table 4.3 Application client profile

	Information element	Status	Description
1.	Default EAS ID	M	The default EAS for the AC
2.	Application client type	M	The category or type of AC (e.g. V2X)
3.	ECSP filter	O	The identity of edge computing service provider(s) that the EEC is willing to connect to. If this field is present, the ECS may filter its response based on this preference.
4.	AC schedule	O	The estimated operation schedule of the AC.
5.	AC service area	O	The expected location(s) (e.g. route)
6.	AC service KPIs	O	KPIs are required for ACs to receive services from the EAS.

Table 4.4 Application client service KPI

	Information element	Status	Description
1.	Connection bandwidth	O	Connection bandwidth needed
2.	Service continuity support	O	Indicates if service continuity support is required or not for the application
3.	Maximum request rate	O	The highest request rate originated from AC
4.	Response time	O	Maximum response time (e.g. latency) is required for the server servicing the requests
5.	Availability	O	Minimum availability required for the server
6.	Compute	O	The maximum compute resources required
7.	Graphical compute	O	The maximum graphical compute resources required
8.	Memory	O	The maximum memory resources required
9.	Storage	O	The maximum storage resource required for ACs
10.	AC type-specific information	O	Information specific to each AC type e.g. video, VR, etc.

describes service characteristics of application clients. The ACS-KPIs are presented in Table 4.4. The Edge Application Server Profiles (EASP) required for cloud-IoT integrated multi-access 5G networks are presented in Table 4.5, and the Edge Application Server Service (EASS) KPIs which may provide information about service characteristics of the EAS is presented in Table 4.6 [13–15].

4.3.3.1 Service Provisioning in Multi-Access 5G Networks

In general, the service provisioning allows the Edge Enabler Clients to be configured with information about edge computing services available in the cloud-IoT integrated distributive computing environment. This procedure provides Edge Enabler Clients with the necessary address information for establishing connections to Edge Enabler Servers.

Table 4.5 EAS profile

	Information element	Status	Description
1.	EAS ID	M	The identifier of the EAS
2.	EAS endpoint	M	Gives information about end points. Including FQDN, URI, IP address etc.
3.	EAS provider identifier	O	The identifier of the EAS provider
4.	EAS type	O	The category or type of EAS (e.g. V2X)
5.	EAS description	O	Human-readable description of the EAS
6.	EAS schedule	O	The availability schedule of the EAS (e.g. time windows)
7.	EAS service area	O	The geographical service area that the EAS serves
8.	EAS service KPIs	O	Service characteristics provided by EAS
9.	Service continuity support	O	It indicates the EAS supports service continuity
10.	EAS availability reporting period	O	The availability reporting period (i.e. heartbeat period)
11.	EAS required service APIs	O	A list of the required service APIs
12.	EAS status	O	Describes the EAS status i.e. enabled or disabled

Table 4.6 EAS service KPIs

	Information element	Status	Description
1.	Maximum request rate	O	Max rate of request received from ACs
2.	Average response time	O	The average response time advertised for ACs' service requests
3.	Availability	O	It describes the server availability percentage time for the ACs use
4.	Available compute	O	The max available computer resource for ACs
5.	Available graphical compute	O	The max graphical computing available resource for ACs
6.	Available memory	O	The max available memory for ACs
7.	Available storage	O	The max available storage resource for ACs

The pre-conditions for service provisioning in a multi-access 5G network will be as follow [16, 17]:

Pre-condition 1: The EEC is pre-configured, and it traced the address of the ECS.
Pre-condition 2: The EEC is authorized to enable the communication with the ECS. The UE Identifier may be preconfigured or it may have received a successful authorization.

The Fig. 4.2 describes the information flow of the service provisioning scheme in a multi-access 5G network and it can be completed using the following three steps:

Step 1: The EEC sends a provisioning request to the ECS. The request message may include the UE identifier such as GPSI and credentials received during EEC authorization procedure and AC Profile information.

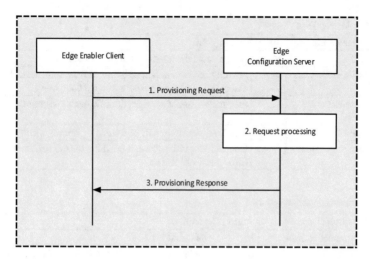

Fig. 4.2 Service provisioning

Step 2: Upon receiving the request from the EEC, the EDNCS performs an authorization check to verify whether the EEC has privileges to perform the operation. The ECS determines the EESs matching AC Profiles (or AC Profile IDs) if provided in step 1. The EES may find some other information like EES endpoints, EDN identification, and service area information,.

Step 3: The ECS responds to the EEC by sending Edge services configuration information, e.g. identification of the EDN, service area information (for LADN), and the information for establishing a connection to the EES (e.g. URI, IP address).

In addition to the above three steps, the EDN configuration information includes a LADN DNN as an identifier to trace the registration procedure of UE.

4.3.3.2 Provisioning Request in Multi-Access 5G Networks

The Table 4.7 describes the information elements for a Provisioning Request in multi-access 5Gfrom the EEC to the provisioning server (i.e. Edge Configuration Server). Please note that it is FFS whether the EEC ID is mandatory or whether the UE ID should be included.

4.3.3.3 Provisioning Response in Multi-Access 5G Networks

The Table 4.8 presents the information elements for a Provisioning Response from the ECS to the EEC in multi-access 5G Networks.

Table 4.7 Provisioning request

	Information element	Status	Description
1.	EEC ID	M	It represents the unique identifier of the EEC.
2.	Security credentials	M	Security recommendations obtained from a successful authorization for the purpose of edge computing.
3.	Application client profile(s)	M	Information about services the EEC wants to connect.
4.	UE identifier	O	The identifier of the UE (i.e. GPSI or identity token)
5.	Connectivity filter	O	Connectivity information related list for the UE. It includes SSID and PLMN ID.

Table 4.8 Provisioning response

	Information element	Status	Description
1.	EDN connection info	M	DNN (or APN)
2.	EES endpoint	M	The address of the endpoint of the EES e.g. IP address and URI etc.
3.	EDN service area (NOTE)	O	Cell list, list of TA, PLMN IDs
4.	ECSP info	O	Information for edge computing service provider
	It should be noted that the EDN service area IE will be included if and only if the EDN is a LADN		

4.4   Registering Edge-Enabler Clients and Server in Multi-Access 5G Networks

The registration procedures permit to use the request of their edge capabilities in multi-access 5G networks. An EEC may perform registration with an EES to use Edge enabling services offered by that EES in multi-access 5G networks, e.g. to discover EASs in an area of interest. The procedure enables initialization of state changes of the EEC context information at the EES in the multi-access 5G networks. It may be used for further analysis and processing [18, 19].

An EAS performs registration with an EES to use edge enabling services offered by that EES, e.g. exposure of its capabilities to Edge Enabler Clients. An EES performs registration with an ECS to use edge configuration services offered by that ECS in a multi-access 5G networking environment, e.g. provisioning with EDN-specific information.

4.4.1   Edge Enabler Client Registration in Multi-Access 5G Networks

In general, the EEC Registration procedure allows an EEC to obtain services from an EES in multi-access 5G networks by providing information regarding its identity and security credentials. The procedure enables the initialization or update of the

EEC context information at the EES. This context may further be used for the purpose of performing analysis, processing, and edge-specific operations [20, 21].

The pre-conditions for EEC Registration in multi-access 5G networks will be as follow:

Pre-condition 3: The EEC is authorized to access the EES to perform registration and has received relevant security credentials
Pre-condition 4: The EEC has received configuration information from the ECS.

The Fig. 4.3 describes the information flow of the EEC registration procedure in multi-access 5G networks and it can be completed using the following four steps [22, 23]:

Step 1: The EEC sends EEC registration request to the EES. The request from the client includes the security credentials received after successful authorization for edge computing services.

> Further, the EEC registration request indicates if the request is a new registration or a registration update. A registration update may be used to send new or updated AC Profile(s) to the EES in a multi-access 5G Networking environment.

Step 2: Upon receiving the request from the Edge Enabler Client, the EES validates the registration request and verifies the security credentials.
Step 3: Upon successful validation of the request, if the received Registration request contains a Context ID and a source EES Identifier, the EES retrieves the

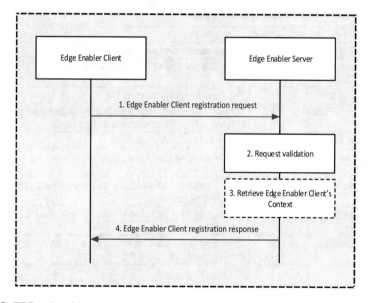

Fig. 4.3 EEC registration procedure

Edge Enabler's Registration Context from the source EES. Otherwise, this step is skipped.

Step 4: The EES can send registration response successful and it may include a newly assigned Context ID. Further, the EEC can store the new Context ID. This new context ID may be used if we need to register with a new EES later on. The EES also provides a registration expiration value to indicate the automatic expiry of registration. The EEC must send a registration request with an Update Indication before the expiration to maintain the current registration. The EES will treat the registration expiration as an implicit de-registration. If the EES is not able to fulfil, or provide, the services that are indicated by AC Profile(s), then the EES will indicate this in the EEC registration response.

4.4.1.1   Edge Enabler Client Registration Request

The Table 4.9 describes about the information elements available in the EEC Registration Request in a multi-access 5G networking environment.

4.4.1.2   Edge Enabler Client Registration Response

The Table 4.10 describes about the available information elements in the EEC Registration Response.

Table 4.9 Edge enabler client registration request

	Information element	Status	Description
1.	EEC ID	M	Unique identifier of the EEC
2.	Registration type indication	M	Indication for new or updated registration
3.	UE identifier	O	The identifier of the hosting UE
4.	Security credentials	O	Security credentials required from a successful authorization to provide computing services at edge level
5.	AC profile(s)	O	It includes the profiles of ACs
6.	Proposed expiration time	O	Proposed registration expiry time
7.	Context ID	O	Identifier of the EEC context which was obtained from a preceding registration
8.	Context ID provider EES ID	O	If a context ID is included, the identifier of the EES that provided it
9.	EAS identifiers	O	Identifiers of already discovered EAS which can support the services needed by the EEC

Table 4.10 Edge enabler client registration response

	Information element	Status	Description
1.	Result	M	Result of the registration operation
2.	Expiration time	M	It represents the time of expiration of the registration
3.	Authorization info	O	Information resulting from any authorization procedure performed by the EES based on the registration request, which can be used for future requests
4.	Context ID	O	Identifies the EEC context information
5.	EAS information list	O	Optional information for the EASs specified in the request or those to which the client information is being forwarded. Each element may include the information detailed below
6.	>EAS ID	M	The identifier of the edge application server
7.	>EAS endpoint	M	Endpoint information that ACs use to send requests to the EAS i.e. IP address, URI, and FQDN.
8.	>EAS provider identifier	O	The identifier of the EAS provider
9.	>EAS available compute	O	The max compute resource available for the AC
10.	>EAS available graphical compute	O	The max available graphical compute resource for the AC
11.	>EAS available memory	O	The max memory resource available for the AC
12.	>EAS available storage	O	The max storage resource available for the AC

4.4.2   Edge Application Server Registration

In general, the EAS Registration procedure permits an EAS for providing information to an EES in order to use the requests of its edge capabilities.

The following are three pre-conditions required for EAS Registration in a multi-access 5G networking environment [24, 25]:

Pre-condition 5: The EAS must be configured with an EAS Identity;

Pre-condition 6: The EAS must be configured with the address (e.g. URI) of the EES; and

Pre-condition 7: EAS and EES must be configured with the necessary credentials to enable communications.

The Fig. 4.4 describes the information flow of the EAS Registration procedure in multi-access 5G networks and it can be completed using the following four steps [26, 27]:

Step 1: The EAS determines that registration to the EES is needed. The EAS may also determine the Edge Application Server's status.

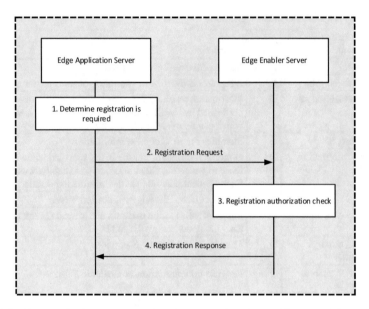

Fig. 4.4 Edge application server registration procedure in multi-access 5G networking environment

Step 2: The EAS sends a Registration Request to the EES. The request indicates if the request is for a new registration or an update to an existing registration.

Step 3: The EES performs an authorization check to verify whether the EAS has the proper privileges to register.

Step 4: Upon successful authorization, the EES stores the Service Profile for later use (e.g. for serving EAS discovery requests received from Edge Enabler Clients, etc.) and replies to the EAS with a Registration Response. The EAS will send a Registration Request message with a Registration Type Indicator of type Update before the expiration to maintain the current registration. The EES will treat the registration expiration as an implicit de-registration.

4.4.2.1   Edge Application Server Registration Request

The Table 4.11 describes about the information elements available in the EAS Registration Request [28, 29].

Further, it is observed that the EAS ID, EAS Instance ID, EAS Provider Identifier, and EAS Type are also included in the EAS Profile. Hence, it is the FFS that describes how to eliminate this duplication.

Table 4.11 Edge application server registration request

	Information element	Status	Description
1.	EAS ID	M	Unique identifier of the edge application server
2.	EAS provider identifier	O	The identifier of the EAS provider
3.	EAS type	O	The category or type of edge application Server (e.g. V2X)
4.	Registration type indication	M	Indication for new or updated registration
5.	Security credentials	O	It includes the security credentials for a successful authorization
6.	Proposed expiration time	O	Proposed time of expiration for the registration
7.	EAS profile(s)	O	EAS profile(s) as described in Table 4.9

Table 4.12 Edge application server registration response

	Information element	Status	Description
1.	Result	M	It represents the result of the registration operation
2.	Expiration time	M	It indicates the expiry time of the registration

4.4.2.2 Edge Application Server Registration Response

The Table 4.12 explains the information elements available in the EAS Registration Response. These information elements were obtained during communication from the EES to the EAS in a multi-access 5G networking environment [30, 31].

4.4.3 Edge Enabler Server Registration

In general terms, the EES Registration procedure permits an EES for providing information to an ECS in order to use the request of its edge configuration capabilities in a multi-access 5G networking environment [32, 33].

The EES Registration (EESR) procedure is described in Fig. 4.5 and it requires the following three steps [34, 35]:

Step 1: The EES will send the EES registration demand to the ECS. The request from the EES should include the EES identity, EES Point of Contact information, EAS Profiles of registered Edge Application Servers, and EES security credentials.

Step 2: Upon receiving the request from the EES, the ECS verifies the security credentials of the EES and stores the EES registration information obtained in step 1. If the ECS already contained the EES registration information corresponding to the EES identity provided in the request, then the stored EES registration information is updated with the received information in step 1.

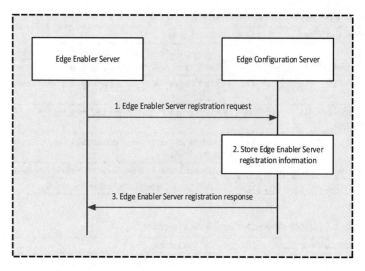

Fig. 4.5   EES Registration procedure

Table 4.13   EES registration request

	Information element	Status	Description
1.	EES ID	M	Unique identifier of the EES
2.	Registration type indication	M	Indication for new or updated registration
3.	Security credentials	M	It describes the security credentials obtained from a successful permission for the edge computing service
4.	EES endpoint	M	Endpoint information for establishing a connection to the EES (e.g. IP address)
5.	EAS information	O	The information of EASs registered with the EES

Step 3: The ECS will send an EES registration answer to indicate the failure or success of the registration procedure.

4.4.3.1   Edge Enabler Server Registration Request

The Table 4.13 provides descriptions about the information elements for an EES Registration Request that may have come from an EES to an ECS in a multi-access 5G networking environment. Further, it may be noted that the subset of EAS information provided by the EES is FFS [36, 37].

4.4.3.2   EES Registration Response

The Table 4.14 provides descriptions about the information elements for an EES Registration Response that may have come from the ECS to the EES in a multi-access 5G networking environment [38, 39].

Table 4.14 EES registration response

	Information element	Status	Description
1.	Result	M	Result of the registration procedure

4.5 Conclusions

The MEC gives cloud-IoT related computing capabilities and an IT service atmosphere at the edge level in a network to the content developers and application developers. This MEC environment provides high bandwidth and ultra-low latency in real-time access to wireless network information which can be leveraged by various users of cloud-IoT technologies of our modern societies including *Society 5.0*. This chapter includes definitions of 5 G-related terms, key issues identified and the corresponding architectural requirements, detailed application architecture for enabling EAs corresponding to the key issues, and other architectural requirements [40, 41]. Further, in this chapter, the authors have described the application layer architecture of Multi-access edge computing for 5G networks with procedures and information flow necessities for enabling EAs over 3GPP networks in the cloud-IoT integrated distributive computing environment.

The described algorithms and approaches include architectural requirements to activate the edge applications, ALA, and fulfilling the procedures and architecture requirements to activate the deployment of EAs for multi-access edge computing in a 5G networking environment [42]. The technical details and information flow of EAS, ECS, EES, edge enabler client, uniform resource identifier, EES, and edge enabler clients in multi-access 5G networking environment are provided in this chapter [43].

References

1. 3GPP TR 21.905: Vocabulary for 3GPP Specifications (2021). https://www.etsi.org/deliver/etsi_tr/121900_121999/121905/04.05.00_60/tr_121905v040500p.pdf. Last Accessed on 2 June 2021
2. 3GPP TS 23.501: System Architecture for the 5G System; Stage 2 (2021). https://www.etsi.org/deliver/etsi_ts/123500_123599/123501/15.03.00_60/ts_123501v150300p.pdf. Last Accessed on 2 June 2021
3. 3GPP TS 23.502: Procedure for the 5G System; Stage 2 (2021). https://www.3gpp.org. Last Accessed on 2 June 2021
4. 3GPP TS 29.522: 5G System; Network Exposure Function Northbound APIs; Stage 3 (2021). https://www.etsi.org/deliver/etsi_ts/129500_129599/129522/15.02.00_60/ts_129522v150200p.pdf. Last Accessed on 2 June 2021
5. 3GPP TS 29.122: T8 reference point for northbound Application Programming Interfaces (APIs) (2021). https://datasheets.globalspec.com/ps/5943/3GPP/7D0DEFED-ED87-470F-9A37-1AA34EC7565E. Last Accessed on 1 June 2021

6. 3GPP TS 23.222: Functional architecture and information flows to support Common API Framework for 3GPP Northbound APIs; Stage 2 (2021). https://www.3gpp.org. Last Accessed on 1 June 2021
7. 3GPP TS 23.271: Functional stage 2 description of Location Services (LCS) (2021). https://portal.3gpp.org/desktopmodules/Specifications/SpecificationDetails. aspx?specificationId=834. Last Accessed on 2 June 2021
8. 3GPP TS 36.305: Evolved Universal Terrestrial Radio Access Network (E-UTRAN); Stage 2 functional specification of User Equipment (UE) positioning in E-UTRAN (2021). https:// patents.google.com/patent/US8761806B2/ar. Last Accessed on 2 June 2021
9. 3GPP TS 23.273: 5G System (5GS) Location Services (LCS); Stage 2 (2021). https://www. archclearing.com/Views/Events/13948.xhtm. Last Accessed on 31 May 2021
10. 3GPP TS 38.305: NG Radio Access Network (NG-RAN); Stage 2 functional specification of User Equipment (UE) positioning in NG-RAN
11. 3GPP TS 23.003: Numbering, addressing and identification (2021). https://suuse02.ch.abb. com/nm/ics_news/ics_news/neuerscheinungen_2021-03_33_fr.html. Last Accessed on 1 June 2021
12. ETSI GS MEC 003 V1.1.1, Mobile Edge Computing (MEC); Framework and Reference Architecture (2016-03) (2021). https://www.etsi.org/deliver/etsi_gs/ mec/001_099/011/01.01.01_60/gs_mec011v010101p.pdf. Last Accessed on 2 June 2021
13. ETSI GS MEC 010-1 V1.1.1, Mobile Edge Computing (MEC); Mobile Edge Management; Part 1: System host and platform management (2017-10) (2021). http://www.mydoc123. com/p-733287.html. Last Accessed on 2 June 2021
14. ETSI GS MEC 010-2 V1.1.1, Mobile Edge Computing (MEC); Mobile Edge Management; Part 2: Application lifecycle, rules and requirements management (2017-07) (2021). https:// www.ibm.com/in-en/cloud/edge-computing?p1=Search&p4=43700055270654354&p5=b& gclid=Cj0KCQjw2NyFBhDoARIsAMtHtZ4EFdUzxylJDQd_6Oc38BHAamumYOArXB_ g2lVGl-n6w9VzN3kFQtQaAkNHEALw_wcB&gclsrc=aw.ds. Last Accessed on 2 June 2021
15. ETSI GS MEC 011 V1.1.1, Mobile Edge Computing (MEC); Mobile Edge Platform Application Enablement (2017-07) ETSI GS MEC 011 (2021). https://docplayer.net/54282826-Etsi-gs-mec-012-v1-1-1.html. Last Accessed on 1 June 2021
16. ETSI GS MEC 012 V1.1.1, 2Mobile Edge Computing (MEC); Radio Network Information (2017-07) (2021). https://www.etsi.org/deliver/etsi_gs/MEC/001_099/012/02.01.01_60/gs_ mec012v020101p.pdf. Last Accessed on 1 June 2021
17. ETSI GS MEC 013 V1.1.1, Mobile Edge Computing (MEC); Location API (2017-07) (2021). https://www.etsi.org/deliver/etsi_gs/mec/001_099/013/01.01.01_60/gs_mec013v010101p. pdf. Last Accessed on 1 June 2021
18. ETSI GS MEC 014 V1.1.1, Mobile Edge Computing (MEC); UE Identity API (2018-02) (2021). https://www.etsi.org/deliver/etsi_gs/MEC/001_099/014/01.01.01_60/gs_mec014v010101p. pdf. Last Accessed on 1 June 2021
19. ETSI GS MEC 015 V1.1.1, Mobile Edge Computing (MEC); Bandwidth Management API (2017-10) (2021). https://standards.iteh.ai/catalog/standards/etsi/763e5752-6943-44aa-b482-6828f63b6429/etsi-gs-mec-ieg-006-v1.1.1-2017-01. Last Accessed on 2 June 2021
20. ETSI GS MEC 016 V1.1.1, Mobile Edge Computing (MEC); UE Application Interface (2017-09) (2021). https://www.hpe.com/hpe_intelligent/edge. Last Accessed on 1 June 2021
21. 3GPP TS 23.501 V15.1.0 (2021) 3rd Generation Partnership Project; Technical Specification Group Services and System Aspects; System Architecture for the 5G System; Stage 2 (Release 15) (2018-03). https://data.epo.org/gpi/EP3701738A4-A-METHOD-FOR-SYNCHRONIZING-STATUS-OF-UE-IN-A-COMMUNICATION-NETWORK. Last Accessed on 2 June 2021
22. ETSI White Paper "MEC deployments in 4G and evolution towards 5G" (2018, February). http://www.etsi.org/images/files/ETSIWhitePapers/etsi_wp24_MEC_deployment_ in_4G_5G_FINAL.pdf. Last Accessed on 2 June 2021

23. 5GAA White Paper (2017, December) Toward fully connected vehicles: edge computing for advanced automotive communications. http://5gaa.org/news/toward-fully-connected-vehiclesedge-computing-for-advanced-automotive-communications/. Last Accessed on 2 June 2021

24. Pekka Pirinen (2014) A brief overview of 5G research activities. In: 1st International Conference on 5G for Ubiquitous Connectivity (5GU), Levi, Finland, pp 1–6

25. Gupta A, Jha RK (2015) A survey of 5G network: architecture and emerging technologies. IEEE Access 3:1206–1232

26. Le NT et al (2016) Survey of promising technologies for 5G networks. Mob Inf Syst 2016:1–26

27. Hossain S (2013) 5G wireless communication systems. Am J Eng Res 2(10):344–353

28. Kachhavay MG, Thakare AP (2013) 5G technology-evolution and revolution. IJCSMC 3(3):1080–1087

29. Asvin G et al (2013) 5G technology of mobile communication: a survey. In: IEEE 2013 international conference on Intelligent Systems and Signal Processing (ISSP), pp 1–6

30. MitraDharma RN, Agrawal P (2015) 5G mobile technology: a survey. ICT Express 1:132–137

31. Attaran M (2021) The impact of 5G on the evolution of intelligent automation and industry digitization. J Ambient Intell Humaniz Comput:1–17

32. Kasper A. et al (2021) StaRe: statistical reasoning tool for 5G network management, pp 1–4. https://seco.cs.aalto.fi/publications/2016/apajalahti-et-al-stare-2016.pdf. Last Accessed on 6 Oct 2021

33. He, C, Gitlin RD (2016) System performance of cooperative massive MIMO downlink 5G cellular systems. IEEE-WAMICON, pp 1–5

34. Shinde S, Nikam A, Joshi S (2016) An overview of 5G technology. IRJET 3(4):2390–2394

35. Fizza M, Shah MA (2015) 5G technology: an overview of applications, prospects, challenges and beyond. In: Proceedings of the IOARP International Conference on Communication and Networks (ICCN 2015), pp 94–102

36. Alexandros K et al (2016) Scenarios for 5G networks. In: 23rd International Conference on Telecommunications (ICT), pp 1–6

37. Ronald N, Wien TU (2017) 5G simulator: FBMC. Technical Report of Brno University of Technology, pp 1–30. https://publik.tuwien.ac.at/files/PubDat_248708.pdf. Last Accessed on 10 June 2021

38. Kamta NM, Navin K (2020) Multi-server multi -CS based deadlock prevention in distributed systems using voting and priority based approaches. Nat Acad Sci Lett 43:1–6

39. Kamta NM (2020) A novel integration of smart vehicles and secure clouds for supervising vehicle accidents on roads/highways. Sadhana J Eng Sci 45:1–21

40. Kamta NM (2021) Fraud detection and prevention in smart cities using k-fold machine learning technique. Wirel Pers Commun 116:1–25

41. Kamta NM (2020) A proficient mechanism for cloud security supervision in distributed environment. Int J Comput Netw Inf Secur 12(6):57–77

42. Kamta NM (2017) Deadlock prevention in single server multi-cs distributed systems using voting and priority based strategies. In: Springer International Conference on Recent Advancement on Computer and Communication (ICRAC-2017), pp 115–123

43. Kamta NM (2016) Voting and priority based mechanism for deadlock prevention in distributed systems. In: 2nd IEEE International Conference on Control Computing Communication and Materials (IEEE ICCCCM – 2016), pp 264–272

Chapter 5
Discovery and Location Reporting of Multi-Access Edge Enabled Clients and Servers for 5G Networks

Abstract In broad terms, the discovery and location reporting procedures of multi-access 5G networks enable entities in the deployed edges for retrieving information about edge servers and services available. Here, the authors have explained the features of multi-access 5G networks like Edge Application Server Discovery (EASD), Edge Application Server Request (EASR), Edge Configuration Server Communication (ECSC), and Edge Enabler Server Communication (EESC) using location reporting application programme interface (API) and User Equipment (UE) detection techniques. In common terms, it can be said that the EASD enables the EEC (Edge Enabler Clients) to get exact information about available Edge Application Servers in a multi-access 5G networking environment. During the study and further analysis of 5G networks, the authors found that the identification of the EAS (Edge Application Servers) is dependent on ACP (Application Client Profiles) or matching query filters.

It was observed by the authors during the experimental analysis of results of multi-access 5G networks that some of the individual solutions were having dependencies on other working groups within 3GPP. These dependencies and their overall evaluations concerning multi-access 5G networks are summarized in this chapter. The ECS (Edge Configuration Server) can provide the supporting functions which are needed by the EEC (Edge Enabler Client) to connect with an EES (Edge Enabler Server) in a multi-access 5G networking environment. Further, the authors have explained the deployment scenarios and involved business relationships of multi-access 5G networks using EvCS (Evolved Charging Suite), communication among EEC, EES, EAS (Edge Application Server), and the 3GPP network.

Keywords 5G networks · Edge application server discovery · Edge application server request · Edge configuration server communication · Edge enabler server communication · Location reporting API · User equipment detection

© The Author(s), under exclusive license to Springer Nature Switzerland AG 2023
K. N. Mishra, S. C. Pandey, *Cloud-IoT Technologies in Society 5.0*,
https://doi.org/10.1007/978-3-031-28711-4_5

5.1   Introduction

In the previous chapter (Chap. 4) we explained the definitions of 5G related terms, key issues identified and the corresponding architectural requirements, detailed application architecture for enabling Edge Applications corresponding to the key issues, and other architectural requirements. Further, in Chap. 4 the authors explained the application layer architecture of Multi-access edge computing for 5G networks with procedures and information flow necessities for enabling edge applications over 3GPP networks in cloud-IoT integrated 5G networks [1–3].

In general, the discovery and location reporting procedures of multi-access edge computing for 5G networks enable entities in an edge deployment to obtain information about edge servers and services available based on specified criteria of interest. In this chapter, the authors have explained Edge Application Server Discovery, Edge Application Server Request, Edge Configuration Server Communication, and Edge Enabler Server Communication using location reporting application programme interface (API) and User Equipment (UE) Detection techniques. The general abbreviation terms and their corresponding descriptions are given in Tables 5.1 and 5.2 [4–6].

5.2   Edge Application Server Discovery for Multi-Access Edge Computing in 5G Networks

In general terms, it can be said that the EASD enables EEC to obtain information about available EAS(s) of interest for MEC in 5G networks. The identification of the EAS(s) is based on matching query filters or ACP(s) provided in the request. The pre-condition requirement of EAS(s) discovery for MEC in 5G networks will be as follow:

Pre-condition 1: The Information related to the EEES is available with the EEC.

Further, the following three steps explain the process of providing EAS discovery of MEC for 5G networks [7, 8]:

Step 1: The EEC sends an EAS discovery request to the EES. The discovery request may have query filters.
Step 2: After receiving the request from the EEC, the EES checks if the EEC has authority to discover the requested EAS(s) or not. The authorization check may apply to an individual EAS, or a category of EAS, or the EDN
The EES determines a set of discovered EAS that match the query filters (e.g. ACPs) provided in the request.
Step 3: The Edge Enabler Server sends an Edge Application Server (EAS) discovery response including information about the discovered Edge Application Servers.

Table 5.1 Abbreviations and the corresponding descriptions

	Abbreviation	Description
1.	AC(s)	Application clients
2.	ACK	Acknowledgment
3.	ACP(s)	Application client profiles
4.	ADT	Application data traffic
5.	API	Application programme interface
6.	ACP	Application client profile
7.	BSF	Binding support function
8.	CAPIF	Common API framework
9.	DNS	Domain name systems
10.	EA(s)	Edge applications
11.	EAS	Edge application server(s)
12.	EASD	Edge application server discovery
13.	EAS ID	Edge application server identity
14.	EASR	Edge application server request
15.	ECI	Edge configuration information
16.	ECS	Edge configuration server
17.	EChS	Evolved charging suite
18.	EDN	Edge data network
19.	EDNCS	Edge data network configuration service
20.	EEC	Edge enabler client
21.	EES	Edge enabler server
22.	e.g.	For example
23.	FFS	For further study
24.	FQDN	Fully qualified domain name
25.	GPS	Global positioning systems
26.	GPSI	Generic public subscription identifier
27.	ID	Identity
28.	i.e.	That is
29.	IEs	Information elements
30.	KPI	Key performance indicator
31.	LADN	Local area data network

The response may include further additional information regarding matched capabilities.

Finally, the EAS discovery procedure of MEC for 5G network performs two operations namely edge application discovery request and edge application discovery response using EEC and EES and the information flow is represented by Fig. 5.1 [9–11].

Table 5.2 Abbreviations and descriptions

	Abbreviations	Descriptions
1.	LCS	Location services
2.	M	Mandatory
3.	MEC	Multi-access edge computing
4.	MNO	Mobile network operator
5.	NEF	Network exposure function
6.	NRF	Network repository function
7.	O	Optional
8.	PCF	Policy control function
9.	PLMN	Public land Mobile network
10.	QoS	Quality of service
11.	SCEF	Service capability exposure function
12.	SIM	Subscriber identification module
13.	SUT	Service under test
14	UE	User equipment
15.	URI	Uniform resource Identifier

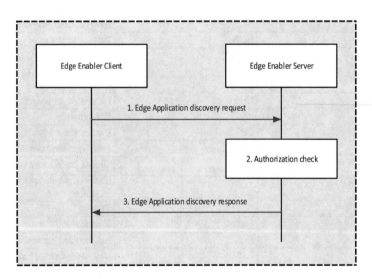

Fig. 5.1 EAS Discovery procedure

5.2.1   Edge Application Server Discovery Request

The Table 5.3 explains information elements for the EASD request that happens between the EEC and EES. Further, Table 5.4 provides full details about the Query Filter information elements. Furthermore, the researchers of 5G networks need to

Table 5.3 Discovery request for edge application server

	Information element	Status	Explanation
1.	EEC ID	M	Unique identifier of the EEC
2.	UE identifier	O	The identifier of the UE
3.	Security credentials	O	Security credentials resulting from a victorious authentication to provide the services at edge computing level
4.	Query filter	O	Characteristics list for the purpose of discovery
5.	Application client ID(s)	O	Identities of AC(s) that may initiate application data traffic with the discovered EAS

Table 5.4 Query filters

	Information element	Status	Explanation
1.	EAS IDs	O	List of EAS IDs to be revealed e.g. gaming
2.	EAS ID list	O	List of EAS to be considered in the discovery request, if available
3.	Application provider(s)	O	Provider of the AC
4.	Service permission level(s)	O	Desired level of service permissions
5.	Desired feature(s)	O	The desired service features
6.	Location availability	O	The desired location(s) where the service can be provided
7.	Application client profile(s)	O	Profiles of AC(s) with used parameters to determine matching EA

find the most appropriate answers to the following queries (*Query 1* to *Query 2*) [12–14]:

Query 1: The logic on how the query filters are applied in conjunction with the ACP (Application Client Profiles) is to be clarified in detail.

Query 2: How complex Information Elements may be broken down into multiple elements? It may be the case of FFS.

5.2.2 Edge Application Server Discovery Response

The Table 5.5 explains information elements for the EASD response from the EES (Edge Enabler Server) to EEC. The use of EAS instance identity (ID) includes an optional facility and it depends on how the ID is defined and assigned. Further, the researchers of EASD response need to find the most appropriate answers to the following queries (*Query 3* to *Query 4*) [15, 16]:

Query 3: If and how complex Information Elements may be broken down into multiple elements?

Table 5.5 EAS discovery response

	Information element	Status	Explanation
1.	Discovered EAS list	O	List of discovered EAS
2.	EAS endpoint	M	Endpoint information for establishing a connection to the EAS (e.g. FQDN, internet protocol (IP) address)
3.	EAS ID	O	EAS IDs to be discovered e.g. gaming
4.	EAS name	O	Name of the EAS
5.	EAS description	O	Human-readable explanation of the EAS
6.	Supported features	O	Supported service features
7.	Service permission levels	O	Supported level of service permissions e.g. trial, gold-class
8.	Location availability	O	The desired location(s)
9.	Time of operation	O	The operation time during which the EAS is available
10.	EAS available compute	O	The max available compute resource for the AC(s)
11.	EAS available graphical compute	O	The max available graphical compute resource for the AC(s)
12.	EAS available memory	O	The max available memory resource for the AC(s)
13.	EAS available storage	O	The max available storage resource for the AC(s)

Query 4: Whether EAS Profiles should replace several of the IEs in the Discovered EAS List or not?

5.3   User Equipment Location Reporting API

In general, the User Equipment Location Reporting API provides the exposure of UE location information to the Edge Application Server. The EAS exposes Location Reporting API to the Edge Application Server to support checking or tracking the valid location of the UE. The location reporting API exposed by the Edge Enabler Server may be relying on the northbound API of SCEF/network exposure function (NEF) for monitoring events of UE location [17, 18].

The Edge Application Server can request location reporting API for one-time reporting to check current user equipment location and it can further be used for continuous tracking the location of UE. The Location reporting API supports both request-response for one-time queries as well as Subscription-Notify modes for reporting UE's location to EAS continuously (as and when the UE location changes) [19, 20].

The following are three pre-conditions (*Pre-condition 2* to *Pre-condition 4*) that may be required for user location equipment location reporting API [21, 22]:

Pre-condition 2: The EAS is authorized to discover and to use the location reporting API provided by the EES.

Pre-condition 3: The Edge Enabler Server is authorized to use SCEF/NEF of Event
   Exposure API for Location Reporting, based on service level agreement with
   mobile network operator.
Pre-condition 4: UE Identifier between Edge Application Server and the Edge
   Enabler Server is authorized for the location reporting API (e.g. appropriate
   access token is received by Edge Application Server based on the consent provided by the user).

5.3.1   Request-Response Model

The Fig. 5.2 illustrates the interactions between the Edge Enabler Server and the
Edge Application Server for one-time reporting of location.
   The following *three steps* can be used by UE API to complete the reporting pro-
cess [23, 24]:

Step 1: The Edge Application Server requests Location Reporting API (UE Identifier,
   Location Granularity) to the Edge Enabler Server. The Edge Application Server
   shall include UE Identifier. Location granularity is an optional parameter to indicate the location format which can be understood by the Edge Application Server.
   It may be noted that the implementation of the trigger condition of the location
   reporting API is up to application service logic which may be independently
   studied by the readers and researchers.
Step 2: The Edge Enabler Server checks the UE location according to the following
   three conditions:

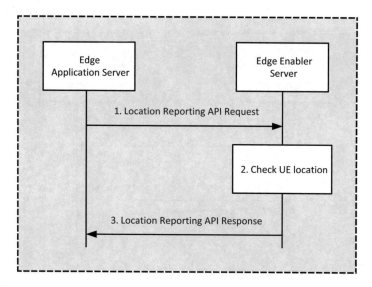

Fig. 5.2 Location reporting API request and response

Condition 1: If the location reporting API request from the Edge Application Server includes the location granularity, then the Edge Enabler Server can consider the LGP (Location Granularity Parameter) to check the actual location of the UE.

Condition 2: If the Edge Enabler Server caches locally the location of the UE as the latest, then the Edge Enabler Server may use this cached UE location to respond to the Edge Application Server.

Condition 3: The Edge Enabler Server may modify the format of the UE location to fit the location granularity requested from the Edge Application Server in the above *Step 1* (if supported).

It may be noted that the readers and researchers may need to put extra effort to get complete knowledge about this specification. The condition 3 can be performed if the EES is deployed by the PLMN operator.

Step 3: The Edge Enabler Server responds to the Edge Application Server with the location of the UE, and optionally the timestamp of the location.

5.3.2   Subscribe-Notify Model

The Fig. 5.3 illustrates the subscribe operation between the Edge Enabler Server and the Edge Application Server and it can be used for continuous User Equipment location reporting [25, 26].

The following *two steps* can be used by UE API to complete the subscribe operation processing of location reporting API:

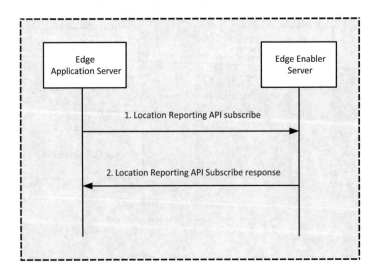

Fig. 5.3 Location reporting API: subscribe operation

Step 1: The Edge Application Server requests Location Reporting subscribe operation (UE Identifier, Location Granularity) for tracking the UE location continuously. The Edge Application Server will include UE Identifier. Location granularity is an optional parameter to indicate the format of location e.g. Tracking Area ID, GPS Coordinates, Cell ID, and civic addresses etc. The Edge Application Server can understand these addresses.

Step 2: The Edge Enabler Server determines that the request from the Edge Application Server is authorized. If it is authorized, the Edge Enabler Server sends ACK as a response to the Location Reporting API subscribe request. If it is not authorized, then the Edge Enabler Server responds to rejection with cause.

The Fig. 5.4 illustrates the *notify operation* between the Edge Enabler Server and the Edge Application Server for continuous location reporting in a multi-access 5G network.

The following *two steps* describe the working of location reporting notify operation API [27]:

Step 1: The Edge Enabler Server detects the location of the UE. The Edge Enabler Server may cache the detected location information locally with a timestamp as the latest location information of the UE. The Edge Enabler Server determines to notify the location information of the UE to the Edge Application Server which has subscribed to the location reporting.

Step 2: The Edge Enabler Server sends Location Reporting notification to the Edge Application Server. The Edge Enabler Server includes the location of the UE and optionally the timestamp of the location.

In addition to the above two steps, the Edge Enabler Server can modify the format of location information for fitting the location granularity obtained from the Edge Application Server during the process of subscribe operation.

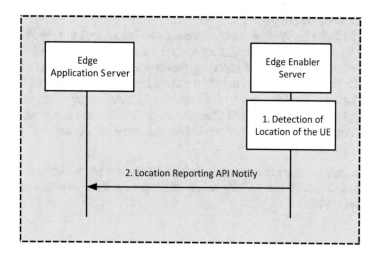

Fig. 5.4 Location reporting API: notify operation

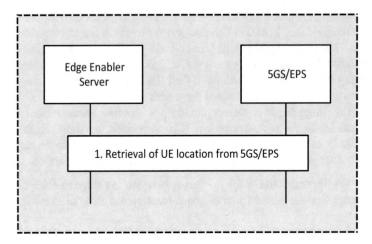

Fig. 5.5 Detection of UE location from the 3GPP system

5.3.3   Detection of UE Location from the 3GPP System

The Fig. 5.5 illustrates the interaction between the Edge Enabler Server and the 3GPP system (e.g., 5GS, EPS) which is needed for detecting the location information of the UE.

The following three steps (*Step 1 to Step 3*) can be used for detecting user equipment (UE) location using 3GPP system [28, 29]:

Step 1: The Edge Enabler Server interacts with the 3GPP system (e.g., 5GS, EPS) to retrieve the location of the UE (e.g. the Edge Enabler Server may use API exposed by SCEF/NEF or LCS (Location Service) as specified in 3GPP TS 23.502 [3], 3GPP TS 23.271 [7], 3GPP TS 36.305 [8], 3GPP TS 23.273 [9] and 3GPP TS 38.305 [10]).

Step 2: The Edge Enabler Server may request continuous location reporting to the 3GPP system to keep informed up to date location information of the UE to avoid repetition of location reporting requests to the 3GPP system so that the Edge Enabler Server always detects the latest location information of the UE.

Step 3: The Edge Enabler Server may consider the location granularity parameter (e.g. Tracking Area ID or GPS Coordinates or Cell ID etc.) requested from the Edge Application Server for retrieving the location of the UE from the 3GPP system.

Further, it may be noted that how to reuse the 3GPP network northbound API (e.g. provided by NEF or SCEF) when the serving Edge Enabler Server is changed is FFS.

Table 5.6 Location reporting API request

	Information element	Status	Explanation
1.	UE ID	M	Identifies the UE for which location will be reported
2.	Location granularity	O	Indicates the format of location i.e. cell ID, GPS coordinates, tracking area ID etc
3.	Location accuracy	O	It indicates the location information accuracy

Table 5.7 Location reporting API response

	Information element	Status	Explanation
1.	UE location	M	It represents the location of the UE
2.	Timestamp	O	It indicates the timestamp and location information of the UE
3.	Location accuracy	O	It indicates the accurateness of the location information

Table 5.8 Location reporting API subscribe

	Information element	Status	Explanation
1.	UE ID	M	Identifies the UE for which location will be reported
2.	Location granularity	O	Indicates the format of location e.g. GPS coordinates, cell ID, tracking area ID, or civic addresses (e.g. streets, districts, etc.) that can be understood by the edge application server
3.	Location accuracy	O	Indicates the accuracy of the location information

5.3.4   Location Reporting API Request and Response

The Table 5.6 represents the information elements used in the processing of *location reporting API requests,* and Table 5.7 represents the information elements used in the processing of *location reporting API response* in multi-access 5G networks [30, 31].

The Table 5.8 presents the information elements descriptions for *location reporting API to subscribe,* Table 5.9 presents the information elements descriptions for *location reporting API to subscribe response,* and Table 5.10 presents the information elements descriptions for *location reporting API to notify* in multi-access 5G networks.

5.4   Results and Discussions

The Edge Enabler Server simulator, its communication with all other major Network Functions (NFs), Edge Configuration Server communication, and the Linux interface-based working of the simulator in a multi-access 5G network environment is discussed in this section. The source code of the EES simulator, major NFs, and

Table 5.9 Location reporting API subscribe response

	Information element	Status	Explanation
1.	ACK	M	Acknowledge for the subscribe request
2.	Rejection cause	O	This indicates that the subscribe request is not authorized

Table 5.10 Location reporting API notify

	Information element	Status	Description
1.	UE location	M	It represents the location of the UE
2.	Timestamp	O	It indicates the timestamp value of the location information
3.	Location accuracy	O	It indicates the accurateness of information received for the location

Linux interface are explained in the form of Sample Json Request and Response in multi-access 5G network and we have presented them in Appendix – I & Appendix – II.

In the current research of MEC module of 5G network, the EES Network Function is one of the major and important role-playing Network Functions. The EES provides supporting functions needed for EAS and EEC in a multi-access 5G computing network. The following are the three functionalities (*Functionality 1* to *Functionality 3*) of Edge Enabler Server [32]:

Functionality 1: Provisioning of configuration information to enable the exchange of ADT with the EAS in a multi-access 5G network.
Functionality 2: Providing information about the Edge Application Servers to the Edge Enabler Client and vice versa.
Functionality 3: It supports the functionalities of Application Programme Interface invoker and Application Programme exposing function in multi-access 5G network.

5.4.1   Edge Enabler Server Communication with Different Network Functions

The Fig. 5.6 explains the Edge Enabler Server Communication with different Network Functions, and Fig. 5.7 explains the Edge Configuration Server Communication with different Network Functions in multi-access edge computing 5G network. It is very clear from Fig. 5.6 that the edge enabler server (EES) is providing communication amongst BSF (Binding Support Function), EEC (Edge Enabler Client), SIM (Subscriber Identification Module), SUT (Service Under Test), EAS (Edge Application Server), PCF (Policy Control Function), NEF (Network Exposure Function), NRF (Network Repository Function), and other clients [33, 34].

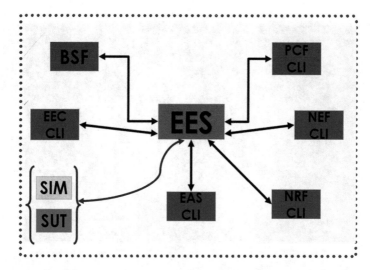

Fig. 5.6 The edge enabler server communication with different network functions in multi-access 5G network

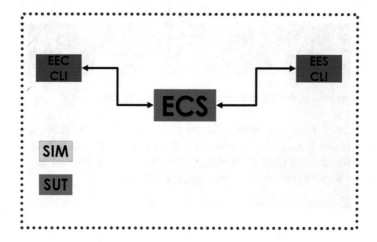

Fig. 5.7 Edge configuration server communication with different network functions in multi-access 5G network

In Fig. 5.7 it can be seen that the evolved charging suite (EvCS) is working as one of the facilitators for communication among EEC, EES, EAS, and the 3GPP network. The ECS provides the supporting functions which are required for the EEC to connect with an EES in a multi-access 5G network. The functionalities of Edge Configuration Server are as follow (*functionality 4* to *functionality 6*) [35]:

Functionality 4: Providing ECI to the EEC. The ECI includes the functionality 5 and functionality 6.

```
##################################
# webminal.org - your linux  ~ #
##################################

     -  Share files with others, See /common_pool/README.txt
     -  See 'Root' menu for Webminal Desktop Root and Webminal Root features
     -  For Students, partial sudo (plus C programming) platform available -
mail us with your college/school id.
[Arunjugran@webminal.org ~]$
[Arunjugran@webminal.org ~]$
[Arunjugran@webminal.org ~]$
[Arunjugran@webminal.org ~]$ls
[Arunjugran@webminal.org ~]$
[Arunjugran@webminal.org ~]$mkdir NfSim_01Feb
[Arunjugran@webminal.org ~]$
[Arunjugran@webminal.org ~]$
[Arunjugran@webminal.org ~]$ls
NfSim_01Feb
[Arunjugran@webminal.org ~]$
[Arunjugran@webminal.org ~]$mkdir NfSim_13Mar
[Arunjugran@webminal.org ~]$mkdir NfSim_07May
[Arunjugran@webminal.org ~]$ls
NfSim_01Feb  NfSim_07May  NfSim_13Mar
[Arunjugran@webminal.org ~]$
[Arunjugran@webminal.org ~]$
[Arunjugran@webminal.org ~]$mkdir NFSimumlator
[Arunjugran@webminal.org ~]$
[Arunjugran@webminal.org ~]$
[Arunjugran@webminal.org ~]$
[Arunjugran@webminal.org ~]$cd NFSimumlator/
[Arunjugran@webminal.org NFSimumlator]$mkdir Networking
[Arunjugran@webminal.org NFSimumlator]$mkdir core
```

Fig. 5.8 Snapshot-1 of working of the simulator with Linux interface

Functionality 5: Providing information for the Edge Enabler Client to connect to the
   Edge Enabler Server (e.g. service area information applicable to LADN); and
Functionality 6: Providing information for establishing a connection with Edge
   Enabler Servers (such as Uniform Resource Identifier).

5.4.2   The Snapshots of the Linux Interface and Working of Simulator in Multi-Access 5G Network

The three snapshots (*snapshot – 1, snapshot – 2, snapshot – 3*) taken from the working model of Linux interface-based simulator in multi-access 5G network are presented in Figs. 5.8, 5.9, 5.10. In Figs. 5.8 and 5.9, the working of NFS (Network
Function Simulator) in a real-time multi-access 5G network environment is shown
whereas in Fig. 5.10 the working with the curl commands is shown.

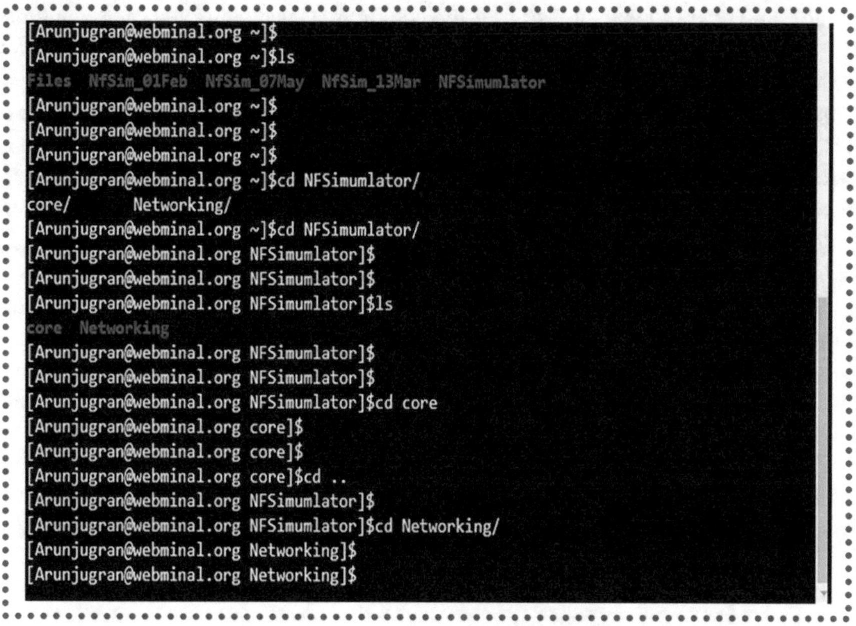

```
[Arunjugran@webminal.org ~]$
[Arunjugran@webminal.org ~]$ls
Files  NfSim_01Feb  NfSim_07May  NfSim_13Mar  NFSimumlator
[Arunjugran@webminal.org ~]$
[Arunjugran@webminal.org ~]$
[Arunjugran@webminal.org ~]$
[Arunjugran@webminal.org ~]$cd NFSimumlator/
core/        Networking/
[Arunjugran@webminal.org ~]$cd NFSimumlator/
[Arunjugran@webminal.org NFSimumlator]$
[Arunjugran@webminal.org NFSimumlator]$
[Arunjugran@webminal.org NFSimumlator]$ls
core  Networking
[Arunjugran@webminal.org NFSimumlator]$
[Arunjugran@webminal.org NFSimumlator]$
[Arunjugran@webminal.org NFSimumlator]$cd core
[Arunjugran@webminal.org core]$
[Arunjugran@webminal.org core]$
[Arunjugran@webminal.org core]$cd ..
[Arunjugran@webminal.org NFSimumlator]$
[Arunjugran@webminal.org NFSimumlator]$cd Networking/
[Arunjugran@webminal.org Networking]$
[Arunjugran@webminal.org Networking]$
```

Fig. 5.9 Snapshot-2 of working of the simulator with Linux interface

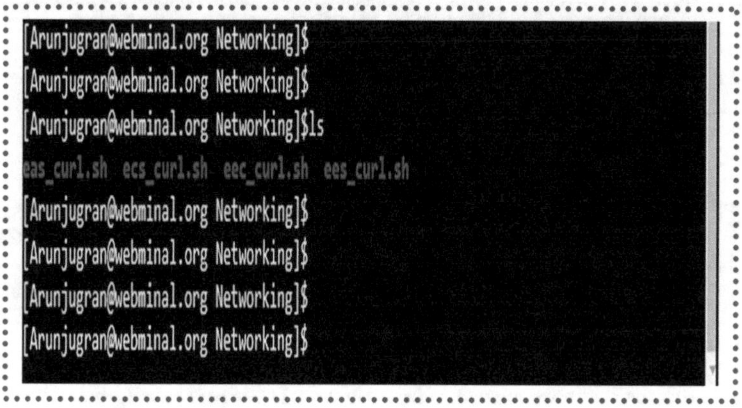

```
[Arunjugran@webminal.org Networking]$
[Arunjugran@webminal.org Networking]$
[Arunjugran@webminal.org Networking]$ls
eas_curl.sh  ecs_curl.sh  eec_curl.sh  ees_curl.sh
[Arunjugran@webminal.org Networking]$
[Arunjugran@webminal.org Networking]$
[Arunjugran@webminal.org Networking]$
[Arunjugran@webminal.org Networking]$
```

Fig. 5.10 Snapshot-3 of working of the simulator with Linux

5.5   Conclusions

The research article of this chapter fulfills the objectives of the study of architectures and applications for enabling edge applications in multi-access 5G networks. This chapter includes the descriptions of architectural requirements of key issues, detailed application architecture for enabling the EAs corresponding to the key issues, and overall evaluations of all the solutions. It was observed by the authors during experiments that some of the individual solutions were having dependencies on other working groups within 3GPP in multi-access 5G networks [36, 37]. These dependencies and their overall evaluations for multi-access computing in 5G networks are summarized in this chapter. The ECS can provide supporting functions needed for the EEC to connect with an EES in a multi-access 5G computing network [38, 39]. Further, the deployment scenarios and involved business relationships using EvCS (Evolved Charging Suite), communication among EEC, EES, EAS, and the 3GPP network are explained in this chapter.

In this chapter, the authors have explained how the EES and the ECS communicate with different Network Functions in multi-access edge computing 5G networks [40, 41]. Further, it was observed by the authors during experiments that the edge enabler server (EES) provides communication amongst BSF (Binding Support Function), EEC (Edge Enabler Client), SIM (Subscriber Identification Module), SUT (Service Under Test), EAS (Edge Application Server), PCF, NEF, NRF, and other clients in multi-access 5G computing networks [42–44]. The new application layer deployment models and their implications are also explained in this chapter.

References

1. 3GPP TR 21.905: Vocabulary for 3GPP Specifications (2021). https://www.etsi.org/deliver/etsi_tr/121900_121999/121905/04.05.00_60/tr_121905v040500p.pdf. Last Accessed on 2 June 2021
2. 3GPP TS 23.501: System Architecture for the 5G System; Stage 2 (2021). https://www.etsi.org/deliver/etsi_ts/123500_123599/123501/15.03.00_60/ts_123501v150300p.pdf. Last Accessed on 2 June 2021
3. 3GPP TS 23.502: Procedure for the 5G System; Stage 2 (2021). https://www.3gpp.org. Last Accessed on 2 June 2021
4. 3GPP TS 29.522: 5G System; Network Exposure Function Northbound APIs; Stage 3 (2021). https://www.etsi.org/deliver/etsi_ts/129500_129599/129522/15.02.00_60/ts_129522v150200p.pdf. Last Accessed on 2 June 2021
5. 3GPP TS 29.122: T8 reference point for northbound Application Programming Interfaces (APIs) (2021). https://datasheets.globalspec.com/ps/5943/3GPP/7D0DEFED-ED87-470F-9A37-1AA34EC7565E. Last Accessed on 1 June 2021
6. 3GPP TS 23.222: Functional architecture and information flows to support Common API Framework for 3GPP Northbound APIs; Stage 2 (2021). https://www.3gpp.org. Drafts. Last Accessed on 1 June 2021
7. 3GPP TS 23.271: Functional stage 2 description of Location Services (LCS) (2021). https://portal.3gpp.org/desktopmodules/Specifications/SpecificationDetails.aspx?specificationId=834. Last Accessed on 2 June 2021
8. 3GPP TS 36.305: Evolved Universal Terrestrial Radio Access Network (E-UTRAN); Stage 2 functional specification of User Equipment (UE) positioning in E-UTRAN (2021). https://patents.google.com/patent/US8761806B2/ar. Last Accessed on 2 June 2021
9. 3GPP TS 23.273: 5G System (5GS) Location Services (LCS); Stage 2 (2021). https://www.archclearing.com/Views/Events/13948.xhtm. Last Accessed on 31 May 2021
10. 3GPP TS 38.305: NG Radio Access Network (NG-RAN); Stage 2 functional specification of User Equipment (UE) positioning in NG-RAN

11. 3GPP TS 23.003: Numbering, addressing and identification (2021). https://suuse02.ch.abb. com/nm/ics_news/ics_news/neuerscheinungen_2021-03_33_fr.html. Last Accessed on 1 June 2021

12. ETSI GS MEC 003 V1.1.1, Mobile Edge Computing (MEC); Framework and Reference Architecture (2016-03) (2021). https://www.etsi.org/deliver/etsi_gs/ mec/001_099/011/01.01.01_60/gs_mec011v010101p.pdf. Last Accessed on 2 June 2021

13. ETSI GS MEC 010-1 V1.1.1, Mobile Edge Computing (MEC); Mobile Edge Management; Part 1: System host and platform management (2017-10) (2021). http://www.mydoc123. com/p-733287.html. Last Accessed on 2 June 2021

14. ETSI GS MEC 010-2 V1.1.1, Mobile Edge Computing (MEC); Mobile Edge Management; Part 2: Application lifecycle, rules and requirements management (2017-07) (2021). https:// www.ibm.com/in-en/cloud/edge-computing?p1=Search&p4=43700055270654354&p5=b& gclid=Cj0KCQjw2NyFBhDoARIsAMtHtZ4EFdUzxylJDQd_6Oc38BHAamumYOArXB_ g2lVGl-n6w9VzN3kFQtQaAkNHEALw_wcB&gclsrc=aw.ds. Last Accessed on 2 June 2021

15. ETSI GS MEC 011 V1.1.1, Mobile Edge Computing (MEC); Mobile Edge Platform Application Enablement (2017-07) ETSI GS MEC 011 (2021). https://docplayer.net/54282826-Etsi-gs-mec-012-v1-1-1.html. Last Accessed on 1 June 2021

16. ETSI GS MEC 012 V1.1.1, 2Mobile Edge Computing (MEC); Radio Network Information (2017-07) (2021). https://www.etsi.org/deliver/etsi_gs/MEC/001_099/012/02.01.01_60/gs_ mec012v020101p.pdf. Last Accessed on 1 June 2021

17. ETSI GS MEC 013 V1.1.1, Mobile Edge Computing (MEC); Location API (2017-07) (2021). https://www.etsi.org/deliver/etsi_gs/mec/001_099/013/01.01.01_60/gs_mec013v010101p. pdf. Last Accessed on 1 June 2021

18. ETSI GS MEC 014 V1.1.1, Mobile Edge Computing (MEC); UE Identity API (2018-02) (2021). https://www.etsi.org/deliver/etsi_gs/MEC/001_099/014/01.01.01_60/gs_mec014v010101p. pdf. Last Accessed on 1 June 2021

19. ETSI GS MEC 015 V1.1.1, Mobile Edge Computing (MEC); Bandwidth Management API (2017-10) (2021). https://standards.iteh.ai/catalog/standards/etsi/763e5752-6943-44aa-b482-6828f63b6429/etsi-gs-mec-ieg-006-v1.1.1-2017-01. Last Accessed on 2 June 2021

20. ETSI GS MEC 016 V1.1.1, Mobile Edge Computing (MEC); UE Application Interface (2017-09) (2021). https://www.hpe.com/hpe_intelligent/edge. Last Accessed on 1 June 2021

21. 3GPP TS 23.501 V15.1.0, "3rd Generation Partnership Project; Technical Specification Group Services and System Aspects; System Architecture for the 5G System; Stage 2 (Release 15)" (2018-03) (2021). https://data.epo.org/gpi/EP3701738A4-A-METHOD-FOR-SYNCHRONIZING-STATUS-OF-UE-IN-A-COMMUNICATION-NETWORK. Last Accessed on 2 June 2021

22. ETSI White Paper "MEC deployments in 4G and evolution towards 5G", February 2018 (2021). http://www.etsi.org/images/files/ETSIWhitePapers/etsi_wp24_MEC_deployment_ in_4G_5G_FINAL.pdf. Last Accessed on 2 June 2021

23. 5GAA White Paper "Toward fully connected vehicles: Edge computing for advanced automotive communications", December 2017 (2021). http://5gaa.org/news/toward-fully-connected-vehiclesedge-computing-for-advanced-automotive-communications. Last Accessed on 2 June 2021

24. Pirinen P (2014) A brief overview of 5G research activities. In: 1st international conference on 5G for Ubiquitous Connectivity (5GU), At: Levi, Finland, pp 1–6

25. Gupta A, Jha RK (2015) A survey of 5G network: architecture and emerging technologies. IEEE Access 3:1206–1232

26. Le NT, Hossain MA, Islam A, Kim D-y, Choi Y-J, Jang YM (2016) Survey of promising technologies for 5G networks. Mob Inf Syst 2016:1–26

27. Hossain S (2013) 5G wireless communication systems. Am J Eng Res 2(10):344–353

28. Kachhavay MG, Thakare AP (2013) 5G technology-evolution and revolution. IJCSMC 3(3):1080–1087

29. Gohil A, Modi H, Patel SK (2013) 5G technology of mobile communication: a survey. In: IEEE 2013 International Conference on Intelligent Systems and Signal Processing (ISSP), pp 1–6
30. MitraDharma RN, Agrawal P (2015) 5G mobile technology: a survey. ICT Express 1:132–137
31. Attaran M (2021) The impact of 5G on the evolution of intelligent automation and industry digitization. J Ambient Intell Humaniz Comput:1–17
32. Apajalahti K, Hyvönen E, Niiranen J, Räisänen V (2021) StaRe: statistical reasoning tool for 5G Network management, pp 1–4. https://seco.cs.aalto.fi/publications/2016/apajalahti-et-al-stare-2016.pdf. Last Accessed on 10 June 2021
33. He C, Gitlin RD (2016) System performance of cooperative massive MIMO downlink 5G cellular systems. IEEE-WAMICON, pp 1–5
34. Shinde S, Nikam A, Joshi S (2016) An overview of 5G technology. IRJET 3(4):2390–2394
35. Fizza M, Shah MA (2015) 5G technology: an overview of applications, prospects, challenges and beyond. In: Proceedings of the IOARP International Conference on Communication and Networks (ICCN 2015), pp 94–102
36. Kostopoulos A, Agapiou G, Kuo F-C et al (2016) Scenarios for 5G Networks. In: 23rd International Conference on Telecommunications (ICT), pp 1–6
37. Nissel R, Wien TU (2017) 5G simulator: FBMC. Technical Report of Brno University of Technology, pp 1–30. https://publik.tuwien.ac.at/files/PubDat_248708.pdf. Last Accessed on 10 June 2021
38. Mishra KN, Navin K (2020) Multi-server multi -CS based deadlock prevention in distributed systems using voting and priority based approaches. Nat Acad Sci Lett 43:1–6
39. Mishra KN (2020) A novel integration of smart vehicles and secure clouds for supervising vehicle accidents on roads/highways. Sadhana J Eng Sci 45:1–21
40. Mishra KN (2021) Fraud detection and prevention in smart cities using k-fold machine learning technique. Wirel Pers Commun 116:1–25
41. Mishra KN (2020) A proficient mechanism for cloud security supervision in distributed environment. Int J Comput Netw Inf Secur 12(6):57–77
42. Mishra KN (2017, May) Deadlock prevention in single server multi-CS distributed systems uisng voting and priority based strategies. In: Springer International Conference on Recent Advancement on Computer and Communication (ICRAC-2017), pp 115–123
43. Mishra KN (2016, October) Voting and priority based mechanism for deadlock prevention in distributed systems. In: 2nd IEEE International Conference on Control Computing Communication and Materials (IEEE ICCCCM – 2016), India, pp 264–272
44. Kamta NM, Bhattacharjee V, Saket S, Mishra SP (2022) Blockchain and machine learning algorithms: a novel approach. Cluster Comp:1–26. https://doi.org/10.1007/s10586-022-03813-x

Chapter 6
Enhancing the Concert of M-health Technologies in Smart Societies Using Cloud-IoT-Based Distributive Networks

Abstract In the recent past, it has been realized that money is being spent on health care at a very fast pace and the general public has very high expectations about health service delivery. Therefore, the sustainability of the existing public health system in the event of a pandemic has become untenable. In 2011, health spending comprised 14.6% of Canada's GDP and approximately $196 billion was spent on e-health care. In addition, the 2005 census found that 15% of Canadians were 65 or older. But, statisticians say that if the situation of all other epidemic diseases remains the same, then by 2036 this figure will reach 30%. It is also observed that policy-makers resist comprehensive e-healthcare reform and they are asking confusing and difficult questions about the ancillary returns of additional spending on care related to infection and illness. It is also being observed that healthcare Managers/Physicians and others associated with the medical world are working towards creating a culture of inter-professional collaboration and further reforms such as reorganizing the e-health services delivery systems and they are continually working towards promoting the evidence-guided based decision-making phenomenon. It is genuine to say that there is a continuous effort to encourage cost-efficiency in the area of e-healthcare systems, and e-health Information Technology (IT) has huge use and potential in this area. Circumstantial evidence suggests that such innovations can further enhance the efficiency, quality, cost-effectiveness, and safety of e-healthcare delivery. It cannot be denied that as integrated multidisciplinary models of care incorporate e-health-related services into human resources, there is a growing curiosity among service providers about e-health information and the role of such information is becoming more and more decisive. The literature survey reveals that the number of e-health implementations in smart cities in developing countries has increased significantly over the past few decades. These growths in patient health monitoring and control systems are also expected to increase soon. However, the need for further careful confirmation by scientific evaluation procedures of the expected increase shortly cannot be ruled out. In reviewing the evaluation done on e-health care implementation in smart city societies of developing countries and making recommendations for future evaluation, it is quite clear that we are not keeping the required pace. It has also been revealed from a literature survey that in developed countries like Canada, only 42% to 45% out of every 2000 Canadian

© The Author(s), under exclusive license to Springer Nature Switzerland AG 2023
K. N. Mishra, S. C. Pandey, *Cloud-IoT Technologies in Society 5.0*,
https://doi.org/10.1007/978-3-031-28711-4_6

physicians use IT-based e-health. After in-depth data analysis, the authors also discussed that the impediments assimilated in e-health information methodologies exist in terms of a huge chunk of data, imbibing of data, and the complications involved in data accuracy. Further, the authors depicted the possible pros and cons of IT-based e-health implementations in smart city societies and provided reasonable suggestions for future directions in the era of COVID-19.

Keywords Collaborative Multidisciplinary Models · e-health recommendations · e-health Delivery · e-healthcare technologies · Smart City Societies

6.1 Introduction

As the population density in cities increases, the pressure of the need for shared urban resources, such as roads, energy, clean air, water, etc. increases. To make cities smart, the use of technology to manage these common resources expediently proves beneficial [1]. Since cities are irregularly structured and urban systems are dynamic systems. Therefore, to practically and effectively implement the multi-dimensional impact of technology in these cities requires a multi-disciplinary approach. Apart from this, it is also to be ensured that the multi-dimensional impact of technology will ultimately lead to an expected improvement in the quality of life of the citizens. Usually, each type of urban resource has to be managed independently. But, it has been found that sometimes there is a need to manage independently even within the same domain. Often different resources interact and these interactions are sometimes positive, for example, increasing the frequency of bus and metro rail reduces private car traffic. On the contrary, sometimes these interactions are also negative, as an increase in the number of buses can lead to a decrease in air quality. For these reasons, smart cities need to move away from traditional methods and adopt a multi-pronged approach by integrating interdependent public and private systems [2]. Shared urban resources can be classified into several areas, such as:

- Mobility (road space)
- Energy (electricity, gas)
- Water
- Pollution (air quality)
- Waste
- Health, etc.

Each category has its own set of challenges inherent in development. For example, to make traffic effective, it is necessary to remove barriers to mobility. Similarly, for public and shared transport to be effective, it is essential to have the provision of suitable transport modes at the right place, at the right time, and the right cost. Similarly, the water domain network should have provision for clean water to be available when and where it is needed.

The concept of smart cities can be said to have come into vogue since 2010. The concept started when IBM launched the idea by providing $50 million in technology and services to 100 cities. A literature survey found the fact that Songdo city of South Korea was declared the world's first smart city in 2014. This city was constructed from the ground up with technological support provided through Cisco Systems. In 2019, the city functioning started but the chunk of habitats in the city was only one-third of the stipulated population and was declared as technology without community [3]. However, nowadays there are more 'new' cities like Songdo and it is assumed that all cities need to be smarter, as 68% of the world population is supposed to be living in urban areas by 2050. The sustainable development of a Smart City can be considered completed in two phases. Initially, technology-promoting private companies pioneered the development of smart cities, resulting in a variety of technological products that helped enhance the quality of life in the city [4]. As a result, it came to be recognized that technological products and technology are important in the larger urban development framework. In [5], three drivers are identified that could catalyze the development of a smart city. These are:

- State-operated
- Private or corporate operated
- Civilian operated.

Indeed, as per the inherent philosophy of the primary driver, it can be conceptualized that the operational logic of a smart city may have its common functionalities as well as implications to create the impetus to citizens of smart city network together with the impact of citizens on the city. It is pertinent to mention that many cities remain concentrated on the advancement of technology whereas others are more susceptible to the governance model. Some domains of researchers are specifically interested in the well-being and engagement of citizens; while others focused their attention on sustainable development. Perhaps, owing to this pervasive paradigm and criteria various indices are used to recognize different cities as being smart. Table 6.1 enumerates the three top-tier smart cities as per three distinct indices.

It is natural for any smart city to have certain characteristics such as health-care, economic efficiency, and sustainable lifestyle. Apart from this, smart cities should also provide political and social inclusiveness and opportunities for the development of all public and private residents. These ideal consequences must be poised with the augmented likelihood of surveillance, lack of control, and assent related to data collection privacy backed with profiling of the 'normal' population [6]. In [7], it is given that in today's modern world of the twenty-first century more than fifty percent population of the globe is a citizen. Moreover, the number of devices connected to the internet per individual is almost six [8]. Therefore, it is explicit that devices and systems used in a city are gigantic. The purpose of using these devices and systems is to cater to the objectives of the smart city. Different objectives of the smart city are depicted in Fig. 6.1. These objectives can be enumerated as [9]:

Table 6.1 Top-ranked smart cities according to separate indices

	Source	Dimensions	First	Second	Third
1.	Strategy Index of Smart City (SISC)	Fields of Various types of Actions; Infrastructure and Policy; Planning of various categories of Strategies	Vienna, Austria	London, UK	St. Albert, Canada
2.	IESE Cities in Motion Index	Economy; Human Capital; Governance; Social Cohesion; Environment; Planning of Urban Areas; Transportation; Technologies; Global Outreach;	New York City, US	London, UK	Paris, France
3.	Statista	Sustainability; transport; governance; innovation of economic reforms; Improving living standard; digitalization; perception of experts	Gothenburg, Sweden	Bergen, Norway	Stockholm, Sweden

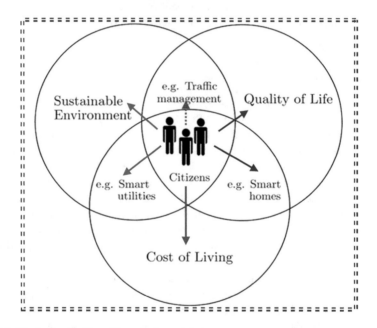

Fig. 6.1 The basic objectives of smart city societies

- Smart Economy
- Smart governance
- Smart people
- Smart mobility
- Smart mobility
- Smart environment
- Smart living

As per the authors' point of view, a hybrid structure to manage the data is basic and of the utmost importance for the devices and systems implanted in a smart city. It is also a fact that flawless, effective management and supply of optimum quality of food, energy, and water resources is of the dire need e.g., the smart and witty hybridization of food and agriculture administration with flawless supervision of raw and processed food quality supplied to the city could effectively and substantially limit or detect the spreading of fatal diseases and bacteria [10]. Likewise, the smart administration of water can detect health-detrimental bacteria and pollutants in water and thus eventually alert municipal authorities before diseases really spread. Also, if energy sectors are managed smartly then it could be possible to manage the variable demand based production of energy major hindrances are precluding precluding the smart city [11].

It is explicit that proper management of data is an essential ingredient for the pragmaIoT-enabledIoT enabled devices in smart cities. Chiefly, it includes three sub-domains. These are:

- Data acquisition
- Data processing
- Data dissemination

The first sub-domain i.e., data acquisition comprises of standards, quality and use of data. Data acquisition is of the paramount importance when the chunk of data is substantially huge. The phenomenon of data standardization ascertains the data consistency when different data acquisition approaches are used. Further, the quality of data ensures sufficient dimensionality in data as well as required granularity so that it can function effectively for the purpose of data fusion and in decision making.

Literature survey reveals the fact that substantial investments are presently being done in the IoT sector to enable the viability of wide range services. In addition, various dimensions of socio-economic life are being researched for IoT in recent past. Indeed, faith in IoT implicates that investors do not abstain to commit to it fiscally. Moreover, communication standards plays vital role in wide implementation of IoT. Several worldwide organizations are involved in standardizing such communications. Further, authors briefly display some of these IoT standards and initiatives in Fig. 6.2. For example, the Internet of Things Standard Global Initiative (IoT-GSI) supported by ITU made two recommendations. Namely: ITU-T Y.2060 and ITU-T Y.2061. The first one gives the general idea related to IoT and second one illustrates the machine interface pertaining to applications [12]. In [13], it is given that at the link layer the suitability of IEEE 802.15.4 standard is better than Ethernet in industrial perspective whereas at the network level the IPv6 is more suitable than the Low power Wireless Personal Area Networks (6LoWPAN). The architectural details of secured payload application data is shown in Fig. 6.3.

Simplified OSI	TCP/IP	6LoWPAN	ZigBee
Application	HTTP	HTTP, COAP, MQTT	ZigBee APL
Transport	TCP	TCP, UDP	
Internet	IP	IPv6, RPL	ZigBee NWK
Link	WiFi	6LoWPAN IEEE 802.15.4 MAC	IEEE 802.15.4 MAC
Physical		IEEE 802.15.4 PHY	IEEE 802.15.4 PHY

Fig. 6.2 Some IoT standards and initiatives

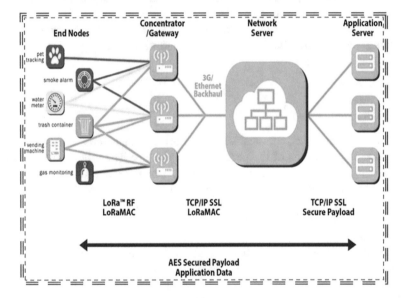

Fig. 6.3 Architectural details of secured payload application data

6.2   Theoretical Foundations & Literature Review

The Internet of Things (IoT) is a topic of great potential for connecting a multitude of digital devices to the Internet. It is playing an important role in increasing the utility of the Internet [14, 15]. Nowadays, the market of IoT is constantly moving towards new horizons as various industrial sectors have started to find and utilize the possibilities and opportunities associated with it. It has been observed from the literature survey that the global IoT business will touch US$1.7 trillion in 2020 while it was US$655.8 billion in 2014. Thus, it is supposed to hike at the rate of 16.9% of compound annual growth.

The smart city is a complex ecosystem that is full of possibilities for the enormous application of information and communication technologies (ICTs). Using ICT, cities can be made comparatively more attractive and more sustainable. In addition, with its help, cities can also be made better centers of innovation, and innovative industries [16]. A high-level illustration of an IoT-based smart city is given in Table 6.2.

In [17], it is mentioned that IoT-based smart city relevances can be classified into several domains based on different parameters such as network type, scalability, exposure, suppleness, heterogeneity and replicability, and participation of end-user. In general, this relevance can be classified into personal and home, utilities, mobile, and enterprises. For example, body area networks (BANs) are being used in personal and home applications for ubiquitous e-healthcare services. Utility applications include smart grids, smart metering/monitoring, and water network monitoring as well as video-based surveillance. The taxonomy of smart cities based on IoT is depicted in Table 6.3.

The inherent concepts and practical start of various tele-healthcares are being seen on the ground for the last few years. In [18, 19], wonderful and informative content about the essential framework of SOA (Service Oriented Architecture), VO (Virtual Organization) concepts, and the underlying infrastructure for practically implementing medical tele-consultations in the healthcare sector has been presented in a captivating manner. In addition, in [20], it has been described with in-depth and detailed information that how mobile computing and wireless communication technologies are used for the analysis of bio-signals to monitor a mobile patient monitoring system. In addition, in [21], it is discussed in detail that how we can use mobile systems based on cloud computing to provide better medical care to respiratory patients living at home. Indeed, in [21], it is illustrated that how reliable and pragmatic implementation of cloud computing can be adopted to securely share the patients' data. Further, how telemedicine (FEST) is being used to improve medical services in European countries is discussed in [22]. A software agent-based paradigm to tele-monitor the patients at home are rendered in [23]. The preliminary studies needed to guide the long-term care, development, and implementation of Taiwan's Tele-Health Pilot Project (TTPP) is given in [24]. TTPP talks about three types of models. These are concerned with improving health, patient care, and quality of life, respectively. It also highlights about home-care, community, and residential care for elderly patients for all three models. In addition to these, in [25] analysis regarding the use and evaluation of clinical guidelines, user controls, and data controls have been performed. In [26], an attempt has been made to assess how existing web-based technology and mobile phones can facilitate balance and coordination between diabetes patients and the primary healthcare team. Several strategies have been presented in [27] for the practical implementation of IoT technology in the health sector. In the literature, IoT technology is mainly discussed in three points. These are related to the application, security, and efficiency domains, respectively. The strategy presented in [27] can help provide success in the field of design and implementation of IoT technology holistically. The technology described in [28] provides an outline of the remote monitoring of elderly people and how the needs of elderly people can be met. The model proposed in [29] also makes expedient use of a machine learning strategy to enhance its quality. In addition, [30] a framework

Table 6.2 High level description of design components of IoT-based smart cities

Feature	Applications	Advantages	Research challenges	Major requirements
Security	ITS, e-healthcare, smart schools, logistics	Safe and attack-free implementation environment for deployment of various types of services.	Secure deployment and integration of cloud-IoT based services at the network and device levels. Lack of standardized security solutions. Early identification of outside and inside threats.	Identification of vulnerabilities in the network.
Risk management	ITS, Indoor e-healthcare	Ensures security by identifying uncertain events and threats in the IoT network.	Low-cost and efficient risk management systems to identify newly emerged attacks effectively. Fast and ultra-efficient risk decision mechanisms to counter identified threats.	It may use detailed threat model for identifying different threats in the network. It may use threat actors and asset-based threat modelling to trace a variety of risks areas.
Low-cost and low power environment friendly communication	Smart e-healthcare, smart meters,	In the case of low cost communication we need to provide a wide range of applications in IoT-integrated smart cities.	How can we extend the life of batteries of IoT devices?	We may use the advancements of wireless communications, and micro-electronics.
Big data	Smart meters, e-healthcare, Information Technology Systems	Increases the performance of IoT networks. Processes the useful information that are traced through authentic sources.	Very little availability of advanced tools to process the big data. Protection of users' security and privacy. Increase the proficiency of data acquisition approaches.	Centralized big data processing centres. Public awareness to utilize resources in the IoT network safely.
Connectivity	ITS, waste management, e-healthcare, smart industry	Ensures that IoT devices can communicate from various domains.	How to ensure connectivity in a wide range of IoT devices during no communication network and high mobility?	Efficient usage of spectrum for IoT devices to communicate. Intelligent usage of every possible communication medium.

Table 6.3 IoT-based smart city taxonomy

S. No.	Parameters	Descriptions
1.	Communication Protocols	Zigbee/Bluetooth; Wi-Fi; 6LoWPAN; IEEE 02.11;SigFax; WiMAX; GSM/GPRS; LTE/LTE-A; Upcoming 5G.
2.	Service Providers	AT&T; Telefonica; Orange; SKtelecom; Nokia; Ericssion; NTT DOCOMO; Vodafone; Telenor.
3.	Network Types	WLANs; WANs; BANs; Mobile Networks; WPANs; MANs;
4.	Activities of Standard Bodies	ETF; SGPP; ETS; EEE; OMA;oneM2M; FIWARE.
5.	Services Offered	Smart Parking; e-healthcare; Waste Management; security and Safety; Smart Electric Metering.
6.	Requirements	LOWCOST; Consumption of very low/ low power; Connectivity/ Interoperability; Privacy and Security.

named 'Help to You (H2U)' has been described in detail for effective monitoring of elderly people and patient status.

Certainly, the importance of remote monitoring for patients is widespread and this topic is explained in [31] in a very comprehensible way. In [32], the fusion of traditional medical frameworks and smart healthcare is interestingly presented. Further, how a rehabilitation system can be developed in an IoT environment that can optimize the resources effectively is proposed with important information in [33]. The model proposed in [33] utilizes semantic information to identify the healthcare-related resources available in the smart medical system. A specific model for maintaining data privacy in electronic health records and location information is given in [34]. However, it is fair to say that the model presented in [34] was mainly limited to the confidentiality of location, patient and treatment-related questions, and the confidentiality of the patient's electronic health record. Furthermore, in addition to the encrypted DES technique, a novel algorithm is proposed for the phenomenon of smart medical care [35]. This improved and modified technique augments the security required for the electronic health records during transmission and while the records reside on the server. Different panoramic views about the use of IoT in the healthcare sector were also seen in [36–39]. In Fig. 6.4, IoT and e-health Platforms are depicted in smart Cities.

6.3 The Proposed Model

Many actors are involved when e-health technologies are implemented for effective development of a smart city. There are essentially a number of actors playing their roles. It would not be wrong to say that without the cooperation of these actors, the expected success cannot be achieved. These actors can mainly be divided into the following categories:

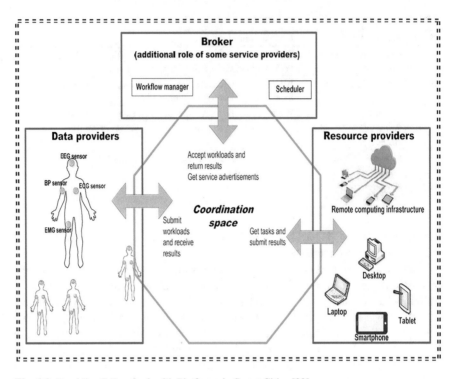

Fig. 6.4 Providing IoT and e-health Platforms in Smart Cities [39]

- Physicians
- Operators
- Patients

The first category of the actor is the physician and he is responsible for the treatment of diseases. Apart from this, he/she also takes the responsibility of analyzing the disease and preventing side effects caused by the disease in the future and continuous care of the patient. It is the responsibility of the medical personnel to visit the patients from time to time or as and when required. It is also the responsibility of the medical personnel to immediately inform the doctor about the serious condition of the patient. Medical personnel act as a bridge between patients and health facilities in a hospital. The role of the medical worker is very important for people with chronic illnesses or those who require long-term recovery.

Indeed, effective e-health systems of smart cities must fulfill the following functionalities.

- Input Data Management
- Data Storage
- Service Development
- Application Development
- Secure Data Access

The e-health system of a smart city deals with the medical data accumulated through the remotely situated sensors. Even more, the e-health system of a smart city adopts the measurement systems needed to observe and detect peculiar physiological patterns and environmental changes. Different subtle and precise devices are used to accumulate the data. These devices are often attached to the patients' attire or sometimes can directly be appended to the patient's bodies. Moreover, certain devices can also be placed at the home of the ill person to accumulate the patients' data automatically. In contrast, some other devices are also used that can be manually operated to collect the patients' data.

Further, it is pertinent and worthy to mention that the patient's medical data thus gathered needs subsequent transmission to a central repository system for benchmarking through precise medical care devices [40]. This central repository system is hosted in a remote server and only authorized users can access this repository for different purposes such as further processing or history tracking. The data available in the central repository plays a vivid role to make the e-health system of the smart city more effective and pragmatic. However, security issues must be taken care of because, in absence of security measures, the system will be vulnerable. To fix this vulnerability there must be strict access policies. In the forthcoming sub-section, the authors will present the architecture to provide the IoT-based e-health system for smart cities as well as a security model.

6.3.1 Architecture of Providing IoT and e-health Platforms in Smart Cities

In this section, the authors will summarize pertinent necessary information to develop comprehensive insights into the proposed architecture. The authors would like to render brief and precise information about the following components:

- IoT Devices
- Wireless Technologies (WT) for IoT
- Web Technologies for IoT

In general, the miniaturization of IoT devices is preferred. Moreover, low power consumption and limited processing attribute are some other characteristics of IoT devices. Further, eight or sixteen-bit processors are frequently used for microcontrollers.

However, these processors are not much effective to deal with planarity and thus sustaining the IoT devices. Therefore, IoT devices need a real-time operating system (RTOS). But, RTOS requires increased energy, processing efficacy, and space to support the functionality of IoT devices. Even more, a peculiar algorithm is used to tackle the various processes simultaneously in a single processor. It is important to mention that devices working in the IoT domain must also have certain characteristics such as compatibility with TCP/IP stack, compatibility with Java Virtual Machine

(JVM) as well as RAM/ROM support for supporting the RTOS. Nowadays, 32-bit microcontrollers are available with these characteristics for supporting IoT devices.

Communication technologies are of paramount importance for the satisfactory functioning of IoT devices so that effective communication can take place between the IoT devices and backend service providers. This communication can take place through wireless connectivity. However, it is tough to single out a standard WT to support an IoT system. It should also be noted that the use of WT is IoT project dependent. The comparative information of some technologies of this domain is enumerated in Table 6.4. In addition, web technologies are also used to enhance the functional efficacy of the IoT paradigm. However, as of date, the compatibility of web technologies is not optimal with IoT systems and thus often the results outputted are not satisfactory. Available web-related protocols can be used in the IoT paradigm. However, several resources are required to support the pragmatic applications of the IoT paradigm. Many goal-specific protocols are also designed and developed. These protocols need a comparatively lesser number of resources to support the IoT systems. In Table 6.5, details of some web technologies are given briefly.

6.3.2   System Components

In this section, different components of the system proposed for the IoT-based smart health system will be discussed. Further, the authors will discuss the functionality of different layers in the proposed model. The prime components of this proposed model are:

Table 6.4 Wireless technologies for IoT systems [39]

Standards	Operating Frequency	Data Rate	Range	Power Consumption	Battery Time
IEEE 802.15.4	868/915 MHz, 2.4 Gz	250 kbps	10 to 300 m	Very Low	Months-year
Wi-Fi	2.4 to 5.8 GHz	11–105 Mbps	10 to 100 m	High	Hours
Bluetooth	2.4 GHz	723 Kbps	10 m	Very Low-Low	Days-Weeks

Table 6.5 Web technology requirements for IoT systems

	Protocol	Transport Mechanism	Method of message passing	Successful Applications
1.	HTTP RESTful	TCP	Request/Response	Smart home and grid
2.	CoAP	UDP	Request/Response	Useful in FAN (Field Area Networks)
3.	MATP	TCP	Request/Response	Used to monitor and control the devices from a remote place.
4.	XMPP	TCP	Request/Response	Management of main appliances from a remote place.

- The Data Collector (DC)
- IoT Gateway (iGW)
- Backend Facilitator (BF)
- Access Applications (AA)

The DC is a sensor device and its purpose in the IoT system is to sense the patient's body, and it also supports various WT to communicate with the IoT system. DC also converts the data sensed into digital values. Further, the IoT gateway is a vital sub-component of the IoT paradigm. It connects the Local Processing Units (LPU) with the remotely situated backend facilitator. IPv4 or IPv6 protocols are often used to establish this connectivity. The other functioning of iGW is to convert the protocols, manage the IoT devices, as well as to give support for temporary storage. Indeed, it acts as an intermediate entity or middleware between the Local Sensor Network (LSN) and the remote IP network. Furthermore, the BF imparts the permanent storage facility for the IoT data and thus facilitates the decisions and analytics on this data. The data integration facility is also incorporated in BF so that different heterogeneous data can be fused. Different security measures are also adopted for BF. The last component of the proposed model is AA and this component facilitates the access mechanism in the IoT paradigm. The AA can be installed on smart devices such as smart mobile phones as well as on desktops.

6.3.2.1 Proposed Layers

The complete functionality of the model is described using following three layers:

- SL (Sensor Layer)
- NAL (Network Access Layer)
- SAL (Service Access Layer)

The SL will address the functionality of the different components. The data collectors are the sensor devices that are used to accumulate and monitor the health information of a patient. Sometimes these data collectors are embedded in the body of a patient to collect the pulse rate and heartbeat. The sensor layer consists of the following components:

- Communication technologies
- RFIDs and Bar Code used for tagging
- Data collectors e.g. sensor devices
- iGW (IoT gateway device)

The NAL is the 2nd of the IoT- based health system. It is used to provide the connection between the IoT gateway and the backend facilitator. It also provides an interface to the backend facilitator and the sensor layer devices where CSP (cloud service provider) supplies backend services. Further, DSL, Dslam, and 4G/5G technologies provide the connection between the backend services and the IoT gateway devices over the cloud with the help of Internet services.

The following components are included in the network access layer:

- Communication and IoT technologies
- Backend cloud services
- IoT-gateway
- Registered remote consultants list.

Thus, it can be said that the network access layer is an essential part of the described model. Medical professionals or doctors can access the health information of any patient whenever it is needed. The following components are included in the service access layer:

- Management authorities
- Medical professionals
- Modern web technologies
- Desktop computers and smart computing devices.
- All types of smart applications

The front-end interface for its users will be provided by the smart health unit of the service access layer.

6.3.3   Security Model

To provide the security to IoT system, it is necessary to use locked racks to make security to physical access possible. Moreover, non-required features and wired connectivity of the system should make disabled. It is also important to have strong passwords instead of default passwords. Further, remote access should be restricted in case of no need, and installation of updates should only be taken when there is availability. Indeed, the IoT paradigm can provide healthcare services vividly. However, there is still not any well-defined framework for IoT services within the realm of health care. But, in a certain scenario, a particular service is difficult to distinguish from a specific solution or application. The service provided by the proposed security model is generic. In addition, it should be noted that the service and protocols provided by the proposed security framework may need subtle modifications for effective functioning in the healthcare domain. However, the critical review of these modifications is outside the scope of this chapter. The readers are suggested to perform the literature survey for these needed modifications to make a deeper insight, if interested. Integration of the Cloud of Things, IoT, and different layers to M-Health Technologies for smart cities to enhance the performance is shown in Fig. 6.5, and m-health services and their applications in the Cloud-IoT environment are depicted in Fig. 6.6.

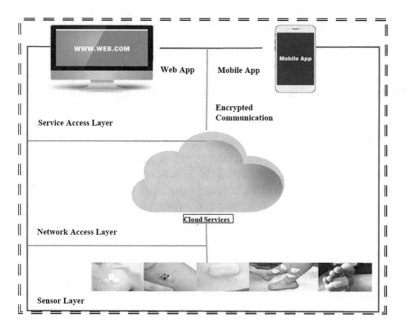

Fig. 6.5 Linking of different layers with cloud and devices

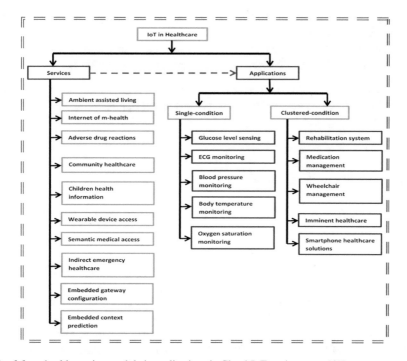

Fig. 6.6 m-health services and their applications in Cloud-IoT environment [41].

6.3.4   Integration of Responsive Technologies in Smart Cities

The persistent advancement over three decades in the technical domain made the phenomenon of smart cities a reality. The advancement in the field of technology extended the multifold help and support such as in the accumulation of data, making effective connectivity, in the analysis of the data, etc.

The dynamic contextualization of data takes place in the proper functioning of smart cities and this dynamic contextualization cannot exist without the help of technological advancement. And no doubt, this dynamic contextualization permits dynamic decision making which is of the utmost importance to augment the efficiency and resiliency in the functioning of government services. Perhaps, this in turn positively affects the performance of the smart city. However, sudden growth in technological advancement cannot take place and it follows an evolutionary pattern and it lets the sifting from technology to the fusion of technology to responsive technology.

This evolutionary phenomenon incorporates five stages as enumerated below.

1. Measurement Technology (MT): This permits the sensors to gather the data. This gathered data can subsequently be used for monitoring the status of the operation.
2. Networked Technology (NT): It permits the connection between the sensors and thus allows the exchange of data.
3. Management of Systems (MS): for allowing the real-time analysis of the gathered data and information.
4. Integration of the Systems (IS): It renders the data analysis possible.
5. Smart Technology (ST): It provides software as a service (SaaS).

Some of the IoT-based M-healthcare products are displayed in Fig. 6.7. Further, an attempt has been made to list miscellaneous actual applications of Cloud-IoT in smart cities in Fig. 6.8.

6.4   Results and Discussions

6.4.1   Challenges of Implementing M-health Technologies in Smart Cities

The subject matter of this chapter elaborates on the functionality of ICT to impart the medical-care in smart cities. Several attempts have already been taken by researchers worldwide to way out the hybridization of ICT with medical care systems in smart cities. In this chapter, the authors tried to analyze how existing works can further be extended to use ICT optimally in the health-care domain. As per the authors' point of view, undoubtedly the further leap in the integration of pervasive computing with machine learning will create a new horizon with broadened scope.

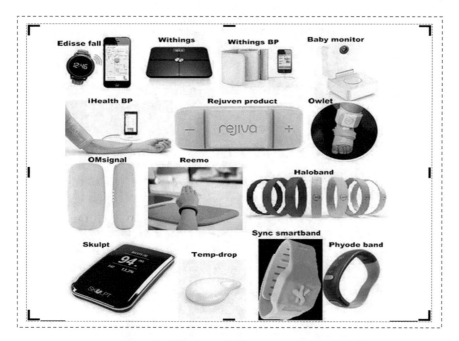

Fig. 6.7   Some examples of IoT-based M-healthcare products

Further, the symbiotic implementation of data accumulation and communication can fortify the scope even wider with effective tackling of privacy issues.

Perhaps, security and privacy are the most substantially concerned issues in the inclusion of ICT in the realm of health care [42, 43]. Researchers have made various measures to avoid these issues but cases of intrusion are still a frequently occurring phenomenon [44]. Often, the intruder somehow gets the details about the living pattern to trespass on the premises, and thus belongings inside the premises become at stake. Sometimes, the chances of intrusion can be generated without malicious intentions. For example, the situation when the software being used in health monitoring systems is not backed with prescribed standards that in turn can jeopardize human lives by not conveying critical information as and when needed. Moreover, it is also possible that sharing information about mobile phone apps can cause severe consequences.

In some countries, even sharing location-related information with third parties is forbidden by law [45]. Encryption of data is indeed done before storage and transferring, however, the efficacy of data to analyze the patterns can only be reflected when it is shared with entire populations. It is also pertinent to mention that the primitive approach to change the names with randomized identifiers is not sufficiently leak proof. In [46], it is given that an analysis of newspaper stories about hospital visits led to identifying the matching health record in 43% of the cases.

Attempts have also been made by the research community to make aware the decision makers regarding the inherent privacy and security issues involved in the

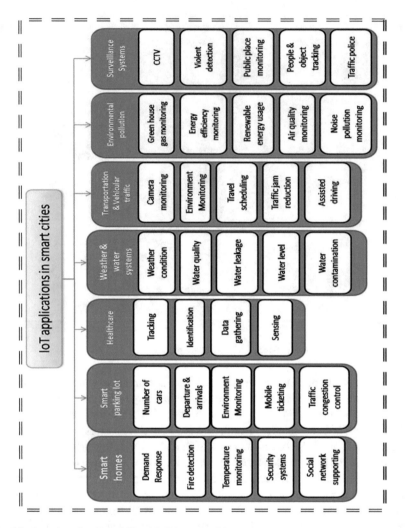

Fig. 6.8 Actual application of Cloud-IoT in smart cities

healthcare sector of smart cities [47, 48]. Moreover, further advancements are being implemented in this direction as well. In [49], it is illustrated how different techniques used for data analytics ensure a certain degree of privacy with the optimal utilization of the data. In literature, this phenomenon is coined as the 'Privacy-Utility Tradeoff'. Three types of 'Privacy-Utility Tradeoffs' are generally used to provide privacy to the citizens of smart cities. These are given below.

- To perturb the data to make it camouflaged [50, 51]
- K-Anomaly of the data [49, 50]
- Modification of the output obtained from the data mining techniques.

Perturbation of gathered data can be performed by creeping in more noises in the original data. This can be done by adding (or multiplying) more noises. While, the phenomenon of camouflaging the data is even yet a domain of further investigation [50, 51]. The second approach is often used when the gathered data is to be shared with a third party. This implicates the insurance that the recognizable features for a particular user are non-differentiable from at least k-1 different users. This approach can be accomplished by the techniques that are enabling the reduction of sensitive features and thus augment the diversity of sensitive features. It can also be achieved by fusing the synthetic data to disguise the real values, thus permitting sensitive data to almost seem to disappear in the crowd. Very often a unique approach is used for mobile data. In this approach, a single constant category of the identifier is assigned to each user with an alternative arrangement to change it frequently and thus render the hacking of the user difficult. The third approach also effectively ignores the chances of leaking sensitive data and information. In this approach, the performance of the classification algorithm is substantially degraded so that its performance just touches the threshold level but in this way mitigates the risk of individual identification. However, it is also important to maintain the consensus between the smart city designers, decision and policymakers, and technocrats before the implementation of a particular approach. Further, awareness must be created among the citizens of smart cities about sensitive data transmission. IoT applications in the health-care sector are shown in Table 6.6.

6.4.2 Effectiveness and Environmental Assessment

Having the required patients' monitored information is used in a variety of ways. This information is also collected for non-optimal management conditions or non-responding patients. It is also useful to do so that appropriate and effective health-related assistance can be provided to them at the right time [52]. This information also helps to reduce misleading and false positive attitudes and helps to take further necessary steps [53, 54]. The expected monitored information of the healthcare system of a smart city includes many aspects. For example, data collected by sensors, patient medical records, the effectiveness of the systems, and chronically ill patient monitoring systems are included. Apart from this, the healthcare system of smart cities also integrates all these aspects. It is also necessary that the sensitivity and effectiveness of the required information monitoring system are regularly and effectively measured [55]. It would certainly be right to say that involving the patients as well as their family members to enhance the quality of management of the healthcare system of smart cities would be the right step. Doing so helps patients to actively participate in the management and consequently allows the patient to cooperate and contribute effectively. Even more, smart health systems should assimilate the use of health-related records and important signs so that effective guidance can be provided about day basis activities, tasks, and habits within the smart city. For example, patients with heart and respiratory diseases can be informed about the

Table 6.6 IoT applications in healthcare

	Infirmity/ Condition	Sensors Used	Operations	IoT Roles/Connections
1.	Management of Diabetes Medication	Non-negative opto-physiological sensor	The sensor's output is connected to the TelosBmote for converting the analog signal into the digital one.	6LoWPAN and IPV6 protocol architectures enable wireless sensor devices for all IP-based wireless nodes.
2.	Injury Analysis for Advance Diabetes Patients	A smartphone camera	Image decompression and segmentation	The app runs on the software platform in the smartphone's System on Chip (SoC) to drive the IoT.
3.	Monitoring of Heart Rate	Capacitive electrodes fabricated on a printed circuit board	Digitized right on top of the electrode and transmitted in a digital chain connected to a wireless transmitter	BLE and Wi-Fi connect smart devices through an appropriate gateway
4.	BP Monitoring	A wearable BP sensor	Oscillometric and automatic inflation and measurement	WBAN connects smart devices through an appropriate gateway
5.	Monitoring of Body Temperature	A wearable body temperature sensor	Skin-based temperature measurement	WBAN connects smart devices through an appropriate gateway
6.	Rehabilitation System	A wide range of wearable and smart home sensors	Coordination, cooperation, event detection, reporting, tracking, and feedback to the system itself.	Interactive heterogeneous wireless networks enable sensor devices to have various access points.
7.	Medication Management	Delaminating materials and a suit of wireless biomedical sensors (Touch, Humidity, and Co_2	The diagnosis and prognosis of vitals recorded by wearable sensors	Database access, GPS (Global Positioning System), RFIDs, Web access, Multimedia transmission, and Wireless links.
8.	Management of Wheelchairs	WBAN Sensors (e.g. Accelerometer, ECG, and Pressure)	Realize abnormality, Nodes process signals, communicate with sink nodes wirelessly, and perceive surroundings.	Smart devices and data center layers with heterogeneous connectivity.
9.	Monitoring of Oxygen Saturation level	A pulse oximeter wrist by using vibration	Intelligent approach for pulse-by-pulse filtering.	Ubiquitous integrated clinical environments
10.	Eye Disorder, Skin Infection	Smartphone cameras	Pattern matching and/ or Visual inspection with a standard library of images.	The cloud-aided app runs on the software platform in the Smartphone's SoC to drive the IoT.

(continued)

Table 6.6 (continued)

	Infirmity/ Condition	Sensors Used	Operations	IoT Roles/Connections
11.	Asthma, Chronic Obstructive Pulmonary Disease, Cystic Fibrosis	A built-in microphone audio system in the smartphone	Calculate the air flow rate and produces the flow time, volume time, and flow-volume graphs.	The apps run on the software platform in the Smartphone's SoC to drive the IoT
12.	Cough Detection	A built-in microphone audio system in the smartphone	An analysis of recorded spectrograms and the classification of rainforest machine learning	The apps run on the software platform in the smart phone's SoC to drive the IoT
13.	Allergic Rhinitis and Nose Related Symptoms	A built-in microphone audio system in the smartphone	Speech recognition and vector machine classification	The apps run on the software platform in the smart phone's SoC to drive the IoT
14.	Melanoma Detection	A smartphone camera	The matching of the suspicious image patterns with a library of images of cancerous skin	The apps run on the software platform in the Smartphone's SoC to drive the IoT
15.	Remote Surgery	Surgical robot systems and augmented reality sensors	The master controller, Robot arms, and feedback sensory system ensure tele-presence.	Information system management and Real-time data connectivity.

localities with an elevated degree of pollution, so that they can choose suitable routes for their daily routine [56, 57]. The author believes that improvement in policy and decision-making also plays an important role in improving the quality of management. There is also a need to amend laws and priorities to improve the policies and decisions so that health hazards can be predicted by including data on population, weather, environment, and accessible infrastructure. The policy reform is also beneficial in the control of epidemics as it fundamentally enhances the state's ability to control and detect possible new cases during a pandemic. Further, it is needed to effectively identify areas of increased risk, and effectively manage outbreaks. Such approaches are also useful to detect and organize different widespread risks to health e.g., radiation/pollution from trade incidents [58]. Smartphone apps for general health care are enumerated in Table 6.7.

Some researchers believe that cost-saving analysis of different sectors can have an effective and favorable effect on reducing essential healthcare costs [59–61]. The money thus generated from the cost savings can be used for other purposes such as increasing the efficiency of the policies and increasing the provision of services.

In addition, optimum prevention and management of diseases can reduce unnecessary pressure on hospitals [62]. Moreover, cost reduction, reduction in response time, and effective public health management at the national level also play a role in

Table 6.7 Smartphone apps for general healthcare

	Apps	Descriptions
1	Health Assistant	Keeps track of a broad range of health parameters e.g. fat and body water, body temperature, weight, lipids, BP, glucose level, etc.
2	Healthy Children	Ability to search for a pediatrician by location and can request their advice.
3	Google Fit	Tracks the user's walking, running, and cycling activities.
4	Calorie Counter	Keeps track of food consumption levels.
5	Water Your Body	Generates the drinking water-related alarm to the user.
6	Noom Walk	Count the user's steps at all times and it may serve as a pedometer.
7	Pedometer	Records and displays the number of steps the user takes and the corresponding burned calories.
8	Period Calendar	Keeps track of the best periods, cycles, and ovulation dates and helps to prevent pregnancy.
9	Period Tracker	Keeps track of periods and forecasts fertility.
10	Instant Heart Rate	Measures the heart rate by using the smartphone's built-in camera to sense changes in the color of the fingertip, which is directly related to the pulse.
11	Cardiax Mobile ECG	Serves as a companion app for Cardiax Windows's full-scale, 12-Channel Personal Computer ECG system.
12	ECG Self-Monitoring	Serves as an automatic ECG device by registering ECG data based on the self-check software.
13	ElektorCardioscope	Displays ECG data through a wireless terminal.
14	Runtastic Heart Rate	Measure the heart rate on a real-time basis.
15	Heart Rate Monitor	Checks the heart rate on a real-time basis.
16	Cardiomobile	Monitors cardiac rehabilitation remotely on a real-time basis.
17	Blood Pressure (BP) Watch	Collects, tracks, analyzes and shares BP data.
18	Finger Blood Pressure Prank	Measure BP based on the fingerprint.
19	On Track Diabetes	Tracks blood glucose and medication to help manage diabetes.
20	Finger Print Thermometer	Determines the body temperature from fingerprint.
21	Body Temperature	Keeps track of body temperature and identifies its severity.
22	Medisafe Meds & Pill Reminder	Reminds the user of medication time.
23	Dosecast Education Reminder	Reminds the user of the medication time, tracks the inventory, and maintains a log for drug management.
24	Rehabilitation Game	Serves as an interactive game facilitating the auditory rehabilitation of patients with hearing loss.
25	iOximeter	Calculate the pulse rate and SpO_2
26	Eye Care Plus	Tests and monitors the vision
27	Skin Vision	Keeps track of skin health and enables the early discovery of skin disorder
28	Asthma Tracker and Log	Keeps track of the patient's asthma

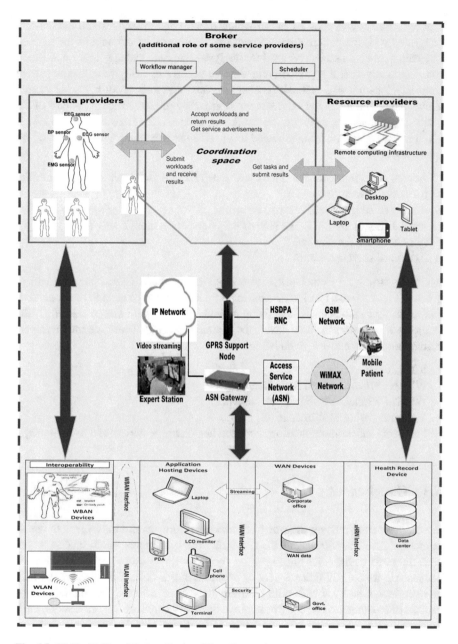

Fig. 6.9 M-Health-Based Patient Care and Data Processing

achieving optimal outcomes [63–66]. In Fig. 6.9, a layout is shown that illustrates the functioning of a heterogeneous computing grid. Authors have attempted to show how a huge amount of data and signs constitutes a typical topology and how a heterogeneous computing grid can be linked with static and mobile electronic devices.

Figure 6.9 also envisages a case in which mobile health devices and sensors are integrated with the patient's body to get the health profile and data of the patient. The data thus obtained can be used for analysis, retrieval, and aggregation. Further, based on analysis and aggregation healthcare takers can easily monitor the patient from any location and can also provide his/her responses accordingly. Over and above, the layout given in Fig. 6.9 incorporates the required structural details of the network topology for enabling the streaming of medical videos e.g., the topology given in Fig. 6.9 can be implemented to provide the streaming with the help of the following entities.

- Access of an interconnected network with WiMAX (worldwide interoperability for microwave access).
- Access of IP (Internet Protocol) network.
- Availability of GNS (Global Network System) for a mobile network
- Access of usual gateways
- Access of service networks.

A similar structural framework is also observed in the IoThNet. The framework given in Fig. 6.10 can be used as a basic approach and can be used in the domain of telehealth and ambient assisted living systems. The pivotal issues related to the framework given in Fig. 6.10 have been identified in [65]. These are the interoperability among the entities given below:

- IoT gateway
- WLAN (Wireless Local Area Network)
- WPAN (Wireless Personal Area Network)
- Streaming using Multimedia
- Providing safe communications between healthcare providers and IoT gateways.

6.5 Conclusions

Researchers from all over the world are making efforts toward the expedient development of health services. And, the researchers have had unexpected success so far. But, the need of the hour is to keep on trying to find various technical solutions because right now still there is a lot of potential in this field. This chapter provides an overview of how to better utilize various IoT-based technologies and the various aspects of IoT that are currently possible in the healthcare sector. Furthermore, various healthcare network architectures and platforms are also depicted preceded by a literature review of various aspects of IoT technologies. Various positive scenarios such as how the transmission and reception of medical data can be improved are also discussed. The direction and prospects of the near future R&D in IoT-powered healthcare services and applications are also described in a comprehensible manner. In addition, this chapter also highlights topics such as how IoT can impact children and elderly people in medicine and care, chronic disease surveillance, personal

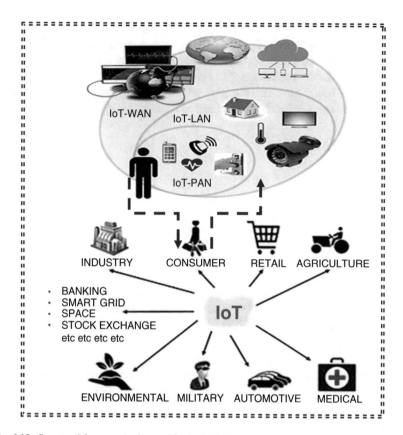

Fig. 6.10 Structural framework observed in the IoThNet

health and fitness management, and a comprehensive view of the essential facts of the industry and technologies impacting it are also provided. Apart from this, this chapter also highlights how the development of sensors, devices, internet applications, and other technologies will prove helpful in expanding health services unbounded.

In this chapter, what security policies should be there in the use of technology in the field of health-care and what challenges can be faced in this direction have also been discussed thoroughly. Potential models are also proposed for how these associated security risks can be mitigated. Several important research topics such as standardization, network types, business models, quality of service, and health data protection are also discussed. No doubt, it will provide better direction for future research. Thus, this chapter will be potentially beneficial towards restructuring the framework of a new horizon for the research workers involved in the field of IoT-based healthcare technologies.

It would not be wrong to say that rapid success has been seen in the development of smart cities due to the extensive practical use of ICT. Apart from this, the combined synergistic use of mobile technology with ICT has also seen promising success in the field of e-health and m-health. This has given rise to the concept of smart health and this concept plays an important role in connecting smart cities with mobile and electronic health services. As a result, making innovative efforts in the direction of S-Health Plus will result in essential research and finding new possibilities to enhance health care. This chapter will prove to help and observe the S-Health concept, and various research areas related to it can be rapidly followed.

References

1. Bouroche M, Dusparic I (2021) Urban computing – the technological framework for smart cities. Handbook of Smart Cities, pp 89–112
2. Naphade M, Banavar G, Harrison C, Paraszczak J, Morris R (2011) Smarter cities and their innovation challenges. In: Computer, vol 44, pp 32–39. https://doi.org/10.1109/MC.2011.187
3. James P et al (2021) Smart cities - fundamental concepts. Handbook of smart cities, pp 1–53
4. Townsend Anthony M (2013) Smart cities: big data, civic hackers, and the quest for a New Utopia. WW Norton and Co.
5. Mosco V (2019) The smart city in a digital world. Emerald, Bingley, UK
6. Sadowski J, Pasquale F (2015) The spectrum of control: a social theory of the smart city. First Monday, [S.l.], June 2015. ISSN 13960466. Available at: https://firstmonday.org/ojs/index.php/fm/article/view/5903/4660. Date accessed: 01 July 2022. https://doi.org/10.5210/fm.v20i7.5903
7. United Nations. (2014) World's population increasingly urban with more than half living in urban areas. Accessed on December 2016. [Online]. Available: http://www.un.org/en/development/desa/news/population/world- urbanization-prospects-2014.html
8. Evans D (2011) The internet of things: how the next evolution of the internet is changing everything. [Online]. Available: http://www.cisco.com/c/dam/en/us/about/ac79/docs/innov/IoT IBSG 0411FINAL.pdf
9. Pellicer S, Santa G, Bleda AL, Maestre R, Jara AJ, Skarmeta AG (2013) A global perspective of smart cities: A survey, in 2013 Seventh International Conference on Innovative Mobile and Internet Services in Ubiquitous Computing, July 2013, pp. 439–444
10. Fernandez-Anez V (2016) Stakeholders approach to smart cities: A survey on smart city definitions. Cham: Springer International Publishing , pp. 157–167. [Online]. Available: https://doi.org/10.1007/978-3-319-39595-116
11. Biggs EM, Bruce E, Boruff B, Duncan JM, Horsley J, Pauli K, McNeill A, Van Neef F, Ogtrop JC et al (2015) Sustainable development and the water–energy–food nexus: A perspective on livelihoods. Environ Sci Pol 54:389–397
12. Next Generation Networks – Frameworks and functional architecture models. (2012) Recommendation ITU-T Y.2060. Overview of the Internet of things. Technical report, International Telecommunication Union
13. Bello O, Zeadally S, Badra M (2017) Network layer inter-operation of device-to-device communication technologies in internet of things (iot). Ad Hoc Netw 57:52–62. Special Issue on Internet of Things and Smart Cities: security, privacy and new technologies
14. Y. Mehmood, F. Ahmad, I. Yaqoob, A. Adnane, M. Imran and S. Guizani, "Internet-of-things-based smart cities: recent advances and challenges," in IEEE Commun Mag, vol. 55, no. 9, pp. 16–24, 2017, 10.1109/MCOM.2017.1600514
15. Zanella A et al (2014) Internet of things for smart cities. IEEE Internet Things J 1(1):22–32
16. Gubbi J et al (2013) Internet of things (IoT): A vision, architectural elements, and future directions. Futur Gener Comput Syst 29(7):1645–1660

17. Gluhak A et al (2011) A survey on facilities for experimental internet of things research. IEEE Commun Mag 49(11):58–67
18. Celesti A et al (2019) How to develop IoT cloud e-health systems based on FIWARE: a lesson learnt. J Sens Actuator Netw 8(7):1–24
19. Łukasz C, Malawski F, Wyszkowski P (2015) Holistic approach to design and implementation of a medical teleconsultation workspace. J Biomed Inform 57:225–244
20. Pawar P, Jones V, van Beijnum BJF, Hermens H (2012) A framework for the comparison of mobile patient monitoring systems. J Biomed Inform 45:544–556. https://doi.org/10.1016/j.jbi.2012.02.007. http://www.ncbi.nlm.nih.gov/pubmed/22406009
21. Risso NA, Neyem A, Benedetto JI, Carrillo MJ, Farías A, Gajardo MJ, Loyola O (2016) A cloud-based mobile system to improve respiratory therapy services at home. J Biomed Inform 63:45–53. https://doi.org/10.1016/j.jbi.2016.07.006. http://www.ncbi.nlm.nih.gov/pubmed/27392646
22. Gerneth M (1994) FEST: Framework for European services in telemedicine. Comput Methods Progr Biomed 45:71–74
23. Rialle V, Lamy JB, Noury N, Bajolle L (2003) Telemonitoring of patients at home: A software agent approach. Comput Methods Progr Biomed 72:257–268
24. Hsu MH, Chu TB, Yen JC, Chiu WT, Yeh GC, Chen TJ, Sung YJ, Hsiao J, Li YCJ (2010) Development and implementation of a national telehealth project for long-term care: A preliminary study. Comput Methods Progr Biomed 97:286–296
25. Shalom E, Shahar Y, Lunenfeld E (2016) An architecture for a continuous, user-driven, and data-driven application of clinical guidelines and its evaluation. J. Biomed. Inform. 59:130–148. https://doi.org/10.1016/j.jbi.2015.11.006. http://www.ncbi.nlm.nih.gov/pubmed/26616284
26. Harris LT, Tufano J, Le T, Rees C, Lewis GA, Evert AB, Flowers J, Collins C, Hoath J, Hirsch IB, Goldberg HI, Ralston JD (2010) Designing mobile support for glycemic control in patients with diabetes. J Biomed Inform 43:S37–S40
27. Sahi MA, Abbas H, Saleem K et al (2017) A survey on privacy preservation in e-healthcare environment. IEEE Access
28. Zhao W, Wang C, Nakahira Y (2011) Medical application on internet of things. In: Proceedings of IET international conference on communication technology and application (ICCTA 2011). Beijing, China, pp 660–665
29. Earley S (2015) Analytics, machine learning, and the internet of things. IT Professional 17(1)., Article ID 7030173:10–13
30. Basanta H, Huang YP, Lee TT (2016) Intuitive IoT-based H2U healthcare system for elderly people. In Proceedings of the Networking, Sensing, and Control (ICNSC), 2016 IEEE 13th International Conference on, pp. 1–6, IEEE
31. Swiatek P, Rucinski A (2013) IoT as a service system for eHealth, In Proceedings of the e-Health Networking, Applications & Services (Healthcom), 2013 IEEE 15th International Conference on, pp. 81–84, IEEE, Lisbon, Portugal
32. Yang G, Xie L, Mäntysalo M et al (2014) A health-IoT platform based on the integration of intelligent packaging, unobtrusive bio-sensor, and intelligent medicine box. IEEE Trans Industr Inform 10(4):2180–2191
33. Fan YJ, Yin YH, Xu LD, Zeng Y, Wu F (2014) IoT-based smart rehabilitation system. IEEE Trans Industr Inform 10(2):1568–1577
34. Ding D, Conti M, Solanas A (2016) A smart health application and its related privacy issues, In Proceedings of the smart city security and privacy workshop (SCSP-W), pp. 1–5,
35. Gong T, Huang H, Li P, Zhang K, Jiang H (2015) A medical healthcare system for privacy protection based on IoT, In proceedings of the parallel architectures, algorithms and pro- gramming (PAAP), 2015 Seventh International Symposium on, pp. 217–222
36. Amrutha KR, Haritha SM, Haritha VM, Jensy AJ, Sasidharan S, Charly JK (2017) IOT based medical home. International Journal of Computer Applications 165(11)
37. Rathore MM, Ahmad A, Paul A, Wan J, Zhang D (2016) Real- time medical emergency response system: Exploiting IoT and big data for public health. J Med Syst 40(12):283

38. Zhang G, Li C, Zhang Y, Xing C, Yang J (2012) SemanMedical, A kind of semantic medical monitoring system model based on the IoT sensors In Proceedings of the e-health networking, applications and services (Healthcom), 2012 IEEE 14th International Conference on, pp. 238–243, IEEE
39. Pasha M, Shah SMW (2018., Article ID 6183732) Framework for E-health systems in IoT-based environments. Wireless Comm Mob Comp 2018:1–11
40. Persico V, Pescapé A, Picariello A, Sperlí G (2018) Benchmarking big data architectures for social networks data processing using public cloud platforms. Future Gener Comput Syst 89:98–109
41. Riazulislam SM et al (2015) The internet of things for health care: a comprehensive survey. IEEE Access:1–12
42. Abelson JS, Kaufman E, Symer M, Peters A, Charlson M, Yeo H (2017) Barriers and benefits to using mobile health technology after operation: A qualitative study. Surgery 162(3):605–611
43. Rashid F (2017) How to secure your (easily hackable) smart home Tom's Guide. [Online]. Available: https://www.tomsguide.com/us/secure-smart-home- how-to,news-19380.html
44. Diaz ED (2016) The new European Union General Regulation on Data Protection and the legal consequences for institutions. Church Commun Cult 1(1):206–239
45. Zang J, Dummit K, Graves J, Lisker P, Sweeney L (2015) Who knows what about me? A survey of behind the scenes personal data sharing to third parties by mobile apps. Technol Sci. 2015103001
46. Sweeney L (2015) Only you, your doctor, and many others may know. Technol Sci 2015092903
47. Bhuyan SS, Kim H, Isehunwa OO, Kumar N, Bhatt J, Wyant DK, Kedia S, Change CF, Dasgupta D (2017) Privacy and security issues in mobile health: Current research and future directions. HealPolicy Technol 6(2):188–191
48. Kotz D, Gunter CA, Kumar S, Weiner JP (2016) Privacy and security in mobile health: A research agenda. Computer (Long Beach Calif) 49(6):22–30
49. Mendes R, Vilela JP (2017) Privacy-preserving data mining: Methods, metrics, and applications. IEEE Access 5:10562–10582
50. Dwork C (2015) Differential privacy: A survey of results. Lect Notes Comput Sci 9076:1–19
51. Peng W, Kanthawala S, Yuan S, Hussain SA (2016) A qualitative study of user perceptions of mobile health apps. BMC Public Health 16(1158):1158
52. Majed KA, Malik BA (2019) Smart city and smart-health framework, challenges and opportunities. Int J Comp Sci Apps 10(2):171–176
53. Singh J (2015) Big data: tools and technologies in big data. Int J Comput Appl 112(15):975–8887
54. Box D, Pottas D (2013) Improving information security behaviour in the healthcare context. Procedia Technol 9:1093–1103
55. Agbele K, Nyongesa H, Adesina A (2010) IeT and infonnation security perspectives in E-health systems. 4(1):17–22
56. Solanas A et al (2014) Smart health: A context-aware health paradigm within smart cities. IEEE Commun Mag 52(8):74–81
57. Jammoul K, Lee H, Lane K (2014) Understanding users' trust and the moderating influence of privacy and security concerns for mobile banking : an elaboration 1–11
58. Gawlik A, Köster L, Mahmoodi H, Winandy M Requirements for integrating end-to-end security into large-scale EHR systems 1–12
59. Glasmeier A, Christopherson S (2015) Thinking about smart cities, Cambridge. J Reg Econ Soc 8(1):3–12
60. Li D, Shan J, Shao Z, Zhou X, Yao Y (2013) Geomatics for smart cities - concept, key techniques, and applications. || Geo-Spatial Inf. Sci 16(1):13–24
61. Fernando JI, Dawson LL (2009) The health information system security threat lifecycle: an informatics theory. Int J Med Inform 78(12):815–826
62. Park I (2010) Essays on information assurance: Examination of detrimental consequences of information security, privacy, and extreme event concerns on individual and organizational use of systems ProQuest LLC

63. Anthopoulos L, Janssen M, Weerakkody V (2016) A unified smart city model (USCM) for smart city conceptualization and benchmarking. Int J Electron Gov Res 12(2):77–93

64. Jin J, Gubbi J, Marusic S, Palaniswami M (2014) An information framework for creating a smart city through internet of things,‖. IEEE Internet Things J 1(2):112–121

65. De I, Díez T, Lopez-coronado M, López-coronado M (2014) Privacy and security in mobile health apps : a review and recommendations privacy and security in mobile health apps: A Review and Recommendations no. October 2017

66. Elkhodr M, Shahrestani S, Cheung H (2011) Enhancing the security of mobile health monitoring systems through trust negotiations 2011 IEEE 36th Conf. Local. Comput Netw:754–757

Chapter 7
Supervision of Communication and Control Services in Societies of Smart Cities Using Sheltered Cloud-Based Confirmation and Access Techniques

Abstract In the existing age of computations and research, the cloud-IoT (internet of things) integrated distributive computing is being broadly used for performing information/data computation and transmission services. In view of the fact that the implementation of cloud-IoT integrated communication and computing services have safety and security-related serious concerns. Therefore, in this chapter, the authors have presented verification and validation entrails for evaluating the transmutation-based usefulness of cloud data/services. The authors believe that this technique can realize the idea of defenselessness evaluation and permeation testing in a further improved way. The described technique of this study work contains information on widespread threats to cloud-IoT integrated services e.g. SaaS (Software as a service), IaaS (Information as a Service), and PaaS (Platform as a Service). These services need to be provided to the cloud-IoT customers. The ideas originated in this chapter are to utilize Internetworked Communication Technology (IwCT), IoT, and Embedded Computing Technology (ECT) for further enhancing the overall performance of safe cloud-based information/data transfer services.

In this chapter, the authors have described innovative and safe cloud-IoT integrated communication and computing services to further enhance the recital of cloud-IoT integrated communication and processing systems. Here, better-quality internetworked communication machineries based on Internet Protocol-Wireless Sensor Network (IP-WSN), web computing, and sprinkled scheme architectures are being used for improving the effectiveness of cloud-IoT integrated distributive data/ information communication and control systems. The cloud-IoT integrated server of described IRTMCCS (Intelligent Road Transport Management and Communication Control & System) will unquestionably offer control and access mechanisms for several types of vehicles on roads/highways and the described IRTMCCS will be very much useful in further improving the safety of drivers and other traveling passengers.

Keywords Cloud-IoT-integrated Computing · Distributive Computing · Embedded Computing Technologies · Secure Cloud · Transportation Services

7.1 Introduction

Web-based computing is a most modern network-reliant computing system that may allocate available amenities in the support of end users distributed over different locations on the earth. Few of the applications of web-based computing are the estimation of platform infrastructure, sharing of networks & associated resources, and sharing of software products through various dynamic paths of network. The actualization of cloud repayments available in the current era of the vibrant market is Google, Amazon, IBM, Microsoft, Eucalyptus, Oracle, VMware, and Citrix. These companies are offering sales power and frame space in a distinguishing cloud-based administration environment [1]. The terms and conditions of an appropriate web-based defense system have become indispensable for looking after uprightness, secrecy, and user-friendliness of transportation conveniences with the gargantuan augment of cloud and internet of things (IoT) based web crime control and management services.

The necessities of real-time interactive data/video transmission and integrating them with ongoing systems for all consumers may wind up essentials to keep up flexibility and improved quality of services (IQoS) in cloud-IoT integrated distributive web systems. If internet service providers need to make available user-welcoming ease of use, trustworthiness, and confidentiality of indispensable data placed on a cloud-IoT integrated web computing arrangement then a diversity of security procedures will be required. If the cloud-IoT integrated internetwork system wishes to maintain an established and protected web internetwork then the web server will need all the indispensable actions to be implemented with suitable faithful access rights and external restrictions will have to be suitably defined [2, 3].

Many of the researchers, experts of industries, and academic scholars have jointly tried to define the word *web-based computing* and its distinctive characteristics. Buyya et al. [4] and Khodadadi et al. [5] have successfully defined it as the cloud which is a gathering of interrelated and interlinked virtualized vigorously provisioned computer systems which may present real-time parallel and distributed computing atmosphere and it may be possible to use one or many amalgamated computing resources which are established through conciliation between the two parties namely internet service provider and clients. Van Bon et al. [6] stated that the clouds are a huge collection of straightforwardly utilizable/reachable virtualized resources which are enthusiastically reconfigured to fiddle with a changeable load and it has the capability of optimized resource consumption. The collections of resources in a cloud-IoT integrated distributive atmosphere are shared as per the rules of the use-per-pay model. Here, assurance is presented by the cloud-IoT infrastructure supplier as per the previously defined agreements. Miller et al. [7] emphasized that the clouds are hardware-dependent services where computing tasks, internetwork access, and data/information storage abilities are offered with decidedly elastic infrastructure capabilities.

The specific information obtained from the University of California, USA reveals that the basic distinctiveness of cloud computing systems is immeasurable internetworked computing resources, up-front promise elimination, and use-per-pay. Similarly, Alger D. et al. [3] described that the cloud is more frequently referred to as the IT-related infrastructure deployed on information as a service (IaaS) data centers. Here, a resource will represent a computation related application including physical components/software components of the system, service platforms, reliable software services, and implicit servers. Web computing is extensively being used by many types of industries including motor vehicles and service sector industries. The cloud-IoT integrated computing systems have a huge number of applications in countless areas like accounts-related applications, CRM (consumer relationship management), transportation-related communications, distributive cooperation, emails, online data/information storage management, management of human resources and employment office management, etc. The cloud-IoT integrated computing systems have a variety of advantages like 24x7 sustainable support, repay as per the need, efficient scalability, and high-speed computing in a virtual and self vibrant environment [8, 9].

The safe keeping services of cloud-IoT integrated communication systems can be minimized in instantaneous situations. The secure cloud integration with information and communication technologies (ICT) may get an interestingly imperative role in establishing links among servers of the clouds available at various locations and vehicle users to further improve accident deterrence in distributive environments [10, 11]. To keep away from these serious problems, the creators have presented a justifiable verification policy to scrutinize the implementation of cloud administering methods [12].

Cloud-based web computation merges certain things like amenity protection, amenity administration, and observations of available internetworked resources. Currently, the authors could not find any standardized rules and guidelines for deploying applications of clients in cloud-IoT-based computing systems. Varieties of new processes have been developed by researchers and are being imposed in cloud-IoT-based web servers. It is also observed by authors that the currently existing techniques are not adequate to guarantee the overall security of clouds because the clouds have dynamic nature. The fundamental issues of data safety, data management, data incomparability, and control of cloud data are discussed by [13] their research paper. Sun et al. [14] discussed the isolation, key protection, and reliance related issues in cloud-IoT based accessible environment and promised to provide help to the clients/customers for identifying the generous and insubstantial fears related to cloud computing problems in their research work. According to the views of researchers, there are three innermost probable problems namely safety, seclusion, and faith which may exist in the cloud-IoT integrated computing surroundings. Out of these innermost problems, safety plays an influential role in the existing age of cloud-IoT integrated distributive computing. The cloud security systems can further be divided into six subsystems i.e. *server monitoring, safety mechanism, web management, data privacy, prohibiting unlawful operations & hijacking of services.*

A records security-related concept for cloud-IoT-based computing networks was presented by [15] where the authors discussed the fortification-related concerns which are linked to data/information storage in the cloud. A variety of patents regarding the safety measures of statistical techniques for cloud-IoT-based distributive computing systems were filed by [16]. Authors Younis and Kifayat provided an in-depth analysis of web-based sanctuary administration for cloud-IoT-related available infrastructures [17]. A safety and segregation structure for RFID (radio frequency identification) in the cloud-IoT integrated web computing environment was described by [18] which can competently amalgamate RFID technology with IoT in a distributive computing atmosphere.

In a confined way, it can be understood that the major issues of cloud-IoT integrated web data indemnity comprise of records ingenuousness, records protection, data assurance, and secure data communication. The primary security issues in distributed computing situations include hazards of location, convalescence of information calamity, discovery, and prevention of insidious assaults [19]. Chen and Zhao [20] provided details about information sanctuary and fortification issues in the cloud-IoT integrated environment and described the distributed processing conditions which may affect fortification insurance, cloud safety, and information remoteness. Further, it can be said that the cloud-IoT integrated information safekeeping issues are primarily concerned with software as a service (SaaS), platform as a service (PaaS), and information as a service (IaaS) levels of operations. Supplementary, it can also be understood that the most challenging situation comes during performing information sharing in a distributed computing environment. The connections between information safekeeping and fortification issues in the cloud-IoT integrated distributive computing circumstances of different types of clouds are described in Fig. 7.1.

To guarantee infrastructure and communication securities certain more features like the cloud, users checklist, firewalls, network infrastructure security, access

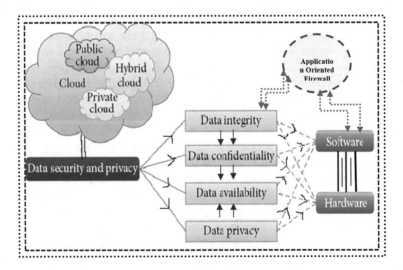

Fig. 7.1 Establishing relationship among protection and information security components in the cloud-IoT integrated distributive computing environment

control lists (ACLs), anti-DoS (Denial of Services), available customers' security policies, virtualization issues, far-off access facility, catastrophe recovery, mobile admittance platforms, and identity validation/authentication are be added in Fig. 7.1. The application-level security using software, hardware, and technical methods are provided in Fig. 7.1 for protecting the applications from possible external threats. The possibilities of access, steal, modify, and delete sensitive/secure data by intruders can be minimized with the help of application firewalls of Fig. 7.1.

The function of some other system components like PKIS (Public Key Infrastructure Systems), IAMS (Identity and Access Management systems), SIS (safety indication services), and other database applications affects the security concerns of the whole system while executing and administering different applications software in the cloud-IoT environment. Hence, high dependencies on these cloud-IoT systems can increase the security and complexity concerns exponentially. In the specific cases of security points like *input data validation, authenticity verifications, session management, security design of life cycle, error handling, data exchange/integration, Patching, and Anti-Malware Vulnerability,* we need to consider the anti-spam with application sandboxing approaches.

With the beginning of cloud-IoT technologies, the anthology and aggregation of network and accounting-related activities are simplified, but it may have increased efforts of security-providing teams who continuously need to scrutinize event log data information for impending threats. With the help of the Amazon Web Services (AWS) security hub, it is easily possible to prioritize and organize the security using Amazon Guard Duty services for detecting threats.

In this chapter, the authors have explained a pioneering and safe cloud-based service to further improve the performance of cloud-IoT integrated communication systems. Here, highly developed internet communication machinery (ICM) based on internet protocols and wireless distributive sensor networks (WDSN), detached framework structures (DFS), and distributive computations, are being used for uplifting the execution performance of cloud-IoT integrated information communication systems. The cloud-IoT integrated server of described intelligent road transport management and communication control system (IRTMCCS) will also be able to present entrée and control management method for numerous types of vehicles moving on the highways/roads and therefore the described IRTMCCS will be able to enhance the safety and security of passengers.

7.2   The Objectives and New Generation Challenges of Cloud-IoT Integrated Investigation Systems

The basic problem related to safety and protection in a cloud-IoT integrated distributive computing environment is described as of the biggest problems. It may become the basic cause for the users to resist the utilization of cloud-IoT integrated distributive computing advancements.

7.2.1   The Primary Objectives

The fundamental intention of this assessment is to realize the security-related dangers and be familiar with the appropriate security systems being used in the cloud-IoT integrated distributive computing environment. Most probably all of us are aware that in an open cloud structure we must have a foundation underlined with plentiful virtual intelligent machines. Many of the existing companies' associations use virtual machines for getting the secret information of their competitors.

7.2.2   Present Challenges

The cloud-IoT integrated distributive computing atmosphere addresses the forthcoming challenges of new generation cloud computing architectures. It also describes the issues related to cloud-IoT integrated application development platforms to take the benefits of the web-based distributive computing environment. Many issues related to security, protection, and efficient accesses of cloud-IoT infrastructure have so far not been addressed while the new challenges are raising their heads on a day-to-day basis. Quite a few of these new challenges are Web Data Management & Security (WDMS), Service Level Agreements (SLAs), Data/information indoctrination, and repositioning of existing virtual Machines [21, 22].

Furthermore, as per the opinion of the authors, we need to uncover the answers to basic questions which are associated with cloud-IoT-dependent data communication and security systems [23–25].

7.3   Admittance Control Mechanism of Cloud-IoT Services

The admittance control is a control access list that is arranged in an appropriate order to indicate that who can get the right of entry & what are the things which can be accessed by the authentic persons/machines/systems. Since, the cloud-IoT integrated distributive systems are used by various users, several enterprises, and non-homogeneous infrastructure. Therefore, new cloud-IoT-based safeties concerns appear in the cloud-IoT integrated distributive computing environment and these are related to information assertion, data/information ownership, data/information privacy, and Multi-tenancy.

The users have to use a variety of cloud safety policies to make the cloud-IoT integrated infrastructures secure. It can be said that in a cloud-IoT integrated environment, the things like computers, networks, and storage space are virtualized for maintaining safety and creating confusion about the location actual location of these devices in the mind of hackers. Figure 7.2 is showing the cloud-IoT integrated safety concerns which apply to all types of cloud-IoT-based distributive communication and internetworked security systems [26–28].

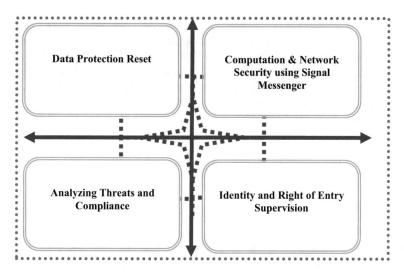

Fig. 7.2 The safety processes of cloud-IoT integrated computing systems

To describe the probable scenarios and test feasibilities of side-channeling-based attacks which may occur in the cloud-IoT integrated computing environment of Fig. 7.2, a multiparty case study was conducted by the University of California, San Diago (UCSD) and Massachusetts Institute of Technology (MIT). The following four flaws were traced during the case study by the researchers and these flaws can be used by intruders to carry out side-channel attacks in a cloud-IoT integrated computing environment:

Flaw 1: It is practically possible to trace out the physical infrastructure of a cloud-IoT integrated system where an instance of virtual machine (VM) resides.

Flaw 2: It is practically possible to find out if two or more VMs instances are residing on the same physical server or not.

Flaw 3: It is practically feasible to purposely create a virtual machine instance that will be located exactly on the same physical server where VMs instances of other users reside.

Flaw 4: It is potentially possible to leak information from one VM to another VM which resides on the same physical server.

With the help of Fig. 7.2, it is possible to provide computation and network security to the end-users using signal messenger LLC where signal messenger utilizes end-to-end encryption and state-of-the-art security for providing Internet-based video/audio calling, chatting using private messaging, and other types of services to the worldwide users. Here, the communication signal can't be decrypted in the path of communication because of using private key encryption. Hence, unauthorized content access of calls or messages is rarely possible. Further, the message history of communication is recorded on the users' own devices. Furthermore, the supplementary technological information of communication is stored on the specified servers using arbitrarily generated certification tokens, and keys which are essential for establishing calls, transmitting, and receiving messages between end-users. The signal may ascertain which particular contacts in the address book are users of the signal with the help of a service intended to look after the privacy of contacts. The contacts-related information/data of your device can be cryptographically hashed before transmission and it may be transmitted to the server for getting information about registered contacts.

7.3.1 Virtual Machine's Security

The currently existing virtual machines (VMs) can be protected by hardening them in the cloud-IoT integrated distributive computing environment. The hypervisor management system (HMS) can be another part that can be attacked by intruders. The VMs software will be able to prevent the HMS from intruder's attacks. The security of VMs can be provided by including two concepts namely VM's isolation and VM's hardening. If one of the VMs has been attacked by intruders and it has been compromised in the cloud-IoT integrated then that particular machine should be secluded from the remaining VMs to ensure that the attackers don't get remotely control over the other VMs or the other infrastructures. The hardening method is used for changing the evasion arrangement to achieve superior safety measures. The authors suggest that virtual machines can avoid denial of services types of attacks by restricting the resources by disabling unused functions and devices on virtual machines [29–32].

To secure VMs, the OS (operating system) and the safety software should be restructured / updated on regular basis. The applications running on virtual machines should also be updated on regular basis for providing a better quality of security. The distinctiveness management is another anxiety of security management in cloud-IoT integrated distributive systems because the public cloud infrastructure may have numerous users who are belonging to various organizations. So, it becomes difficult to ensure the authorization of these users in a cloud-IoT integrated distributive environment. The addition of multi-layer safety schemes like multifactor authenticity verification and multi-layer biometric authenticity verification may ensure that only approved users may enter into our system through specific login IDs and passwords [33, 34].

7.3.2 Various Operations and Governance of Services in Cloud-IoT Environment

Governance refers to the commanding rules, process, and policies of institution/ organization that illustrate the arrangements and interrelationships by which corporations are planned and managed. Each institution must have its security and regulation policies in a cloud-IoT integrated distributive computing environment e.g. the banking sector operates under its own set of governing rules to ensure that the top-secret data/information like online transaction passwords must not be compromised in any situation. Similarly, the electronic and mobile healthcare industries possess their own set of rules and regulations. In general, the organizations follow in-house and peripheral regulations of state governments and central government. In the cases of conventional data centers,' the IT (information technology) section of that corporation will have to take care of it. Further, in the case of a cloud-IoT integrated environment, the cloud service provider (CSP) with the institution's IT department needs to make sure that the institution's policies are implemented in a cloud-IoT integrated atmosphere [34].

At the present time, web-integrated computing processes can crate challenging situations in our day-to-day life. Some of these examples are: withdrawing and depositing money from an ATM of one bank whereas in an actual sense the money belongs to another bank. In these situations, the agreements between banks and countries play a very important role where inter-country and inter-continent rules need to be defined. The authors observe that the conformity requirements may include privacy and law of land; necessities of debit and credit card industries; and economic law coverage [35, 36].

It might be possible that the information about an accurate convincing point cannot be predicted in the cloud-IoT environment. In the dissimilar modern swarm computing systems, the endeavor knows correctly where the positions of their business statistics exist. In the web-based computing representations, the foremost cloud-IoT integrated inspection supplier may ranch out the ability to a third party, who may ranch out the curative process capabilities. This situation will turn out to be very difficult when the main cloud-IoT integrated service supplier doesn't eventually hold the information/data. Figure 7.3 and 7.4 illustrate the summary of cloud safe-keeping and cloud protection framework of cloud-IoT integrated distributed communication systems through special types of layers namely protract layer, network layer, internetworking layer, percept layer, and application layer [37–39].

7.4   Security Issues for Cloud-IoT Integrated Communication Systems and Servers

Web-based information processing is being used in diversified ventures and it is receiving a remarkable response from our rural and urban societies. The important components of cloud-IoT-based web processing include access framework, an exhaustive examination of existing things/information, speedy adaptability, and online booking of all types of tickets/hotels/doctor's appointments. The online requests are available for local administrations and other general public to access and evaluate the assets in the cloud-IoT integrated distributive computing environment. The local administration may get appropriate directions from higher

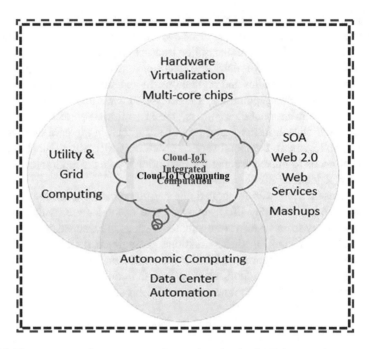

Fig. 7.3 The summary of governance and operations in cloud-IoT integrated communication networks

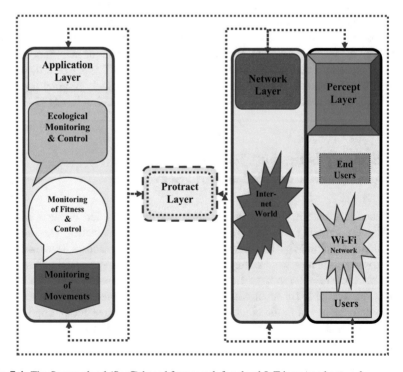

Fig. 7.4 The Secure cloud (SecC) based framework for cloud-IoT integrated networks

authorities to incorporate the government decisions and adequately utilize the manpower & other assets using a cloud-IoT-based environment in the welfare of human societies.

The most important building blocks which are regularly used in the distributive cloud computing environment are infrastructure as a service (IaaS), platform as a service (PaaS), and software as a service (SaaS). The IaaS will provide the framework for information/data preparing and system assets as per the requirements of cloud customers. The PaaS will provide a platform as per the interests of cloud customers for developing new programs / new software by using the libraries and instruments of expert organizations. Hence, the PaaS will strengthen the arrangement settings of programming/software development atmosphere creation for clients in the cloud-IoT-based environment. The SaaS will provide the products and applications as per the requests of the client in the cloud-IoT integrated environment and hence the expenses of programming and other software purchase can be minimized. The association and arrangement of the cloud-IoT integrated computing model are presented in Fig. 7.5 [40, 41].

The cloud-IoT integrated computing systems are getting further better recognition in the industry and research world but the securities of these systems have always been a worrying point of concern. As per the reports of National Institute of Standard Technology (NIST), USA, any cloud computing environment is made up of five types of organizational model namely Public, Protected, Private, community, and Hybrid clouds where community cloud model is free of cost

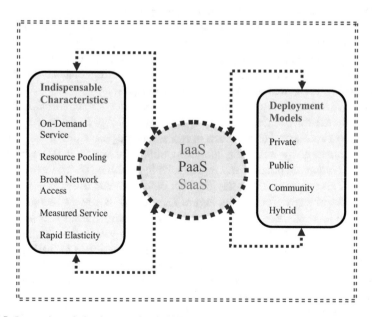

Fig. 7.5 Interaction of cloud-computing building blocks with other components in a distributed environment

accessible by the overall community of internet world. The private cloud provides personal space saved to numerous customers' associations for performing storage and computation-related tasks individually after paying the usage and storage costs [8, 40, and 41].

7.4.1 Security Concerns of Cloud-IoT Server Communications in IRTMCCS

Nearly all cloud users are not conscious of the risk factors associated with the storage and transmission of confidential data/information in a public environment. Thus, the major technical constraints e.g. intelligibility, multi-ownership, information security, attack speed, privacy, cryptography, agreement, and reliability should be addressed cautiously. Hence, it can be said that the clients are not safe from Internet-generated threats and this may necessitate a suitable and safe cloud-IoT integrated mechanism to review and manage the existing cloud and other communication technologies developments periodically. To access the data/information of highly secured cloud-IoT integrated servers, it is most important that every client/regulator in the cloud computing network is safe and aware of types of forthcoming threats. In the denial of service (DoS) attacks [12] one or many machines attack a sufferer machine in a cloud-IoT integrated environment and attempt to stop the sufferer machine from performing functional tasks. In general terms, it can be said that the DoS attacks can be traced by a thorough analysis of the behavior of sufferer's communication networks. The most successful defenses against distributed denial of services (DDoS) and DoS attacks is that the DDoS and DoS should regularly filter routers, immobilize IP address transmissions, implement security patches and render inoperative services that execute intrusion uncovering related tasks in distributed cloud-IoT integrated computing environment [42].

Figure 7.6 describes four key processes namely *induction, interaction, intervention*, and *search* for each client to recognize and test separately in the cloud-IoT integrated environment. Here, *induction* represents the procedure of understanding the main intention by analyzing the surroundings in which it is positioned. In Fig. 7.6, the *induction* procedure is represented by variable 'Z'. The *search* conception in fig. 7.6 is represented as the identifier called 'C' and it represents the search process of the objective finding. In. Figure 7.6, 'A' and 'B' are the recognized interaction identifiers and these identifiers are just representing the answers to agitations or queries raised by the analysts during intrusion analysis in the distributed communication network e.g. the internet control message protocol (ICMP) tracks and responds the corresponding route related operations. Lastly, it can be said that the intervention is the process followed by analysts who reproduce a few resources and services that are required by the objective to perform a specific operation. This procedure may help the network analysts to discover some tremendous levels at which

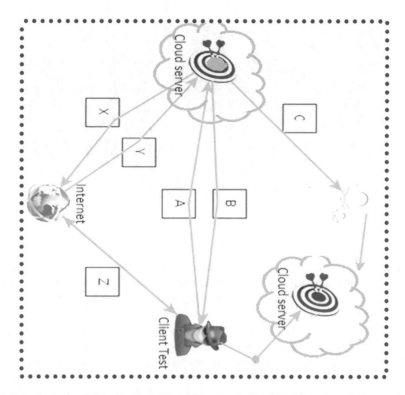

Fig. 7.6 The interaction mechanism of four key processes in intelligent road transport communication control and management system

the target could still operate and these tremendous levels are represented by variables 'X', 'Y' & 'Z' in Fig. 7.6. Multi-ownership is an important cloud-IoT network security-related problem where the exterior attacks are significantly augmented because of the co-location of several virtual machines to a particular server.

7.4.2 Probable Architecture of Safe Cloud-IoT-Based Communication Model

In today's age of 5G communication networks, the economic capability of almost every country is rising at a remarkable rate. The persons in almost all parts of this earth have their vehicles like motorbikes, scooters, and luxurious cars to travel. Few of them consider cars and other luxurious vehicles as their status symbol whereas others consider the vehicles as a transportation-related necessity of their life. Many times we find that a huge number of cars and other vehicles are crawling on the roads in metro cities of developing and advanced countries. On the other side, vehicle accidents are rapidly increasing in our day-to-day life and a lot of persons in our

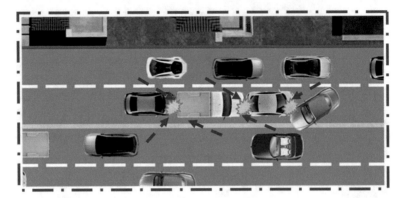

Fig. 7.7 The conventional transportation system without using a cloud-IoT integrated consultative control system

world are being killed in a fraction of seconds in road accidents. Figure 7.7 is representing a model of road accidents that are occurring in the present era of conventional transportation systems without using a cloud-IoT integrated consultative control system.

To reduce the collisions of vehicles described in Fig. 7.7, the authors described an authentication appliance for the vehicular network which will work in a cloud-IoT integrated communication environment and it is presented in Fig. 7.8. Figure 7.8 shows that the deployment of Bluetooth / Wi-Fi module associated with other types of equipment and interfaces can transmit required information and pictures to the specialists within the predefined time to the coordinating processor and, in this way, the lives of several folks trapped in serious episodes of accidents can be saved. The projected cloud-IoT topology of Fig. 7.8 can be introduced within each vehicle to provide information about accidents to concerned authorities including nearby hospitals, police stations, and relatives of persons caught in an accident. This type of advanced cloud-IoT integrated distributed computing-based transport communication and control framework will be tremendously precious to prevent deaths during vehicular accidents on roads of cities, highways, and streets.

7.4.3   Secure Cloud-IoT Integrated Test Setup Model

The system model of safe cloud-IoT integrated testing for testifying the cloud-IoT dependent communication frame structure is presented in Fig. 7.8 where the consumer executes reliable cloud-IoT topology to perform his / her needful tasks. The test setup display of the cloud-IoT server provides the interface between client-cloud-interaction and coordinates with important business norms. It utilizes leveled approach which is dependent on key usefulness and versatility in the connection totaling. There are two types of associations between interior and all other kinds of appropriation switches which are described in Fig. 7.8. The VLANs (virtual local

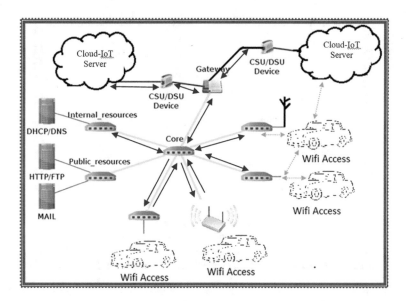

Fig. 7.8 The structural design of a secure cloud-IoT integrated transport communication system

area networks) are being used in the wireless networks of the described cloud-IoT server-based transport communication model. The implementation of VLANs in the described IRTMCCS shows that the described system can assist the passengers or driver of the vehicles in getting help from nearby available hospitals, police stations, and relatives (in specific cases) through an automatic response and control system. To provide flawlessness-related confidence to the vehicle passengers, the important transport convention (ITP) server has been used in the described system as a server and hence a passenger/driver can communicate with the nearby helping centers through the available gadgets from the place of accident.

Further, the virtual LANs planned in the focal control switch and the ITP server transmits blinking updates to the concerned authorities which can promise that the concerned persons are getting indispensable information through the available gadgets inside the vehicle and virtual LAN. These types of communication systems enclose an amendment digit which can reveal to the concerned authorities that how many times the persons of accidental vehicles have tried to communicate with emergency service provider agencies for getting immediate help. The true association between the control center of IRTMCCS and each vehicle are designed by providing VLAN based traffic control and management system where every association can underpin the neighboring virtual LAN to allow the means of transportation to tag a lesser amount of virtual LAN traffic between various units of the IRTMCCS [7, 12, 42].

The relationship of transportation-related information/data transfer between a variety of vehicles/clients of the described cloud-IoT-based IRTMCCS framework are presented in Fig. 7.9. In Fig. 7.9, the system address elucidation (SAE), internet control message protocol (ICMP), Enhanced Internal Gateway Routing Protocol

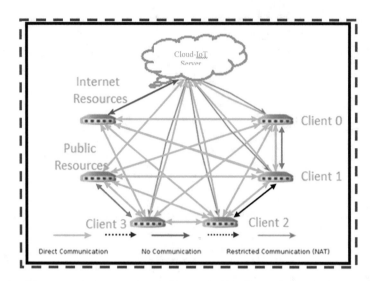

Fig. 7.9 The Communication components are used for providing interaction between cloud-IoT integrated servers and clients in a distributive computing environment

(EIGRP) are being used to perform the steering between virtual LANs which can help the vehicle drivers in preventing accidents in dense population area and accident-prone area. Furthermore, the residential areas or accident-prone areas can be protected from unusual accidents by sending special messages like *"Dense Population Here: Drive Slow"* and *"Accident Prone Area: Drive Slow"* to the drivers of vehicles in described cloud-IoT integrated IRTMCCS. In Fig. 7.9, the communication components like cloud-IoT integrated server, internet resources, and specific public resources are being used for providing communication between clients (drivers/passengers of vehicles) and IRTMCCS. In an actual sense, each one of these components can be linked to a diversified testing environment in the cloud-IoT integrated computing atmosphere. This type of rigorous testing of IRTMCCS may provide improved performance while its implementation and installation in the real-time environment [43, 44]. The cloud components communication arrangement of Figs. 7.8 and 7.9 uses computerized control signals for providing a large range of communication between vehicles and control systems.

7.4.4   Performance Analysis and Result Comparison of Described Cloud-IoT Integrated IRTMCCS with Other Systems

The cloud-IoT based infrastructure and the corresponding linked smart vehicles pretense noteworthy safety challenges that have to be addressed to persuade the acceptance of secure cloud-based IRTMCCS *(Intelligent Road Transport*

Management and Communication Control System) integrated technologies and the associated services. These challenges of IRTMCCS include privacy & localization, certification, validation, mobility, steadfastness, stumpy error patience, and resolving the conflict of interests. The secure cloud-based IRTMCCS needs to have very efficient end-to-end contact between its users and reliable validation of all participating entities to guarantee the legitimacy of exchanged messages in the cloud-IoT-based distributed computing environment. This type of action permits a vehicle to move forward with high self-assurance for a received message which may direct the need to thwart camouflaged and other types of spoofing attacks. In certain cases where continuous attacks take place, the strapping message certification and authenticity mechanisms may act as forensic proof for the intention of pursuing lawful proceedings.

A variety of cloud-IoT-based vehicular networks and their applications executions depend on precise localization schemes. Thus, it becomes very imperative to attain well-organized and consistent authenticity verification of all participating components of secure cloud-based IRTMCCS to guarantee the high-level accuracy of interchanged messages. The vital communications between the components of IRTMCCS based vehicular applications engage greatly reliable and mostly accessible real-time communications which are provided in the described IRTMCCS. It was observed in the experiments that most of the vehicular networks and their applications are self-organized. After considering security issues and the attachment of human lives it becomes important that the vehicular networks and their applications must avoid malevolent and other types of online/offline attacks on an immediate basis for the reason that, prevention is always better than cure. Hence, if the malicious attacks have already brought the vehicle into an accidental state then it cannot be reverted to normal condition effortlessly.

The researchers and inventors of smart road transportation system (SRTS) related fields have received a lot of attention from the research community in the previous few years [43–46]. The extraordinary challenges of intelligent transport communication systems are being currently considered as a societal obstruction to the universal acceptance of SRTS. The basic objective of developing SRTS technology was to further improve road safety, passengers' safety, and traffic efficiency. But, several cloud-IoT-based threats can severely affect the working of SRTS because of its dependency on wireless communication systems, and hence it may lead to road accidents. The main threats/attacks which may influence the intelligent transportation system (ITS) with their counteractions are provided in Fig. 7.10 [47, 48].

The malicious attackers may attempt to contravene the security of IRTMCCS. These highly sensitive attackers can be categorized into several categories. The categories of threats and the equivalent remedial actions taken by the projected IRTMCCS are presented in Table 7.1. The performance evaluation of described cloud-IoT based IRTMCCS with other existing *road traffic accident preclusion systems (RTAPS)* in the terms of accessible features and uniqueness is presented in Table 7.2. The result analysis of Table 7.2 shows that the described cloud-IoT-based IRTMCCS gives hopeful performance and it includes almost all

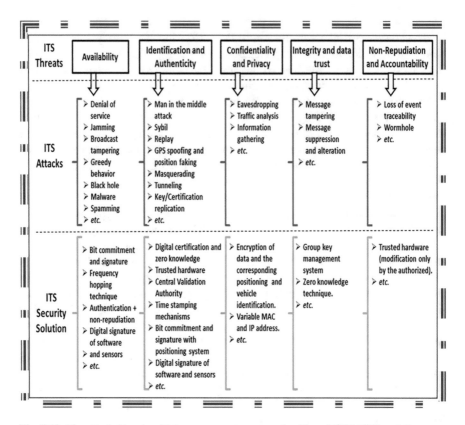

Fig. 7.10 The attacks/threats which may occur to secure cloud-based IRTMCCS and the corresponding countermeasures

the important features which are mandatory for an answerable, trustworthy, and unblemished RTAPS.

7.4.5   *Executing the Results of Described IRTMCCS*

The Metasploit tool is a precious deployment and limitation testing tool which can help in separating the saturation testing workflow into smaller units of supplementary manageable tasks. The researchers of cloud computing specializations can control the power of the Metasploit framework with the help of available features. The Metasploit tool helps us in automating the process of in-depth deployment of cloud networks. Further, the Metasploit tool provides the required tools to the users/specialists for performing manual testing of penetration test cases in the cloud-IoT integrated distributed computing environment. The cloud computing researchers can use the Metasploit tool to scan the unlocked ports and services of

Table 7.1 Categorization of attacks/threats and the types of actions taken by secure cloud-IoT based IRTMCCS ('Y': Yes, and 'N': No)

S. No.	Threats Categories	Refutation of Services	Revelation	Manipulation	Information Hiding	Respond
1.	Natural disaster related threats	Y	N	N	N	N
2.	Accidental disclosure related threats	N	Y	N	N	N
3.	Errors related to configuration	Y	Y	Y	N	N
4.	Creation of electrical disturbances	Y	N	Y	N	Y
5.	Electrical interruption related threats	Y	N	N	N	N
6.	Fire related threats	Y	N	N	N	N
7.	Hardware failure related threats	Y	N	Y	N	Y
8.	Liquid leakage related threats	Y	N	N	N	N
9.	Threat related to user/ operator error	Y	Y	Y	Y	N
10.	Threats related to software error	Y	Y	Y	Y	Y
11.	Telecommunication interruption related threats	Y	N	Y	N	Y
12.	Data alteration related threats	Y	Y	Y	Y	Y
13.	Software alteration related threats	Y	Y	Y	Y	Y
14.	Bomb related threats	Y	N	N	N	N
15.	Employee sabotage related threats	Y	N	Y	N	N
16.	Enemy overrun related threats	Y	Y	Y	N	N
17.	Fraudulent related threats	N	N	Y	Y	Y
18.	Threats related to consumption of resources	Y	N	N	N	N
19.	Terrorism related threats	Y	Y	Y	N	N
20.	Threats related to theft	Y	Y	Y	N	N
21.	Unauthorized use related threats	Y	Y	Y	Y	Y
22.	Threats related to vandalism	Y	Y	Y	N	N

Table 7.2 Available features based performance of described IRTMCCS ('Y': Yes, and 'N': No)

	Available Features								
Algorithm / Method Name	Accessibility of Video cameras	Availability of Parallel Processing	Availability of GPS dependent mishap site searching	GPS integrated adjoining police station for phone tracing	GPS integrated nearby hospital searching and their phone number tracing	Availability of driver's family members phones in the database	Voice-based alert generation & reminder call availability	Transmission of Video images & voice signals to nearby police stations	transmission of video images & voice signals to relatives of the vehicle driver
1. NGM for Future Internet & IoT [49]	Y	N	Y	N	N	N	N	N	N
2. IPTMS [50]	Y	N	Y	N	N	N	N	N	N
3. ADS [51]	Y	N	Y	Y	Y	N	N	N	N
4. ITS for Smart Cities [52]	Y	N	Y	N	N	N	N	N	N
5. ADTRS [53]	Y	N	Y	N	N	N	N	N	N
6. Internet of Vehicles for Safe Driving [54]	Y	N	Y	N	N	N	N	N	N
7. Traffic Accidents Analyzer [55]	Y	N	Y	N	Y	N	N	N	N

8.	RAPV Ad-Hoc Networks [56]	Y	N	Y	Y	Y	Y	N	N	N	N
9.	ITIS [57]	Y	N	Y	Y	N	N	N	N	N	N
10.	ADRS [58]	Y	N	Y	Y	N	N	N	N	N	N
11.	Cloud-Based AADMS [59]	Y	N	Y	Y	Y	Y	N	N	N	N
12.	Geo-Based MVNs [60]	Y	N	Y	Y	N	N	N	N	N	N
13.	Accident Prevention Using VANET [61]	Y	N	Y	Y	N	N	N	N	N	N
14.	*Described secure cloud-based IRTMCCS*	Y	Y	Y	Y	Y	Y	Y	Y	Y	Y

cloud-IoT-based computing networks; The Metasploit tool can generate detailed reports of test results by utilizing the vulnerabilities and gathered pieces of evidence.

The Metasploit tool's version Pro is being considered as a multi-user collabora- tive tool that can help us in the allocation of tasks/information to other group mem- bers of any dispersal testing group in the cloud-IoT integrated computing atmosphere. To perform the diffusion testing-related tasks in a cloud-IoT integrated environ- ment, the team members will be able to distribute the host's data with each other, scrutinize the collected evidence, and create host notes to dispense wakefulness about a particular or any target. The Metasploit tool was initially used by cloud-IoT researchers for the objective of basic data/information gathering in the execution proving environment.

The experimental results obtained from the Metasploit tool are assembled in the form of reports. But, these reports may have surplus data that may not be fully uti- lized for evaluation and analysis purposes in the experimentation work. The authors performed the testing and result analysis of IRTMCCS in a self-created cloud-IoT integrated test set-up environment where customers were permitted to employ dis- similar types of operating systems (OS) for interacting with each other and servers. The outcomes obtained during testing, and result analysis of the described IRTMCCS corresponding to client-client interaction, client-server interaction, and server- server interaction concerning used operating systems are offered in Fig. 7.11 [12, 42, and 62]. The results of Fig. 7.11 show that the hosts of four operating systems namely Cisco IOS, Microsoft Windows, Netgear Embedded OS, and an unknown OS were able to communicate with each other in the IRTMCCS based cloud com- puting environment where Cisco IOS used the highest number of hosts and Microsoft Windows OS used the highest number of services.

The CDPs (Cisco Discovery Packets)-Snarf is a network sniffer tool and it was utterly written for smelling out information from the CDP packets. It is a Linux- dependent package that can be used for selecting the data of connected gadgets in the system and can sniff CDPs. The CDP-Snarf can provide almost every type of

Discovered Operating Systems		
Operating System	Hosts	Services
Cisco IOS	6	16
Microsoft Windows	3	34
Netgear embedded	4	5
Unknown	1	1

Fig. 7.11 The interaction details of IRTMCCS in the created test set-up environment

information through a command *"show CDP neighbors detail"*. This particular command can be executed on each type of Cisco router. The CDP-Snarf can be straightforwardly tested with the IPV4 (internet protocol version 4) and IPV6 in the cloud-IoT integrated distributive computing environment. The data/information which can be displayed using CDP-Snarf in the distributive cloud computing surroundings are: Software version, CDP Version, Time intervals between CDP address, Source MAC address (media access control address), Device ID, Checksum, Platform, Port ID, Read packets from packet capture (PCAP) dump files, Save packets in PCAP dump file format, and Debugging information. Fig. 7.12 is presenting a snapshot where the described IRTMCCS is interacting with the network gateway successfully to provide communication between patrons. The corresponding source address, platform, protocol type, and port ID for conducted experiments are also shown in Fig. 7.12. The CGE.pl is a package of purl which works efficiently in a Linux-based cloud computing environment. This package can perhaps overload the ports of system gadgets and therefore thinks of them as unusable connection points.

Figure 7.13 describes the activities of specific adventures that have been performed in the cloud-IoT integrated described communication framework using

Fig. 7.12 The outputs obtained from CDPSnarf experiments.

Fig. 7.13 The maximum load efficiency testing of described cloud-IoT integrated communication networks using CGE.pl packet

CGE.pl devices [12, 27, and 42]. The results of Fig. 7.13 show that the described system can check the status of target servers. Further, the IRTMCCS is capable to send videos/data packets of large sizes starting from 100 KiloBytes (KB) to 1 Gigabyte (GB) can be transmitted through the communication systems described IRTMCCS in the cloud and IoT based environment. The Zenmap is an innovative probing apparatus that can be used for creating an interactive graphical map (IGM) of the network. The IGM can be used for inspection and identification of errors in networked systems. The Fern WiFi Cracker is customized equipment that can use additional bundles of characters, digits, and special symbols to crack the passwords from far-off passageways by using distinct strategies like lexicon documents.

As per the obtained experimental reports, version 2.0 (v2.0) of SNMP (Simple Network Management Protocol) is susceptible to exploitation. Hence, it can be effortlessly wrecked if we use it in cloud-IoT integrated distributive communications. In this way, the gadgets associated with network channels that are being utilized by the SNMP can be accessed by other unknown customers including intruders. Therefore, the session users SNMP v2 may face privacy problems while using the cloud networks because any skillful network robber can control the arrange setups of SNMP v2 by getting specialized SNMP certifications and can originate denial of services related assaults [12, 62–64].

A supplementary but essential viewpoint to be considered for security enhancement of cloud-IoT integrated computing system would be the inclusion of an expanded version of CDPs into the system. In every anomalous condition, the master/ruffian can indisputably decide on the open ports and the special functionalities of the gadgets using the data/information included in these bundles can prevent unauthorized use of available ports of gadgets. Further, the authors observed that the programming parts of Cisco gadgets are promoted on the CDPs. Therefore, the intelligent internetwork robbers can explore the adventures which are representing the impressions of the cloud system interconnection framework. To oppose this type of dent, the authors advise for crippling of CDPs reports on all of the Cisco gadgets. To maintain the accessibility after intruders attacks, the authors recommend the use of directing conventions e.g. the fringe portal informing convention (FPIC) can keep up many doors available in the cloud-IoT integrated communication environment without thinking whether one of the existing doors is blocked or not.

The Zenmap tool is a marvelous data/information gathering tool that may be used by cloud-IoT researchers to bring together a colossal sum of data/information about the objective system. Although, the Zenmap tool is not a highly intelligent apparatus for system testing and it can efficiently identify partial topology charts, working framework fingerprints, and open ports in a cloud-IoT integrated environment [65–68].

7.5 Conclusions

This chapter presents the innovative security and privacy-related developments of cutting-edge cloud-IoT integrated distributive computing technologies. In terms of positive developments, the cloud-IoT integrated computing environments provide safety, security, and privacy to private cloud, public cloud, protected cloud, community cloud, and hybrid cloud customers. The cloud-IoT integrated servers of described IRTMCCS are certainly providing access and control mechanisms for several types of vehicles on roads/highways and the described IRTMCCS is supportive in further improving the safety and physical security of drivers/passengers. The safety and services of cloud-IoT integrated IRTMCCS can be used in a real-time environment for optimizing accident and death rates. The significance of cloud-IoT integrated IRTMCCS is that the drivers and passengers of vehicles can get guidelines regarding routes related information and they can approach the nearby medical health centers and police stations in emergencies. Further, the described IRTMCCS provides synchronization between securities-related dangers and the connecting countermeasures. But, still, the described IRTMCCS has more focus on identifying and jamming dangers instead of hiding crucial system resources from intruders/hackers. Finally, it can be truly stated that cloud-IoT-based distributive computing organizations have a reduced amount of openness in comparison to others. Hence, there is always a chance of security and safety-related dispute occurrences between the executives of the corporate framework.

References

1. Albeshri A Caelli W (2010) Mutual protection in a cloud computing environment, 12th IEEE international conference on high-performance computing and communications (HPCC), pp. 641–646
2. Sedigh A, Radhakrishnan K, Campbell CE-A, Singh D (2014) Trust Evaluation of the Current Security Measures Against Key Network Attacks. MAGNT Res Report 2(4):161–171
3. Alger D (June 2005) Build the best data Center Facility for Your Business. Cisco Press Book, Indianapolis, USA
4. Buyya R, Yeo CS, Venugopal S (2008) Market-oriented cloud computing: vision, hype, and reality for delivering IT services as computing utilities, In Proceedings of the 10th IEEE international conference on high-performance computing and communications (HPCC 2008, IEEE CS Press, Los Alamitos, CA, USA), Dalian, China, September 25-27, pp. 1–9
5. Khodadadi F, Calheiros RN, Buyya R (2015) A data-centric framework for development and deployment of internet of things applications in clouds, Proceedings of the 10th IEEE international conference on intelligent sensors, sensor networks and information processing (ISSNIP 2015), Singapore, April 7–9, pp. 1–6
6. Van Bon J, Van Der Veen A (2007) Foundations of IT service management based on ITIL, vol 3. Van Haren Publishing, Zaltbommel
7. Miller M (2008) Cloud computing: web-based applications that change the way you work and collaborate online. Que Publication
8. Mell P, Grance T (2009) The NIST definition of cloud computing, version 15, National Institute of Standards and Technology (NIST), Information Technology Laboratory, pp. 1–3. Online Available On: www.csrc.nist.gov, Last Accessed On 21 July 2017
9. Khalid U, Ghafoor A, Irum M, Awais Shibli M (2013) Cloud-based secure and privacy enhanced authentication and authorization protocol. Procedia Comp Sci 22:680–688
10. Plummer DC, Smith D, Bittman TJ, Cearley DW, Cappuccio DJ, Scott D, Kumar R, Robertson B (2009) Gartner highlights five attributes of cloud computing. Gartner Report G00167182:1–5
11. Singh I, Rai R, Murarker S (2015) Password authentication in cloud. Int J Eng Res Appl 9, No. 2 (Part – I):56–59
12. Singh I, Mishra KN, Alberti A, Singh D, Jara A (2015) A novel privacy and security network for the cloud network services, 17th IEEE International Conference On Advanced Communication Technology, pp. 355–359
13. Mahmood Z., "Data location and security issues in cloud computing", proceedings of the 2nd IEEE international conference on emerging intelligent data and web technologies (EIDWT '11), 49–54, 2011
14. Sun D., Chang G., Sun L., Wang X. (2011) Surveying and analyzing security, privacy and trust issues in cloud computing environments, Proceedings of the International Conference on Advanced in Control Engineering and Information Science (CEIS '11, pp. 1–5)
15. Pandey A, Tugnayat RM, Tiwari AK (2013) Data security framework for cloud computing networks. Int J Comp Eng Technol 4(1):178–181
16. Klein DA (2013) Data security for digital data storage, U.S. Patent Application 14/022,095,
17. Younis MYA, Kifayat K (2013) Secure cloud computing for critical infrastructure: a survey. UK Liverpool John Moores University
18. Kardaş S, Çelik S, Bingöl MA, Levi A 2013 A new security and privacy framework for RFID in cloud computing, Proceedings of the 5th IEEE international conference on cloud computing technology and science (CloudCom '13), pp. 1–5
19. Behl A (2011) Emerging security challenges in cloud computing: an insight to cloud security challenges and their mitigation, Proceedings of the World Congress on Information and Communication Technologies (WICT '11), pp. 1–5
20. Chen D., Zhao H. (2012) Data security and privacy protection issues in cloud computing, Proceeding of the international conference on computer science and electronics engineering (ICCSEE '12), pp. 1–5

21. Wijaya C (2011) Performance analysis of dynamic routing protocol EIGRP and OSPF in IPv4 and IPv6 network, First International Conference on Informatics and Computational Intelligence (ICI), pp. 355–360
22. Handley M, Rescorla E (2006) Internet denial-of-service considerations, Internet Engineering Task Force, Tech. Rep, pp. 1–38
23. Hogan M, Liu F, Sokol A, Tong J (2011) NIST cloud computing standards roadmap – version 1.0, Natl. Inst Stand Technol Spec Pub:1–83
24. Almulla S, Chon YY 2010 Cloud computing security management, 2nd international conference on engineering systems management and its applications, pp.1–7
25. Tan Y, Sengupta S, Subbalakshmi KP (2011) Analysis of coordinated denial-of-service attacks in IEEE 802.22 networks, Selected Areas in Communications. IEEE J 29(4):890–902
26. http://searchsecurity.techtarget.com/definition/authentication-**author**ization-and-accounting. Last Accessed On: 5 May 2017
27. Ahmed I, James A, Singh D (2013) Critical analysis of counter mode with cipher blockchain message authentication mode protocol—CCMP. Secur Commun Netw 7(2):293–308
28. Hogan M, Liu F, Sokol A, Tong J (2011) NIST cloud computing standards roadmap – version 1.0, Natl. Inst Stand Technol Spec Publ 500–291:1–63
29. Ahuja R (2011) SLA based scheduler for cloud storage and computational services, International conference on computational science and applications (ICCSA), pp.258–262
30. Albeshri A, Caelli W (2010) Mutual protection in a cloud computing environment, 12th IEEE International Conference on High-performance Computing and Communications (HPCC), pp. 641–646
31. Bellare M, Kohno T, Namprempre C (2002) Authenticated encryption in SSH: provably fixing the SSH binary packet protocol. In: Altari V, Jajodia S, Sandhu R (eds) Proceedings of 9th annual conference on computer and communications security – CCS 2002, held 18–22 November 2002 in Washington, USA. ACM Publication, New York, pp 1–11
32. Bellare M, Kilian J, Rogaway P (2001) The security of the cipher block chaining message authentication code. J Comp Syst Sci 61(3):362–399
33. http://cloudcomputing.sys-con.com/node/612375/print Accessed on 5 May 2016
34. Alger D (June 2005) Build the best data Center Facility for Your Business. Cisco Press, Indianapolis, USA
35. Alani MM (2010) Testing randomness of block-ciphers using diehard test. Int J Comp Sci Netw Secur 10(4):53–57
36. Whiting D, Housley R, Ferguson N (2017) AES encryption & authentication using CTR Mode & CBC-MAC. http://csrc.nist.gov/groups/ST/toolkit/BCM/current_modes.html#03 (Online available 6 May 2017)
37. Chadwick DW, Fatema K (2012) A privacy-preserving authorization system for the cloud. J Comput Syst Sci 78(5):1359–1373
38. Saldhana A, Marian R, Barbir A, Jabbar SA (2014) OASIS cloud authorization (CloudAuthZ). Int J Multimedia Ubiquitous Eng 9(9):81–90
39. Whiting D, Housley R, Ferguson N AES encryption & authentication using CTR mode & CBC-MAC" http://csrc.nist.gov/groups/ST/toolkit/BCM/current_modes.html#03. Online available 6 May 2017
40. Whiting D, Housley R, Ferguson N (2017) AES encryption & authentication using CTR mode & CBC-MAC http://csrc.nist.gov/groups/ST/toolkit/BCM/current_modes.html#03. Online available On 6 May 2017
41. NIST Publication 2001 Statistical Test Suite for Random and Pseudorandom Number Generators for Cryptographic Applications. http://csrc.nist.gov/publications/nistpubs/800-22/sp-800-22-051501.pdf. Online available 6 May 2017
42. Caballero J, Yin H, Liang Z, Song D (2007) Polyglot: automatic extraction of protocol message format using dynamic binary analysis. In: Ning P (ed) Proceedings of the 14th ACM conference on computer and communications security - CCS 2007, held 28–31 October 2007 in whistler, Canada. ACM Publication, New York, pp 317–329

43. Pietro RD, Guarino S, Verde N, Domingo-Ferrer J (2014) Security in wireless ad-hoc networks—a survey. Comput Commun 51:1–20
44. Mejri MN, Ben-Othman J, Hamdi M (2014) Survey on VANET security challenges and possible cryptographic solutions. Vehicular Commun 1(2):53–66
45. Engoulou RG, Bellaiche M, Pierre S, Quintero A (2014) VANET security surveys. Comput Commun 44:1–13
46. Petit J, Shladover S (2015) Potential cyber-attacks on automated vehicles. IEEE Trans Intell Transp Syst 16:546–556
47. Kaveh B, Kelarestaghi MF, Heaslip K, Gerdes R (2019) Intelligent transportation system security: Impact-oriented risk assessment of vehicle networks. IEEE Intelligent Transportation Systems Magazine, pp. 1–14
48. Hamida EB, Noura H, Znaidi W (2015) Security of cooperative intelligent transport systems: standards threats analysis and cryptographic countermeasures. Electronics 4:380–423
49. Alberti MA, Singh D (2014) Developing a Nova genesis architecture model for service oriented future internet and IoT: an advanced transportation system scenario. IEEE world forum on internet of things 2014, Seoul, Korea, pp. 6–8
50. Bhayya G., Raghava Rao K (2015) Intelligent public transport management system using embedded technologies. National conference on advancements in embedded systems and sensor networks, pp. 189–193
51. James A (2013) Accident detection and reporting system using GPS, GRS, & GSM technology. A seminar report of Amal Jyoti College of Engineering, pp:1–21
52. Balasubramaniam A, Paul A, Hong W-H, Seo HC, Kim JH (2017) Comparative analysis of intelligent transportation systems for sustainable environment in smart cities. MDPI J Sustain 9:1–12
53. Ramya Keerthi C, Shanmukh G, Sivaram R (2013) Various accident detection technologies and recovery systems with victim analysis. Int J Adv Trends Comp Sci Eng 2(3):7–12
54. Singh D, Singh M (2015) Internet of vehicles for smart and safe driving. IEEE International Conference on Connected Vehicles and Expo pp. 328–329
55. Abdullah E, Emam A (2015) Traffic accidents analyzer using big data. IEEE Int Conf on CSCI:392–397
56. Gokulakrishnan G (2015) Road accident prevention with instant emergency warning message dissemination in vehicular Ad-Hoc network. PLoS ONE J 10(2):1–36
57. Hasan Omar Al-Sakran (2015) Intelligent traffic information system based on the integration of the internet of things and agent technology. Int J Adv Comp Sci Appl 6(2):37–43
58. Md. Amin S, Jalil J, Reaz MBI (2012) Accident detection and reporting system. Proceedings of International Conference on Informatics Electronics and Vision, pp. 640–643
59. autam R, Choudhary S, Surbhi IK, Bhusry M (2015) Cloud-based automatic accident detection and vehicle management. 2nd Int. Conf on Science Technology and Management:341–352
60. Wang S, Yan Z, Geng G, Zhang Y (2016) Geo-based content naming and forwarding mechanism for vehicular networking over CCN. Int J Int Technol Secured Transact 6(4):291–301
61. Khandelwal SA, Abhale AB, Nagraj U (2014) Accident prevention and air pollution control using VANET under cloud environment. Proceedings of 3rd International Conference on Recent Trends in Engineering & Technology, pp. 900–804
62. Black, J., Rogaway, P. "A suggestion for Handling Arbitrary-Length Messages with the CBC-MAC". In Bellare, M. (Ed.) Proceedings of 20th Annual International Conference of Advances in Cryptology – CRYPTO (2000) Lecture notes in computer science 1880, held 20–24 august 2000 in Santa Barbara, USA. Springer, Berlin, pp 197–215
63. Rogaway, P. and Black, J. "A Block-Cipher Mode of Operation for Parallelizable Message Authentication". In Knudsen, L. R. (Ed.) Proceedings of the International Conference on Theory and Applications of Cryptographic Techniques, Advances in Cryptology - EUROCRYPT (2002) Lecture notes in computer science 2332, held 28 April −2 may 2002 in Amsterdam, Holland. Springer, Berlin, pp 384–397

64. Robert AE, Manivasagam G, Sasirekha N, Hemalatha M (2011) Reverse engineering for malicious code behaviour analysis using virtual security patching. Int J Comp Appl 26(4):41–45
65. Johnson DH (1999) The insignificance of statistical significance testing. J Wildl Manag 63(3):763–772
66. Mishra KN et al. (2023) Supervising communication activities in Smart City societies using sheltered cloud based validation and access control approach, Personal Ubi Comp J, pp. 1–24
67. Mishra KN (2020) Supervising data transmission services using secure cloud-based validation and admittance control mechanism, Springer Book on Internet of Things(IoT) - Concepts and Applications, pp. 1–23
68. Mishra KN (2020) A novel integration of smart vehicles and secure clouds for supervising vehicle accidents on roads/highways. Sadhana Proc Eng Sci 45:1–21

Chapter 8
Life Quality Improvement in Smart City Societies Using Cloud–IoT and Deep Machine Learning (CIDML) Technologies

Abstract While the definition of a smart city is still evolving in the current era of the twenty-first century, a few things have become very clear that the use of information and communication technologies (ICT) can enhance service levels, citizen well-being, sustainability, and eco-friendly economic developments. Hence, the life quality of smart city societies can be further improved where the people can live a stress-less life. But, it is another unfortunate truth that the urban population is growing rapidly at an enormous speed. This rapid growth of population in urban cities may lead to the exponential increase of pressure in the day-to-day life of urban people. Therefore, there is a serious need of thinking about developing smart cities and the corresponding societies where technologies will assist the people of urban societies in improving the quality of life by providing a stress-less and eco-friendly working and living environment.

In this article, the authors have described the hardware, software, and other technological requirements needed for developing a smart city and the corresponding society. The intellectuals and technocrats have more responsibility to contribute towards the development of better and further advanced technologies that can enhance the life quality of smart city societies. In this chapter, the authors have described how we can use cloud-IoT and intelligent machine learning technologies to improve the overall life quality of smart cities and the corresponding societies using cloud-IoT integrated machine learning technologies. We have taken certain basic facilities like traffic management, accident prevention, accident death minimization, city crowd management, stadium crowd management, vehicle parking management, video surveillance, and waste management activities of smart city societies. Further, the authors have tried to find how these mentioned things can be managed and controlled using cloud-IoT integrated technologies.

Keywords Cloud-IoT Technologies · Crowd Control System · Eco-friendly Environment · Machine Learning · Road Traffic Management · Smart City Societies · Vehicle Accident Prevention · Video Surveillance · Waste Processing System

8.1   Introduction

Improving the urban life quality needs the improvement in five things namely improving public safety, making daily commutes faster, better public health, cleaner, and appropriately sustainable environments, and enhance social connectedness. These are the first five basic requirements for life quality improvement in any smart city [1]. Without fulfilling these criteria no city can be called a "Smart City". Without public safety, no one can call any city the smart city. The people residing in a smart city must always feel safe and secure [2, 3]. As far as security is concerned, we cannot even tolerate a minor threat to the general public. To prevent these threats and dangers we require the installation of 24x7 cloud-IoT and AI (artificial intelligence) integrated video cameras based monitoring system at all the sensitive points and corners in the city. To improve the life quality in a smart city, we need to improve the means of transport and the traffic management systems, because in a fast-moving world one cannot like to wait in traffic jams and chaotic situations. To avoid any such event, we need better and efficient traffic management and control systems that would be connected to the cameras placed at important places all over the city to provide route-related guidance for commuters [4, 5].

Better public health facility is achievable in any smart city within a short duration due to the technological advancements in the field of medical science and research and hence the increased social awareness about any spreading disease in the general public can be provided at a very high speed. In a smart city, it is expected that every person is to be connected and to the outside world either physically or through audiovisual digital technologies and gazettes [6]. A cleaner and appropriately sustainable environment is primarily needed for the people of any smart city and it is doable through creating environment cleanness awareness programs and conducting physical activities for reducing pollution, managing our daily wastes efficiently, and cutting down the aspects which may harm nature. The life of the people of metro cities is very much hectic [7]. Almost every time these people are busy doing business and piling up money. They don't know when to stop running behind money and their whole life is spoiled in just spending time doing business and piling up money. So, usually, they don't find enough time for social activities. Hence, there is an urgent and immediate requirement for enhancement in the social connectedness of the people of smart city societies. The deep machine learning (DML) based approaches can be used to compute the daily and overall money / other requirements of a person of a smart city [8, 9]. Further, the people of smart cities should be encouraged to stop running behind materialistic things after a certain limit using DML approaches. Social connectedness may play a vital role in improving the mental health of smart city societies. To enhance social connectedness, we must provide social connections to the smart city people through various cultural and life improvement awareness programs. The imagination of a smart city without 24x7 health connectedness, transport connectedness, and video surveillance of all sensitive places are impossible. Before further enhancing the quality of life in smart cities, we need to ensure that the basic components of a smart city are

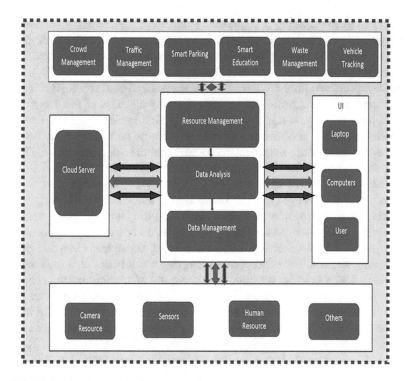

Fig. 8.1 The basic things required to be upgraded in smart city society

properly functioning. The basic things required to be upgraded in a smart city are presented in Fig. 8.1 [10, 11].

8.2   Theoretical Foundations

Increased urbanization is putting a strain on the limited shared urban resources, for example, road space, energy, clean air, and water. Smart cities leverage technology to manage such shared resources more efficiently, thereby improving citizens' quality of life. This chapter introduces and discusses technical challenges in managing city-scale resource infrastructures and potential solutions. We frame the discussion within the Sense-Analyze-Actuate paradigm, a model leveraged by most smart city solutions [12, 13]. The Sense step entails gathering data from existing or newly deployed dedicated sensors, owned by public agencies and businesses, as well as contributed by citizens. In the analysis step, these disparate and often unreliable sources of data are fused to further improve the authenticity of data (improving reliability, detection, confidence, and reducing ambiguity) as well as extending its spatial and temporal coverage. In this step, optimization techniques, and artificial intelligence in particular, allow to reason on the data, making resource management decisions in a centralized or decentralized approach. In the Actuate step, the results of the analysis can be presented to human operators, i.e., visualized for decision support, or used to directly actuate the changes, adapted to the specific urban resource [14, 15].

In the most recent fifteen to twenty years, the perception of the smart city society has become too much well-liked in approximately all areas of this earth, and in general, the citizens have started searching the ground-breaking ways of developing smart city societies. The research articles and reports on smart city societies'life improvements have been exponentially increased in the last few decades. The general tendency about publishing investigable articles associated with smart city societies and its indexing in customary databases like DBLP and Scopus has become a passion in the present age [16–18]. The discovery and classification of foundation elements in smart city society development are dreadfully important for the researchers to realize that how various components of metro / urban city areas recommend nonconventional EDI (electronic data interchange) dependent electronic services and communications. The concept of a smart city was introduced at the time when the entire world was under pressure for coming out of the most horrible economic disaster and the countries desired the help and collaboration of each other for the objective of their survival. At the starting of the twenty-first century, IBM initiated the concept of the smarter planet where smart communication and interface between various components of smart cities were planned. Further, by the start of 2009, the thought of a smart planet became very popular in the whole world [19–21].

The proposal of becoming a smart city was initially proposed by European countries because their cities started becoming compactly populated. Hence, they started giving a stronger focus on low-carbon emissions and sustainability. Nowadays, the climate is varying significantly because of global warming. Thus, significant thinking on the development of eco-friendly communication systems is needed in the present era of innovative technology developments. The swift increase in population and resource collapse are some other areas of concern for which a lot of planning and efforts are required [22, 23].

Currently, with the help of the internet and cloud-IoT technology, it is becoming easily achievable for everybody to learn whenever and wherever he/she wants and it doesn't necessitate the viewer's presence at any specific time. Therefore, it can be said that cloud-IoT Technologies help the customers and the manufacturers (both) in the current era. Today, there is an urgent need for a long-term method of developing sustainable cities by appropriately supervising the lifecycles of smart cities. The introduction of healthy competition in terms of online services like education, waste management, safety, healthcare, and transportation management systems, etc. may further enhance the quality of life in smart cities [24, 25]. The initial success of Cloud-IoT deployments in smart city society-related applications will depend on the availability of test-beds of desired scales and its suitability for the validation of most recent research outcomes. It is observed by the researchers that most of the accessible test-beds of smart cities usually offer a limited testing environment which may work up-to to a very small area of particular cases of deployments [26, 27].

8.3   Objectives of Life Quality Improvements in Smart Societies

The objectives of life quality improvement in smart city societies are described as follow:

Objective 1: Making the governance and infrastructure development of smart city activities citizen-friendly and cost-effective.

Objective 2: Reduce congestion on roads, air pollution, and resource depletion, boost the local economy, promote interactions, ensure security, giving an identity to the city based on its main economic activity, such as local cuisine, health, education, arts, and craft, culture, sports goods, furniture, hosiery, textile, and dairy, etc.

Objective 3: Providing proper surveillance and traffic/crowd management technologies for the city to function without any breakdowns.

Objective 4: The rate of migration from rural to urban areas is increasing across the world day by day. By 2050, around 70% of the people will be living in cities and India will not be an exception in this regard. So, there is an emerging need for the cities to be smarter in terms of basic infrastructure development, and tackle the issues related to large-scale urbanization.

Objective 5: Smart cities should have a dynamic and lucrative environment. So, the infrastructure and other developments should be environmentally friendly.

8.4   Smart City Life Quality Improvement Related Problems

The concept of a '*smart city*' might become an icon of a new digitally facilitated form of living in urban cities. In this chapter, the authors cover the wide aspects of solving the basic needs of the community in a smart city. To improve the quality of life in smart city societies following problems are to be addressed appropriately:

1.1 *Problem of Surveillance*

The cameras positioned all around the smart city give us access to all the sensitive areas, roads, transportation systems, and important buildings within the periphery of the city and provides us a complete physical view of the city. The updated views of the smart city received through various interconnected video cameras and their corresponding analysis through available machine learning tools may be very much useful for providing 24×7 surveillance. Further, the received analysis reports may also be useful for sending alerts and triggers as and when required [28, 29].

1.2 *The problem of In-City Crowd and Traffic Management*

In a smart city, we cannot afford to have a situation where the crowd is out-of-hands and starts creating a situation where proper functioning of all other components of the city is disturbed. Hence, a *smart video surveillance and intelligence input* (SVSII) based crowd management system is needed for a smart city society. Traffic management and control is a common major concern for all the emerging smart cities of the globe. The described *SVSII* should direct the people to go through the less crowded route and it should assist the law enforcement agencies in controlling the crowd [30].

1.3 *The problem of Stadium Crowd Management*

These days entering into a stadium and getting a seat inside the stadium is as tough as playing the game. Further, getting out of the stadium is equally difficult and can create a ruckus. Therefore, entering into a stadium and coming out of the stadium if once the event is over needs to be managed and controlled using cloud-IoT integrated machine learning approaches for tracking an object where the allocated seat in the stadium may be considered as the object [31].

1.4 *The Problem of Vehicle Tracking*

The theft of two / three / four / six-wheeled vehicles is a major concern of smart city society where the people's vehicles are being theft by the thieves at one place and are being sold at another place. It is an incredible challenge to recover the vehicle where we need to minimize the time difference between the start and completion of the investigation process. Sometimes, we may need to track vehicle's customers for deliveries and regular services. The cloud-IoT integrated distributive machine learning technologies may be useful for solving vehicle tracking, vehicle deliveries, and regular servicing of vehicles related problems [32].

1.5 *The Problem of Accident Prevention / Detection*

In a smart city, we need to provide medical facilities on an urgent basis on a phone call. Vehicle accidents may abruptly occur and are the serious concerns of smart city societies where immediate medical help is needed to save the life. A little delay in providing medical help to the accident-affected persons may result in loss of life. Unfortunately, more than 1.6 million people lose their life on this earth during accidents every year because of the non-availability of in-time medical facilities. Vehicle accidents can be prevented by providing accident-related information/warnings to the drivers and passengers during the travel and before arriving in the accident-prone areas [33].

1.6 *Smart Parking Problem*

Finding a parking slot in a marketplace is a very typical, tiring, and time-consuming activity. Thus, we need an automated cloud-IoT integrated system smart parking system to get information and guidance about the availability of parking places. The system is expected to help the vehicle drivers in searching a parking place and should guide while the driver is parking his/her vehicle at the parking place [34].

1.7 *Digital Library Access Related Problem*

Rather than having a library with fixed seating capacity, the smart cities require a much more efficient and modern digital library where the library users have access to almost all the books of the world through a mouse click. Further, the digital library should provide searching of books/ magazines/ newspapers/journal articles through various types of keywords and phrases.

The digital library should accommodate a huge number of public logins at any time [35].

1.8 *The Problem of Live Monitoring of Hospital Services*

In a smart city, we mainly focus on reducing the consumption of time taken to complete a given task like visiting a doctor, making an appointment with a doctor for diagnosis or surgery. To improve the quality of life in the smart city we need to enhance the medical facility and monitoring of hospital services provided in the city. For this purpose, we need an appropriate hospital service live monitoring system for vacant beds, equipment, medicines, doctors, nurses, and other medical staff members. The hospital information and management system may also provide information about the availability of a particular medicine in the medical store and its exact location in the store [35].

1.9 *Smart Transportation Management and Control System Related Problem*

Travelling and transportation is another major component of a smart city. The people of smart cities should be provided appropriate information about the availability of public transport and the people should be updated about the latest changes in the smart city transport services such as bus routes, bus timing, train routes, trains timings, and metro trains related information [36].

1.10 *The Problem of Smart Education and Smart Governance*

Education is the basic right for each person of any society including smart city societies. A very famous slogan said about the value of education in ancient India is as follow:

"A king is worshipped in his country".
Whereas, *"A knowledgeable or a person with wisdom is worshipped everywhere".*

To educate our next generation, we need to have good schools. Good schools should include three things namely good infrastructures in the schools, honest teachers with high moral values, and an unbiased system to run the school. The students should be asked to follow up on the guidelines of the school and the offline/online study materials should be provided to the students for their holistic development. In a smart city, people should be motivated towards a paperless working environment [37].

1.11 *The Problem of Waste Management*

Any city cannot be called a smart city unless it has an appropriate plan for the management of wastes within the city. An appropriate wastes management plan should be provided to the residents of the smart city where different types of wastes should be collected from different parts of the smart city using various means of transport. Finally, the overall wastes of the smart city societies should be forwarded to the waste-treatment plants. The outputs of the waste-treatment plants may be further useful for plants and trees of smart cities. The specific wastes that cannot be used by waste-treatment plants may be disposed of in much smarter and safer ways. The waste-management plants should follow the guidelines of green computing [38, 39].

The overall problems of a smart city and its connectedness can be represented by Fig. 8.2 [40, 41].

8.5   Described Work Model

In this chapter, the authors have described eleven problems related to smart city societies. The major problems of smart cities like smart transportation and traffic surveillance, accident detection, death prevention, smart parking, waste management, and smart garbage collection/disposal and the corresponding feasible solutions of smart city model-based approaches are discussed in this section.

The responsibility of the common medium is incredibly crucial in achieving smart city-related goals. The presently existing communication and transportation services that are being regularly utilized in smart city infrastructure developments are namely 4G, ZigBee, Long-term evolution (LTE), cable television, Wireless fidelity (Wi-Fi), satellite-based communication systems, and worldwide interoperability for microwave access (WiMAX).

The presented described architectural model of Fig. 8.3 may help the smart city societies in their day-to-day activities by repeatedly sending time-to-time alarming messages and warnings to remember and recall the daily life-related tasks. The described system may work as an intelligent platform that is equipped with deep machine learning techniques for the persons living in smart city societies. After combining data obtained from different domains of smart cities, it can be said that

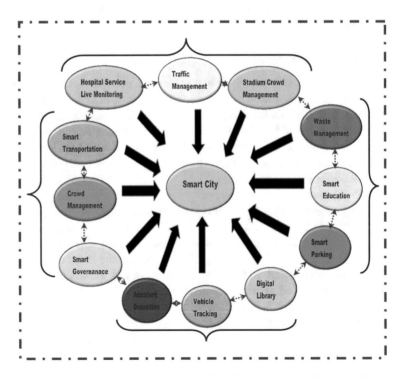

Fig. 8.2 Diagrammatical representation of overall problems of a smart city and their connected components [40–43]

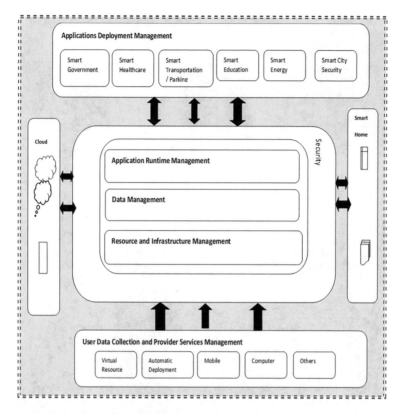

Fig. 8.3 The described architectural model for improving life quality in smart cities using Cloud-IoT and Deep Machine Learning Technologies [37–40]

the described architectural model of Fig. 8.3 will assist the smart city societies in managing their day-to-day activities in an intelligent way e.g. the smart fridge may send alerts and warnings for purchasing household food-related items, the smart television, may send information related to its recharge dates and channels to be subscribed for the next coming months.

The described architectural model of Fig. 8.3 may assist the drivers in selecting another route in traffic jams-like situations. It may automatically alert the heart disease /chronically ill patients about their oxygen level, and heart bit rates (if it crosses significantly over a threshold value) while the patients perform their day-to-day duties. In this model (Fig. 8.3), the unprocessed data will be collected and processed to make it internet responsive then only the data will be forwarded for vagueness and effectiveness checking. Similar types of intelligent machine learning techniques can also be useful in unfolding the customized services that can provide 24 × 7 feedback reports to the smart city societies in the form of various types of specific warnings and alerts.

Figure 8.4 describes the energy consumption and management of the smart city societies as demonstrated by the Toshiba group of Japan [35, 36]. Few additional

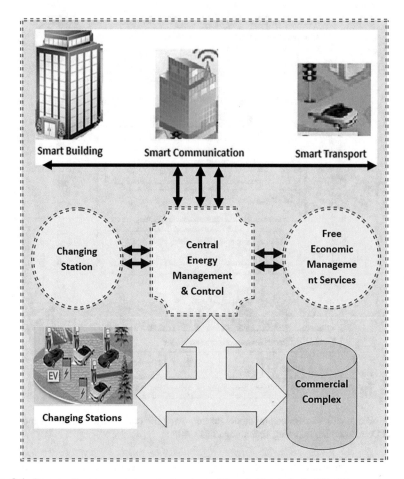

Fig. 8.4 Community energy management system of Smart cities in India [39, 40]

groups like the Hitachi group in Japan have also been dynamically working in the vicinity of human care where eco-friendly smart cities will have very low carbon production.

8.5.1 Traffic Surveillance in Smart City Societies

The camera-related methodology used in the smart city for crowd management, traffic management, accident detection can be outlined providing the following key features:

Key Feature 1: Providing Camera (Tag and calibrate cameras for installation locations, set calibration parameters and other usage pattern information)

Key Feature 2: Camera Discovery (Discover and register internet protocol (IP) cameras on specified IP blocks. Registered cameras automatically participate in the analytics activities)

Key Feature 3: Recording of Events (Record and manage segmented camera footage for preview or later review purpose)

Key Feature 4: Analytics (Perform analytics on the live/recorded camera streams. Latency-sensitive analytics are performed on the Edge while others are on the cloud)

Key Feature 5: Triggers and Alerts (Manage triggers on analytics data and respond with actions on triggered alerts.)

Key Feature 6: Smart Upload and Archive (Trans-code and upload only critical data to the cloud-IoT integrated distributive system for archival or further offline analysis.)

Key Feature 7: Statistical Computations (Perform statistical computations for planning/monitoring purposes based on data analysis.)

Key Point 8: Provide Data through User Interface (Present analyzed data of smart city and the corresponding societies to the end-users, administrators, and city planners.)

The traffic and video surveillance of various activities about the happenings in a smart city can be expressed by the following Fig. 8.5 and the complete flowchart of video camera-related activities is presented in Fig. 8.6. Crowd management and

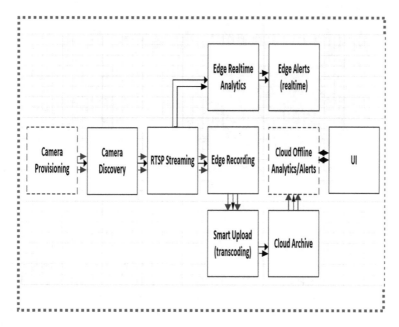

Fig. 8.5 Representing traffic and video surveillance of various activities about the happenings in a smart city

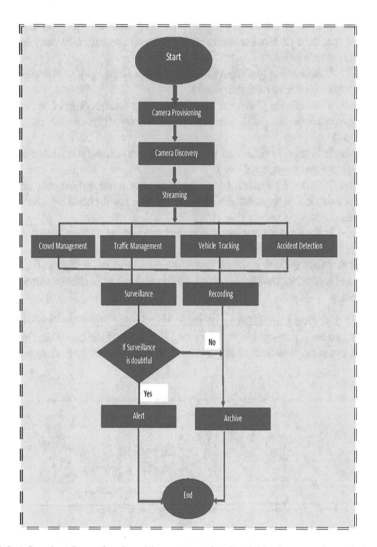

Fig. 8.6 A flowchart for performing video camera-related activities in smart city societies using the Deep Machine Learning Approaches

control-related activities can be divided into two types namely crowd management, and crowd monitoring. The crowd management activities can be performed using IP Cameras and cloud-IoT technologies in a distributive environment. The crowd monitoring activities can further be divided into three categories namely crowd counting, crowd localization, and crowd behavior analysis. Soft computing techniques like fuzzy logic can be useful for counting crowds. But, for analyzing the behavior of the crowd we may use video cameras based on intelligent machine learning techniques. The competent authorities may take appropriate decisions to prevent further damages in the specific case based on outcomes of intelligent machine learning

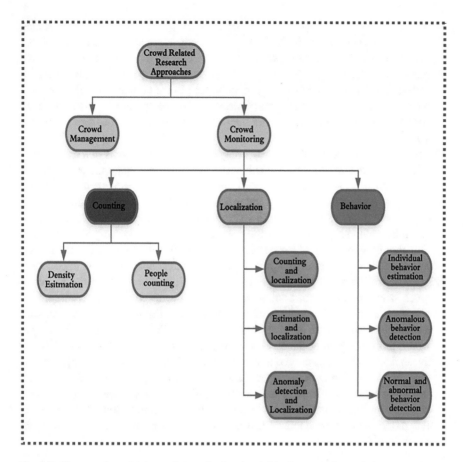

Fig. 8.7 The crowd monitoring and control-related activities in smart city societies

techniques which have been used for behavior analysis of crowd in a smart city. The crowd monitoring and management-related approaches are presented in Fig. 8.7.

8.5.2   Accident Detection and Death Prevention in Smart City Societies

The objective of described methodology for accident detection and death prevention is to provide rapid support to any accident location in the cloud-IoT integrated distributive environment using modern audio-visual technology. In any smart city, several types of sensors may be placed all around the vehicles to monitor the activities. These sensors are connected to smart communication and monitoring devices in the cloud-IoT integrated distributive environment. Some of the sensors which can be used in vehicles of smart city are as follow:

Acceleration Sensors: These sensors are used to record the force at impact. Hence, it will be possible to know the average force experienced in the case of an accident situation. In specific cases if the accelerometer sensors reading exceeds a certain limit then an automatic alert may be generated by the accident prevention system and an automatic message may be sent to the concerned authorities like nearby police stations, nearby hospitals, and relatives of the people seating in the vehicle and hence the deaths in the accidents can be prevented using acceleration sensors.

Pressure Sensors: The pressure sensors may be fixed in the chassis of a car and they will provide detailed information about the pressure applied on the chassis of the car in case of accident occurrence. We may use soft computing techniques to get the average pressure applied on the sensors in case of a major accident through experimental analysis of pressure sensors data. So, whenever any vehicle in the city meets with an accident then the pressure sensor provides very clear information about the intensity of the accident and the corresponding alert will be raised by the accident detection and prevention system available in the vehicle.

Microphones: The Microphones would be placed in vehicles to confirm the occurrence with the help of unusual noise generated during the accident. The microphones placed in the vehicle would sense the intensity level of noise generated during the occurrence of accidents and its machine learning-based analysis would help in knowing the level of damages which may have happened during the accident. Thus, based on outputs of machine learning analysis an appropriate amount of alerts may be generated and forwarded to the concerned authorities including relatives of concerned persons seating in the vehicle, police stations, and nearby hospitals. The accident detection and prevention in a cloud-IoT Integrated distributive environment can be represented by the flowchart of the following Fig. 8.8.

8.5.3   Solving Parking Problems of Smart City Societies Using Sensors and ML Techniques

Following steps and approaches may be useful To solve the parking problems of smart city societies:

Step 1: Install pressure sensors for recording the presence of any car at a given parking spot in all the parking places within the city.

Step 2: Record the sensors' data of the parking places to know whether a particular parking place is empty or occupied and use machine learning and soft computing techniques for the analysis of obtained results.

Step 3: If the parking slot in a parking place is empty then the car driver will be provided the exact map of the parking along with the mark of empty and occupied parking slots.

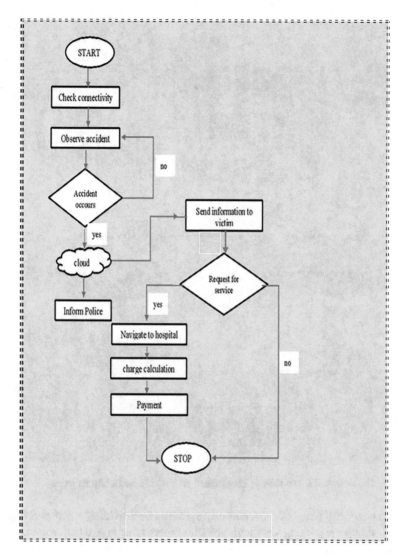

Fig. 8.8 The flowchart for accident detection and death prevention and cloud-IoT integrated distributive environment using intelligent machine learning techniques

Step 4: If the output of step 3 is 'Yes' then the driver may decide about a parking slot to be picked for parking the vehicle and further record the time of arrival and the time of exit.

Step 5: Compute the total time for parking and then calculate the total parking charges using machine learning techniques (The parking charges may vary according to the traffic rush situations and timings).

The above five steps can be described by the flowchart of Fig. 8.9 from which we can get complete information about the availability / non-availability of parking

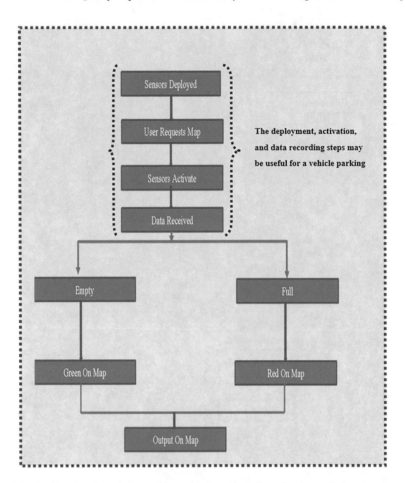

Fig. 8.9 The flowchart for solving parking-related problems in smart city societies

slots in a parking place of the smart city system. For providing smart parking, we need to set up the parking slots with pressure sensors that give us information as to whether a parking spot is empty or occupied. In this case, we need to make it sure that the sensors are working appropriately and enough parking slots have been covered for the parking of vehicles of smart society people. Further, the authorities must ensure that the parking slots are recognized by the deployed pressure sensors.

8.5.4 Waste Management and Garbage Collection in Smart City Societies

The waste management in any smart city is done through implementing a planned garbage collection procedure where citizens of the smart societies will have complete information where, when, and which type of wastes/garbage should be kept.

The wastes may be categorized into basic two categories biological wastes and non-biological wastes where each of these may further be categorized in dry wastes and wet wastes. The special waste collection points all around the smart city may be provided to the citizens for collecting biodegradable-dry, biodegradable wet, non-biodegradable-dry, and non-biodegradable-wet wastes. A separate collection point may be provided for each of the four types of wastes. Further, the dustbins of each type of waste will be attached with sensors to indicate the level of waste available in the dustbins. The level of wastes may be either low or medium or full. Furthermore, the waste collection agencies may be informed through the alert messages through the cloud-IoT integrated distributive system about the status of dustbins in a particular part of the smart city, and accordingly, they may fix up their routes of waste collection. Finally, the wastes will be disposed of in the dumping yards for recycling and producing biomaterial products.

In the waste management process of smart cities, the tanks in which the wastes are being collected needs to be immediately drained out as soon as it reaches the danger level i.e. Just before the overflow condition. Hence, we need to place sensors on the garbage collection tanks which will inform us about the filling level of the tank and will send us alerts as soon as the tank reaches close to the *tank full level*. In this case, we need to keep the sensors connected to garbage tanks always in good condition to get precise and correct data about the status of tanks.

8.5.5 *Implementation Details*

In the case of traffic surveillance, the users get an overview of the traffic conditions of the areas for which they requested. Hence, it becomes easy for them to make decisions and judgments based on the analytics. The deep machine learning-based techniques will be useful for analyzing decisions about traffic routes in the smart city. But, in this case, we need proper connectivity throughout the city using IP Cameras, and the maintenance of these cameras on the regular basis will also be needed to execute the requests of users without any failure. Further, in the case of any accident detection, the use of different types of sensors will help to analyze the probable happenings of accidents. If an accident occurred at a place then with the help of traffic management and control system it could be possible to know the intensity. Further, it could be possible to send information to the concerned authorities and departments including nearby hospitals and police stations using cloud-IoT integrated distributive traffic management and accident prevention system. Here, the authorities of smart cities need to ensure that the sensors used in vehicles are appropriately configured and are calibrated to send precise data about the accident happenings as and when needed.

The initial registration window of described life quality improvement system using the CIDML technique may look like Fig. 8.10 where an independent button

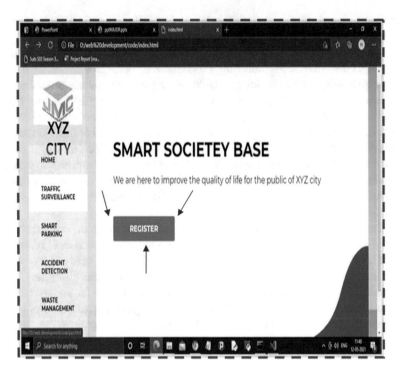

Fig. 8.10 The initial registration window of smart city life quality improvement software

like *traffic surveillance button*, *smart parking button*, and *waste management buttons*, etc. will be provided to the users and authorities of smart city society. With the help of these buttons, the users and authorities of a smart city may execute their tasks related to the management and control of a smart society.

For the traffic surveillance part, we need to perform video footage analytics using machine learning approaches. The machine learning approach of video surveillance is to implement machines using Python and OpenCV libraries. The obtained sample videos can be segmented into frames. The deep machine learning-based analysis may provide clear information about any movements of vehicles and suspicious objects. Further, the two consecutive frames can be differentiated in terms of pixels. So, to remove the non-moving items in the video footage frames the pixels-based differentiation method may be used. The noise removal from the obtained video may help in improving the analysis results. After getting the outlines of the moving vehicles we may start comparing and analyzing the vehicles in a particular zone using a contour-based approach to achieve the pre-defined objectives. Fig. 8.11 is representing a frame (frame number 13) of video footage of vehicles, and Fig. 8.12 is representing another frame (frame number 14) of video footage of vehicles in the daytime.

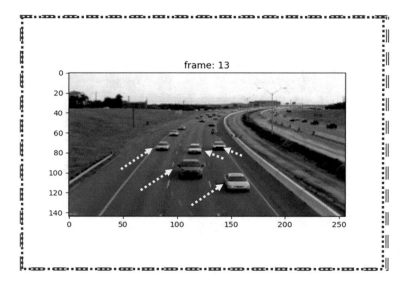

Fig. 8.11 A frame of video footage of vehicles

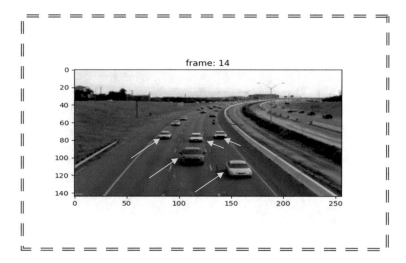

Fig. 8.12 Another frame of video footage of vehicles

Fig. 8.13 is representing a frame of video footage of vehicles in the night, and Fig. 8.14 is representing the BW (black & white) image of a video footage frame of vehicles obtained in the night. After playing and analyzing the videos using deep

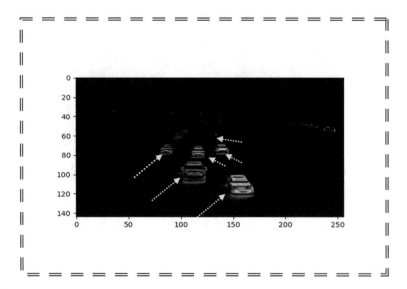

Fig. 8.13 A frame of video footage of vehicles in the night

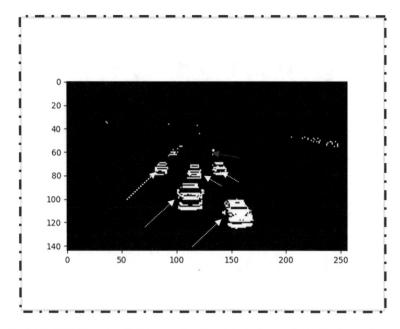

Fig. 8.14 The BW (black & white) image of a video footage frame of vehicles obtained in a night

machine learning approaches in the cloud-IoT integrated environment, the obtained best results are presented in Fig. 8.15. The Fig. 8.15 shows that the vehicles coming across a specific point are being tracked by the system.

Fig. 8.15 The vehicles traced by video surveillance system after coming across a specific point in a cloud-IoT integrated environment

8.6 Conclusions

The cloud-IoT integrated smart city development agenda entails improving the citizens' quality of life, strengthening, and diversifying the economy while prioritizing environmental sustainability through the adoption of smart technological solutions. This article recommends using cloud-IoT integrated machine learning techniques to identify and collect data required for proper management of the city including the future development plans of the city. Any smart city requires actual and appropriate data sets for managing the smart city societies. The use of intelligent machine learning techniques for policymaking and taking community-related decisions may further enhance the performance of smart cities and the corresponding societies. The authors believe that this article will help to improve the overall life quality of smart city societies by taking the help of cloud-IoT, and intelligent machine learning technologies in managing the day-to-day life to execute tasks and thoughtful planning.

References

1. Allwinkle S, Cruickshank P (2011) Creating smarter cities: an overview. J Urban Technol 18(2):1305–1453
2. Baqir MN, Kathawala Y (2004) Ba for knowledge cities: a futuristic technology model. J Knowl Manag 8(5):83–95
3. Caragliu A, del BoC NP (2011) Smart cities in Europe. J Urban Technol 18(2):65–82

4. Chourabi H, Nam T, Walker S, Gil-Garcia JR, Mellouli S, Nahon K, Scholl HJ (2012) Understanding smart cities: an integrative framework in system science. HICSS 2012, 45th Hawaii international conference, IEEE, pp. 2289-2297
5. Cocchia A (2014) Smart and digital city: a systematic literature review. In: Dameri RP, Sabroux C (eds) Smart city: how to create public and economic value with high technology in urban space. Springer International Publishing, Switzerland, pp 13–43
6. Marinova D, Philimore J (2003) Models of innovation. In: Shavinina LV (ed) The international handbook on innovation. Elsevier, pp 44–53
7. Schuler D (2002) Digital cities and digital citizens. In: Tanabe M, van den Besselaar P, Ishida T (eds) Digital cities ii: computational and sociological approaches. Springer, Berlin Heidelberg, pp 71–85
8. Harrison C, Eckman B, Hamilton R, Hartswick P, Kalagnanam J, Paraszczak J, Williams P (2010) Foundations for smarter cities. IBM J Res Develop 54(4):350–365
9. Yoshihito Y, Sato Y, Hirasawa A, Takahashi S, Yamamoto M (2012) Hitachi's vision of the Smart City. Hitachi Rev 61(3):111–118
10. Faisal R (2012) Spamming the internet of things: a possibility and It's probable solution. The 9th international conference on Mobile web information systems. Procedia CompSci 10:658–665
11. Anthopoulos L, Fitsilis P (2009) From online to ubiquitous cities: the technical transformation of virtual communities. In A. B. Sideridis & C. Z. Patrikakis (Eds.), Next generation society: technological and legal issues. Proceedings of the third international conference, eDemocracy, Athens, Greece, 26: pp. 360-372
12. Borja J (2007) Counterpoint: intelligent cities and innovative cities. Universitat Oberta de Catalunya (UOC) papers. E-J Knowl Soc 5:1–12
13. Edvinsson L (2006) Aspects of the city as a knowledge tool. J Knowl Manag 10(5):6–13
14. Klein C, Kaefer G (2008) From smart homes to smart cities: opportunities and challenges from an industrial perspective. In: Proceedings of the 8th international conference, NEW2AN and 1st Russian conference on smart spaces, ruSMART 2008. St. Petersburg, Russia, pp 260–270
15. Jennings P (2010) Managing the risks of smarter planet solutions. IBM J Res Dev 54(4):1–9
16. Moser MA (2001) What is smart about the smart communities movement?. Elect J, 10(1): pp. 1–11. Available Online at http://www.ucalgary.ca/ejournal/archive/v10-11/v10-11n1Moser-print.html. Last Accessed On: July 15, 2021
17. Smart Cities Final Report - European smart cities http://www.smart-cities.eu/download/smart_cities_final_report.pdf, Last Accessed On: 01.06.2021
18. UT_Smart_Model_FINAL.pdf https://static1.squarespace.com/static/5527ba84e4b09a3d0e 89e14d/t/55aebffce4b0f8960472ef49/1437515772651/UT_Smart_Model_FINAL.pdf, Last Accessed On: 01.04.2021
19. Smart City Architecture and its Applications Based on IoT http://www.sciencedirect.com/science/article/pii/S1877050915009229, Last Accessed On 27.05.2017
20. Stanford/ Yonsei Universities – Towards A Smart City Framework: is-db.stanford.edu/evnts/7239/Jung_Hoon_Lee_final.pdf, Last Accessed On: 16 July 2021
21. Connected Smart Cities Network (EU): projects.cavi.au.dk domain
22. Smart City Information Architecture and Functional Platform: http://www.epic-cities.eu/sites/default/files/documents/D3.2%20Smart%20City%20Info%20Architecture.pdf, Last Accessed On 15.04.2021
23. Smart Cities in India - ENVIS Centre on Renewable Energy and http://terienvis.nic.in/WriteReadData/links/Smart%20Cities%20in%20India_Report_pagewise-5937837909069130880.pdf, Last Accessed On: 21.05.2021
24. Smart Cities Final Report - European smart cities http://www.smart-cities.eu/download/smart_cities_final_report.pdf, Last Accessed On 01.06.202021
25. Smart city research highlights- VTT. http://www.vtt.fi/inf/pdf/researchhighlights/2015/R12.pdf, Last Accessed On 01.06.2021

26. Yousif A, Farouk M, Bashir MB (2015) A cloud-based framework for platform as a service. In: Cloud computing (ICCC), international conference on, Riyadh, pp 1–5

27. Alam AFB, Soltanian A, Yangui S, Salahuddin MA, Glitho R, Elbiaze H (2016) A cloud platform-as-a-service for multimedia conferencing service provisioning. In: IEEE symposium on computers and communication (ISCC), Messina, Italy, pp 289–294

28. Doukas C, Antonelli F (2014) A full end-to-end platform as a service for smart city applications. IEEE 10th international conference on wireless and Mobile computing, networking, and communications (WiMob), Larnaca, pp. 181-186

29. Ribas M, Sampaio LA, Neuman de Souza J, de Rubens CSF, Oliveira ML (2016) A platform as a service billing model for cloud computing management approaches. IEEE Lat Am Trans 14(1):267–280

30. Hong LT, Schahram D, Georgiana C, Alessio G, Waldemar H, Duc HL, Daniel M (2014) CoMoT - a platform-as-a-Service for Elasticity in the cloud. In: Cloud engineering (IC2E), IEEE international conference on, Boston, MA, pp 619–622

31. Sami Y, Pradeep R, Ons B, Roch HG, Monique JM, Paul AP (2016) A platform-as-a-service for hybrid cloud/fog environments. In: IEEE international symposium on local and metropolitan area networks (LANMAN), Rome, Italy, pp 1–7

32. Graubner P, Baumgärtner L, Heckmann P, Müller M, Freisleben B (2015) Dynalize: dynamic analysis of mobile apps in a platform-as-a-service cloud. In: IEEE 8th international conference on cloud computing, New York City, NY, pp 925–932

33. Dhuldhule PA, Lakshmi J, Nandy SK (2015) High-performance computing cloud -- a platform-as-a-service perspective. International conference on cloud computing and big data (CCBD), Shanghai, pp. 21-28

34. Vanhove T, Vandensteen J, Seghbroeck JV, Wauters T, De TF (2014) Kameleo: design of a new platform-as-a-service for flexible data management. IEEE Network Operations and Management Symposium (NOMS), Krakow:1–4

35. Zhao S, Zhang Y, Shen B, Shen X, Chen R (2014) Mass data processing and personalized services in Shanghai e-commerce credit evaluation platform. Progress in informatics and computing (PIC), international conference on, Shanghai, pp. 481-485

36. Zhu J, Sha C (2015) Multi-stage scheduling with scalable resources for automated deployment in platform as a service cloud. Parallel architectures algorithms and programming (PAAP). Seventh international symposium on, Nanjing, pp. 204-209

37. Mishra KN, Chakraborty C (2020) A novel approach towards using big data and IoT for improving the efficiency of m-health systems. In: Gupta, D., Hassanien, A., Khanna, A. (eds) Advanced computational intelligence techniques for virtual reality in healthcare. Studies in computational intelligence, Vol 875

38. Singh I et al (2015) A novel privacy and security framework for the cloud network services, *2015 9th international conference on innovative Mobile and internet services in ubiquitous computing*. Santa Catarina, Brazil 2015:301–305

39. Mishra KN, Pandey SC (2021) Fraud prediction in smart societies using logistic regression and k-fold machine learning techniques. Wireless Personal Comm 119:1341–1367

40. Kamta NM, Chakraborty C (2020) A novel approach towards enhancing the quality of life in smart cities using clouds and IoT based technologies. Digital Twin Technol Smart Cities:19–33

41. Web Link: smartcityhub.com /problems-and-solutions Last accessed On: May 27, 2021

42. Web Link: storyblocks.com. Last accessed On: May 27, 2021

43. Web Link: shutterstock.com. Last accessed On: May 27, 2021

Chapter 9
Multiple Disease Infection Prediction in Smart Societies Using Intelligent Machine Learning Techniques

Abstract In the described intelligent machine learning (IML) based healthcare diseases prediction/monitoring system of this chapter, the medical dataset is divided into test & train data sets and the machine learning algorithms are trained on the training data which produces the model. Further, the produced model can be implemented in the described IML based healthcare diseases prediction/monitoring system. Here, the end-user will be asked to select any five symptoms from a large number of symptoms. If once the selection is done then the end-user will be is permitted to select the machine learning algorithms for the prediction of disease.

The three supervised learning algorithms that have been described and implemented in this chapter are Decision Tree, Random Forest, and Naive Bayes algorithm. Out of the three algorithms, the Naive Bayes has produced the highest accuracy followed by Random Forest and decision tree. Further, the medical dataset taken into consideration is a binary dataset with each column referring to a symptom and each row corresponding to a disease. The symptoms corresponding to disease have the numeric value '1' in that row otherwise it will have the numeric value '0'. It is observed by the authors that this binary dataset ('1' / '0') makes the implementation of mathematical functions and machine learning algorithms much easier. Furthermore, it is possible in the described system to select all three algorithms and in this situation; the system produces the result of each algorithm along with its accuracy.

The SQLite database used in the described IML based healthcare diseases prediction/monitoring system will allow the end-user (including patients) to register them in the system. A unique user ID is generated and the symptoms, as well as predicted diseases, are recorded for each end user/patient. In any specific case if the actual diagnosis of the disease is different from the predicted diseases of the system, then the user/patient can come back and record his actual disease in the system. The medical records of the patients are integrated with the medical datasets for increasing the transparency and efficiency of the described system. The described IML based healthcare diseases prediction/monitoring system can be used as a prototype by authors/researchers for the development of more sophisticated and better systems to predict.

© The Author(s), under exclusive license to Springer Nature Switzerland AG 2023
K. N. Mishra, S. C. Pandey, *Cloud-IoT Technologies in Society 5.0*, https://doi.org/10.1007/978-3-031-28711-4_9

Keywords Confusion matrix · Convolution neural network · Decision trees · Intelligent machine learning, m-health disease prediction system · Pandas libraries · Supervised learning · Transfer learning · Unsupervised learning

9.1   Introduction

The recent spread of the Coronal Virus (Covid-19) has brought this lightning-paced world to a standstill state. Around 80% of the world population has been under lockdown for several days due to this unprecedented crisis. The Covid-19 is a cruel reminder of our internal dishonesty and the fragile healthcare system. Therefore, there is an urgent need to establish an honest and robust healthcare system. Further, the Covid-19 has forced us to rethink the priorities of human life and the efficiency of our healthcare systems including m-heath and e-health components. In our day-to-day life, we often tend to ignore our healthcare needs for obtaining technical/professional gains [1, 2]. The healthcare system of developing and developed countries (with high population density including India) fails to cater to the health-related needs of the vast population. A large section of the population has no access to hospitals or doctors even after having huge amounts of cash into their hands. A recent study suggests that only 25% of people in India and abroad have access to proper healthcare services during peak days Covid-19. With the population growing at an unbridled pace, it has become extremely important to leverage technology to address the issue of healthcare systems in developing and developed countries. The introduction and adoption of machine learning (ML) and artificial intelligence (AI) approaches have made it possible to automate the process of diagnosis and even cure some diseases up to a certain extent. There are many tools available that are related to multiple disease predictions. But, it is unfortunate that the focus of most of the available tools, technologies, researches, and automation systems has been on terminal and serious diseases like tuberculosis, heart disease, cancer, and brain stroke, etc. But, there are very few tools available for the prediction of general diseases like viral fever, cough & cold, and Covid-19 [3–5].

To reduce the large-scale deaths of humans due to lack of an appropriate healthcare system, a quick and efficient prediction technique is to be discovered for predicting the spread of viral fever, cough & cold, and Covid-19. Hence, this chapter is aimed to develop an intelligent system for predicting the general symptomatic diseases like viral fever, cough & cold, and Covid-19 based on easily diagnosed symptoms. The main objective of this research article is to predict general diseases including Covid-19 of a patient using soft computing and machine learning algorithms. The comparative studies of the performance of various machine learning algorithms are possible through the graphical and mathematical representation of the results. The authors have applied multiple algorithms for predicting diseases to further improve the overall accuracy of the system. The large historical datasets of diseases and symptoms currently available have been used to train the described algorithms [6, 7].

Now, these days doctors are adopting many scientific technologies and methodologies for both identification and diagnosis of a common and fatal disease. Successful treatment is always attributed to the right and accurate diagnosis of disease. Many times the medical doctors and healthcare experts fail to trace the cause of sickness of the vast population. Therefore, the current era needs machine learning and AI-based disease prediction systems to assist medical doctors and other healthcare workers in the diagnosis of diseases. It is observed that the existing healthcare system fails to cater to the needs of the vast population of our country. In the existing healthcare systems, a patient has to book an appointment with the doctor to whom he/she wants to consult. In some cases, the waiting time to consult a doctor can be very long (maybe up to a week). In pandemic situations, patients have to wait for a long time to get an appointment with a doctor for regular check-ups and general symptomatic diseases also. The cost involved in this whole process of booking an appointment, visiting the doctor, waiting for the doctor, and meeting the doctor becomes very high if the doctor is unavailable or very much busy. Indeed, some healthcare automated systems do exist. But, they are mostly used for the study and diagnosis of heart diseases, tuberculosis, brain disorder, and kidney-related diseases, etc. In the recent era, the applications of AI and ML have been limited to terminal diseases. Further, the developed algorithms are mostly focused on the minute details of specific chronic diseases to develop a cure for these diseases in the future. Furthermore, the spread of Covid-19 led many agencies to develop chatbots that can be used for consultation on receiving specific symptoms of the virus. If we could develop AI and ML-based disease prediction systems with high accuracy then it would be possible to reduce the workload of doctors, nurses, and other healthcare experts [8–10].

In general, it is observed that in developing countries that most of the patients are forced to go to the hospitals and meet the doctor directly for even the simplest of diseases in pandemic situations. So, usually, the patients have to wait for an average of one week to get an appointment in the pandemic situation. Hence, more people are getting untimely deaths because of not being attended by doctors. Moreover, the doctors also find it very difficult to administer the hundreds of patients every single day. So, a better system is needed for predicting the infection spread of multiple infectious diseases using machine learning (ML) and AI Techniques. The authors have used the scientific approaches to design and develop multiple disease infection prediction systems which can analyze and predict terminal and more serious diseases like cancer, liver diseases, and cardiovascular diseases [11, 12].

Overall, this chapter can be divided into the following three parts [13, 14]:

Part 1: In the first part of the intelligent machine learning (IML) algorithms are to be studied and reviewed for initial short-listing and then various data visualization and analysis techniques are to be used to analyze the performance of these algorithms. This can be achieved by finding appropriate data sets of medical science and then running the selected IML algorithms on those specific datasets to measure the accuracy in terms of performance.

Part 2: Based on the results of the first part, the most appropriate and accurate IML algorithms are to be further shortlisted for the implementation of the disease prediction system. Here, multiple IML algorithms are to be shortlisted to ensure higher accuracy and better performance of the developed system. During the development of algorithms, it would be better to have *two to three* options for further diagnosis of diseases and in this way increase the accuracy and decrease the chances of system failure.

Part 3: In the third part the patient can record his/her symptoms and diagnosis reports in the described IML based healthcare diseases prediction/monitoring system for providing training and testing in the live environment. In actual diagnosis, if the disease is different from the ones predicted by the described IML based healthcare diseases prediction/monitoring system then the corresponding user can record the actual diseases and symptoms in the database which can further be used to train and further improve the performance of described healthcare system.

9.2   Background and Theoretical Foundations

Most of the systems that have been developed are used to predict a single disease. Moreover, such systems are highly complicated and are mostly used by experts for recommendation purposes. Therefore, there is an urgent need to develop simple healthcare prediction/guidance systems that can be directly used by little intelligent patients to predict the diseases based on symptoms and diagnosis results which can be given as input by the user. The development of such types of healthcare prediction/guidance systems is still in incipient stages. However, few disease prediction/guidance systems have been proposed by various scholars. But, most of them are either used for heart or other respiratory diseases whereas other systems which are used for the prediction/guidance of multiple diseases are based on a single algorithm. These diseases prediction/guidance systems generally have a low accuracy score [15, 16].

In the field of medical science, accuracy is of much bigger concern than other factors and only the most accurate algorithms must be chosen for implementation. The main objective of this chapter (research article) is to study and compare the performance of various intelligent machine learning (IML) algorithms on medical science data sets and then provide an IML based healthcare prediction/guidance system for automated disease prediction with high accuracy. The developed healthcare system can overwhelm all the restrictions of the manual healthcare assessment systems [17, 18].

To specify the requirements of the described system, we need to specify the technical feasibility, operational feasibility, functional requirements, and non-functional requirements. Here, the technical feasibility aims to study and analyze the technical requirements, costs, and gains of the described system. It involves the study of the accurateness of the described system and its comparison with other systems (if exists). The overall technical feasibility study and analysis includes a brief description of the language used to develop the IML based healthcare prediction/guidance system for automated diseases prediction; Hardware and software requirements of the system; Overview of the medical dataset used; Study of algorithms to be implemented in IML based healthcare system, and measuring the accuracy of the developed system. The operational feasibility plays an important role in the success of a system as it directly impacts the users of the system. The operational feasibility evaluation focuses on the management, working, and maintenance of the developed system. The IML based multiple diseases prediction systems must be easy to use, easily maintainable, and manageable. Further, the interface of the described system should be user-friendly and informative [19–21].

In general, large-size software is divided into independent/less dependent modules. A good software requirement specification (SRS) defines how the modules of the software component interact with each other and with the end-user. It includes the flow of necessary information through different modules and their interconnectivity. The test cases for the software are developed by keeping the details of SRS in the mind. The software requirements for developing and installation of the IML based multiple diseases prediction/guidance systems are: Windows XP or later; Linux/Ubuntu (Excluding Kali Linux)/Mac Software; Python Version 3.5 or higher; SQLite with GUI Manager [22, 23].

Technically, a functional requirement defines the functionalities that a system is expected to perform. In general, a function is described as a set of inputs given, the processing tasks performed, and the outputs obtained. Some of the basic functional requirements of the IML based multiple diseases prediction/guidance systems are: Obtaining a complete dataset; Keeping track of all the attributes and their values required for analysis; Analysis of the performance of various algorithms to be implemented; Keeping details of the healthcare system to be used for prediction; Defining database schema for storage purpose, and Maintaining/regularly updating the database [24, 25].

Apart from functional requirements, we need to have non-functional requirements/quality requirements, which impose constraints on the design or implementation of performance, security, and reliability related requirements. The non-functional requirements specify the overall characteristics of the described system e.g. cost, and reliability. Both of the functional and non-functional requirements must be well-defined for a software product. Some of the basic non-functional requirements of the IML based multiple diseases prediction/guidance systems are: *Performance-related requirements* (All data entered shall be up to mark and properly cleaned. There should be no null or missing values in the dataset); *Platform constraints* (The main target is to generate the system such that it runs on all platforms and operating systems)**;** *Accuracy and Precision* (The developed system must improve the accuracy of existing systems)*;* *Portability* (The software should be portable so that it can be transferred from one system to another system as per needs); *Reliability* (Requirements about how often the software fails. The software must be easy to maintain so that it does not breakdown or malfunctions); *Security* (The individual data of each patient must be secured); and *Usability* (Requirements about how

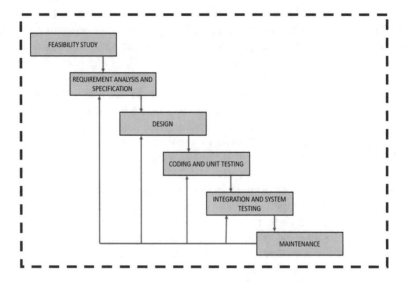

Fig. 9.1 An iterative water flow development of disease prediction system

difficult it will be to learn and operate the system. The requirements are often expressed in learning time or similar metrics). For developing the IML based multiple diseases prediction/guidance systems the iterative waterfall model of software development can be used. The steps of the iterative waterfall model are shown in Fig. 9.1 [26, 27].

9.3   The Tools, Technologies, and Algorithms

The tools and technologies used for developing the IML based multiple diseases prediction/guidance systems are Python, Python Libraries, Pandas, Numpy, Matplot, MatplotLib, Tkinter, SQLite, and other machine learning technologies/algorithms.

9.3.1   The Python, Pandas and their Libraries

Since Python is an open-source language and easily understandable. Therefore, it is chosen for the development of the based multiple diseases prediction/guidance systems. Multiple intelligent machine learning algorithms have been used for the prediction of results. The outputs of these algorithms and the accuracy of the described system are discussed in much detail in later sections of this chapter. The graphical user interface (GUI) for the IML based multiple diseases prediction/guidance systems have been developed using Tkinter which is an open-source python library.

The Tkinter provides the best user experience and it is the most popularly used python GUI library. The main features of Python are: Simple and Easy to Learn; Interpreted Language; Cross-platform language; Free and Open Source; Object-Oriented language; Extensive Libraries; Easily Integrated; Better Databases Connectivity; Portability, and compatibility with other High-Level Languages [28, 29].

There are a plethora of options available in terms of technology to visualize large datasets in terms of Python libraries. However, the IML based multiple diseases prediction/guidance system is to be developed using Python languages and its rich support libraries. The Python language offers ease of understanding and writing code and have better interconnectivity with recently developed Microsoft and other technologies for better handling of the medical data. The chapter involves extensive use of various libraries of the language to plot and present data in the form of graphs and tables. Some of the major tools used for this purpose are Pandas, NumPy, Matplotlib, ScikitLearn, and Tkinter [30, 31].

Pandas is an open-source library that permits us to perform data manipulation and management in Python. The Pandas library is built on the crest of NumPy. Some of the frequently used data structures in pandas are Series objects; Data Frame objects (Generate 2D tables like a spreadsheet); and Panel objects. The Pandas Series object can be created using *pd.Series* function. Here, each row is provided with an index value and by default, the assigned numerical values starting from 0. The Pandas Data Frame objects are represented by a spreadsheet with cell values, row index labels, and column names, etc. The rows and columns of Data Frame objects are simple and can be accessed spontaneously. The Pandas is capable to provide SQL-like functionality to filter and sort the rows based on specific conditions [32, 33].

9.3.2   The Numpy, MatPlot, Scilit, Tkinetr, SQLite, and their Libraries

The NumPy stands for Numerical Python. It provides a high-performance multidimensional array of objects and tools for working with these arrays. It includes powerful mathematical tools which can be used to simplify calculations and visualization of mathematical data. The NumPy is much more memory efficient and its data structures save a lot of memory as compared to other fundamental Python data structures. Some of the important attributes of a NumPy object are *Ndim* (It displays the dimension of the array); *Shape* (It returns a tuple of integers indicating the size of the array); *Size* (It returns the total number of elements in the NumPy array); and *Dtype* (It returns the type of elements in the array, i.e., int64, character).

The MatPlotLib is a fundamental Python library that can be extensively used for plotting different types of graphs and curves for data. The Matplotlib can be used for the 2-dimensional plotting of graphs and curves. It provides various features and a very simple user interface. Thus, it makes itself the most popular Python library for data visualization and analysis. Some of the plots built by MatPlotLib are Histograms, Power spectra, Error charts, Bar charts, and Scatter Plots. The Scikit-learn is a library in Python that provides many supervised and unsupervised learning algorithms. The functionality that scikit-learn provides include Regression, including Linear and Logistic Regression; Classification, including K-Nearest Neighbours; Clustering, K-Means and K-Means++; Model selection; Preprocessing, and Min-Max Normalization. In this research article, the authors have used ScikitLearn to implement Random Forest, Decision Tree, and Naive Bayes algorithms on the dataset. We have also used it to validate the result and publish it in a user interactive format [34, 35].

The Tkinter is a python interface to the Tk GUI Toolkit. Out of the numerous libraries provided by Python for GIS development, the Tkinter is the most commonly used. It provides the fastest and easiest ways to develop GUI applications. Some of the major benefits of Tkinter are: free of cost available for business usage; Featured in Python library; Creating executables for Tkinter apps is more accessible because of its inclusion in Python; Minimum interdependencies; and Simple to understand. The SQLite is a software library that includes self-contentedness, zero-configuration, and a transactional SQL database engine. The SQLite3 may be integrated with Python using the sqlite3 module. Some of the Python Sqlite3 module application program interfaces are *Sqlite3.connect()*, *Connection.cursor()*, *Cursor.execute()*, *Connection.execute()*, *Connection.commit()*, *Connection.rollback()*, and *Connection.close()*.

9.3.3   The Machine Learning Algorithms

In formal terms, machine learning is a branch of artificial intelligence that gives computer systems the ability to learn on their own without being explicitly programmed. The diagram in Fig. 9.2 shows the working of a machine learning algorithm. It can be observed from the Fig. 9.2 that apart from the input, we also give the expected output as a parameter to the machine learning algorithms. This approach can be very much useful for the models and patterns which can be used for prediction, and classification [36, 37].

Machine learning (ML) has been widely used across domains to improve and automate the functioning of various systems. Some of the important applications of machine learning include *Healthcare* (To predict the diagnosis of a patient based on clinical data); *Finance* (To predict stock prices and detect fraudulent transactions); *Business* (Study customer's behavior & preferences and develop recommendation systems); *Automobile industry* (To power self-driving cars); and *Computer Visions* (Object detection and image classification).

In broad terms, the machine learning algorithms can be classified into three different categories namely supervised, unsupervised, and reinforcement algorithms. The classification of ML algorithms can be represented by Fig. 9.3.

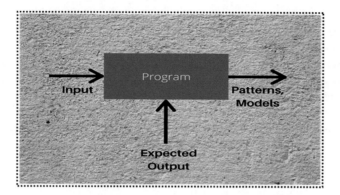

Fig. 9.2 Working of a Machine Learning Algorithm

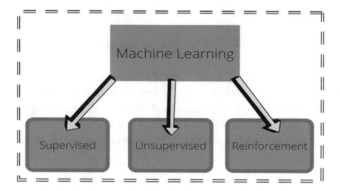

Fig. 9.3 Classification of machine learning algorithms

In supervised learning, the algorithm is trained on a labeled dataset which is also known as a training dataset. This training dataset allows the algorithm to find patterns and characteristics in the general/medical data which can be used to map unknown inputs to correct outputs. This type of training produces a model which can further be used to predict the output for the unlabelled dataset. In unsupervised learning, the algorithm is trained on an unlabelled dataset and then the algorithm is left to work in a way. It may try to find similarities, differences, and patterns in the data to group or cluster them accordingly. The output of the unsupervised learning algorithm can be considered as clusters of similar instances in the target dataset. The reinforcement learning algorithms involve making a sequence of decisions in an interactive and complex environment. In reinforcement algorithms, the input to a particular stage is dependent on the output of the preceding stage. The trial and error methods are most commonly used for reinforcement learning of tasks.

The experiments and result analysis of this chapter are based on supervised learning algorithms. Here, the algorithms are trained on a labeled dataset of symptoms and diseases and then used for the prediction of diseases based on inputs obtained from the end-users [38, 39].

The various algorithms implemented in the IML based multiple diseases prediction/guidance model are Decision Tree, Random Forest, and Naive Bayes. The *Decision Tree* is the most intuitive algorithm for the prediction of diseases. Whenever a patient visits patient a doctor, he/she asks few questions to the doctors and the doctors also ask few questions to the patients. Sometimes, the next question may be decided based on the answer to the previous questions. This process is repeated till the doctor reaches a satisfactory conclusion. This is exactly how the decision tree algorithm works. At each stage, some attribute values are analyzed and then the algorithm decides about the course of actions to be taken.

The course of action may be in terms of giving medicines with few valuable suggestions or asking the patient to go for further laboratory tests. This process is repeated till a leaf node is reached which is one of the output classes. In Decision Trees, we start from the root node for predicting a class label for a record. Based on comparisons, we move to a branch corresponding to a value and then we jump to the next node. The diagram of Fig. 9.4 pictorially represents the working of a decision tree algorithm.

The Random Forest algorithm consists of a large number of individual decision trees that operate as an ensemble. Each decision tree in the random forest spits out a class prediction and the class with the most votes may be selected as the prediction model for the IML based multiple diseases prediction/guidance system. The diagram in Fig. 9.5 represents the working of the random forest algorithm [40].

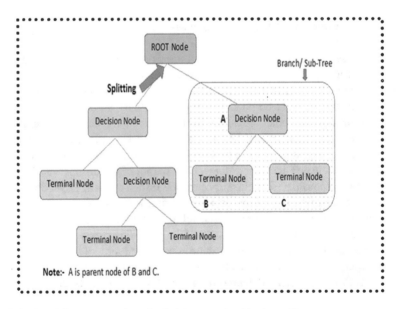

Fig. 9.4 Pictorially representation of a decision tree algorithm's working

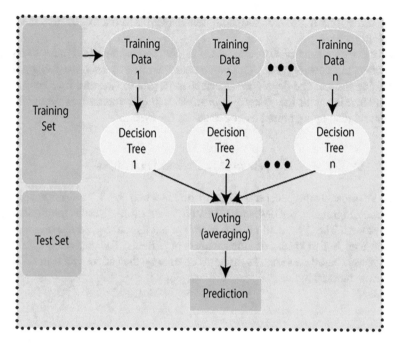

Fig. 9.5 The working of random forest machine learning algorithm

9.3.4 The Steps and Implementation Details of Described Algorithms

9.3.4.1 The Steps of Described Algorithms

The major steps involved in the development of the multiple disease infection prediction using intelligent machine learning techniques are as follow:

Step 1: *Data collection and dataset preparation* (This step will involve the collection of medical information from various data sources. Further, the pre-processing and cleaning are performed to remove errors from the dataset and then we make it fit for analysis and development).

Step 2: *Data visualization and performance prediction* (The medical-related dataset is to be used to apply various machine learning algorithms and analyze their performance. It involves fitting the models and performance evaluation to measure the accuracy of different algorithms.)

Step 3: *Short-listing the algorithms* (Based on the accuracy analysis reports of results obtained from *Step 2*, some of the machine learning algorithms are to be shortlisted for the development of the multiple diseases prediction systems.)

Step 4: *Use of suitable dataset to fit the final model* (An extensive dataset with required features to be used to fit the final model of the described system. Further, this dataset should contain the maximum possible diseases and their symptoms to ensure the improved and comprehensive performance of the developed system.)

Step 5*: Development of User Interface to the Underline ML Model* (This step involves the development of a simple user interface to the underlying machine learning model. The developed interface must provide the end-user an easy way of interacting with the system. It involves taking symptoms as input from the user and displaying output as generated by the system.)

9.3.4.2   Implementation Details of Described Algorithms

Figure 9.6 presents the general Use-Case processes and Fig. 9.7 presents the general Sequence diagram of the described IML based multiple diseases prediction/guidance systems. The described system has main actors namely admin and end-user. The end-user is also known as general users or patients. The described system predicts diseases based on various symptoms entered by the patient/end user during the process of interaction.

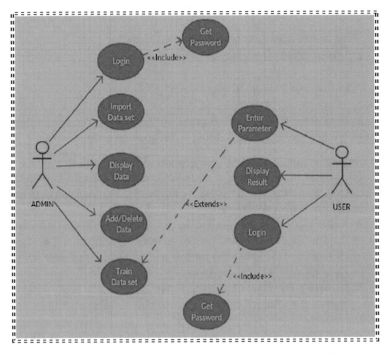

Fig. 9.6 General Use-Case diagram for the described IML based multiple diseases prediction/guidance model

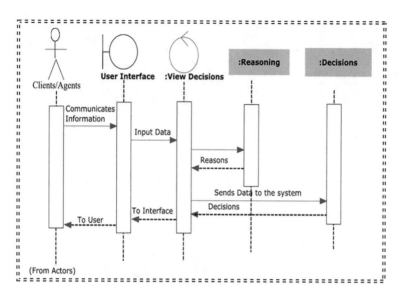

Fig. 9.7 General Sequence Diagram for the described IML based multiple diseases prediction/guidance model

9.4   Experimental Discussions

9.4.1   Implementation of Typhoid/Pneumonia/Viral Fever/ Covid Detection for Severe Symptoms

For detecting Typhoid/Pneumonia/Viral Fever/Covid Detection with Severe Symptoms, the authors have used a different deep learning library **for** implementing the desired convolution neural network in Python. The code consists of fourteen parts (Part 1 to Part 14).

9.4.1.1   Import Python Libraries for Performing Pre-processing Tasks

First, the authors have imported the libraries required for performing the preprocessing tasks on the data. The dataset for this module dealing with Pneumonia detection has been fetched/downloaded into the system from Kaggle [10]. This dataset will be later referenced in the code. The Python codes for importing libraries are as follow:

```
import pandas as pd
import cv2
import numpy as np
import os
from random import shuffle
from tqdm import tqdm
import scipy
import skimage
from skimage.transform import resize
```

9.4.1.2   Dividing Medical Data into Test, Train, and Validation Data Sets

The print statements written below is showing the directory structure of the area where we need to store our dataset.

```
print(os.listdir("./input/chest_xray/chest_xray"))

['chest_xray', 'test', 'train', 'val', '__MACOSX']

print(os.listdir("./input/chest_xray/chest_xray/train/"))

['NORMAL', 'PNEUMONIA']
```

Here, the dataset is divided into 3 subcategories namely *Test*, *Train*, and *Val* ('Val' means validation). The *Train* folder contains the X-ray images which the authors have used in the codes to train the described model. The *Test* folder contains X-ray images for testing the described model for which training has already been provided. The *Val* (validation) folder contains the X-ray over which the described model will be finally validated. Each of the *test*, *train*, and *validation* folders contains two subfolders namely *PNEUMONIA*, and *NORMAL*, where the *PNEUMONIA* folder contains the X-ray images of pneumonia affected Chests, and the NORMAL folder, contains the X-ray image of a normal person with no pneumonia symptoms.

9.4.1.3   Define the Path Variables for the Input Medical Datasets

In this part, the authors define the path variables for the input dataset. The Python code for defining the path variables for the input dataset will be as follow:

```
TRAIN_DIR = "./input/chest_xray/chest_xray/train/"
TEST_DIR =  "./input/chest_xray/chest_xray/test/"
VAL_DIR =   "./input/chest_xray/chest_xray/val/"
```

9.4.1.4 Design of Functions for Performing Pre-processing on the Input Data

The below part displays the function designed for preprocessing the input data for the described system.

```
def get_data(Dir):
    X = []
    y = []
    for nextDir in os.listdir(Dir):
        if not nextDir.startswith('.'):
            if nextDir in ['NORMAL']:
                label = 0
            elif nextDir in ['PNEUMONIA']:
                label = 1
            else:
                label = 2

            temp = Dir + nextDir

            for file in tqdm(os.listdir(temp)):
                img = cv2.imread(temp + '/' + file)
                if img is not None:
                    img = skimage.transform.resize(img, (150, 150, 3))
                    |
                    img = np.asarray(img)
                    X.append(img)
                    y.append(label)

    X = np.asarray(X)
    y = np.asarray(y)
    return X.v
```

The above function *"get_data(Dir)"* takes the directory path as an input argument, instantiates two empty arrays namely X *(X array will be containing the images)* and Y *(Y array will be containing the label of the corresponding image present in the X array)* in the beginning and returns two Numpy arrays. It includes two for loops where one *for loop* is enclosed within the other. The outer *for loop* iterates over each subdirectory present in the given directory whose path is mentioned in the input argument. Further, during the iteration, it creates a variable named label whose value is set to Zero ('0') if the subdirectory's name is normal or One ('1') if the sub directory's name is pneumonia. In other cases, value Two ('2') is assigned.

In the inner *for loop*, we iterate over the files present in each subdirectory. The files present in each subdirectory are imaged files. We can move forward through every image in the directory and resize it to *150 x 150 x 3*. Further, it can be converted into a Numpy array. After resizing the image we can append the converted image and its respective label into the X-array and Y-array. At last, we can convert the arrays 'X' and array 'Y' into a Numpy array, and then it can be returned to the *get_data(Dir)* function.

9.4.1.5   Call the Defined Function of Sect. 9.4.1.4 Using Different Path Variables

Here, the function defined in Sect. 9.4.1.4 is called over the three path variables namely *TRAIN_DIR*, *TEST_DIR*, and *VAL_DIR* which we have defined in Sect. 9.4.1.3 (Part 3). After applying the function, we would get six Numpy arrays where three of them will contain the images and the other three will contain labels. The Python description of the same is given below:

```
X_train, y_train = get_data(TRAIN_DIR)
100%|██████████| 1341/1341 [11:12<00:00,  1.99it/s]
100%|██████████| 3875/3875 [13:09<00:00,  4.91it/s]

X_test , y_test = get_data(TEST_DIR)
100%|██████████| 234/234 [02:27<00:00,  1.58it/s]
100%|██████████| 390/390 [00:48<00:00,  7.97it/s]

X_val , y_val = get_data(VAL_DIR)
100%|██████████| 8/8 [00:03<00:00,  2.58it/s]
100%|██████████| 9/9 [00:01<00:00,  6.86it/s]
```

From the shape of the array, we can infer the number of images present in the array. To print the shape/dimensions of the resultant array we can use the following Python code:

```
print(X_train.shape,'\n',X_test.shape)
(5216, 150, 150, 3)
 (624, 150, 150, 3)

print(y_train.shape,'\n',y_test.shape)
(5216,)
 (624,)
```

9.4.1.6   Performing the On-Hot-Encoding and Printing the Shape of NumPy Array

In this part, we are importing the *to_categorically* function from *the Keras utils* package for *on-hot-encoding* the input data sequence. The *on-hot-encoding* is a representation of categorical variables as binary vectors. Here, first, we need to map the categorical values to the integer values and then each integer value is represented as a binary vector that is all zero values except the index of the integer where the index of an integer is marked as '1'. The Python code for the same is given below.

```
from keras.utils.np_utils import to_categorical

y_train = to_categorical(y_train, 2)
y_test = to_categorical(y_test, 2)

Using TensorFlow backend.

print(y_train.shape,'\n',y_test.shape)

(5216, 2)
 (624, 2)
```

The authors are converting the one-dimensional array containing the labels into two-dimensional arrays. This fact is depicted from the above print statement which prints the shape of the *y_train* Numpy array after performing *on-hot-encoding)*, and it would look like Table 9.1. Here, the top row is showing the classes of output categories and the first column is depicting the index of the item. Since, we have only two classes of output. Therefore, only two columns are present apart from the index column. The value '1' for the respective index under the column means it belongs to the category or class depicted by the column, and the value '0' says that it does not belong to the category depicted by the column. In our case, the column represented by '0' belongs to the normal class, and the column represented by '1' belongs to the Pneumonia class. The Python code for defining the exact path variables to the Pneumonia and the normal directory present in the train directory will be as follow:

```
Pimages = os.listdir(TRAIN_DIR + "PNEUMONIA")
Nimages = os.listdir(TRAIN_DIR + "NORMAL")
```

Table 9.1 Printing the shape of the y_train Numpy array after performing on-hot-encoding

0	1	
0	1	
0	1	
1	0	
1	0	

9.4.1.7   Visualization of Medical Data and Images Using ML Techniques

In this part of the chapter, the authors have visualized the available medical data. The Python code for visualizing the available medical data will be as follow:

```python
import matplotlib.pyplot as plt
def plotter(i):
    imagep1 = cv2.imread(TRAIN_DIR+"PNEUMONIA/"+Pimages[i])
    imagep1 = skimage.transform.resize(imagep1, (150, 150, 3) , mode = 'reflect')
    imagen1 = cv2.imread(TRAIN_DIR+"NORMAL/"+Nimages[i])
    imagen1 = skimage.transform.resize(imagen1, (150, 150, 3))
    pair = np.concatenate((imagen1, imagep1), axis=1)
    print("(Left) - No Pneumonia Vs (Right) - Pneumonia")
    print("--------------------------------------------------------------
    plt.figure(figsize=(10,5))
    plt.imshow(pair)
    plt.show()
for i in range(0,5):
    plotter(i)
```

In the above Python code, the authors have used *matplotlib* for displaying X-ray images of normal and Pneumonia affect chest of a person. It can be observed after implementing ML techniques that the X-ray of a normal person is different than the Pneumonia suffering person.

Now, let us define a function named plotter which takes an integer input argument and is representing the index of scanned images. The open CV's pre-defined function *imread()can be used* for reading the image. The authors can use using *Scikit* image library's predefined function for resizing the image. Further, both images can be concatenated using the Numpy library's concatenate function and at last, we can plot the concatenated image in a graph by using matplotlib's functions. In the *"for"* loop of the above Python code the defined function *plotter ()* is called five times to draw/plot five processed images. The five processed images to differentiate between the chest of a normal person and a Pneumonia person are presented in Fig. 9.8a and Fig. 9.8b. In Fig. 9.9, the authors have displayed visualized number of different classes of data that are is present in the training dataset along with its count using the predefined count plot function of *sea born data visualization library*.

9.4.1.8   Defining Checkpoints and Layers

Now, in this part of the experimental setup, the authors have defined the checkpoints and layers of the experimental setup of the described system. The checkpoints are used to optimize the code.

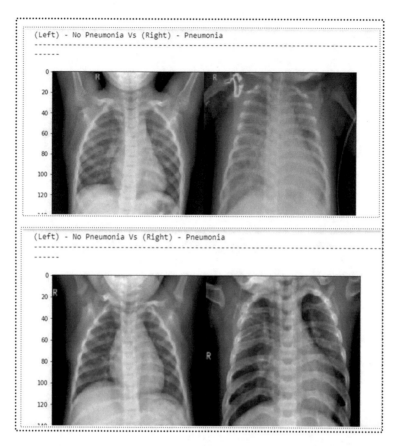

Fig. 9.8a Differentiation between the chest of a normal person and Pneumonia suffering person (person 1) using processed images

```
from keras.callbacks import ReduceLROnPlateau , ModelCheckpoint
lr_reduce = ReduceLROnPlateau(monitor='val_acc', factor=0.1, epsilon=0.0001, patience=1, verbose=1)

C:\Users\Navin Stark\anaconda3\envs\dl\lib\site-packages\keras\callbacks\callbacks.py:998: UserWarning: `
eprecated and will be removed, use `min_delta` instead.
  warnings.warn('`epsilon` argument is deprecated and '

filepath="weights.hdf5"
checkpoint = ModelCheckpoint(filepath, monitor='val_acc', verbose=1, save_best_only=True, mode='max')
```

In the above Python code, we call *Reduce LR On Plateau* and *Model Check point*. The *Reduce LR On Plateau* monitors the validation accuracy factor and reduces the learning rate by 0.1 if no improvement is seen in the monitored value. The *Model Check point* monitors the validation accuracy value and saves the best weight in the file '*weights.hdf5*'.

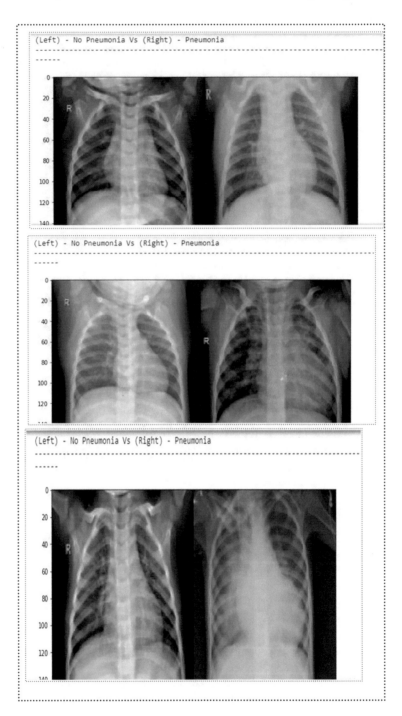

Fig. 9.8b Differentiation between the chest of a normal person and Pneumonia suffering person (person 2) using processed images

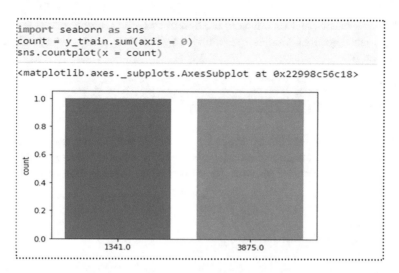

```
import seaborn as sns
count = y_train.sum(axis = 0)
sns.countplot(x = count)

<matplotlib.axes._subplots.AxesSubplot at 0x22998c56c18>
```

Fig. 9.9 Data visualization of the number of different classes available in the training data set

9.4.1.9 Add and Import Libraries to Build Convolution Layer of Neural Network

In this section, the authors will be adding and importing libraries that are essential for building the convolution layers of the neural network (NN).

```
from keras.models import Sequential
from keras.layers import Dense , Activation
from keras.layers import Dropout
from keras.layers import Flatten
from keras.constraints import maxnorm
from keras.optimizers import SGD , RMSprop
from keras.layers import Conv2D , BatchNormalization
from keras.layers import MaxPooling2D
from keras.utils import np_utils
from keras import backend as K
K.common.set_image_dim_ordering('th')
from sklearn.model_selection import GridSearchCV
from keras.wrappers.scikit_learn import KerasClassifier
```

It can be seen in the above Python code that the authors have imported the *Keras libraries* that were needed for building the different convolution layers. The *Keras* is one of the leading high-level neural network APIs. It is written in Python and it supports multiple back-end neural network computation engines. Initially, the API was designed for human beings (not for machines), and it follows the best practices for reducing cognitive load. The Neural layers, cost functions, optimizers, initialization schemes, activation functions, and regularization schemes are all standalone modules that we can combine to create new models. The new modules are simple to add as new classes and functions in the described based multiple diseases prediction/guidance systems. Models are defined in Python code, not separate model configuration files.

```
X_train=X_train.reshape(5216,3,150,150)
X_test=X_test.reshape(624,3,150,150)
```

We can reshape the Numpy arrays which contain the training and the test data that is required by the convolution layer's input. To reshape we can use Numpy's predefined function called *reshape( )* described in the above Python code.

```
from keras.utils import get_custom_objects

def swish_activation(x):
    return (K.sigmoid(x) * x)

get_custom_objects().update({'swish_activation': Activation(swish_activation)})
```

In the above Python code, we have defined a swish activation function and a custom activation function that we need to use in convolution layers. We are making this swish activation function as a global variable so that we can load the saved model from an external file and the program can understand what the swish activation function means? Further, to make this a global variable we are using the *get_custom_object( )* function from *the Keras utils package*.

9.4.1.10   Building the Layers of Convolution Neural Network

In this section, we build the layer of the convolution neural network. Here, we will use the libraries and functions that were imported in Sect. 9.4.1.9 while building different layers of convolution neural networks. Further, we are creating a variable model in which we are instantiating the sequential model using the predefined function of Keras (*Sequential( )*). After creating a sequential model we can add different layers that make up the convolution neural network. We can see from line number 2 of the below code that the function *model.add()* is adding new layers to the existing sequential model and the argument given to the add method tell us perfectly which type of layer is to be added where the type of layer is evident from the name of the input argument function.

```
model = Sequential()
model.add(Conv2D(16, (3, 3), activation='relu', padding="same", input_shape=(3,150,150)))
model.add(Conv2D(16, (3, 3), padding="same", activation='relu'))
model.add(MaxPooling2D(pool_size=(2, 2)))
```

In the second line of the above Python code, the first argument tells us about the depth of the layer i.e. the number of filters used which is sixteen (*'16'*) in the described case. The second argument of the second line of the above Python code tells us about the size of the kernel/filter used in the described model which is (3,3) in this case. The third argument of the second line of the above Python code tells us about the activation function that we are going to use in our layer. The fourth argument of the second line of the above Python code tells about the padding type that we are going to use in the described model and it is *the 'same'* in our case which means that we are adding the padding feature to the image such that the size of the output and input images remain the same. The fifth argument of the second line of the above Python code tells us about the input shape of the image and it is 3 x 150 x 150 in the described model.

Similarly, all the subsequent layers are added using the same Keras API but with different attributes i.e. input arguments. Since we have discussed the various types of layers and types of activation function in the convolution neural network explanation part of the code. Therefore, we can now easily add the subsequent layers to the model using the *APIs* but with different input arguments. The subsequent layers that have been added in the described model are displayed using the below Python code.

```python
model.add(Conv2D(32, (3, 3), activation='relu', padding="same", input_shape=(3,150,150)))
model.add(Conv2D(32, (3, 3), padding="same", activation='relu'))
model.add(MaxPooling2D(pool_size=(2, 2), padding='same'))


model.add(Conv2D(64, (3, 3), activation='relu', padding="same"))
model.add(Conv2D(64, (3, 3), padding="same", activation='relu'))
model.add(MaxPooling2D(pool_size=(2, 2), padding ='same'))


model.add(Conv2D(96, (3, 3), dilation_rate=(2, 2), activation='relu', padding="same"))
model.add(Conv2D(96, (3, 3), padding="same", activation='relu'))
model.add(MaxPooling2D(pool_size=(2, 2), padding ='same'))


model.add(Conv2D(128, (3, 3), dilation_rate=(2, 2), activation='relu', padding="same"))
model.add(Conv2D(128, (3, 3), padding="same", activation='relu'))
model.add(MaxPooling2D(pool_size=(2, 2), padding ='same'))
```

In the above Python code, we have constructed the Input, Convolution Layer, ReLU Layer, and Pooling Layer. Now, we are going to connect these layers to form the fully connected layered network with a lot node which is also known as a convolution neural network. But, before joining **the** connected layers we need to flatten the model output which is done with the help of the below Python code.

```
model.add(Flatten())
```

The above line of code flattens the layers i.e. it converts the two-dimensional input to one-dimensional input which is required by the fully connected layer.

```
model.add(Dense(64, activation=swish_activation))
model.add(Dropout(0.4))
model.add(Dense(2 , activation='sigmoid'))
```

The 1st line of the above python code adds the dense/fully connected layer to the described model with 64 neurons in the input layer. 2nd line of the above Python code adds a dropout to the described model where 0.4 is used to introduce regularization. The 3rd line of the above Python code adds another layer of dense/fully connected layer in the described model using sigmoid activation function where two ('2') neurons will be in the input layer. We can use the following Python code to compile the above-constructed model with binary cross entropy as its loss function, optimizer as RMSprop, learning rate as 0.0005, and accuracy as the metric over which loss is to be calculated.

```
model.compile(loss='binary_crossentropy',
              optimizer=RMSprop(lr=0.00005),
              metrics=['accuracy'])
```

The below line of Python code will print the summary of the model that we have just created. The output of the below code is given in *Appendix – IV.*

```
print(model.summary())
```

9.4.1.11   Providing Training to Convolution Neural Network

To provide training to convolution neural networks, we need to define *batch size* and *epochs* to train the described model. The below code of Python defines the *batch size* and *epochs*.

```
batch_size = 256
epochs = 6
```

In the below Python code, the function *Model.fit( )* is used to train the described model. The function takes *training data, training labels, validation data, callbacks,* and *epochs* as its input parameters. Here, in the *callbacks* part, we are passing the two *callbacks* that have been defined in Sect. 9.4.1.9 of this chapter. Further, the trained model is passed to a variable called *'history' and the 'history'* variable will be used to analyze the accuracy of results.

```
history = model.fit(X_train, y_train, validation_data = (X_test , y_test) ,callbacks=[lr_reduce,checkpoint] ,
          epochs=epochs)
```

The outputs obtained in terms of loss, accuracy, validation accuracy, and validation loss of the described model over each epoch for the function *model.train( )* is presented in Fig. 9.10.

9.4.1.12   Visualizing Output Metrics of the Trained Model

To visualize the output metrics of the trained model we can use various visualization libraries of Python. The below Python code displays the output metrics of the trained model for the described IML based healthcare diseases prediction/monitoring system. In the below code, the authors have used the *matplotlib* as the visualization library for visualizing the accuracy, and the validation accuracy of the described model. In general, the generated plot will represent accuracy at its 'Y' axis and epoch at its 'X' axis. The graphical representation of obtained outputs for the described IML based healthcare diseases prediction/monitoring system is presented in Fig. 9.11.

```python
import matplotlib.pyplot as plt



plt.plot(history.history['accuracy'])
plt.plot(history.history['val_accuracy'])
plt.title('model accuracy')
plt.ylabel('accuracy')
plt.xlabel('epoch')
plt.legend(['train', 'test'], loc='upper left')
plt.show()
```

The below code is the exact copy of the previous code that was used to plot the graph of accuracy and validation accuracy, the only difference is that instead of accuracy we are plotting the graph around training loss and validation loss. The graph in Fig. 9.12 is representing the output of the Python code.

```
Train on 5216 samples, validate on 624 samples
Epoch 1/6
5216/5216 [==============================] - 148s 28ms/step - loss: 0.5936 - accuracy: 0.7411 - val_loss: 0.6699 - val_accurac
y: 0.6250
Epoch 2/6

C:\Users\Mavin Stark\anaconda3\envs\dl\lib\site-packages\keras\callbacks\callbacks.py:1042: RuntimeWarning: Reduce LR on platea
u conditioned on metric `val_acc` which is not available. Available metrics are: val_loss,val_accuracy,loss,accuracy,lr
  (self.monitor, ','.join(list(logs.keys()))), RuntimeWarning
C:\Users\Mavin Stark\anaconda3\envs\dl\lib\site-packages\keras\callbacks\callbacks.py:707: RuntimeWarning: Can save best model
only with val_acc available, skipping.
  'skipping.' % (self.monitor), RuntimeWarning)

5216/5216 [==============================] - 40s 8ms/step - loss: 0.5391 - accuracy: 0.7429 - val_loss: 0.6109 - val_accuracy:
0.6250
Epoch 3/6
5216/5216 [==============================] - 39s 8ms/step - loss: 0.4209 - accuracy: 0.7682 - val_loss: 0.4900 - val_accuracy:
0.7147
Epoch 4/6
5216/5216 [==============================] - 40s 8ms/step - loss: 0.3490 - accuracy: 0.8452 - val_loss: 0.4338 - val_accuracy:
0.8125
Epoch 5/6
5216/5216 [==============================] - 59s 11ms/step - loss: 0.3109 - accuracy: 0.8821 - val_loss: 0.5577 - val_accuracy:
0.7644
Epoch 6/6
5216/5216 [==============================] - 39s 8ms/step - loss: 0.2678 - accuracy: 0.8961 - val_loss: 0.4853 - val_accuracy:
0.7981
```

Fig. 9.10 Computing the values of loss, accuracy, validation accuracy, and validation loss of the described model over each epoch

```
# summarize history for loss
plt.plot(history.history['loss'])
plt.plot(history.history['val_loss'])
plt.title('model loss')
plt.ylabel('loss')
plt.xlabel('epoch')
plt.legend(['train', 'test'], loc='upper left')
plt.show()
```

Now, we can visualize the output metrics with the help of a trained model by constructing a confusion matrix. The Python code is given below and the corresponding confusion matrix is given in Fig. 9.13.

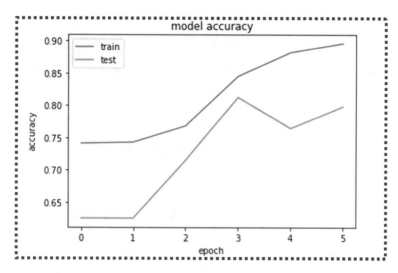

Fig. 9.11 Graphical representation of obtained output for the described model in terms of accuracy

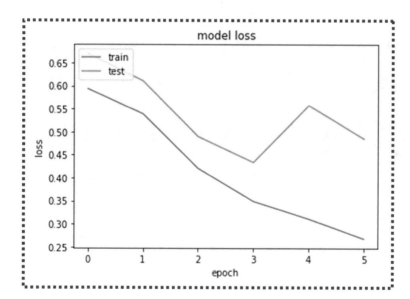

Fig. 9.12 Graphical representation of obtained output for the described model in terms of training loss

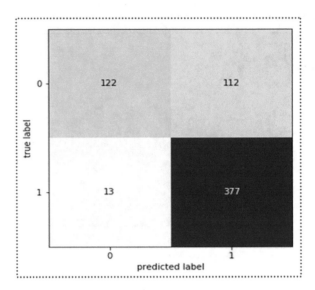

Fig. 9.13 The outputs of the described model in the form of a confusion matrix

```
from sklearn.metrics import confusion_matrix
pred = model.predict(X_test)
pred = np.argmax(pred,axis = 1)
y_true = np.argmax(y_test,axis = 1)
```

```
CM = confusion_matrix(y_true, pred)
from mlxtend.plotting import plot_confusion_matrix
fig, ax = plot_confusion_matrix(conf_mat=CM , figsize=(5, 5))
plt.show()
```

9.4.1.13   Save the Output

The obtained output can be saved using the below Python code and the saved output can be used for classifying the image without training it again and again.

```
model.save("./saved_pnemonia_conv.h5")
print("Model Saved")
```
```
Model Saved
```

```
import cv2
import numpy as np
from keras.models import load_model

img_row, img_height, img_depth = 150,150, 3
classifier = load_model('./saved_pnemonia_conv.h5')
color = True
scale = 2

def draw_test(name, res, input_im, scale, img_row, img_height):
    BLACK = [0,0,0]
    res = int(res)
    if res == 0:
        pred = "NORMAL"
    if res == 1:
        pred = "PNEUMONIA"


    expanded_image = cv2.copyMakeBorder(input_im, 0, 0, 0, imageL.shape[0]*2 ,cv2.BORDER_CONSTANT,value=BLACK)
    if color == False:
        expanded_image = cv2.cvtColor(expanded_image, cv2.COLOR_GRAY2BGR)
    cv2.putText(expanded_image, str(pred), (300, 80) , cv2.FONT_HERSHEY_COMPLEX_SMALL,1, (0,255, 0), 1)


    cv2.imshow(name, expanded_image)
```

9.4.1.14 Classify the Medical Image Using Saved Data

To test whether the classifier is working or not, we can use the saved model to classify the medical images that have been provided to the classifier as input. We are loading the saved mode using the load_model() function of the *keras.models* package. Further, we are defining the name/title (to be displayed on the window), result, an input image, and the dimension of the medical image as input arguments. Furthermore, the input images are displayed in a separate window after putting labels like *normal* or *Pneumonia affect* chest X-ray. The Python code for performing these above tasks is given above.

In the below Python code, we are using a *for loop* and iterating it over the code 10 times. The code over which we are iterating the *for loop* is taking a random medical image from the '*X_val*' Numpy array and classifying the medical image using the predict_classes() function of the described model. The obtained medical images in the form of the output of the below code are given in Fig. 9.14. We can observe from Fig. 9.14 of the described model that the model can predict whether the person is affected with pneumonia or not just by applying the described approach at the chest X-ray images.

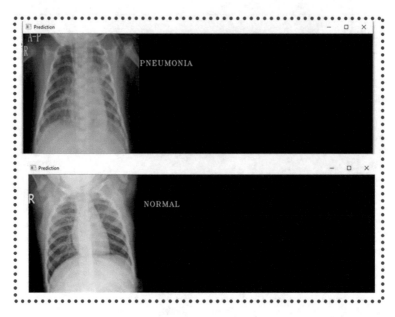

Fig. 9.14 The outputs obtained for the inserted medical images using the described model

```
for i in range(0,10):
    rand = np.random.randint(0,len(X_test))
    input_im = X_test[rand]
    imageL = cv2.resize(input_im, None, fx=scale, fy=scale, interpolation = cv2.INTER_CUBIC)
    input_im = input_im.reshape(1, img_depth, img_row, img_height)

    ## Get Prediction
    res = str(classifier.predict_classes(input_im, 1, verbose = 0)[0])

    draw_test("Prediction", res, imageL, scale, img_row, img_height)
    cv2.waitKey(0)

cv2.destroyAllWindows()
```

9.4.1.15   Transfer Learning

For increasing the accuracy of the described IML based healthcare diseases prediction/monitoring model, the authors have introduced the concept of transfer learning approach in this described model. The transfer learning can be applied by the researchers using the *GoogleLeNet teams developed model* which is the inception v3 model and its brief description has already been given in this chapter in the previous sections. The inception V3 model has been developed by the authors as an entirely separate program files itself so that we could compare the performance of both the models with each other.

The Python programming part of *transfer learning* is exactly similar to the above/previously described model up to Sect. 9.4.1.9 (part 9). Therefore, in the next few pages of this section, we will discuss the code part of the inception v3 model which is different from the previously implemented part.

In the general inception model, we need to import the *InceptionV3 class* from the *keras.application.inception_v3* package. This approach may harbor the entire application program interfaces (APIs) required for developing a model that resonates with inception V3.

```
from keras.applications.inception_v3 import InceptionV3

base_model = InceptionV3(weights=None, include_top=False , input_shape=(150, 150,3))
```

The above line of code creates a base model which has the skeleton structure of *inception* v3 architecture. The skeleton structure is passed to the variable *base_model* using the function InceptionV3() which takes three parameters as input. Here, the 1st parameter says that we are not including the weight into our inception v3 skeleton model, the second 2nd parameter says that we are not adding the fully connected layer of the *inception v3 architecture*, and the 3rd parameter takes in the dimension of the input image.

The below Python code (1st line) defines the fully connected/dense layer of the convolution model as the authors have not taken the fully connected layer of the *inception v3 model*. This dense layer is exactly similar to the last dense layer of the previous model of this chapter because both of them have been built for the same purpose.

```
base_model.load_weights("./input/inceptionweights/inception_v3_weights.h5")

x = base_model.output
x = Dropout(0.5)(x)
x = GlobalAveragePooling2D()(x)
x = Dense(128, activation='relu')(x)
x = BatchNormalization()(x)
predictions = Dense(2, activation='sigmoid')(x)
```

In the above line of Python code (2nd line onwards), we are loading the weight to the base model. These weights are being taken from *inception_v3_weight.h5 file* which is an open-source weights file for inception v3, and anyone can download it from the web.

In the below line of code, the authors are defining the entire *inception v3 model* and compiling it with categorical cross entropy as its *loss function* and *'adam'* as its optimizer over the accuracy metric for the described model. Further, the print statement of the below Python code prints the summary of the described model whose outputs are displayed in *Appendix V, Appendix VI, Appendix VII, Appendix VIII, Appendix IX, Appendix X, Appendix XI,* and *Appendix XII* of this book.

```python
model = Model(inputs=base_model.input, outputs=predictions)

model.compile(loss='categorical_crossentropy',
              optimizer='adam',
              metrics=['accuracy'])

print(model.summary())
```

In the Inception v3 Model, the authors will provide training to the *inception v3* based convolution neural network model. The below Python code will be used to declare the batch size and epochs that the authors will use in the inception model while the training is being provided.

```python
batch_size = 64
epochs = 10

history = model.fit(X_train, y_train, validation_data = (X_test , y_test) ,callbacks=[lr_reduce,checkpoint] ,
          epochs=epochs)
```

In the above Python code *Model.fit ()* is used to train the described model, and the function takes *training data, training labels, validation data, callbacks,* and *epochs* as its input parameters. Here, in the *callbacks* part, the authors are passing the two callbacks that have been defined in Sect. 9.4.1.9 of this chapter, and then the trained model is passed to a variable called *'history'* that will be used to analyze the resultant accuracy. Figure 9.15 represents the output for the code *model.train()*. Further, we can also analyze the values of the loss, accuracy, validation accuracy, and validation loss obtained from Fig. 9.15.

9.4.2 Implementation of Corona Virus Detection Part for Mild Symptoms

In Covid-19 cases also the lungs infection and chest infections occur. In some cases, the symptoms of Covid-19 are very similar to Pneumonia and Typhoid. To implement Covid-19 detection the authors need to import certain libraries of Python.

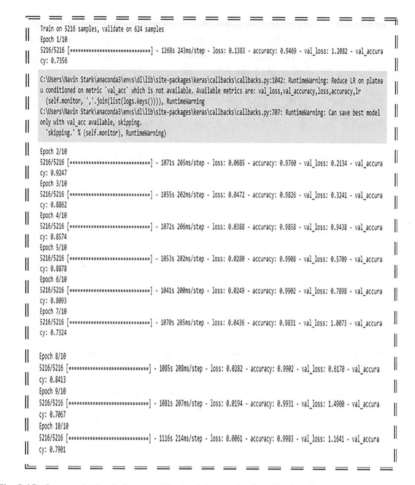

Fig. 9.15 Output obtained after providing training to the described model

Importing a library means loading certain built-in functions of Python into the memory. To import Pandas library, the authors need to run the below code.

```
In [2]: import pandas as pd
```

In the above Python code, usually, we would add the second part ('*as pd*') so that we could access *Pandas* with '*pd.command*' instead of every time writing '*pandas. command*'. *Pandas library* is the most popular Python library that is being used for medical data analysis. It provides highly optimized performance with back-end source code.

The authors may use the below command to read data. Here, the CSV (comma-separated value) files are a common file format for transferring and storing data. The basic process of loading data from a CSV file into a *Pandas Data Frame* is achieved using *the "read_csv"* function of the Pandas library.

```
In [2]:  df = pd.read_csv('data.csv')
```

The *head( )* function is used to get the first 'n' rows. This function returns the first 'n' rows for the object based on position. It is useful for quickly testing if the object has the right type of data in it or not. The output for *df.head( )* command is presented in the below Python code.

```
In [3]:  df.head()
```

Out[3]:

	fever	bodyPain	age	runnyNose	diffBreath	infectionProb
0	101.292240	0	76	0	0	0
1	98.716326	1	4	1	1	0
2	99.471792	0	6	1	1	1
3	98.336311	0	99	0	0	1
4	101.966568	0	71	1	1	1

```
In [4]:  df.tail()
```

Out[4]:

	fever	bodyPain	age	runnyNose	diffBreath	infectionProb
2994	99.658794	0	61	1	-1	1
2995	98.856782	0	46	1	0	1
2996	99.516272	1	33	1	1	0
2997	101.396909	1	32	0	-1	0
2998	98.489700	0	71	0	1	1

Further, the *tail( )* function is being used by authors to return the last 'n' rows. It is useful for quickly verifying data after sorting or appending rows or columns of a table. The output for *df.tail( )* command is presented in the above Python code.

```
In [5]:  df.info()

         <class 'pandas.core.frame.DataFrame'>
         RangeIndex: 2999 entries, 0 to 2998
         Data columns (total 6 columns):
         fever              2999 non-null  float64
         bodyPain           2999 non-null  int64
         age                2999 non-null  int64
         runnyNose          2999 non-null  int64
         diffBreath         2999 non-null  int64
         infectionProb      2999 non-null  int64
         dtypes: float64(1), int64(5)
         memory usage: 140.7 KB
```

The above Python code *"df.info( )"* can be used by the authors to print a concise summary of a data frame for the described IML based healthcare diseases prediction/monitoring system. This function *"df.info( )"* prints information about a data frame including the index *'dtype'* and column *'dtypes'* with non-null values and memory usage.

```
In [6]:  df['fever'].value_counts()
Out[6]:  99.086041      1
         101.579084     1
         100.479451     1
         101.521794     1
         99.210540      1
                       ..
         100.449320     1
         99.635310      1
         99.749880      1
         99.062194      1
         99.142071      1
         Name: fever, Length: 2999, dtype: int64
```

```
In [7]:  df['diffBreath'].value_counts()
Out[7]:  -1      1018
          1       999
          0       982
         Name: diffBreath, dtype: int64
```

In the above Python code, the *value_counts( )* function is used to get a series containing counts of unique values. The resultant object will be in descending order so that the first element will be the most frequently- occurring element. It excludes "NA" values by default.

In the below Python code, the *describe( )* function is used to generate descriptive statistics that summarize the central tendency, dispersion, and shape of a dataset's distribution excluding NaN values.

In [8]: df.describe()

Out[8]:

	fever	bodyPain	age	runnyNose	diffBreath	infectionProb
count	2999.000000	2999.000000	2999.000000	2999.000000	2999.000000	2999.000000
mean	99.976169	0.499833	51.082361	0.486829	-0.006335	0.491497
std	1.162645	0.500083	28.408242	0.499910	0.820208	0.500011
min	98.001196	0.000000	1.000000	0.000000	-1.000000	0.000000
25%	98.977132	0.000000	27.000000	0.000000	-1.000000	0.000000
50%	99.949935	0.000000	51.000000	0.000000	0.000000	0.000000
75%	100.996606	1.000000	76.000000	1.000000	1.000000	1.000000
max	101.994285	1.000000	100.000000	1.000000	1.000000	1.000000

9.4.2.1 The Splitting of Training Tests

The Numpy is the core library for scientific computing in Python. It provides a high-performance multidimensional array object and tools for working with these arrays. The Numpy package is bound to the local variable. Further, the below Python syntax *"import as"* allows us to bind the import to the local variable.

```
In [3]:  import numpy as np
```

```
In [4]:  def data_split(data, ratio):
             np.random.seed(42)
             shuffled = np.random.permutation(len(data))
             test_set_size = int(len(data) * ratio)
             test_indices = shuffled[:test_set_size]
             train_indices = shuffled[test_set_size:]
             return data.iloc[train_indices], data.iloc[test_indices]
```

In the above Python code, a function *"data_split()"* is created for dividing the medical data into a *training dataset* and *test dataset*. If we set the *"np.random. seed(a_fixed_number)"* and every time if the Numpy calls another random function, then the result will always be the same.

The below function *"np.random.permutation(len(data))"* randomly permute a sequence or it returns a permuted range. If '*x*' is a multi-dimensional array then it can be only shuffled along with its first index. After performing these steps the medical dataset is divided into two data sets namely *train_indices* and *test_indices*. Further, by using *the "data_split"* function in the below code the authors are dividing the medical dataset into *train* and *test data* in the ratio "80::20".

```
In [8]:  np.random.permutation(7)
Out[8]:  array([1, 2, 4, 5, 6, 0, 3])
In [12]:  train, test = data_split(df, 0.2)
```

9.4.2.2   Visualizing Training and Test Datasets

The obtained *train dataset* and *test dataset* for the described IML based healthcare diseases prediction/monitoring system are presented in Figs. 9.15, 9.16, and 9.17.

The Python command *"DataFrame.to_numpy"* converts the data frame to a NumPy array. By default, the *dtype* of the returned array will be the common NumPy *dtype* of all types in the data frame. In the below Python code, the *"numpy. reshape()"* gives a new shape to an array without changing its data whereas the logistic regression class implements logistic regression in described IML based healthcare diseases prediction/monitoring environment.

In [13]:   train

Out[13]:

	fever	bodyPain	age	runnyNose	diffBreath	infectionProb
1103	101.671122	1	34	1	-1	0
1569	99.744172	1	39	0	1	0
2229	99.025243	1	16	0	1	1
2296	98.007871	0	35	1	0	1
1800	100.249150	1	13	0	-1	1
…	…	…	…	…	…	…
1638	100.421278	1	21	1	-1	1
1095	99.515225	0	46	1	1	0
1130	98.426670	1	70	0	1	1
1294	98.762656	1	38	0	0	1
860	100.586216	0	97	0	0	0

2400 rows × 6 columns

Fig. 9.16 The training dataset for the described IML based healthcare diseases prediction/monitoring system

In [14]:   test

Out[14]:

	fever	bodyPain	age	runnyNose	diffBreath	infectionProb
1376	100.226787	0	93	1	-1	1
932	100.487583	1	32	1	0	0
144	99.125496	1	12	0	-1	0
1752	101.940294	1	27	1	-1	0
51	100.124193	1	24	0	-1	1
…	…	…	…	…	…	…
842	99.351153	0	22	0	1	0
637	100.622575	0	80	0	1	0
695	101.596964	1	81	1	0	1
226	99.503233	1	100	0	1	0
2603	99.947371	0	27	1	1	0

599 rows × 6 columns

Fig. 9.17 The training dataset for the described IML based healthcare diseases prediction/monitoring system

```
In [15]: X_train = train[['fever', 'bodyPain', 'age', 'runnyNose', 'diffBreath']].to_numpy()
         X_test = test[['fever', 'bodyPain', 'age', 'runnyNose', 'diffBreath']].to_numpy()

In [16]: Y_train = train[['infectionProb']].to_numpy().reshape(2400,)
         Y_test = test[['infectionProb']].to_numpy().reshape(599,)

In [17]: Y_train

Out[17]: array([0, 0, 1, ..., 1, 1, 0], dtype=int64)

In [18]: from sklearn.linear_model import LogisticRegression
```

The logistic regression (LR) is a machine learning classification algorithm that is used to predict the probability of a categorical dependent variable. In the LR approach, the dependent variable is a binary variable that contains data coded as '1' (yes, success, etc.) or '0' (no, failure, etc.). In other words, it can be said that the LR model predicts $P(Y = 1)$ as the function of X.

Further, the below Python code computes the logistic regression values where the authors can fit the training features and training labels. In this way, the classifier is provided training for the medical data.

```
In [ ]: clf = LogisticRegression()
        clf.fit(X_train, Y_train)
```

In the below Python code, we are taking random inputs to predict the probability of Covid-19, and the infection probability is being visualized using *the "infprob"* command/function. As per the obtained results, the infection probability for the Covid-19 cases for the selected training and test datasets is 0.477834 i.e. 47.78%.

```
In [27]: inputFeatures = [101, 1, 22, -1, 1]
         infProb =clf.predict_proba([inputFeatures])[0][1]

In [21]: infProb

Out[21]: 0.4778345928320831
```

9.5   Results and Discussions

9.5.1   *Discussions of Pneumonia and Normal Chests Classifications*

In this chapter, the authors have described the work of two different machine learning models. The 1st model is a simple convolution neural-based on a hit and trial architecture and the 2nd model is a convolution neural network based on Inception v3 architecture. Both of these models can be compared with each other based on precisions, recall values, and the f_1 score where the f_1 score is generally used to measure the performance of the neural network. The below Eqs. (9.1) and (9.2) are being used to calculate. Now, if we put the same in the confusion matrix then its parts will be represented by Table 9.2.

$$Precision = \frac{(True\ Positive)}{(True\ Positive + False\ Positive)} \tag{9.1}$$

$$Recall = \frac{(True\ Positive)}{(True\ Positive + False\ Negative)} \tag{9.2}$$

The *precision* is a good measure to determine the result if the cost of *False Positive* is high. Further, the *Recall* calculates how many of the *Actual Positives* of the described IML based healthcare diseases prediction/monitoring system can be captured through labeling them as *True Positive*. Furthermore, the value of function F_1 can be calculated using Eq. (9.3), and it is a function of *Precision* and *Recall*.

$$F_1 = 2\ X\ \frac{(Precision\ X\ Recall)}{(Precision + Recall)} \tag{9.3}$$

In Eq. (9.2), the F_1 score will be used if there is uneven class distribution and we need to seek a balance between *precision* and *recall* values**.** Now, let us look at the confusion matrix values of both the models which are given in Fig. 9.18. Further, the authors can compare both models concerning their *precision*, *recall*, and F_1 *scores*.

Table 9.2   Representation of actual and predicted values for a confusion matrix

		Predicted	
		Negative	Positive
Actual	Negative	True Negative	False Positive
	Positive	False Negative	True Positive

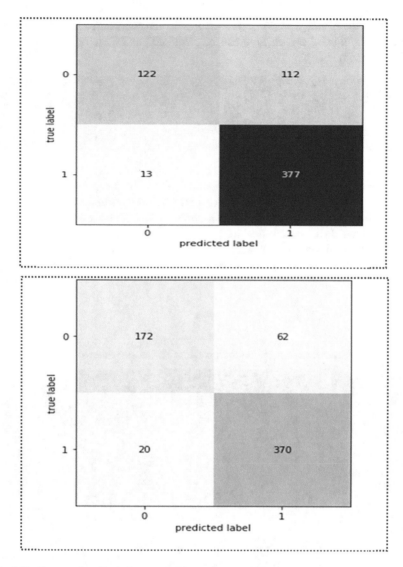

Fig. 9.18 Constructing Confusion matrix for normal convolution neural network model and convolution neural network implementing inception v3 architecture model. (**a**) Confusion matrix of normal convolution neural network model. (**b**) The confusion matrix of convolution neural network implementing inception v3 architecture model

To compare both the models, the *recall, precision,* and *F₁ scores* for the *normal convolution model* can be calculated as following using Eqs. (9.1), (9.2), and (9.3):

Precision Score = 374/(374 + 112) = 0.7695473251028807
Recall Score = 374/(374 + 1) = 0.9973333333333333
F₁ Score = 2x0.9973x0.7695/(0.9973 + 0.7695) = 0.8687144555127915

Further, the *recall*, *precision*, and F_1 *scores* for the *convolution model implementing the inception v3 architecture* can be calculated as following using Eq. (9.1), (9.2), and (9.3):

> *Precision Score* = 370/(370 + 62) = 0.8564814814814815
> *Recall Score* = 370/(370 + 20) = 0.9487179487179487
> *F₁ Score* = 2x0.9487x0.8564/(0.9487 + 0.8564) = 0.9001902166084982

It is very clear from the above computations that the *inception v3 architecture* has better *precision* and F_1 scores in comparison to the normal model. Hence, the authors can conclude that *inception v3 architecture model* has better suitability for the described IML based healthcare diseases prediction/monitoring system. Hence, the inception v3 architecture-based model can successfully classify the *normal* and *Pneumonia* diseases based on chest X-Rays and the same can be seen in Fig. 9.19.

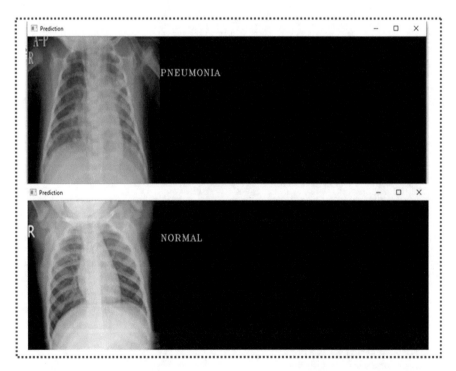

Fig. 9.19 Classifying the normal and Pneumonia diseases based on chest X-Rays using inception v3 architecture model

9.5.2   Discussions of Covid-19 Virus Detection for Mild Symptoms

The viruses and bacteria attack from outside of the human body to make a person ill. These viruses and bacteria convert themselves into multiples after entering into the human body which is called Antigen. To protect the body from these Antigens the human body creates equivalent numbers of antibodies. If the human body could not create enough amount of antibodies to counter the antigens created by a virus then the reflection will be in terms of a rise in human body temperature which brings a person into an illness state. To create an appropriate number of antibodies corresponding to the antigens, the human body needs an immunity booster. The vaccines work as immunity boosters for the human body.

The viruses are of many types and the Corona is one of them. The disease corresponding to Coronal is called Covid-19 or SARS-Cov-2 where SARS stands for Severe Acute Respiratory Syndrome. This virus may be natural or artificial. Although there is no very clear evidence about its origin, the majority of scientists and researchers say that the Coronavirus is not natural and it was developed in a Chinese lab through genetic modification of a few of the existing viruses available in Chinese bats. In the initial stage, the symptom of Covid-19 is like common cough and cold. But, on later days it attacks the respiratory system (lungs), kidney, heart, and liver, etc.

In the described Corona Virus Probability Detector assistance, the authors have taken random inputs like *Body Temperature = 98F*, *Age Value = 18*, *Body Pain = No Pain*, *Runny Nose = Yes*, and *Breathing Difficulty = Severe Difficulty*. After submitting the inputs we will get outputs. The inputs structure is presented in Fig. 9.20a and the structure of the corresponding output is presented in Fig. 9.20b. Here, the patient's probability of infection is 48%.

Further, by training the database and importing the described IML based healthcare diseases prediction/monitoring model into an HTML environment with the Flask (web framework), the authors can perform the execution of described model in a cloud-IoT integrated distributive internet computing environment. The authors tested the described model with available medical data and observed that the accuracy of the model is 81% accuracy for the training data sets and 80% for the test data sets. The Fig. 9.21a describes the view of medical database structure for Coronal Virus Prediction, Figs. 9.21b, 9.21c, and 9.21d are showing the snapshots of the working model of the described IML based healthcare diseases prediction/monitoring system.

The three supervised learning algorithms that have been described and implemented in this chapter are Decision Tree, Random Forest, and Naive Bayes algorithm. Out of the three algorithms, the Naive Bayes has produced the highest accuracy followed by Random Forest and decision tree. The dataset is a binary dataset with each column referring to a symptom and each row corresponding to a disease. The symptoms corresponding to disease have the numeric value '1' in that row otherwise it has the numeric value '0'. It is observed by the authors that this

Fig. 9.20 Inputs and outputs formats for Coronavirus probability detection system. (**a**) Inputs format for Corona Virus Probability Detector. (**b**) Outputs format for Corona Virus Probability Detector

binary dataset ('1' / '0') makes the implementation of mathematical functions and machine learning algorithms much easier [31, 37, 40].

In the described IML based healthcare diseases prediction/monitoring system of this chapter, the medical dataset is divided into test and train data, and the machine learning algorithms are trained on the training data which produces the model and the produced model can be implemented in the described system. Here, the end-user is asked to select any five symptoms from a large number of symptoms. If once the selection is done then the user is allowed to select the algorithm for the prediction of disease. Further, it is possible in the described system to select all three algorithms and in this situation, the system produces the result of each algorithm along with its accuracy [24, 25].

The SQLite database used in the described system allows users to register themselves in the system. For each user, a unique user ID is generated and the symptoms, as well as predicted diseases, are recorded. In any specific case if the actual

```
sqlite> .schema
CREATE TABLE patient(PID Integer Primarykey, Name text);
CREATE TABLE PatientSymptom(PID Integer Primarykey, symptom1 text, symptom2 text, symptom3 text, symptom4 text, symptom5 text);
CREATE TABLE Prediction(PID Integer Primarykey, decisiontree text, randomforest text, naivebayes text);
CREATE TABLE ActualDisease(PID Integer Primarykey,Actualdisease text);
CREATE TABLE credential(userID varchar(6), password varchar,designation text);
sqlite> select * from patient Natural Join PatientSymptom Natural Join Prediction Natural Join ActualDisease;
1|Mukund|dischromic _patches|congestion|inflammatory_nails|family_history|bruising|Varicoseveins
|Fungal infection
|Fungal infection
|NA
2|neha|extra_marital_contacts|dizziness|depression|loss_of_balance|None| Migraine
|Hypertension
|Hypertension
|NA
4|Param|dizziness|depression|coma|fluid_overload|None|Cervical spondylosis
|Hepatitis E
|Hypertension
|NA
5|paul|congestion|depression|irritability|back_pain|fast_heart_rate| Migraine
| Migraine
| Migraine
|NA
sqlite>
```

Fig. 9.21a A medical database structure's view for Coronal Virus Prediction

diagnosis of the disease is different from the predicted diseases by various algorithms of the system, then the user can come back and record his actual disease in the system. This functionality of the described system can be used for further improvement of the system. The records from the database can be integrated into the medical datasets for increasing the efficiency of the system. The described IML based healthcare diseases prediction/monitoring system can be used as a prototype by authors/researchers for the development of more sophisticated and better m-health systems to predict the diseases.

9.6 Conclusions

This chapter describes a simple system called IML based healthcare diseases prediction/monitoring system to predict diseases based on symptoms. It can be used by patients as well as doctors for consultation purposes in the cloud-IoT integrated distributive computing environment. The described system is developed by

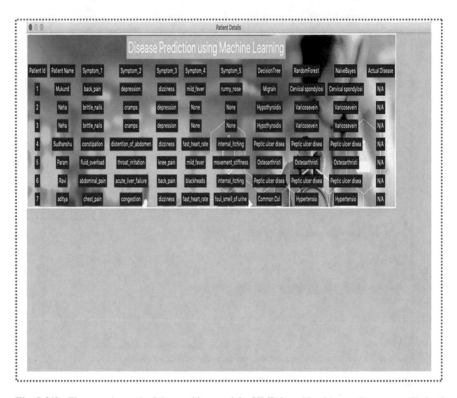

Fig. 9.21b The snapshot – 1 of the working model of IML based healthcare diseases prediction/monitoring system

applying historical medical healthcare data to supervised machine learning algorithms. The choice of algorithms for this purpose is based on their comparative study to measure accuracy and efficiency. The measured performances of various machine learning algorithms are reproduced in the form of charts and graphs for a better understanding and comparison of described methods. However, it was observed by the authors that different algorithms produce marginally variable accuracy in predicting different types of diseases. In this chapter, multiple algorithms have been implemented to further improve the performance and overall accuracy of the described system.

The described IML based healthcare diseases prediction/monitoring system accepts symptoms inputs objectively from the end-users. The list of symptoms is exhaustive and based on the available medical datasets. Thus, it may not accept new symptoms from the user. Although, the described system produces reasonable accuracy and there is always some scope for improvement through the use of more adaptive techniques such as neural network computations. The described IML based healthcare diseases prediction/monitoring system can become a stepping stone towards the development of such next-generation m-health systems.

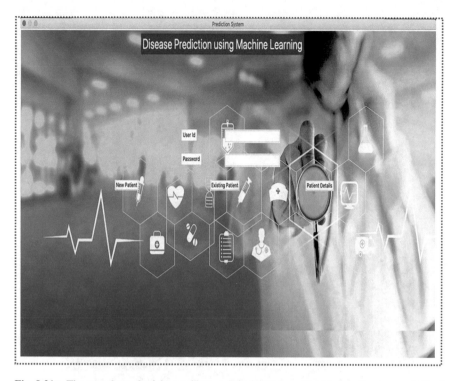

Fig. 9.21c The snapshot – 2 of the working model of IML based healthcare diseases prediction/monitoring system

With the rapid advancements in technologies, there is always vast room for improvement. The current system uses a binary dataset for the application of mathematical operations and simplicity. With the development of new algorithms in ML and AI, it may be possible to develop systems that can work on categorical data types. For the prediction of diseases, the described system works objectively and takes input from an exhaustive set of symptoms. However, a system that can interact with the user as an expert doctor will be better for the forthcoming societies.

There has been a major shift in the way data is stored and accessed. The world is quickly moving towards cloud storage. This functionality has been leveraged in the described IML based disease predicting system. The authors have a fear that the easily available Coronavirus genomes can be further modified (Genome Modification) and misused by the terrorists' laboratories of the world. Hence, genetically modified versions of Coronavirus strains with severe life-threatening diseases and high spreading speed can be seen in the forthcoming days and months.

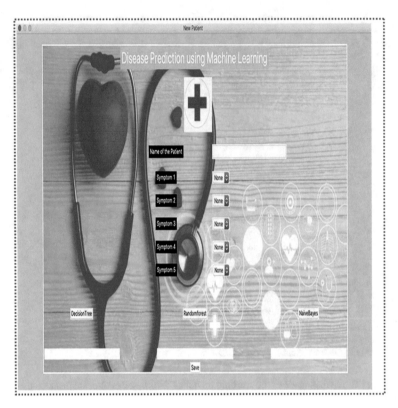

Fig. 9.21d The snapshot – 3 of the working model of IML based healthcare diseases prediction/monitoring system

References

1. Web Link: www.kaggle.com. Last Accessed 26 June 2021
2. Web Link: www.towardsdatascience.com. Last Accessed 26 June 2021
3. Web Link: www.researchgate.com. Last Accessed 26 June 2021
4. Puliafito C, Mingozzi E, Longo F, Puliafito A, Rana O (2019) Fog computing for the internet of things: a survey. ACM Trans Internet Technol 19(2)., Article 18 (April 2019), 41 pages. https://doi.org/10.1145/3301443
5. Raja A (2019) Healthcare cloud on the ground: fog computing powers the IoMT. https://getreferralmd.com/2018/11/fog-computing-powers-iomt-healthcare/
6. Pedroza ADS et al (2016) A motivational study regarding IoT and middleware for health systems. UBICOMM 2016: the 10th international conference on Mobile ubiquitous computing, systems, services, and technologies
7. Sun Get al (2016) Research on Mobile intelligent medical information system based on the internet of things technology. 2016 8th IEEE international conference on information technology in medicine and education (ITME), pp 260–266
8. Ullah K, Shah MA, Zhang S (2016) Effective ways to use the internet of things in the field of medical and smart health care. In 2016 international conference on intelligent systems engineering (ICISE), pp 372–379

9. Yannuzzi M et al (2014) Key ingredients in an IoT recipe: fog computing, cloud computing, and more fog computing. In: 19th international workshop on computer-aided modeling and Design of Communication Links and Networks (CAMAD). IEEE, pp 325–329

10. Web Link: https://www.kaggle.com/paultimothymooney/chest-xray-pneumonia. Last Accessed 25 June 2021

11. Łukasz C, Malawski F, Wyszkowski P (2015) Holistic approach to design and implementation of a medical teleconsultation workspace. J Biomed Inform 57:225–244

12. Pawar P et al (2012) A framework for the comparison of mobile patient monitoring systems. J Biomed Inform 45:544–556

13. Risso NA, Neyem A, Benedetto JI, Carrillo MJ, Farías A, Gajardo MJ, Loyola O (2016) A cloud-based mobile system to improve respiratory therapy services at home. J Biomed Inform 63:45–53

14. Gerneth M (1994) FEST: framework for European services in telemedicine. Comput Methods Progr Biomed 45:71–74

15. Rialle V et al (2003) Telemonitoring of patients at home: a software agent approach. Comput Methods Progr Biomed 72:257–268

16. Hsu MH et al (2010) Development and implementation of a national telehealth project for long-term care: a preliminary study. Comput Methods Progr Biomed 97:286–296

17. Shalom E, Shahar Y, Lunenfeld E (2016) An architecture for a continuous, user-driven, and data-driven application of clinical guidelines and their evaluation. J Biomed Inform 59:130–148

18. Harris LT et al (2010) Designing mobile support for glycemic control in patients with diabetes. J Biomed Inform 43:S37–S40

19. Bagula A, Mandava M, Bagula H (2018) A framework for healthcare support in the rural and low-income areas of the developing world. J Netw Comput Appl 2018(120):17–29

20. FI-WARE Cost-Effective Creation and Delivery of Future Internet Applications. Available online: http://www.fi-ware.eu/. Last Accessed 1 Oct 2014

21. Celesti A, Tusa F, Villari M, Puliafito A (2012) How the data web can support cloud federation: service representation and secure data exchange. In: 79 (ed) Proceedings of the 2012 second symposium on network cloud computing and applications, London, 3–4 December 2012, p 73

22. Fazio M et al (2016) Open issues in scheduling micro-services in the cloud. IEEE Cloud Comput 2016(3):81–88

23. Li W et al (2018) Graph-based semantic evolution for context information management platforms. In: Proceedings of the 2018 global internet of things summit (GIoTS), Bilbao, 4–7 June 2018, pp 1–6

24. Steinmetz C et al (2017) Ontology-driven IoT code generation for FIWARE. In: Proceedings of the 2017 IEEE 15th international conference on industrial informatics (INDIN), Emden, 24–26 July 2017, pp 38–43

25. Zahariadis T et al (2014) FIWARE lab: managing resources and Services in a Cloud Federation Supporting Future Internet Applications. In: Proceedings of the 2014 IEEE/ACM 7th international conference on utility and cloud computing (UCC), London, 8–11 December 2014, pp 792–799

26. Mamra A (2017) A proposed framework to investigate the user acceptance of personal health records in a proposed framework to investigate the user acceptance of personal health records in Malaysia using UTAUT2 and PMT. Int J Adv Comput Sci Appl March 2017

27. Alazzam MB et al (2016) Pilot study of EHRS accepted in Jordan hospitals by UTAUT2. J Theor Appl Info Tech 85(3):378–393

28. Alazzam MB et al (2016) Trust in stored data in EHRs acceptance of medical staff: using UTAUT2. Int J Appl Engg Res 11(4):2737–2748

29. Alazzam MB, Al-sharo YM, Ali MK (2018) Developing (UTAUT2) model of adaption Mobile health application in Jordan E-government. J Theor Appl Inf Technol 96(12):3846–3860

30. Alazzam MB (2015) Physicians' acceptance of electronic health records exchange: an extension of the with UTAUT2 model institutional trust. Adv Sci Lett 21:3248–3252

31. Alazzam ASMB (2015) Review of studies with Utaut as conceptual framework. Eur Sci J 10(3):249–258
32. Ramli MR et al (2018) Enhanced convergence of Bat algorithm based on dimensional and inertia weight factor. J King Saud Univ Comput Inf Sci 31(4):452–458
33. Rasmi M, Alazzam MB, Alsmadi MK, Ibrahim A, Alkhasawneh RA, Alsmadi S (2018) Healthcare professionals' acceptance electronic health records system: critical literature review (Jordan case study). Int J Healthc Manag:1–13
34. Mamra A et al (2017) Theories and factors applied in investigating the user acceptance towards personal health records: review study. Int J Healthc Manag:1–8
35. Alazzam SM (2015) BASARI EHRs acceptance in Jordan Hospitals By UTAUT2 model: preliminary result. Int J Theor Appl Inf Technol 3178(3):473–482
36. Doheir M et al (2015) Structural design of secure transmission module for protecting patient data in cloud-based healthcare environment. Middle-East J Sci Res 23(12):2961–2967
37. Mohammad Al-Sharo Y et al (2018) Classification of big data: machine learning problems and challenges in network intrusion prediction. Int J Eng Technol 7(4):3865–3869
38. Fernández-Alemán JL et al (2013) Security and privacy in electronic health records: a systematic literature review. J Biomed Inform 46(3):541–562
39. Hollands RG (2015) Critical interventions into the corporate smart city. Cambridge J Reg Econ Soc 8(1):61–77
40. Inukollu V, Arsi S, Ravuri S (2014) Security issues associated with big data in cloud computing. Int J Netw Secure Its Appl 6(3):45–56

Chapter 10
Societal Opinion Mining Using Machine Intelligence

Abstract The rapid growth in the chunk of social media messages has generated the dire need to architecture more reliable and robust techniques to mine the social opinion with the help of social media messages related to a particular realm. Machine learning techniques of recent scenarios can successfully be implemented for this pursuit. In this chapter, the authors presented a critical review and performance of different machine learning approaches for social opinion mining (SOM). Indeed, this chapter presents a beautiful amalgamation of different aspects related to SOM such as indispensable and inevitable concepts, implementation details, and efficiency to mine the opinion of society with the help of social media messages in the light of machine learning techniques. The basic discussion and theoretical background of this chapter attempt to explore the application of machine learning strategies in the phenomenon of SOM. Moreover, the chapter renders the discussion on the usual opinion mining process and the attempts performed by different researchers to tackle the pertinent problems of SOM with the help of social media and the implementation of machine learning techniques. Moreover, the chapter also discusses different challenges associated with this task. The mathematical models of social opinion mining are also proposed based on fuzzy concepts and linear algebra. Further, this chapter entails the algorithmic details of ten machine learning techniques for SOM. Finally, experimentations have been carried out for these ten machine learning techniques using Google embeddings and Amazon embeddings on two datasets and it has been observed that convolutional neural network (CNN) based deep learning outperforms other machine learning techniques in the pursuit of SOM.

Keywords Opinion mining · Social opinion mining · Machine learning · Social network · Word embeddings

© The Author(s), under exclusive license to Springer Nature Switzerland AG 2023
K. N. Mishra, S. C. Pandey, *Cloud-IoT Technologies in Society 5.0*,
https://doi.org/10.1007/978-3-031-28711-4_10

10.1   Introduction

Perhaps, social media plays a vital role in modern society. It rendered unprecedented impetus for the citizens to raise their opinions publically and thus created the need before the policymakers to analyze these public opinions so that a real-time visualization and understanding becomes possible. The analysis of public opinions from social media is termed social opinion mining (SOM) and is often considered a synonym of sentiment analysis. However, there is a subtle difference between these two terms. Opinion mining is an active area of research in the present scenario. In [1], it is defined as a phenomenon to analyze the public opinion, appraisals, attitudes, and emotions related to given entities. This entity may be anything like individuals, issues, events, etc. However, as of date, public opinion mining (OM) with the help of social media is in a nascent stage, but the attempt is being made by researchers in this pursuit because of several reasons. Indeed, the realm of opinion mining is of paramount importance because they are directly linked with our behavior [1]. Further, it is also an obvious fact that the internet has made it easy to share the public opinion worldwide about any entity that was a difficult task in past. Precisely, one can say that an enormous volume of opinionated data regarding any entity is available in the social media on the Web first time in human civilization [2]. But, it is also true that the policy-makers and citizens don't yet have substantial, cost-effective, and pragmatic means to obtain sensible and useful information from this huge mass conversation exists in social media and perhaps this is the reason that many experts ponder social media as a lagging opportunity for taking better policy decisions.

In a broader perspective, SOM can be visualized as a sub-domain of computational linguistics that strives to extract the public's opinion from the Web. The current advancement of the web motivates the users to reveal their opinion through various means such as blogs, social networking sites, etc., and thus influences the impetus of research on SOM. Indeed, all these platforms impart a voluminous amount of precious information worthy to analyze. However, SOM is also associated with many pertinent challenges and thus renders it an indispensable research domain. Intuitively, there is a trade-off between the challenges and opportunities of voluminous information on the Web. This voluminous information can provide the efficacy to identify the problems soon they arise. Moreover, it is also pertinent to mention that opinions are subjective entity and analysis of one opinion may not produce a succinct outcome. Therefore, a substantial collection of opinions often needs to be analyzed in SOM that renders it an invaluable and evitable avenue for different application domains of OM.

Furthermore, open data available on data repositories play a succinct role in the phenomenon of SOM. These open data, as well as government data, is easily accessible to the public and thus they can access new information which in turn influences public opinions. Several technological innovations have been developed using the techniques of machine learning (ML) for analyzing this gigantic amount of available data. It is imperative to state that OM is a different phenomenon than pure data and text mining. SOM is a subjective endeavor unlike pure data and text mining and attempt is being made by researchers to develop it as a novel discipline that can deal with unstructured information extraction that was earlier chiefly working with objective data like data related to natural disasters or information about bibliography. It is also true that the exponential growth in user-generated content broadens the scope of application of SOM tools and these SOM tools are considerably pervasive and agile to the bulk of the public.

Social media mining (SMM) can be considered as the sub-domain of SOM and this SMM can analyze all the data and thus no need to select a sample. It is obvious that the social media data are typically the textual content, rating scores, like/dislike indications, web search queries, tags, and profile information [4]. But, as is already stated this huge amount of data is a challenge so some sort of summary is of the utmost importance for analysis. This summary can be of different formats such as it may be in the form of classifications of binary sentiment, opinions of positive or negative types, sentiments of multiclass, etc.

Further, SOM can vividly be used in arrays of applications like to recognize know the online reputation of various companies, to identify the recent trends, to analyze the intents of the users and to retrieve the knowledge, and many commercial and fiscal applications as well. In [3, 4], SOM is used to analyze political opinions. Further, in [5], it is proposed to use SOM to identify the significant participants and groups and how users shift from one service to another. Moreover, in [6], it is used to detect the polarity of mood. In [6–10], it is also implemented for predictive analysis. Some other applications of SOM are enumerated below:

- It can be used in argument mapping software.
- It can be used in voting advice applications.
- It can be used in automated content analysis.

SOM is frequently used in the first two application domains maturely. However, there is an emerging trend of its use in the third application domain with relevant research issues.

It has already been stated that SOM can be visualized as a sub-domain of computational linguistic and thus we can consider different problems of SOM as the problems of natural language processing (NLP). Undoubtedly, it is a multi-disciplinary research domain that entails the realms of computer science, linguistics, and psychology. In [11], NLP is defined as the field of research and application that attempts to search how machines can be used to realize and maneuver natural language text or speech to do useful things. SOMs linked with every aspect of NLP such as to avoid the ambiguity in the implication of words, and the resolutions of co-reference or negation handling. A brief review of SOM is rendered in forthcoming Sect. 10.2.

10.2 Theoretical Background of Social Opinion Mining (SOM)

Opinion can be defined as the individual's belief, ideas, evaluation, and assessment of a specific entity. Perhaps, it is an individual's state of mind. It is also explicit that an individual's opinion also creates substantial impetus on the opinions of other individuals, social communities, and organizations as well as on the government agencies and consequently influences their decision-making process. Actually, during this decision-making process living beings require swift, precise, and succinct information in an attempt to enable and help them to take fast and precise decisions. Even more, in this decision-making phenomenon living beings can fuse varied approaches, empirical facts, perceptions, knowledge, etc. It is fairly usual for a human to take participation in discussions and reflect their viewpoints. Human beings often ask their kiths and kin and the domain experts to receive the information in this process of decision-making. It is also obvious that their opinions and perspectives are based on empirical facts, perceptions, knowledge, etc. It is inquisitive that a human's perspective about an entity can either be positive or negative and this is known as the opinion's polarity. Moreover, opinions can be reflected in different manners. Opinion possesses three chief ingredients as given below:

- The source of opinion.
- The object of opinion.
- Evaluation of opinion.

Indeed, opinions can be accumulated from discrete sources such as newspapers, the Internet, social media, etc. However, all these ingredients are important for the proper identification of opinions. It is also a fact that before the existence of the World Wide Web (www), opinions were gathered manually, and to gain social opinion organizations and institutions often used to conduct surveys through intent groups. However, this way of social opinion mining was expensive, difficult, and cumbersome. In today's scenario because of the Internet, this can be done with extreme ease and cost-effective manner. Hence, the Internet emerged forth as a worthy source for different purposes. In [12], it is mentioned that forty-five new blogs are generated on daily basis with more than one million new posts every day. Further, the information retrieved from these services is used for different purposes of decision-making. Intuitively, the indispensable feature behind this decision-making process is opinion. No doubt, the Internet is an enormous source of opinions with voluminous information. However, it is also linked with certain drawbacks such as the Web data are characteristically unstructured text and thus cannot suitably be used directly for knowledge representation. Moreover, it is not possible to process this huge data manually. Therefore, efficient machine learning tools and techniques are the requirement of the time so that one can extract and summarize the entailed opinions in real-time. Researchers are consistently and persistently striving to develop the techniques that can transform this Web information into knowledge requisition efficiently so that users can use this knowledge succinctly and lucidly. Indeed, Web 2.0 has rendered different tasks such as posting and gathering opinions through the Web considerably easy. However, different pertinent fringe tasks such as processing, compilation, summarization of opinions, etc. are still posing problems and are considered as substantial research problems. The term OM is first coined in [13]. However, some earlier works had already been focused on OM like the works given in [14–18]. Further, many researchers considered the task of OM similar to the review analysis of entities and rendered it as a model for classification of document polarity i.e., being either recommended or not. This work paved the way for a new horizon as the applied research in the domain of NLP and text mining. Subsequently, in few years extensive research had been observed in this pursuit [19–22]. With the emergence of this applied research in the domain of NLP, the definition of SOM is reconfigured as [12]:

> SOM is a recent discipline at the crossroads of information retrieval, text mining and computational linguistics which tries to detect the opinions expressed in natural language texts.

Precisely, SOM is a domain of knowledge discovery and data mining (KDD) and it also incorporates NLP, statistics as well as ML techniques so that opinionated text can be differentiated from the factual text. Further, to perform this differentiation SOM is supposed to perform miscellaneous tasks such as:

- Opinion identification.
- Opinion classification (positive, negative, and neutral).
- Target identification.
- Source identification.
- Opinion summarization.

Therefore, to perform all these tasks OM requires approaches from different domains like NLP, information retrieval, and text mining. However, it is of the prime concern that how to automate the phenomenon of identification of different ingredients of opinion from the purview of unstructured text and subsequently summarize the opinion of an entity from the gigantic quantity of unstructured text. Undoubtedly, this is a challenging task because textual information can be categorized into two sub-domains. These sub-domains are objective and subjective. It is inquisitive that objective textual information implicates facts contrary to subjective textual information that implicates perceptions or opinions. An extensive literature survey reveals the fact that the NLP researches are mainly concentrating on the tasks of mining that are focused on the extraction of factual information from the text and it is an important domain with several applications. However, the emergence of Web 2.0 let the users create the Web content, and thus in this consequence researchers developed innovative techniques to extract knowledge from this Web content. Moreover, the emergence of Web 2.0 also extends the opportunity to gain information by applying the techniques of information retrieval and knowledge discovery for the pursuit of miscellaneous applications. Furthermore, researchers observed that mining huge reviews available on the Web can resolve various quests of research. Over and above, mining the knowledge from users' created corpus on the Web can be treated as the subjective analysis. This subjective analysis can further be sub-divided into two categories. These are:

- Opinion Mining (OM)
- Sentiment Analysis (SA)

In [1], it is mentioned that some researchers used these two terms interchangeably. However, in [23], it is given that some other researchers visualized sentiment analysis as a sub-domain of OM. In [23], it is stated that there is a subtle difference between sentiment analysis and OM. Indeed, within the purview of SA, the analysis or classification of the text takes place and it merely renders the positive or negative attitudes of the source of opinion. Indeed, SA is related to the extraction and analysis of emotions and sentiments contained in the text. A novel, innovative, and motivating progress in this domain is the generation of a cognitive model with the help of NLP and ANN architecture in a brain-like discourse to mine the opinions using customer reviews [24]. However, contrary to SA, OM is linked with any other phenomena such as information retrieval, analysis of the source of opinion, rating of the source of opinion about an entity.

But, it is also pertinent to mention that still the domain of subjectivity analysis is in a nascent phase and different pertinent problems are yet to be resolved. In [12], it is stated that despite intellectual difficulties associated with SOM, it is undoubtedly extremely useful in pragmatic applications.

In subsequent Sect. 10.3, an attempt has been made to render the mathematical model of SOM using the concept of fuzzy set theory and linear algebra.

10.3   Mathematical Model of SOM

Mathematical modeling is to strive to convert the problems from one application domain to tractable mathematical formulations. The theoretical and numerical analysis of these mathematical formulations imparts in-depth insight, answers, and guidance useful for the originating application. Further, mathematical modeling is vividly used in different application domains and renders precise guidelines to solution approaches. Moreover, it provides a better understanding of the modeled system and also facilitates design modification or control over the entity modeled and thus permits the effective implementation of the system in the machine. In this section, the authors attempted to construct the mathematical model for social opinion mining using fuzzy and linear algebra-based approaches. In sub-sect. 10.3.1, a fuzzy-based approach is given and a further linear algebra-based approach is rendered in sub-sect. 10.3.2.

10.3.1   Fuzzy Logic-Based Mathematical Model of SOM

The concept of a fuzzy set is of the utmost importance in mathematics, science, and engineering. Many authors studied the pragmatic use of fixed points in the domain of fuzzy sets [25–29]. In this sub-section attempt has been made to construct the mathematical model of SOM with the help of a fuzzy concept.

Let S be a fuzzy memory space of SOM consisting of different opinions with a general opinion of S denoted by O_p: A fuzzy sub-memory space M of S is characterized by its membership function

$$\mu_M : S \to [0,1]$$

and $\mu_M(O_p)$ is interpreted as the degree of membership of opinion O_p in fuzzy sub-memory space M of S for every $O_p \in S$. Let M and M^* be two fuzzy sub-memory spaces of S: We say that M is included in M^* and we can write $M \subseteq M^*$ if $\mu_M(O_p) \leq \mu_{M^*}(O_p)$, for all $O_M \in S$. In particular, if $O_p \in S$ and M is a fuzzy sub-memory space of opinion in S, then $\{O_p\} \subseteq M$ if $\mu_M(O_p) = 1$. It is intuitive that opinion mining renders the fuzzy order relation. It is due to the fact that a fuzzy order relation on S is a fuzzy subset R of $S \times S$ satisfying the following three properties:

(i) $\forall O_p \in S, r(O_p, O_p) \in [0, 1]$ (Reflexivity).
(ii) $\forall O_p, O_{p1} \in S, r(O_p, O_{p1}) + r(O_{p1}, O_p) > 1$. It implies $O_p = O_{p1}$ (Antisymmetry).
(iii) $\forall O_p, O_{p1}, O_{p2} \in S^3, [r(O_p, O_{p1}) \geq + r(O_{p1}, O_p)$ and $r(O_{p1}, O_{p2}) \geq r(O_{p2}, O_{p1})]$.

   It implies $r(O_p, O_{p2}) \geq r(O_{p2}, O_p)$ (f– Transitivity).

Further, it is intuitive to consider the sub-memory space M as a fuzzy chain because the fuzzy ordered relation of opinion is said to be total if $\forall O_p \neq O_{p1}$ implicates either $r(O_p, O_{p1}) > r(O_{p1}, O_p)$ or $r(O_{p1}, O_p) > r(O_p, O_{p1})$.
   Let M be a fuzzy sub-memory space of S. It is natural to say that an opinion $O_p \in S$ will be an upper bound of M if $r(O_{p1}, O_p) \geq r(O_p, O_{p1}) \ \forall O_{p1} \in M$. Further, if opinion O_p is an upper bound of M and $O_p \in M$ then the opinion O_p will be the greatest element of M. Furthermore, the opinion $O_p \in M$ is called a maximal element of M if there is no $O_{p1} \neq O_p$ in M for which $r(O_p, O_{p1}) \geq r(O_{p1}, O_p)$. similarly, we can define lower bound, minimal and least opinion elements of M. Moreover, it is obvious that the supremum of fuzzy sub-memory space M i.e., sup (M) will be the least element of upper bound of M (if it exists). Similarly, infimum i.e., inf(M) will be the greatest element of lower bound of M (if it exists).
   Further, in this sequel we can say that if we consider S as fuzzy order set then it can generate a map of fuzzy multifunction $T : S \to [0,1]^S / \{\phi\}$ such that for every opinion $O_p \in S$, $T(O_p)$ is a nonempty fuzzy sub-memory space of S. Furthermore, the fuzzy multifunction $T : S \to [0,1]^S / \{\phi\}$ is said to be fuzzy monotone if and only if $\forall O_p, O_{p1} \in S, r(O_p, O_{p1}) \geq r(O_{p1}, O_p)$ and it implicates that for all $\{a\} \subseteq T(O_p) \ \exists \ \{b\} \in T(O_{p1})$ such that $r(a,b) \geq r(b,a)$.

10.3.2   Linear Algebra Based Mathematical Model of SOM

In this sub-section, attempt has been made to model the societal opinion mining with the help of linear algebra using the concept of group, field, and vector space.
   Let A be the set of societal opinion. If a and b be the two opinions of the society i.e., $a, b \in A$ & $\forall a, b \to a^*b \in A$ and $a * b$ is unique then $*$ is said to be an 'internal composition' in the set A of the societal opinion.

Similarly, let V and F be any two sets. If $a¿\alpha \in V \forall a \in F$ and $\forall \alpha \in V$ and $a¿\alpha$ is unique, then $¿$ is said be an 'external composition in V over F. Here a is an element of the set F and α is an element of the set V and the resulting element $a¿\alpha$ is an element of the set V.

Indeed, the set F is a field and thus can be taken as algebraic structure $(F, +, -)$, the elements of F are called scalars. Let V be a non-empty set and its elements are social opinions. In linear algebra, the elements of V are treated as vector. It should be noted that here vector does not implicate the quantity with magnitude and direction. But, here vector implicates any object or entity. In this case, the set V of social opinion will form a vector space over the field F, if:

1. There is defined an internal composition in V, the set of social opinion called addition of vectors and denoted by '+'. It is also pertinent to mention that for this composition, V will also form an abelian group because its elements will display the commutative property i.e.,

    (a) $\alpha + \beta \in V \forall \alpha, \beta \in V$.
    (b) $\alpha + \beta = \beta + \alpha \forall \alpha, \beta \in V$.
    (c) $\alpha + (\beta + \gamma) = (\alpha + \beta) + {}^3 \forall \alpha, {}^2, {}^3 \in V$.
    (d) an element $0 \in V : \alpha + 0 = \alpha \forall \alpha \in V$. This element $0 \in V$ will be called the zero vector.
    (e) $\forall \alpha \in V, \exists$ a vector $-\alpha \in V : \alpha + (-\alpha) = 0$

2. There is an external composition in V over F called 'scalar multiplication' and denoted multiplicatively i.e., $a \times \alpha \in V \forall a \in F$ and $\forall \alpha \in V$. In other words, the set of social opinion V is closed with respect to scalar multiplication.

3. The two compositions i.e., scalar multiplication and addition of vectors satisfy the following postulates:

    (a) $a(\alpha + \beta) = a\alpha + a\beta \forall a \in F$ and $\forall \alpha, \beta \in V$.
    (b) $(a + b)\alpha = a\alpha + b\alpha \forall a, b \in F$ and $\forall \alpha \in V$.
    (c) $(ab)\alpha = a(b\alpha) \forall a, b \in F$ and $\forall \alpha \in V$.
    (d) $1\alpha = \alpha \forall \alpha \in V$ and 1 is the unity element of the field F.

When the set of social opinion V is a vector space over the field F, we shall say that $V(F)$ is a vector space. If the field F is understood we can simply say that V is a vector space. If F is the field R of real numbers, V can be called as the real vector space of social opinion. Similarly, if F is Q or F is C, we can say rational vector space of social opinion or complex vector space of social opinion.

In the above definition of a vector space of social opinion V over the field F, authors have denoted the addition of opinions (vectors) by the symbol '+'. This symbol also denotes the addition composition of the field F i.e., addition of scalars. There should be no confusion about the two compositions though authors used the same symbol to denote each of them. If $\alpha, \beta \in V$, then $\alpha + \beta$ represents addition of V that is addition of vectors. If $a, b \in F$ then $a + b$ represents addition of scalars that is addition in the field F. Similarly, there should be no confusion in multiplication of scalars that is multiplication of the elements of F and in scalar multiplication that is multiplication of an element of V by an element of F. If $a, b \in F$, then ab represents multiplication of F and $ab \in F$. If $a \in F$ and $\alpha \in V$, then $a\alpha$ represents scalar multiplication and $a\alpha \in V$. Since $1 \in F$ and $\alpha \in V$, therefore 1α represents scalar multiplication. Again, $a\alpha \in V, a\beta \in V$, therefore $a\alpha + a\beta$ represents addition of vectors and thus $a\alpha + a\beta$ is an element of set of social opinion V. Further, $a \in F$ and $\alpha + \beta \in V$, therefore $a(\alpha + \beta)$ represents scalar multiplications and we have $a(\alpha + \beta)$ represents scalar multiplication and we have $a(\alpha + \beta) \in V$.

Note 1. It should be noted that the set of social opinion will form the algebraic structure $(V, +)$ and this algebraic structure will be an abelian group. Therefore, all the properties of an abelian group will hold in set of social opinion V. A few of them are as follows:

(a) $\alpha + {}^2 = \alpha + {}^3 \rightarrow {}^2 = {}^3$ (*Left cancellation law*)
(b) ${}^2 + \alpha = {}^3 + \alpha \rightarrow {}^2 = {}^3$ (*Right cancellation law*)
(c) $\alpha + \beta = 0 \rightarrow \alpha = -\beta$ *and* $\beta = -\alpha$
(d) $-(\alpha + \beta) = -\alpha - \beta$ *where by* $\alpha - \beta$ *we mean* $\alpha + (-\beta)$
(e) $-(-\alpha) = \alpha$
(f) $\alpha + \beta = \alpha \rightarrow \beta = 0$
(g) $\alpha + (\beta - \alpha) = \beta$
(h) *The additive identity* **0** *will be unique.*
(i) *The additive inverse of each vector will be unique.*
(j) *if* $\alpha + {}^2 = {}^3$, *then* $\alpha + {}^2 - {}^3 = \mathbf{0}$

Note 2. There should be no confusion about the use of the word vector. Here by vector we do not mean the vector quantity which we often use in vector algebra as a directed line segment. Here we shall call the elements f the set of social opinion V as vectors.

Note3. In the vector space of social opinion, authors use two types of zero elements. One is the zero vector and the other is zero element of the field F that is 0 scalar. To distinguish between the two, authors used the zero letter in bold type to represent the zero vector. Also, the authors use the lower case Greek letters α, β, γ etc., to denote vectors that is the opinions from the set of social opinion V and the lower case Latin letters a, b, c etc., to denote the scalars that is the elements of the field F.

10.4 Effective Machine Learning Tools for SOM

Of recent, there are different ML techniques used for the purpose of SOM. These ML techniques perform the task of SOM in an automated and adaptive manner. In [30], it is given that ML entails the efficacy to perform well owing to their experience. In this section, authors will discuss some frequently used ML techniques for the purpose of SOM.

10.4.1 Clustering Technique (CLT)

Unsupervised ML techniques can perform the task of clustering. Clustering implicates the division of objects, instances, or entities into reasonably alike collections. The clustering techniques have been applied in different fields of application including clustering of e-mail spam datasets [31]. Two types of clustering approaches can be effectively used for SOM. These two approaches are density-based clustering and k-nearest neighbors (k-NN). In [32], density-based clustering is used for document clustering. Contrary to the density-based approach, k-NN is independent of distribution. It is also mentioned in [33] that the k-NN approach is independent of the hypothesis that the data is drawn from a given probability distribution. Indeed, k-NN is a non-parametric algorithm and is also known as the lazy learner and is also associated with an overhead cost of both time and memory. Actually, in the k-NN model, more memory is needed for storing entire training data neighbors [34]. The prime merit of this algorithm is that it does not entail an explicit training phase [35]. Or, if there is a training phase then it is substantially minimal. Different steps required in a naïve k-NN technique for SOM are given in Table 10.1. In this algorithm, the neighbors (n) return the k nearest neighbors of n, Closest (n,t) returns the closest elements of t in n, and test Class (SOM) return the class label of SOM.

Table 10.1 k-NN algorithm for SOM

begin
1: Find SOM class labels.
2: **Input** k, the number of nearest neighbors
3: **Input** N, the set of SOM test message from social media;
4: **Input** T, the set of training SOM Message from social media.
5: C, the concept set of SOM in test message obtained from social media..
6: **Read** T
7: **Read** N
8: **for** each n in N and each t in T **do**
9: $Neighbors\ (n) = \{\ \}$
10: **if** $|Neighbours\ (n)| < k$ **then**
11: $Neighbors\ (n) = Closest\ (n,t) \cup Neighbors(n)$
12: **end if**
13: **if** $|Neighbours\ (n)| \geq k$ **then**
14: restrain (SOM, x_j, y_j)
15: **end if**
16: **end for**
17: **return** final opinion from SOM
end

10.4.2   Naïve-Bayes Classifier (NBC)

This is also a supervised learning technique and it uses a statistical approach to perform the task of classification. In [36], it is given that this technique can be implemented to obtain the solution for problems that are analytical and predictive. This algorithm can be considered as a pragmatic learning approach that is fused with the previous knowledge and experimental data. Further, it is a simple and computationally effective technique to solve many real-world problems with acceptable performance. Perhaps, this is the reason many researchers attempted to use this algorithm for sentiment analysis, opinion mining, text classification task, etc. In [37–40], it is implemented for performing the task of spam Email classification. Indeed, this algorithm attempts to find the exact likelihood, and even more it is robust to noisy input data. An in-depth insight about the algorithm is given in [41, 42] (Table 10.2).

Table 10.2 NBC algorithm for SOM

---

begin
1: **Input** SOM message from social media
2: Parse each message into tokens of opinion $O_{T_i} : i = 1,2,3$ (i.e., components of
    opinion like positive, negative, and neutral)
3: Compute probability for each token of opinions e.g. probability of positive
    opinion $P(O_p) = Number\ of\ positive/$
    $Total\ opinions\ including\ positive, negative, and\ neutral$
4: Store probability values to a database
5: **for** each SOM message O_M **do**
6: **while** $(O_M$ not end) **do**
7: scan SOM message for the next token of opinion O_{T_i}
8: query the database for the probability of O_{T_i}
9: compute probabilities of SOM message collected O_{T_i} for $i = 1,2,3$
10: compute the total SOM message filtering signal by: $I[O_M] =$
    $f(SOM[O_M, (Total - O_M)])$
11: $I(O_M) = (I + SOM[O_M] - (Total - O_M))/2$
12: **if** $I(O_M) >$ threshold **then**
13: SOM message is labeled as O_p
14: **else**
15: SOM message is labeled as O_N (negative) or $O_{Neutral}$
16: **end if**
17: **end while**
18: **end for**
19: **return** final opinion from SOM.
end

10.4.3   Artificial Neural Network (ANN)

Artificial Neural Network (ANN) mimics the functionality of the biological neural network. ANN contains small processing units called neurons interconnected with each other through weighted synaptic links. The neurons of one layer accept the inputs from the neurons of the preceding layer. ANNs are the efficient ML method often used to perform the task of classification [43]. However, this technique is not generally used for sentiment analysis and opinion mining, unlike NBC. But, it is true that large numbers of interconnected neurons in ANN function in symphony and thus impart solutions to many real-world problems. Some researchers also used the ensemble model of ANN and NBC to improve the performance of spam filters. In [44], it is given that there are usually three types of layers in ANN.

- Input Layer: This layer receives input signals from surrounding.
- Output Layer: This layer produces the final outputs of ANN.
- Hidden Layer: This layer receives and propagates the signals within the ANN.

The ANN is trained with the help of training data and this phenomenon is termed as learning of ANN. There are different approaches to learning but mainly it can be categorized into two domains. Namely: supervised and unsupervised learning. There are two traditional categories of neural networks often implied in the context of ANN. They are the single-layer perceptron (SLP) and the multilayer perceptron (MLP). The SLP and MLP use the attribute vector $f(x) = W^T x + b : f(x) > 0$ for opinion vectors of one category [45], and $f(x) < 0$ for opinion vectors of other categories. It is pertinent to mention that $W = (w_1, w_2 \ldots w_m)$ are the weights and b is the biased value. The categories are assigned the numbers $+1$ and -1, so search for a function $d(x) = sign\ (w^T x + b)$ takes place. The learning of SLP and MLP is commenced by random selection of parameters (w_0, b_0) and subsequently the values are updated. Precisely, in SLP and MLP, a training instance (x, c) is selected at the nth iteration of the algorithm to the extent that the current opinion decision function now categorizes it as incorrect (i.e. $sign(w_n x + b_n \neq c)$. Further, the rule is given in Eq. (1) is used to modify the parameters (w_n, b_n).

$$W_{n+1} = W_n + C_x\ b_1 = b_n + c\,(1)$$

The algorithm is finally terminated after meeting the termination criterion that is the opinion decision function must be observed to classify all the training instances into different opinion domains. Often, it is not possible to classify the training data linearly, in such a scenario it is a common practice to terminate the training algorithm once the number of messages obtained from the social media that are incorrectly categorized is considerably small [46, 47]. A perceptron algorithm is given in Table 10.3 for SOM. The architectural details of ANN for SOM are given in Fig. 10.1.

Table 10.3 Perceptron neural network algorithm for SOM

begin
1: **Input** *SOM* message from social media.
2: Initialize w and b with random values or 0.
3: Find a training instance of *SOM* messages (x, c) obtained from social media such that $sign(w^T x + b)$.
4: **if** there is no such instance, **then**
5: Training phase is completed
6: Save the final w and stop.
7: **else**
8: update (w, b): $w = w + cx$,
9: $b = b + c$
10: **go to** step 8
11: **end if**
12: Determine the opinion class as $sign(w^T x + b)$
13: **return** final opinion from *SOM*.
end

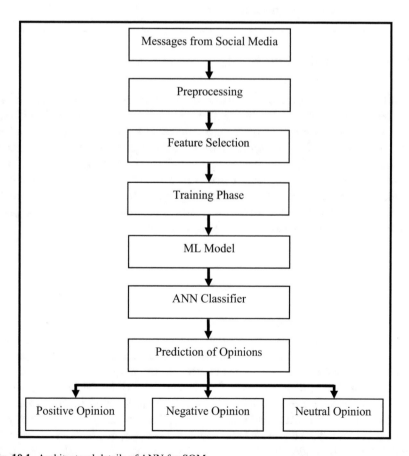

Fig. 10.1 Architectural details of ANN for SOM

Table 10.4 Firefly algorithm for SOM

begin
1: **Input** SOM message from social media with N number of attributes
2: Set $i = 0$
3: Get population of messages (fireflies) P
4: Find N
5: Initialize P
6: **for** each SOM message
7: Choose the SOM message whose fitness is best.
8: Choose matching attributes from the test SOM message obtained from social media.
9: Test the SOM message for opinion.
10: $i = i + 1$
11: Update each SOM message.
12: Classify the SOM message as positive, negative, or neutral.
13: **end for**
14: **return** final opinion from SOM.
end

10.4.4   Firefly Algorithm (FA)

In [48], a population-based metaheuristic algorithm inspired by the sparkly behavior of firefly is proposed that is known as the 'firefly algorithm'. In this algorithm, a direct search is performed to preserve and increase so many candidate solutions [49]. The algorithm is based on the intriguing concept of communication among fireflies when they are getting ready for copulation, and instantly they are exposed to risk. Indeed, the sparkling feature makes them enable to share information [50]. In [50, 51], it is mentioned that their sparkling feature for attraction and movement is similar to an optimization technique in which solutions chase better (brighter) solutions. The firefly algorithm for SOM is shown in Table 10.4.

10.4.5   Rough Set (RS) Classifiers

In [52, 53], rough set theory is proposed for automatic transformation of inexact, ambiguous, and partially correct data obtained from experience into knowledge and it can be treated as the recent mathematical tool to deal with fuzzy concepts and uncertainty. It can even deal with quantitative as well as qualitative data. The core concept behind the rough set theory is that some sort of knowledge is related to every object of the universe. Intuitively, any inappropriate model can be evaluated by subsuming from beneath and by considering the overhead and subsequently by attempting to establish an invisible association. However, this theory requires realizing the inter-dependencies between the features as well as redundancy [54].

Table 10.5   Rough set algorithm for SOM

begin
1: **Input** Testing dataset from SOM message obtained from social media (SOM _test data), Decision rule (DL), b
2: **for** $x \in SOM$ _test data **do**
3: **while** $DL(x) = 0$ **do**
4: $Uncertain = Uncertain \cup \{x\}$;
5: **end while**
6: Let all $o \in DL(x)$ cast a number in favor of a positive opinion.
7: Predict membership degree based on the DL;
8: $O = o \in DL(x)\|$ o predicts positive opinion;
9: Estimate Relation (SOM _test data $\| x \in$ positive opinion);
10: Relation(SOM _test data $\| x \in$ positive opinion) $= \sum o \in O$ Predicts (positive opinion);
11: $Certainty_x = \frac{1}{Cer} \times Relation(SOM$ _test data $\| x \in$ positive opinion);
12: **while** $Certainty_x \geq 1 - b$ **do**
13: $Uncertain = Uncertain \cup \{x\}$;
14: **end**
15: positive opinion = positive opinion $\cup \{x\}$;
16: **return** final opinion from SOM as $positive, negative, and$ $neutral.$
end

Further, a rough set possesses the efficacy to easily recognize the relationship between the attributes as compared to other traditional statistical methods and can perform the task of estimation of a minimum set of data required for clustering jobs. Unlike the fuzzy set concept, this theory does not use the membership grade to represent imprecision or uncertainty. Rather, it uses the concept of borderline section for this purpose.

The empty borderline section of the set implicates that the set has explicitly been described or the set is exact otherwise the set is treated as rough or inexact. Contrary to this, if the borderline section of the set entails at least one member or element then it implicates that we do not know exactly about the set. Furthermore, it permits the automatic formation of decision rules from data. Moreover, it renders the users imbibe and evaluate the importance and significance of data [55]. Rough set theory has also been used for spam email classification [56]. In [57], it is given that this theory can pragmatically be used for parallel and distributed (i.e., concurrent) processing. Table 10.5 represents the algorithmic details of this algorithm for SOM.

10.4.6   Support Vector Machine (SVM) Classifiers

In [58], a supervised learning algorithm is proposed that is very suitable for the classification of non-linearly classifiable datasets and can also be used for regression problems. Indeed, it can effectively be used for solving quadratic programming problems that include inequality constraints and linear equality. It distinguishes different classes using a hyperplane and entertains substantial advantage of boundary

Table 10.6 SVM algorithm for SOM

begin
1: **Input** SOM message m from social media to classify
2: A training set($SOM\_Training$), a kernel function,
$\{(C_1, \gamma_1), (C_2, \gamma_2), ..., (C_{num}, \gamma_{num})\}$.
3: Number of nearest neighbors.
4: **for** $i = 1$ to num
5: set $C = C_i$;
6: **for** $j = 1$ to q
7: set $\gamma = \gamma$;
8: produce a trained SVM classifier $f(x)$ through the recent merger parameter (C, γ);
9: **if** $(f(x))$ is the first produced discriminant function) **then**
10: keep $f(x)$ as the most ideal SVM classifier $f^*(x)$;
11: **else**
12: compare classifier $f(x)$ and the recent best SVM classifier $f^*(x)$ using k-fold cross validation
13: keep classifier with a better accuracy.
14: **end if**
15: **end for**
16: **end for**
17: **return** final opinion
from SOM as $positive, negative, and$ $neutral.$
end

[59]. This technique is not fast in comparison to many other techniques but its accuracy is generally high. In [60], a binary C-SVM is also proposed, where, C is the cost parameter for regulating the modeling error. In this approach, the merger parameter (C, γ) is used during the training phase. Usually, the Grid-search technique is used for C and γ [60]. This algorithm is given in Table 10.6 for SOM.

10.4.7   Decision Tree (DT)

The decision tree belongs to the category of supervised learning. In [61, 62], it is given that this can effectively be used to perform the classification task. However, it can also be used to perform the regression task. There are three types of nodes in the decision tree. Namely: root nodes, intermediate nodes, and leaf nodes. The intermediate nodes represent the different attribute values of the dataset [63]. The leaf nodes implicate the concept or classes. DT produces classification rules by traversing from the root node to the leaf node. Often, pruning of DT is also required to avoid the phenomenon of overfitting of the algorithm. There are different types of DT as given below:

- Naïve Bayes (NB) Tree classifier
- ID3/C4.5/J48 DT
- Logistic model tree (LMT) induction

NB tree is the ensemble model of naïve Bayes classifier and DT. NB tree is very useful for the dataset of big size. Moreover, it can even perform well if the dataset is non-uniformly distributed and the dataset attributes are dependent. In [64], it is mentioned that in this technique the DT divides the data into different divisions, and subsequently, the naïve Bayes technique is applied.

C4.5 is the modified version of the ID3 algorithm. ID3 uses the concept of information gain whereas C4.5 uses the concept of gain ratio. Further, J48 is a modified version of C4.5. In [65], it is claimed that the C4.5 is the most effective and abundantly used DT algorithm. The DT constructed by C4.5 is applicable for solving miscellaneous classification problems. C4.5 selects the attributes of the dataset that it can further split into subclasses at each node. Finally, the result obtained from this division is represented by a leaf node [61].

LMT uses logistic regression models on leaf nodes and it possesses a high degree of accuracy and robustness. This technique is also easy to decode and translate in comparison to C4.5. However, this technique renders a trade-off between accuracy and computational complexity. It is worthy to mention that because of the inclusion of logistic regression the time needed to train the model is considerably less than the naïve Bayes classifier as well as the classification accuracy is also high than the naïve Bayes classifier in many problems including the task of SOM. The authors will take the ID3 technique for SOM in the forthcoming section for experimentation. By dividing the SOM dataset about least entropy, the resultant SOM dataset will have the maximum information gain and thus the impure opinion (SOM messages that contains all opinion i.e. positive, negative, and neutral) of the SOM dataset is reduced. Further, the SOM dataset can be tested with the help of the DT technique once the tree has been produced from the training SOM dataset. The ID3 DT method to perform the task of SOM is given below in Table 10.7.

Table 10.7 DT algorithm for SOM

begin
1: **Input** SOM message from social media to classify
2: Compute entropy for SOM message dataset.
3: **while** conditions **do**
4: for every attribute/feature of the SOM message dataset
5: compute entropy for all categorical values of *the SOM* message dataset.
6: Find means information entropy for the current attribute of *the SOM* message dataset.
7: compute gain for the current attribute of *the SOM* message dataset.
8: select the attribute of highest information gain.
9: **end for**
10: **end while**
11: **return** final opinion from SOM as $positive, negative, and\ neutral.$
end

10.4.8   Ensemble Classifier (EC)

The ensemble model is also known as the committee of multiple hypotheses. In this method, different models are trained and then ensemble to further enhances the classification accuracy. Ensemble models are efficiently used for different purposes including e-mail spam filtering. In [66], it is stated that the cascading of different filters is an excellent approach for this purpose. Two indispensable techniques of the ensemble model are bagging and boosting [67]. In the bagging approach, the training dataset is divided into different groups and then these groups are used for training the different classifiers. Further, the outputs produced by different classifiers are combined. In [68, 69], rigorous analysis has been performed to show various approaches to render the ensemble model and how ensemble models perform better than a single classifier. Bagging is an ensemble meta-learning algorithm that is usually implemented in DT techniques. It is also termed bootstrap aggregating. Random forest (RF) is an ensemble model because in RF many DTs are created for a given problem and subsequently the results obtained from them are hybridized in an attempt to find the most suitable decision on the whole [70]. RF entails the bagging technique. In [71, 72], RF is used to perform the e-mail spam identification task.

Boosting is a technique of substantial efficacy that entails a cascade of weak learners and eventually produces a single model that is considerably more effective than the individual one [73]. The AdaBoost system is an example of boosting technique and is proposed in [74]. It is also fast, easily programmable, and can be integrated easily with other learning techniques. Moreover, the non-requirement of parameter tuning (excluding T) renders it straightforward and less cumbersome.

The tenet of this technique is to obtain the more accurate decision rule or hypothesis by merging several comparatively less accurate hypotheses or decision rules. Indeed, in boosting the learner is trained every stage of classification phenomenon and consequently, the outcome obtained in each stage is used to increase the credence to data for the forthcoming stage [75]. It is revealed from the literature survey that the ensemble model can produce higher classification accuracy in comparison to NB and DT techniques [75]. In [76], it is argued that it has some sort of association with logistic regression and probability maximization. Even more, boosting the preceding knowledge of a weak classifier is also not required and its expanded version can also be used to tackle the learning problems lying beyond the binary classification. Over and above, it can be used with different data types like textual, numeric, discrete in nature, etc. The AdaBoost technique for SOM is shown in Table 10.8. This algorithm is architecture with the help of the algorithm given in [77] to accomplish the task of e-mail spam classification.

10.4.9   Random Forest (RF)

RF was initially proposed in [78]. As already stated in sub-section 10.4.8, it is an ensemble model and can be used to solve the task of classification and regression [79]. In this approach, predictions are performed with the help of DTs. Actually,

Table 10.8 AdaBoost Algorithm for SOM

begin
1. **The input** set of SOM message M obtained from social media
2. **while** condition **do**
3. implement the labeled SOM message M (labeled) to train the model
4. implement the model to test the SOM message M (unlabeled) and obtain the score with the help of a score function
5. relate each SOM message with the matching score as obtained above
6. label the SOM message with the minimum scores
7. include the currently labeled SOM message into SOM message M (labeled)
8. remove the currently labeled SOM message M from SOM message M (unlabeled)
9. **end while**
10. train the SOM message M (labeled)
11. given $(p_1, q_1) \dots (p_n, q_n) \in R_t: q_1 = 0.1$
12. weights $w_1 \dots w_f = \frac{1}{f}: f =$ number of attributes in SOM message M
13. **for** $t = 1\ to\ T$ **do**
14. $\sum_i w_i = 1$
15. error $e_j = \sum_i w_{i\beta}$ where $\beta = |h_j(p_i) - q_i|$
16. Select model h_j with the minimum error
17. Update weights $w_{t+1,i} = w_{t,i}\gamma_t^{1-ei}: e_i =$
$\begin{cases} 0 & if\ classified\ correctly \\ 1 & Otherwise \end{cases}$
18. $\gamma_t = \frac{e_t}{1-e_t}$
19. $\sigma_t = \log\left(\frac{1}{\gamma_t}\right)$
20. **end for**
21. **return** final opinion
from SOM as $positive\ or\ negative\ and\ neutral$

$$h(p) = \begin{cases} 1 & if\ \sum_{t=1}^{T} \sigma_t h_t(p) \geq \frac{1}{2}\sum_{t=1}^{T}\sigma_t \\ 0 & Otherwise \end{cases}$$

end

during the training phase; some DTs are created by the programmer. Further, these DTs are used to predict the hypotheses or class. This prediction is performed by considering specific groups of DTs thus created and eventually selecting the specific groups from every DTs and the group having the highest vote count is considered as the final result. Indeed, the classification of new data from an input vector commences by placing the input vector along each of the DTs in the forest. Subsequently,

Table 10.9 RF algorithm for SOM

> **begin**
> 1: **Input** X: number of nodes
> 2: **Input** N: number of attributes in the SOM message obtained from social media
> 3: **Input** Y: number of DTs to be grown
> 4: **while** termination conditions are not true **do**
> 5: Select a self-starting SOM message M indiscriminately from the training DTs Y
> 6: Create DT R from the selected self-starting SOM message M
> 7: Select n attributes randomly from N such that $n \ll N$
> 8: Find the optimal separation point for node d among the n attributes
> 9: Split the parent node into two child nodes through the optimal separation
> 10: iterate steps 1 to 3 till the maximum number of nodes (x) is generated
> 11: Create forest by repeating steps 1 to 4 for Y number of times
> 12: **end while**
> 13: produce the result of every generated DTs $\{R\}_1^Y$
> 14: take a new SOM message obtained from social media for every generated DTs commencing at the root node
> 15: assign the SOM message obtained from social media to the group well-suited with the leaf node of DT.
> 16: combine the votes/results of every DT
> 17: **return** final opinion
>   *from SOM as positive or negative and neutral*
>   consisting of the highest vote (H_V)
> **end**

each DT will render its classification that is usually termed as DT 'votes' for that group. Literature survey reveals the fact that it has been implemented to solve the problems analogous in nature [80–82]. Furthermore, in comparison to simple DT, RF produces less classification error associated with high f-scores and its performance is also good for the noisy dataset. Moreover, its performance, in general, is like or even superior to SVMs. RF permits the user to develop as many DTs as possible and its execution speed is also considerably high. Finally, the algorithm computes the group having the highest voting score in the forest. Table 10.9 shows the algorithmic details of different steps required by RF to accomplish the SOM task.

10.4.10 Deep Learning (DL) Algorithms

Deep learning is a novel and merging domain of machine intelligence. It utilizes AI and ML and attempts to imbibe the attributes directly from data by many non-linear processing layers. In [83], different DL approaches have been discussed in the context of classification tasks as well as its various application domains such as in computer vision, NLP, text processing, ensemble learning, information retrieval, etc. DL can be used in different ML strategies including hybrid deep network keeping in view the architecture and application domain-specific requirements. The basic ingredient of DL is its incorporation of multilayered hierarchical data representation classically in the form of an artificial neural network (ANN) which comprises more than two layers and it also renders spontaneous hybridization of higher-level data features with the lower-level data features. Further, in [83], it is mentioned that DL can be categorized as given below:

- Unsupervised DL network/Generative learning (GL)
- Supervised DL network
- Hybrid DL network

An unsupervised DL network is also termed genetic learning (GL) because unsupervised DL can vividly be used to create samples by sampling from the networks. In unsupervised DL, classes or concepts are not needed during the training phase and the sole objective is to represent a function. Further, this function is implemented to represent unseen structures from unlabeled data. Moreover, unsupervised DL is also suitable to deal with a huge quantity of unlabelled datasets.

A supervised DL network is a very suitable technique for pattern classification. Labeled data is required during the training phase of this network and subsequently used to represent the unseen structure from unlabeled data. The examples of supervised DL are (1) The sum-product network (SPN) (2) the Convolutional neural network (CNN). Finally, the hybrid DL network is the hybridization of unsupervised and supervised DL networks. The deep belief network (DBN) belongs to this category.

In [84], it is stated that CNN is an emerging research domain because of its inherent features of reliability, fault tolerance, capability to process in parallel, and the efficacy of self-learning. Further, in [85], Deep-CNN is considered as a type of feed-forward network. Indeed, the functioning of CNN differs from the conventional back-propagation network (BPN). Perhaps, BPN uses the features of the isolated hand-crafted image. Contrary to this, the CNN functions precisely on an email message to mine the useful and vital features to perform the classification tasks. CNN algorithm to perform the SOM task is depicted in Table 10.10. This algorithm is adapted from [86] where it is used for e-mail spam classification.

10.5   Experimental Results and Discussions

In this section, the authors will illustrate the experimental results of different ML techniques obtained to accomplish the task of SOM.

Table 10.10 CNN algorithm for SOM

---

begin
1: **Input** Pretreatment of *SOM* message from social media to classify
2: **Input** parameters *N*
3: *file = getfile( )* //Find the *SOM* message from social media
4: *label = getlabel(file)* //Find the labeled *SOM* message
5: *test = gettest(file)* //Find the unlabeled *SOM* message
6: *vec = getword2vec( )* //Load the word vector
7: random = random (label) //Randomized
 8: **while** condition **do**
9: $N_f = CV(len\ (xshuffle), nf)$ //Cross-validation
10: **for** *trindex, teindex in kf* **do**
11: *xtotal, ytotal =*
xshuffle[trindex], yshuffle [trindex]
12: *xtrain, xdev, ytrain, ydev = split(xtotal, ytotal)*
13: //Divide the *SOM* message dataset
14: **for** *i < N* **do**
15: *conv = getconv( )* //Convolution layer
16: *h = sigmoid(conv)*
17: *N = getk( )* //Get the value of *N*
18: *tensorr = gettensor( )*
19: **for** *x, y in xtrain, ytrain* **do**
20: *value, indice = topk(tensorr)*
21: //Get the *SOM* message feature and location information
22: *tensors = get(value, indice)*
23: //Get the corresponding tensor
24: *tensora = append(tensors)*
25: **end for**
26: **end for**
27: *con = con(tensorp)*
28: *conn = sigmoid(con)* //Sigmoid
29: *getsoftmax(conn)* //*softmax*
30: **end for**
31: **if** *getdev( )* **then**
32: *tr = false*
33: **end if**
34: **end while**
35: **return** final opinion
from *SOM as positive, negative, and neutral.*
end

10.5.1 The Datasets

In this sub-section, different aspects of datasets used for experimentation will be presented. The technique of 'word embeddings' will also be used in this experimentation. This technique renders the distributed representation of the text and very useful to encode the word's semantic and syntactic characteristics. In general, they are vectors of dense and low dimensionality. In this experimentation, two-word embedding datasets will be used. These are:

- Google embeddings
- Amazon embeddings

In [87], two different ANN models are used for 'word embedding'. These are (1) CBOW and (2) Skip-gram models. The first one is a bag-of-words-based model whereas in the second the current word is used to predict the word embeddings of surrounding words. Further, a publically available dataset word2vec is also used. These vectors having dimensionality of three hundred were trained using a hundred-billion-word corpus from Google News with the use of CBOW architecture.

In this experimentation, the CBOW architecture is trained on a huge Amazon product review dataset. This dataset is developed in [88]. Different characteristics of this dataset are as under:

(a) Number of reviews = 34,686.770
(b) Number of words = 4.7 billion
(c) Number of Amazon products = 2,441,053
(d) Timespan = June 1995 to March 2013

The word embedding is maintained at 300-dimensional. It is available at http://sentic.net/AmazonWE.zip.

10.5.2 Features and Linguistic Patterns Used

Following features are used in this experimentation:

- Word embeddings are used as features for the network. Further, each word is encoded as a vector with a dimensionality of three hundred and subsequently inputted into the network.
- Part of speech (POS) tags is used as an added feature. Different POS used are nouns, verbs, adjectives, adverbs, prepositions, and conjunction. These POS are encoded as a binary vector of dimensionality six. Moreover, Stanford Tagger is used for POS tagger. Furthermore, these two feature vectors are integrated and inputted to CNN. It is thus explicit that the final dimensionality of each word is 306.

- Linguistic patterns (LPs) are also used. More about LPs are given in [89–91]. In [92], affective computing is used to make a knowledge base for opinion mining and sentiment analysis.

It is also pertinent to mention that the Stanford parser is used to observe the syntactic relations in the sentences. Moreover, authors joined the LPs and CNN in the following manner: both LPs and CNN-based classification models are executed on the text, and thereafter every term marked by either of the classification models is declared as aspect terms.

10.5.3 Comparative Mining Efficacy of Different ML Techniques

For training and evaluation purposes of different ML algorithms, the dataset given in [93] is used. This is shown in Tables 10.11 and 10.12. It entails training and test set from two fields. These are laptops and Restaurant as shown in Table 10.12. Further, IOB2 is used for coding. This coding scheme is frequently used to present the sequences.

It is explicit from Table 10.11 that CNN outperforms in comparison to other ML techniques considered in this experimentation for given datasets. However, the performances of SVM, EA, and RF are also considerably satisfactory and the performances of these ML techniques are also near to the results of CNN. Table 10.12 renders the training and test part of the SemEval dataset for evaluation. Further, Table 10.13 shows the F-score of the SemEval 2014 dataset concerning random

Table 10.11 Characteristics of the dataset given in [93] and comparison of different ML techniques; P represents precision and R recall

Dataset (Domain)	No. of Reviews	No. of Sentences	No. of Aspects	CT		NBC		Perceptron		FA		RS	
				P (%)	R (%)	P (%)	R (%)	P (%)	R (%)	P (%)	R (%)	P (%)	R (%)
Canon	48	600	82	82	69	85	76	81	72	81	72	80	72
Nikon	37	349	99	81	75	76	79	81	73	82	74	80	72
DVD	44	549	70	84	75	82	76	83	74	82	73	82	74
Mp3	98	1719	60	84	69	85	81	82	71	83	70	83	71
Cellphone	102	743	52	85	73	87	87	83	69	83	69	83	68
Dataset (Domain)	No. of Reviews	No. of Sentences	No. of Aspects	SVM		DT		EA		RF		CNN	
				P (%)	R (%)	P (%)	R (%)	P (%)	R (%)	P (%)	R (%)	P (%)	R (%)
Canon	48	600	82	83	74	82	73	86	75	84	74	86	76
Nikon	37	349	99	83	73	81	74	86	77	84	74	87	76
DVD	44	549	70	85	75	81	71	85	75	86	75	87	77
Mp3	98	1719	60	84	75	84	74	86	76	85	76	89	77
Cellphone	102	743	52	85	76	85	73	87	76	86	77	88	77

Table 10.12   Training and test data of SemEval dataset for evaluation

Domain	Training	Test	Total
Laptop	3000	841	3841
Restaurant	3000	845	3845
Total	6000	1689	7686

Table 10.13   F-score of SemEval 2014 dataset concerning random features, Google embeddings, and Amazon embeddings

Domain	Feature	F-Score (%)
Laptop	Random	68.30
Laptop	Google embeddings	74.22
Laptop	Amazon embeddings	**78.57**
Restaurant	Random	75.04
Restaurant	Google embeddings	81.32
Restaurant	Amazon embeddings	**83.68**

Table 10.14   Detailed feature analysis specifically for CNN

Domains	Features	Recall (%)	Precision (%)	F-Score (%)
Laptop	Word embeddings	73.31	84.04	78.57
Laptop	Word embeddings +Part of Speech	**74.33**	**84.38**	**79.10**
Restaurant	Word embeddings	82.21	85.34	83.67
Restaurant	Word embeddings +Part of Speech	**83.02**	**85.45**	**84.05**

features, Google embeddings as well as Amazon embeddings. It is explicit from Table 10.13 that Amazon embeddings produce a high F-score for both the domains i.e., 'Laptop' and 'Restaurant'. Since the performance of CNN is superior to other ML techniques considered so an elaborated analysis of CNN is done. This analysis is shown in Table 10.14. It is obvious from Table 10.14 that the integrated features of word embeddings and part of speech produce high recall, precision, and F-score for the domains of 'Laptop' and 'Restaurant'.

10.6   Conclusions

Social media plays a vital role in opinion acquisition and dissemination and can be considered as a genesis for observing societal opinion on particular issues. In this chapter, the authors critically reviewed the prospects and advantages of using social media for SOM. Further, different ML techniques have been proposed with concepts, algorithmic details, and experimentation. The basic architecture of the opinion mining system and the processes involved are also contemplated. Moreover, different ML approaches have been reviewed in the direction of their pragmatic applications to the domain of SOM and have been implemented to categorize the social media messages as positive, negative, and neutral opinions. The chapter also includes the nuances of various methods and experimentation on some publically available datasets and different performance metrics are used to evaluate the effectiveness of different techniques. The experimentation is performed using Google embeddings and Amazon embeddings with ten state-of-art ML techniques and it is observed that the performance of CNN is better than other techniques for both the domains of 'Laptop' and 'Restaurant'. In general, an extensive literature review reveals the fact that substantial advancement has been made and will still a lot of work be needed in this domain. Further research in this pursuit to augment the efficacy of SOM methods need to be done.

References

1. Liu B (2011) Web data mining: exploring hyperlinks, contents, and usage data, 2nd edn. Springer, Heidelberg
2. Liu B (2012) Sentiment analysis and opinion. Morgan & Claypool, Mining
3. Kaschesky M, Sobkowicz P, Bouchard G (2011) Opinion mining in social media: modeling, simulating, and visualizing political opinion formation in the web. In: Proceedings of the 12th annual international digital government research conference: digital Government innovation in challenging times, College Park, pp 317–326
4. Stieglitz S, Dang-Xuan L (2013) Social media and political communication: a social media analytics framework. Soc Netw Anal Min 3(4):1277–1291
5. King D. Introduction to mining and analyzing social media minitrack, pp 3108–3108
6. Asur S, Huberman BA. Predicting the future with social media, pp 492–499
7. Bollen J, Mao H, Zeng X-J (2010) Twitter mood predicts the stock market. J Comput Sci 2:8
8. Siganos EV-N, Verwijmeren P (2014) Facebook's daily sentiment and international stock markets. J Econ Behav Organ no. 0:730–743
9. Kalampokis E, Tambouris E, Tarabanis K (2013) Understanding the predictive power of social media. Internet Res 23(5):544–559
10. Porshnev A, Redkin I, Shevchenko A. Machine learning in prediction of stock market indicators based on historical data and data from twitter sentiment analysis, pp 440–444
11. Preeti, Sidhu BK (2013) Natural language processing. Int J Comput Technol Appl 4:751–758
12. Pang B, Lee L (2008) Opinion mining and sentiment analysis. Found Trends Inf Retr 2(1–2):135
13. Kushal D, Steve L, Pennock MD (2003) Mining the peanut gallery: opinion extraction and semantic classification of product reviews. Paper presented at the www2003, Budapest
14. Carbonell JG (1979) Subjective understanding: com-puter models of belief systems. Doctor of Philosophy, YaleUniversity New Haven
15. Bo P, Lee L, Kumar VS (2002) Thumbs up? Sentiment classification using machine learning techniques. Paper presented at the ACL-02, conference on empirical methods in natural language processing, vol 10
16. Peter T (2002) Thumbs up or thumbs down? Semantic orientation applied to unsupervised classification of reviews. Paper presented at the proceedings of the 40th annual meeting on Association for Computational Linguistics, Philadelphia
17. Wiebe JM (1994) Tracking point of view in narrative. Comput Linguist 20(2):233–287
18. Yorick W, Janusz B (1984) Beliefs, points of view, and multiple environments. Paper presented at the international NATO symposium on artificial and human intelligence, Lyon
19. Abbasi A, Chen H, Salem A (2008) Sentiment analysis in multiple languages: feature selection for opinion classification in web forums. ACM Trans Inf Syst 26(3):1–34

20. Hsinchun C, Zimbra D (2010) AI and opinion mining. Intell Syst IEEE 25(3):74–80. https://doi.org/10.1109/mis.2010.75
21. Minqing H, Bing L (2004) Mining and summarizing customer reviews. Paper presented at the 10th ACM SIGKDD international conference on knowledge discovery and data mining, Seattle
22. Wei W (2011) Analyzing text data for opinion mining. In: Muñoz R, Montoyo A, Métais E (eds) Natural language processing and information systems, vol 6716. Springer, Berlin/Heidelberg, pp 330–335
23. Tang H, Tan S, Cheng X (2009) A survey on sentiment detection of reviews. Expert Syst Appl 36(7):10760–10773
24. Cambria E, Schuller B, Xia Y, Havasi C (2013) New avenues in opinion mining and sentiment analysis. IEEE Intell Syst 28:15–21
25. Heilpern S (1981) Fuzzy mapping and fixed point theorem. Jour Math Anal Appl 83:566–569
26. Hadzic O (1989) Fixed point theorems for multi-valued mapping in some classes of fuzzy metric spaces. Fuzzy Sets Syst 29:115–125
27. Fang JX (1992) On fixed point theorems in fuzzy metric spaces. Fuzzy Sets Syst 46:107–113
28. Beg I (1998) Fixed points of fuzzy multi-valued mappings with values in fuzzy orders sets. J Fuzzy Math 6(1):127–131
29. Beg I (2001) A general theorem on selector of fuzzy multi-functions. J Fuzzy Math 9(1)
30. Mitchell TM (1997) Machine learning, 1st edn. McGraw-Hill
31. Whissell JS, Clarke CLA (2011) Clustering for semi-supervised spam filtering. In: Proceedings of the 8th annual collaboration, electronic messaging, anti-abuse, and spam conference (CEAS '11), pp 125–134
32. Dipika S, Kanchan D (2016) Spam e-mails filtering techniques. Int J Tech Res Appl 4(6):7–11
33. Saravanan T A detailed introduction to K-Nearest Neighbor (KNN) algorithm. Retrieved on August 8, 2017, from, 2010, https://saravananthirumuruganathan.wordpress.com/2010/05/17/a-detailed-introduction-to-k-nearest-neighborknn-algorithm/
34. Tan PN, Steinbach M, Kumar V (2006) Introduction to data mining. Pearson Addison Wesley, Boston, p 0321321367
35. Zhu S, Dong W, Liu W (2015) Hierarchical reinforcement learning based on KNN classification algorithms. Int J Hosp Inf Technol 8(8):175–184
36. Bandana G (2013) Design, and development of Naïve Bayes classifier, the North Dakota State University of agriculture and applied science. Graduate Faculty of Computer Science. Master thesis
37. Ray S 6 easy steps to learn naive Bayes algorithm (with code in python), retrieved on august 9, 2017, from, 2015., https://www.analyticsvidhya.com/blog/2015/09/naive-Bayes-explained/
38. Marsono MN, El-Kharashi MW, Gebali F (2008) Binary LNS-based Naïve Bayes inference engine for spam control: noise analysis and FPGA synthesis. IET Comput Digit Tech 2:56
39. Marsono MN, El-Kharashi MW, Gebali F (2009) Targeting spam control on middleboxes: spam detection based on layer-3 e-mail content classification. Elsevier Computer Networks
40. Li K, Zhong Z (2006) Fast statistical spam filter by approximate classifications, in proceedings of the joint international conference on measurement and modeling of computer systems, Saint-Malo
41. Biju JJW (2009) Implementing spam detection using Bayesian and porter stemmer keyword stripping approaches. In TENCON 2009–2009 IEEE region 10 conference, pp 1–5
42. Wu J, Deng T (2008) Research in an anti-spam method based on bayesian filtering. In: Computational Intelligence and Industrial Application, 2008. PACIIA '08. PacificAsia Workshop on, 2, pp 887–891
43. Edstrom A. Detecting spam with artificial neural networks, retrieved on august 10, 2017, from, 2016., http://homepages.cae.wisc.edu/~ece539/project/s16/Edstrom_rpt.pdf
44. Chandra A, Mohammad S, Rizwan B (2015) Webspam classification using supervised artificial neural network algorithms. Adv Comput Intell Int J 2(1):21–30
45. Awad M, Foqaha M (2016) Email spam classification using a hybrid approach of RBF neural network and particle swarm optimization. Int J Netw Secure Appl 8(4)

46. Carpinteiro OAS, Lima I, Assis JMC, de Souza ACZ, Moreira EM, Pinheiro CAM (2006) A neural model in anti-spam systems, Lecture notes in computer science. Springer, Berlin
47. Ndumiyana D, Magomelo M, Sakala L (2013) Spam detection using a neural network classifier, online J. Phys. Environ Sci Res 2(2):28–37. ISSN 2315-5027
48. Yang XS (2009) Firefly algorithms for multimodal optimization. In: Watanabe O, Zeugmann T (eds) Proceedings of 5th symposium on stochastic algorithms, foundations, and applications, Lecture notes in computer science 5792, pp 169–178
49. Dugonik J, Fister I (2014) Multi-population firefly algorithm. In: Proceedings of the 1st student computer science research conference, Ljubljana, pp 19–23
50. Khan WA, Hamadneh NN, Tilahun SL, Ngnotchouye JM (2016) A review and comparative study of firefly algorithm and its modified versions. Intech Publishing House, pp 281–313. Chapter 13
51. Kundur A (2013) Evaluation of firefly algorithm using benchmark functions, Department of Computer Science. The North Dakota State University of Agriculture and Applied Science. Master thesis
52. Pawlak ZI (1991) Rough sets: theoretical aspects of reasoning about data. Kluwer Academic, New York
53. Roy SS, Viswanatham VM, Krishna PV, Saraf N, Gupta A, Mishra R (2013) Applicability of rough set technique for data investigation and optimization of the intrusion detection system. In: Quality R (ed) Security, and robustness in heterogeneous networks. Berlin/Heidelberg, Springer, pp 479–484
54. Perez-Díaz N, Ruano-Ordas D, Fdez-Riverola F, Mendez JR (2012) Rough sets for spam filtering: selecting appropriate decision rules for boundary classification. Appl Soft Comput 13(8):1–8
55. Agnieszka NB (2016) Mining rule-based knowledge bases inspired by rough set theory. Fundam Inf 148(1–2):35–50. 37
56. Awad WA, Elseuofi SM (2011) Machine learning methods for spam E-mail classification. Int J Comput Sci Inf Technol 3(1):173–184
57. Perez-Díaz N, Ruano-Ordas D, Fdez-Riverola F, Mendez JR (2016) Boosting accuracy of classical machine learning antispam classifiers in real scenarios by applying rough set theory. Hindawi Publishing Corporation, Scientific Programming, Article ID 5945192, 10 pages
58. Vapnik V (1995) The nature of statistical learning theory. Springer
59. Torabi ZS, Nadimi-Shahraki MH, Nabiollahi A (2015) Efficient support vector machines for spam detection: a survey. Int J Comput Sci Inf Secure 13(1):11–28
60. Chen SK, Chang YH (2014) SVM classifier algorithm. In: Proceedings of 2014 international conference on artificial intelligence and software engineering(AISE2014), 6. DEStech Publications, Inc, p 655
61. Christina V, Karpagavalli S, Suganya G (2010) Email spam filtering using supervised machine learning techniques. Int J Comput Sci Eng 02(09):3126–3129
62. Balakumar C, Ganeshkumar D (2015) A data mining approach on various classifiers in email spam filtering. Int J Res Appl Sci Eng Technol 3(1):8–14
63. Holmes G, Pfahringer G, Kirkby B, Frank R, Hall EM (2002) Multiclass alternating decision trees. ECML:161–172
64. Chakraborty S, Mondal B (2012) Spam mail filtering technique using different decision tree classifiers through data mining approach – a comparative performance analysis. Int J Comput Appl 47(16):26–31, 0975–888
65. Masud K, Rashedur MR (2013) Decision tree and naïve Bayes algorithm for classification and generation of actionable knowledge for direct marketing. J Softw Eng Appl 6:196–206
66. Guerra PHC, Guedes D, Meira JW, Hoepers C, Chaves MHPC, StedingJessen K (2010) Exploring the spam arms race to characterize spam evolution. In: Proceedings of the 7th collaboration, electronic messaging, anti-abuse and spam conference (CEAS), Redmond
67. Breiman L (1996) Bagging predictors. Mach Learn 24(2):123–140

68. Dietterich TG (1857) Ensemble methods in machine learning. Lect Notes Comput Sci 2000:1–15
69. Adeva JJG, Beresi UC, Calvo RA. Accuracy and diversity in ECOC ensembles of text categorizers, available: Retrieved on 9 Aug 2017, from, 2000. http://citeseer.ist.psu.edu/732806.html
70. Breiman L (2001) Random forests. Mach Learn 45(1):5–32
71. Debarr D, Wechsler H (2009) Spam detection using clustering, random forests and active learning. In: CEAS 2009 sixth conference on email and anti-spam
72. Lee SM, Kim DS, Kim JH, Park JS (2010) Spam detection using feature selection and parameters optimization. In: 2010 International conference on complex, intelligent and software intensive systems, vol 1, pp 883–888
73. Biggio B, Corona I, Fumera G, Giacinto G, Roli F (2011) Bagging classifiers for fighting poisoning attacks in adversarial classification tasks. In: Multiple classifier systems. Springer, Berlin/Heidelberg, pp 350–359
74. Freund Y, Schapire RE (1997) A decision – theoretic generalization of online learning and an application to boosting. JCSS 55:119–139
75. Friedman J, Hastie T, Tibshirani R (2000) Additive logistic regression: a statistical view of boosting. Ann Stat 38(2)
76. Schapire S (1999) Improved boosting algorithms using confidence-rated predictions. Mach Learn Mach Learn 37
77. Sahil P, Dishant G, Mehak A, Ishita K, Nishtha J (2013) Comparison and analysis of spam detection algorithms. Int J Appl Innov Eng Manag 2(4):1–7
78. Breiman L, Cutler A (2007) Random forests-classification description. Department of Statistics Homepage. http://www.stat.berkeley.edu/~breiman/RandomForests/cchome.htm
79. Akinyelu AA, Adewumi AO (2016) Classification of phishing email using random forest machine learning technique. J Appl Math 6:Article ID 425731, Retrieved on July 12, 2017, from
80. Koprinska I, Poon J, Clark J, Chan J (2007) Learning to classify e-mail. Inf Sci 177(10):2167–2187
81. Fette I, Sadeh N, Tomasic A (2007) Learning to detect phishing emails. In: Proceedings of the 16th international World Wide Web conference (WWW '07), Alberta, Canada, May 2007, pp 649–656
82. Whittaker C, Ryner B, Nazif M (2010) Large-scale automatic classification of phishing pages. In: Proceedings of the 17th annual network & distributed system security symposium (NDSS '10). The Internet Society, San Diego
83. Deng L, Yu D (2014) Deep learning: methods and applications. Now Publishers, Boston
84. Zhao S, Xu Z, Liu L, Guo M (2017) Towards accurate deceptive opinion spam detection based on Word Order-Preserving CNN, arXiv:1711.09181v1 [cs.CL] 25 Nov 2017, pp 1–8. Available at: https://pdfs.semanticscholar.org/1687/0bed28831f6bd49a0228177351d1870fafd1.pdf. Last Accessed 5 Jun 2022
85. Albelwi S, Mahmood A (2017) A framework for designing the architectures of deep convolutional neural networks. Entropy 19(6):242
86. Dada EG, Bassi JS, Chiroma H, Abdulhamid S'i M, Adetunmbi AO, Ajibuwa OE (2019) Machine learning for email spam filtering: review, approaches, and open research problems. Heliyon 5
87. Mikolov T, Yih W-T, Zweig G (2013) Linguistic regularities in continuous space word representations. HLT-NAACL:746–751
88. McAuley J, Leskovec J (2013) Hidden factors and hidden topics: understanding rating dimensions with review text, in proceedings of RecSys'13, Hong Kong
89. Cambria E, Olsher D, Rajagopal D (2014) SenticNet 3: a common and common-sense knowledge base for cognition-driven sentiment analysis. In: AAAI, Quebec City, pp 1515–1521
90. Poria S, Gelbukh A, Cambria E, Yang P, Hussain A, Durrani T (2012) Merging sentient and wordnet-affect emotion lists for sentiment analysis. In: Signal processing (ICSP), 2012 IEEE 11th international conference on, vol 2. IEEE, pp 1251–1255

91. Poria S, Gelbukh A, Cambria E, Das D, Bandyopadhyay S (2012) Enriching SenticNet polarity scores through semi-supervised fuzzy clustering. In: IEEE ICDM, Brussels, pp 709–716
92. Cambria E, Hussain A (2015) Sentic computing: a common-sense-based framework for concept-level sentiment analysis. Springer, Cham
93. Qiu G, Liu B, Bu J, Chen C (2011) Opinion word expansion and target extraction through double propagation. Comput Linguist 37(1):9–27

Appendix I

Input:

```
{
 "Objects": [{
  "dMarketValueBeforeTrade": "10216333.000000",
  "price": "950.000000",
  "transaction": [
  {
   "account": [{
    "maxPctHiYield": "35.000000",
    "dPositionHiYield": "330000.000000",
    "dPositionHiGrade": "819167.000000",
    "securityPosition": [
    {
     "quantity": "5000",
     "dMarketValue": "819167.000000",
     "security": [{
      "symbol": "PMBND",
      "yield": "6.000000",
      "daysInHolding": "23",
      "dMarketValue": "164.000000",
      "dProfile": "HI-GRD",
      "dAnnualInterestAmt": "60.000000",
      "price": "160.000000",
      "issuer": "Phillip Morris",
      "sin": "Y",
      "dAccruedInterest": "4.000000",
      "faceValue": "1000.000000",
```

© The Editor(s) (if applicable) and The Author(s), under exclusive license to
Springer Nature Switzerland AG 2023
K. N. Mishra, S. C. Pandey, *Cloud-IoT Technologies in Society 5.0*,
https://doi.org/10.1007/978-3-031-28711-4

```
  "rating": "A",
  "__metadata": {
   "#id": "Security_id_1",
   "#type": "Security"
   }
  }],
 "__metadata": {
  "#id": "SecurityPosition_id_1",
  "#type": "SecurityPosition"
  }
 },
 {
 "quantity": "3000",
 "dMarketValue": "330000.000000",
 "security": [{
  "symbol": "3MBND",
  "yield": "12.000000",
  "daysInHolding": "40",
  "dMarketValue": "110.000000",
  "dProfile": "HI-YLD",
  "dAnnualInterestAmt": "90.000000",
  "price": "100.000000",
  "issuer": "3M",
  "sin": "N",
  "dAccruedInterest": "10.000000",
  "faceValue": "1000.000000",
  "rating": "B",
  "__metadata": {
   "#id": "Security_id_3",
   "#type": "Security"
   }
  }],
  "__metadata": {
   "#id": "SecurityPosition_id_2",
   "#type": "SecurityPosition"
  }
 }
 ],
 "warnMargin": "3.000000",
 "name": "Boeing",
 "restricted": "false",
 "maxPctHiGrade": "75.000000",
 "number": "1640",
```

```
    "dMarketValue": "1149167.000000",
    "__metadata": {
    "#id": "Account_id_1",
    "#type": "Account"
     }
   }],
}
```

Appendix II

Output:

```
{
  "Messages": {
    "Message": [
      {
        "entityReference": "Trade_id_1",
        "text": "[AccountConstraint,5] A restricted account [ Sears
] can't be involved in a trade.",
        "severity": "Warning",
        "__metadata": {"#type": "#RuleMessage"}
      },
      {
        "entityReference": "Trade_id_1",
          "text": "[AccountConstraint,4] No account [ Airbus ]
involved in a trade can exceed
              its maximum percentage [ 70.000000 ] for High Yield
securities [ 86.156842 ].",
        "severity": "Warning",
        "__metadata": {"#type": "#RuleMessage"}
      },
      {
        "entityReference": "Trade_id_1",
        "text": "[AccountConstraint,4] No account [ Sears ] involved
in a trade can exceed
              its maximum percentage [ 65.000000 ] for High Yield
securities [ 79.980241 ].",
        "severity": "Warning",
```

© The Editor(s) (if applicable) and The Author(s), under exclusive license to
Springer Nature Switzerland AG 2023
K. N. Mishra, S. C. Pandey, *Cloud-IoT Technologies in Society 5.0*,
https://doi.org/10.1007/978-3-031-28711-4

```
        "__metadata": {"#type": "#RuleMessage"}
      },
      {
        "entityReference": "Trade_id_1",
           "text": "[AccountConstraint,4] No account [ Boeing ]
involved in a trade can exceed
                its maximum percentage [ 35.000000 ] for High Yield
securities [ 42.253808 ].",
        "severity": "Warning",
        "__metadata": {"#type": "#RuleMessage"}
      }
   ],
   "__metadata": {"#type": "#RuleMessages"},
   "version": "0.0"
  },
  "Objects": [{
    "dMarketValueBeforeTrade": 20432666,
    "price": "950.000000",
    "transaction": [
      {
        "dPositionHiGrade": 0,
        "dPositionHiYield": 269397.538944,
        "dAccruedInterest": 2249.666294,
        "dActualQuantity": 281.208287,
        "account": [{
          "dPctHiYield": 42.253808,
          "dPositionHiYield": "330000.000000",
          "dNewPositionHiGrade": 819167,
          "maxPctHiGrade": "75.000000",
          "restricted": "false",
          "dMarketValue": "1149167.000000",
          "number": "1640",
          "dPositionHiGrade": "819167.000000",
          "maxPctHiYield": "35.000000",
          "dNewPositionHiYield": 599397.538944,
          "name": "Boeing",
          "warnMargin": "3.000000",
          "securityPosition": [
            {
              "quantity": "5000",
              "dMarketValue": "819167.000000",
              "security": [{
              "symbol": "PMBND",
              "yield": "6.000000",
              "daysInHolding": "23",
```

```
            "dMarketValue": "164.000000",
            "dProfile": "HI-GRD",
            "dAnnualInterestAmt": "60.000000",
            "price": "160.000000",
            "issuer": "Phillip Morris",
            "sin": "Y",
            "dAccruedInterest": "4.000000",
            "faceValue": "1000.000000",
            "rating": "A",
            "__metadata":
             {
               "#id": "Security_id_1",
               "#type": "Security"
             }
          }],
          "__metadata":{
             "#id": "SecurityPosition_id_1",
             "#type": "SecurityPosition"
           }
        },
        {
        "quantity": "3000",
        "dMarketValue": "330000.000000",
        "security": [{
            "symbol": "3MBND",
            "yield": "12.000000",
            "daysInHolding": "40",
            "dMarketValue": "110.000000",
            "dProfile": "HI-YLD",
            "dAnnualInterestAmt": "90.000000",
            "price": "100.000000",
            "issuer": "3M",
            "sin": "N",
            "dAccruedInterest": "10.000000",
            "faceValue": "1000.000000",
            "rating": "B",
            "__metadata":{
               "#id": "Security_id_3",
               "#type": "Security"
             }
          }],
          "__metadata":{
             "#id": "SecurityPosition_id_2",
             "#type": "SecurityPosition"
```

```
           }
         }
       ],
       "__metadata":{
          "#id": "Account_id_1",
          "#type": "Account"
       },
       "dNewMarketValue": 1418564.538944,
       "dPctHiGrade": 57.746192
     }],
     "dMarketValue": 269397.538944,

"security": [{"__metadata": {"#ref_id": "Security_id_2"}}],
       "dQuantity": 281.208287,
       "__metadata":{
          "#id": "Transaction_id_1",
          "#type": "Transaction"
       },
       "dPrice": 950
     },
     {
     "dPositionHiGrade": 0,
     "dPositionHiYield": 777065.429329,
     "dAccruedInterest": 6489.064129,
     "dActualQuantity": 811.133016,
     "account": [{
        "dPctHiYield": 79.980241,
        "dPositionHiYield": "2495556.000000",
        "dNewPositionHiGrade": 819167,
        "maxPctHiGrade": "45.000000",
        "restricted": "true",
        "dMarketValue": "3314722.000000",
        "number": "1920",
        "dPositionHiGrade": "819167.000000",
        "maxPctHiYield": "65.000000",
        "dNewPositionHiYield": 3272621.429329,
        "name": "Sears",
        "warnMargin": "3.000000",
        "securityPosition": [{
           "quantity": "5000",
           "dMarketValue": "819167.000000",
                        "security": [{"__metadata": {"#ref_id":
"Security_id_1"}}],
              "__metadata": {
```

```
                "#id":  "SecurityPosition_id_3",
                "#type": "SecurityPosition"
              }
          },
          {
            "quantity": "2000",
            "dMarketValue": "295556.000000",
                        "security":  [{"__metadata":  {"#ref_id":
"Security_id_2"}}],
            "__metadata": {
              "#id": "SecurityPosition_id_4",
              "#type": "SecurityPosition"
            }
          },
          {
            "quantity": "20000",
            "dMarketValue": "2200000.000000",
                        "security":  [{"__metadata":  {"#ref_id":
"Security_id_3"}}],
            "__metadata": {
              "#id": "SecurityPosition_id_5",
              "#type": "SecurityPosition"
            }
          }
        ],
        "__metadata":{
          "#id": "Account_id_2",
          "#type": "Account"
        },
        "dNewMarketValue": 4091787.429329,
        "dPctHiGrade": 20.019784
      }],
      "dMarketValue": 777065.429329,

"security": [{"__metadata": {"#ref_id": "Security_id_2"}}],
      "dQuantity": 811.133016,
      "__metadata": {
        "#id": "Transaction_id_2",
        "#type": "Transaction"
      },
      "dPrice": 950
    },
    {
      "dPositionHiGrade": 0,
```

```
        "dPositionHiYield": 1348537.031727,
        "dAccruedInterest": 11261.269577,
        "dActualQuantity": 1407.658697,
        "account": [{
          "dPctHiYield": 86.156842,
          "dPositionHiYield": "4769444.000000",
          "dNewPositionHiGrade": 983000,
          "maxPctHiGrade": "35.000000",
          "restricted": "false",
          "dMarketValue": "5752444.000000",
          "number": "2750",
          "dPositionHiGrade": "983000.000000",
          "maxPctHiYield": "70.000000",
          "dNewPositionHiYield": 6117981.031727,
          "name": "Airbus",
          "warnMargin": "2.000000",
          "securityPosition": [{
              "quantity": "6000",
              "dMarketValue": "983000.000000",
                        "security": [{"__metadata": {"#ref_id":
"Security_id_1"}}],
              "__metadata": {
                "#id": "SecurityPosition_id_6",
                "#type": "SecurityPosition"
                }
            },
            {
              "quantity": "2500",
              "dMarketValue": "369444.000000",
                        "security": [{"__metadata": {"#ref_id":
"Security_id_2"}}],
              "__metadata": {
                "#id": "SecurityPosition_id_7",
                "#type": "SecurityPosition"
                }
            },
            {
              "quantity": "40000",
              "dMarketValue": "4400000.000000",
                        "security": [{"__metadata": {"#ref_id":
"Security_id_3"}}],
              "__metadata": {
                "#id": "SecurityPosition_id_8",
                "#type": "SecurityPosition"
```

```
                        }
                      }
                  ],
                  "__metadata": {
                     "#id": "Account_id_3",
                     "#type": "Account"
                    },
                  "dNewMarketValue": 7100981.031727,
                  "dPctHiGrade": 13.843158
              }],
              "dMarketValue": 1348537.031727,

"security": [{"__metadata": {"#ref_id": "Security_id_2"}}],
              "dQuantity": 1407.658697,
              "__metadata": {
                 "#id": "Transaction_id_3",
                 "#type": "Transaction"
              },
              "dPrice": 950
          }
      ],
      "dAccruedInterest": 40000,
      "quantity": "5000.000000",
      "security": {
        "symbol": "BGBND",
        "yield": "11.000000",
        "daysInHolding": "40",
        "dMarketValue": "148.000000",
        "dProfile": "HI-YLD",
        "dAnnualInterestAmt": "80.000000",
        "price": "140.000000",
        "issuer": "Boeing",
        "sin": "N",
        "dAccruedInterest": "8.000000",
        "faceValue": "1000.000000",
        "rating": "BBB",
        "__metadata": {
         "#id": "Security_id_2",
         "#type": "Security"
        }
      },
      "__metadata": {
        "#id": "Trade_id_1",
        "#type": "Trade"
```

```
    }
  }],
  "__metadataRoot": {
    "#restrictInfoRuleMessages": "true",
    "#restrictViolationRuleMessages": "true",
    "#restrictWarningRuleMessages": "false"
  }
}
```

Appendix III

Source Code

```
# import the necessary packages
import multiprocessing
import face_recognition
import threading
import argparse
import numpy as nmp
import pickle
import cv2
import os
encodings=[0]*128
encodings=nmp.array(encodings)
# load the known faces and embeddings
print("[INFO] loading encodings...")
data = pickle.loads(open("ENCODINGS.pickle", "rb").read())

def func():
    cap=cv2.VideoCapture(0)
     print("PLEASE KEEP YOUR FACE STRAIGHT, WHILE THE CAMERA IS
READING !!!")
    cv2.waitKey(4000)
    # os.system("cls")
    print("READING YOUR IMAGE.....")
    while(True):
        # Capture frame-by-frame
        ret,image = cap.read()
        # # Our operations on the frame come here
        rgb = cv2.cvtColor(image, cv2.COLOR_BGR2RGB)
```

© The Editor(s) (if applicable) and The Author(s), under exclusive license to
Springer Nature Switzerland AG 2023
K. N. Mishra, S. C. Pandey, *Cloud-IoT Technologies in Society 5.0*,
https://doi.org/10.1007/978-3-031-28711-4

```
        rgb = cv2.resize(rgb, (0, 0), fx=0.25, fy=0.25)
        # detect the (x, y)-coordinates of the bounding boxes
corresponding
        # to each face in the input image, then compute the facial
embeddings
        # for each face
        # This boxes here will return a list of tuples of found
face locations in css (top, right, bottom, left) order

b              o           x              e              s
=
face_recognition.face_locations(rgb,number_of_times_to_
upsample=2)
        # This encodings here will return a list of 128-dimensional
face encodings (one for each face in the image)
        encodings = face_recognition.face_encodings(rgb, boxes)
        # initialize the list of names for each face detected
        names = []
        count=0
        # loop over the facial embeddings
        for encoding in encodings:
            # attempt to match each face in the input image to
our known
            # encodings
            # Here this returns the TRUE/FALSE values onthe basis
of correct matching against tolerance
            matches = face_recognition.compare_faces(data["encodi
ngs"],encoding,tolerance=0.40)
            name = "Unknown"
            # check to see if we have found a match
            # enumerate them as to get the index of the "TRUE"
match which further used to detect names
            for (i,b) in enumerate(matches):
                if b==True:
                    # As if true at that particular index than
apend the name in the "names" list
                    names.append(data["names"][i])
                    count+=1
                    # Now here the face distance is calculated,
which is eucledian distance between the two facial encodings
                    # and then the confidence is showed
                conf = round((1.0-nmp.linalg.norm(data["encodings"]
[i]-encoding))*100,2)
                    # stopEvent = threading.Event()
                # thread = threading.Thread(target=savedetails,
```

```
args=())
                              # thread.start()
                         break
              # update the list of "names" as if count=0 which means
that "No Match" with database
                 if count==0:
                     names.append(name)
           # loop over the recognized faces
         for ((top, right, bottom, left), name) in zip(boxes, names):
                 top *= 4
                 right *= 4
                 bottom *= 4
                 left *= 4
                 # draw the predicted face name on the image
                 if name=="Unknown":
                     cv2.rectangle(image, (left, top), (right, bottom),
(0, 255, 0), 2)
                        cv2.rectangle(image, (left, bottom - 35), (right,
bottom), (0, 255, 0), cv2.FILLED)
                        cv2.putText(image, name, (left+15, bottom-6), cv2.
FONT_HERSHEY_DUPLEX,  1.0,  (255,  255,  255),  5,  lineType=cv2.
LINE_AA)
                 else:
                     cv2.rectangle(image, (left, top), (right, bottom),
(0, 0, 255), 2)
                        cv2.rectangle(image, (left, bottom - 35), (right,
bottom), (0, 0, 255), cv2.FILLED)
                        cv2.putText(image, name, (left+15, bottom-6), cv2.
FONT_HERSHEY_DUPLEX,  1.0,  (255,  255,  255),  5,  lineType=cv2.
LINE_AA)
                        cv2.putText(image, str(conf) , (right, top), cv2.
FONT_HERSHEY_DUPLEX, 1.0, (0, 0, 255), 3, lineType=cv2.LINE_AA)
              # This is to show the image as frame-by-frame in terms
of video
             cv2.imshow('FRAME',image)
             if cv2.waitKey(1) & 0xFF== ord('q'):
                 break
      # When everything done, release the capture
      cap.release()
      # stopEvent.set()
      cv2.destroyAllWindows()

func()
```

Appendix IV

```
Model: "sequential_2"

_____
Layer (type)                  Output Shape             Param #
=================================================================
conv2d_11 (Conv2D)            (None, 3, 150, 16)         21616

conv2d_12 (Conv2D)            (None, 3, 150, 16)          2320

max_pooling2d_6 (MaxPooling2  (None, 1, 75, 16)             0

conv2d_13 (Conv2D)            (None, 1, 75, 32)           4640

conv2d_14 (Conv2D)            (None, 1, 75, 32)           9248

max_pooling2d_7 (MaxPooling2  (None, 1, 38, 32)             0

conv2d_15 (Conv2D)            (None, 1, 38, 64)          18496

conv2d_16 (Conv2D)            (None, 1, 38, 64)          36928

max_pooling2d_8 (MaxPooling2  (None, 1, 19, 64)             0

conv2d_17 (Conv2D)            (None, 1, 19, 96)          55392

conv2d_18 (Conv2D)            (None, 1, 19, 96)          83040

max_pooling2d_9 (MaxPooling2  (None, 1, 10, 96)             0

conv2d_19 (Conv2D)            (None, 1, 10, 128)        110720


conv2d_20 (Conv2D)            (None, 1, 10, 128)        147584

max_pooling2d_10 (MaxPooling  (None, 1, 5, 128)             0

flatten_2 (Flatten)          (None, 640)                   0

dense_3 (Dense)              (None, 64)                41024

dropout_2 (Dropout)          (None, 64)                    0

dense_4 (Dense)              (None, 2)                   130
=================================================================
Total params: 531,138
Trainable params: 531,138
Non-trainable params: 0
_____

None
```

© The Editor(s) (if applicable) and The Author(s), under exclusive license to
Springer Nature Switzerland AG 2023
K. N. Mishra, S. C. Pandey, *Cloud-IoT Technologies in Society 5.0*,
https://doi.org/10.1007/978-3-031-28711-4

Appendix V

```
Model: "model_1"

Layer (type)                    Output Shape         Param #    Connected to
==================================================================================
input_1 (InputLayer)            (None, 150, 150, 3)  0

conv2d_1 (Conv2D)               (None, 74, 74, 32)   864        input_1[0][0]

batch_normalization_1 (BatchNor (None, 74, 74, 32)   96         conv2d_1[0][0]

activation_1 (Activation)       (None, 74, 74, 32)   0          batch_normalization_1[0][0]

conv2d_2 (Conv2D)               (None, 72, 72, 32)   9216       activation_1[0][0]

batch_normalization_2 (BatchNor (None, 72, 72, 32)   96         conv2d_2[0][0]

activation_2 (Activation)       (None, 72, 72, 32)   0          batch_normalization_2[0][0]

conv2d_3 (Conv2D)               (None, 72, 72, 64)   18432      activation_2[0][0]
```

```
batch_normalization_3 (BatchNor (None, 72, 72, 64)   192        conv2d_3[0][0]

activation_3 (Activation)       (None, 72, 72, 64)   0          batch_normalization_3[0][0]

max_pooling2d_1 (MaxPooling2D)  (None, 35, 35, 64)   0          activation_3[0][0]

conv2d_4 (Conv2D)               (None, 35, 35, 80)   5120       max_pooling2d_1[0][0]

batch_normalization_4 (BatchNor (None, 35, 35, 80)   240        conv2d_4[0][0]

activation_4 (Activation)       (None, 35, 35, 80)   0          batch_normalization_4[0][0]

conv2d_5 (Conv2D)               (None, 33, 33, 192)  138240     activation_4[0][0]

batch_normalization_5 (BatchNor (None, 33, 33, 192)  576        conv2d_5[0][0]

activation_5 (Activation)       (None, 33, 33, 192)  0          batch_normalization_5[0][0]

max_pooling2d_2 (MaxPooling2D)  (None, 16, 16, 192)  0          activation_5[0][0]
```

© The Editor(s) (if applicable) and The Author(s), under exclusive license to
Springer Nature Switzerland AG 2023
K. N. Mishra, S. C. Pandey, *Cloud-IoT Technologies in Society 5.0*,
https://doi.org/10.1007/978-3-031-28711-4

Appendix VI

conv2d_9 (Conv2D)	(None, 16, 16, 64)	12288	max_pooling2d_2[0][0]
batch_normalization_9 (BatchNor	(None, 16, 16, 64)	192	conv2d_9[0][0]
activation_9 (Activation)	(None, 16, 16, 64)	0	batch_normalization_9[0][0]
conv2d_7 (Conv2D)	(None, 16, 16, 48)	9216	max_pooling2d_2[0][0]
conv2d_10 (Conv2D)	(None, 16, 16, 96)	55296	activation_9[0][0]
batch_normalization_7 (BatchNor	(None, 16, 16, 48)	144	conv2d_7[0][0]
batch_normalization_10 (BatchNo	(None, 16, 16, 96)	288	conv2d_10[0][0]
activation_7 (Activation)	(None, 16, 16, 48)	0	batch_normalization_7[0][0]
activation_10 (Activation)	(None, 16, 16, 96)	0	batch_normalization_10[0][0]
average_pooling2d_1 (AveragePoo	(None, 16, 16, 192)	0	max_pooling2d_2[0][0]
conv2d_6 (Conv2D)	(None, 16, 16, 64)	12288	max_pooling2d_2[0][0]
conv2d_8 (Conv2D)	(None, 16, 16, 64)	76800	activation_7[0][0]
conv2d_11 (Conv2D)	(None, 16, 16, 96)	82944	activation_10[0][0]
conv2d_12 (Conv2D)	(None, 16, 16, 32)	6144	average_pooling2d_1[0][0]
batch_normalization_6 (BatchNor	(None, 16, 16, 64)	192	conv2d_6[0][0]
batch_normalization_8 (BatchNor	(None, 16, 16, 64)	192	conv2d_8[0][0]
batch_normalization_11 (BatchNo	(None, 16, 16, 96)	288	conv2d_11[0][0]
batch_normalization_12 (BatchNo	(None, 16, 16, 32)	96	conv2d_12[0][0]
activation_6 (Activation)	(None, 16, 16, 64)	0	batch_normalization_6[0][0]
activation_8 (Activation)	(None, 16, 16, 64)	0	batch_normalization_8[0][0]
activation_11 (Activation)	(None, 16, 16, 96)	0	batch_normalization_11[0][0]
activation_12 (Activation)	(None, 16, 16, 32)	0	batch_normalization_12[0][0]
mixed0 (Concatenate)	(None, 16, 16, 256)	0	activation_6[0][0] activation_8[0][0] activation_11[0][0] activation_12[0][0]
conv2d_16 (Conv2D)	(None, 16, 16, 64)	16384	mixed0[0][0]
batch_normalization_16 (BatchNo	(None, 16, 16, 64)	192	conv2d_16[0][0]
activation_16 (Activation)	(None, 16, 16, 64)	0	batch_normalization_16[0][0]
conv2d_14 (Conv2D)	(None, 16, 16, 48)	12288	mixed0[0][0]
conv2d_17 (Conv2D)	(None, 16, 16, 96)	55296	activation_16[0][0]

Appendix VII

batch_normalization_14 (BatchNo	(None, 16, 16, 48)	144	conv2d_14[0][0]
batch_normalization_17 (BatchNo	(None, 16, 16, 96)	288	conv2d_17[0][0]
activation_14 (Activation)	(None, 16, 16, 48)	0	batch_normalization_14[0][0]
activation_17 (Activation)	(None, 16, 16, 96)	0	batch_normalization_17[0][0]
average_pooling2d_2 (AveragePoo	(None, 16, 16, 256)	0	mixed0[0][0]
conv2d_13 (Conv2D)	(None, 16, 16, 64)	16384	mixed0[0][0]
conv2d_15 (Conv2D)	(None, 16, 16, 64)	76800	activation_14[0][0]
conv2d_18 (Conv2D)	(None, 16, 16, 96)	82944	activation_17[0][0]
conv2d_19 (Conv2D)	(None, 16, 16, 64)	16384	average_pooling2d_2[0][0]
batch_normalization_13 (BatchNo	(None, 16, 16, 64)	192	conv2d_13[0][0]
batch_normalization_15 (BatchNo	(None, 16, 16, 64)	192	conv2d_15[0][0]
batch_normalization_18 (BatchNo	(None, 16, 16, 96)	288	conv2d_18[0][0]
batch_normalization_19 (BatchNo	(None, 16, 16, 64)	192	conv2d_19[0][0]
activation_13 (Activation)	(None, 16, 16, 64)	0	batch_normalization_13[0][0]
activation_15 (Activation)	(None, 16, 16, 64)	0	batch_normalization_15[0][0]
activation_18 (Activation)	(None, 16, 16, 96)	0	batch_normalization_18[0][0]
activation_19 (Activation)	(None, 16, 16, 64)	0	batch_normalization_19[0][0]
mixed1 (Concatenate)	(None, 16, 16, 288)	0	activation_13[0][0] activation_15[0][0] activation_18[0][0] activation_19[0][0]

Appendix VIII

conv2d_23 (Conv2D)	(None, 16, 16, 64)	18432	mixed1[0][0]
batch_normalization_23 (BatchNo	(None, 16, 16, 64)	192	conv2d_23[0][0]
activation_23 (Activation)	(None, 16, 16, 64)	0	batch_normalization_23[0][0]
conv2d_21 (Conv2D)	(None, 16, 16, 48)	13824	mixed1[0][0]
conv2d_24 (Conv2D)	(None, 16, 16, 96)	55296	activation_23[0][0]
batch_normalization_21 (BatchNo	(None, 16, 16, 48)	144	conv2d_21[0][0]
batch_normalization_24 (BatchNo	(None, 16, 16, 96)	288	conv2d_24[0][0]
activation_21 (Activation)	(None, 16, 16, 48)	0	batch_normalization_21[0][0]
activation_24 (Activation)	(None, 16, 16, 96)	0	batch_normalization_24[0][0]
average_pooling2d_3 (AveragePoo	(None, 16, 16, 288)	0	mixed1[0][0]
conv2d_20 (Conv2D)	(None, 16, 16, 64)	18432	mixed1[0][0]
conv2d_22 (Conv2D)	(None, 16, 16, 64)	76800	activation_21[0][0]
conv2d_25 (Conv2D)	(None, 16, 16, 96)	82944	activation_24[0][0]
conv2d_26 (Conv2D)	(None, 16, 16, 64)	18432	average_pooling2d_3[0][0]
batch_normalization_20 (BatchNo	(None, 16, 16, 64)	192	conv2d_20[0][0]
batch_normalization_22 (BatchNo	(None, 16, 16, 64)	192	conv2d_22[0][0]
batch_normalization_25 (BatchNo	(None, 16, 16, 96)	288	conv2d_25[0][0]
batch_normalization_26 (BatchNo	(None, 16, 16, 64)	192	conv2d_26[0][0]
activation_20 (Activation)	(None, 16, 16, 64)	0	batch_normalization_20[0][0]
activation_22 (Activation)	(None, 16, 16, 64)	0	batch_normalization_22[0][0]
activation_25 (Activation)	(None, 16, 16, 96)	0	batch_normalization_25[0][0]
activation_26 (Activation)	(None, 16, 16, 64)	0	batch_normalization_26[0][0]
mixed2 (Concatenate)	(None, 16, 16, 288)	0	activation_20[0][0] activation_22[0][0] activation_25[0][0] activation_26[0][0]
conv2d_28 (Conv2D)	(None, 16, 16, 64)	18432	mixed2[0][0]
batch_normalization_28 (BatchNo	(None, 16, 16, 64)	192	conv2d_28[0][0]
activation_28 (Activation)	(None, 16, 16, 64)	0	batch_normalization_28[0][0]
conv2d_29 (Conv2D)	(None, 16, 16, 96)	55296	activation_28[0][0]
batch_normalization_29 (BatchNo	(None, 16, 16, 96)	288	conv2d_29[0][0]

Appendix IX

Layer	Output Shape	Param #	Connected to
activation_29 (Activation)	(None, 16, 16, 96)	0	batch_normalization_29[0][0]
conv2d_27 (Conv2D)	(None, 7, 7, 384)	995328	mixed2[0][0]
conv2d_30 (Conv2D)	(None, 7, 7, 96)	82944	activation_29[0][0]
batch_normalization_27 (BatchNo	(None, 7, 7, 384)	1152	conv2d_27[0][0]
batch_normalization_30 (BatchNo	(None, 7, 7, 96)	288	conv2d_30[0][0]
activation_27 (Activation)	(None, 7, 7, 384)	0	batch_normalization_27[0][0]
activation_30 (Activation)	(None, 7, 7, 96)	0	batch_normalization_30[0][0]
max_pooling2d_3 (MaxPooling2D)	(None, 7, 7, 288)	0	mixed2[0][0]
mixed3 (Concatenate)	(None, 7, 7, 768)	0	activation_27[0][0] activation_30[0][0] max_pooling2d_3[0][0]
batch_normalization_35 (BatchNo	(None, 7, 7, 128)	384	conv2d_35[0][0]
activation_35 (Activation)	(None, 7, 7, 128)	0	batch_normalization_35[0][0]
conv2d_36 (Conv2D)	(None, 7, 7, 128)	114688	activation_35[0][0]
batch_normalization_36 (BatchNo	(None, 7, 7, 128)	384	conv2d_36[0][0]
activation_36 (Activation)	(None, 7, 7, 128)	0	batch_normalization_36[0][0]
conv2d_32 (Conv2D)	(None, 7, 7, 128)	98304	mixed3[0][0]
conv2d_37 (Conv2D)	(None, 7, 7, 128)	114688	activation_36[0][0]
batch_normalization_32 (BatchNo	(None, 7, 7, 128)	384	conv2d_32[0][0]
batch_normalization_37 (BatchNo	(None, 7, 7, 128)	384	conv2d_37[0][0]
activation_32 (Activation)	(None, 7, 7, 128)	0	batch_normalization_32[0][0]
activation_37 (Activation)	(None, 7, 7, 128)	0	batch_normalization_37[0][0]
conv2d_33 (Conv2D)	(None, 7, 7, 128)	114688	activation_32[0][0]
conv2d_38 (Conv2D)	(None, 7, 7, 128)	114688	activation_37[0][0]
batch_normalization_33 (BatchNo	(None, 7, 7, 128)	384	conv2d_33[0][0]
batch_normalization_38 (BatchNo	(None, 7, 7, 128)	384	conv2d_38[0][0]
activation_33 (Activation)	(None, 7, 7, 128)	0	batch_normalization_33[0][0]
activation_38 (Activation)	(None, 7, 7, 128)	0	batch_normalization_38[0][0]
average_pooling2d_4 (AveragePoo	(None, 7, 7, 768)	0	mixed3[0][0]
conv2d_31 (Conv2D)	(None, 7, 7, 192)	147456	mixed3[0][0]
conv2d_34 (Conv2D)	(None, 7, 7, 192)	172032	activation_33[0][0]

Appendix X

conv2d_39 (Conv2D)	(None, 7, 7, 192)	172032	activation_38[0][0]
conv2d_40 (Conv2D)	(None, 7, 7, 192)	147456	average_pooling2d_4[0][0]
batch_normalization_31 (BatchNo	(None, 7, 7, 192)	576	conv2d_31[0][0]
batch_normalization_34 (BatchNo	(None, 7, 7, 192)	576	conv2d_34[0][0]
batch_normalization_39 (BatchNo	(None, 7, 7, 192)	576	conv2d_39[0][0]
batch_normalization_40 (BatchNo	(None, 7, 7, 192)	576	conv2d_40[0][0]
activation_31 (Activation)	(None, 7, 7, 192)	0	batch_normalization_31[0][0]
activation_34 (Activation)	(None, 7, 7, 192)	0	batch_normalization_34[0][0]
activation_39 (Activation)	(None, 7, 7, 192)	0	batch_normalization_39[0][0]
activation_40 (Activation)	(None, 7, 7, 192)	0	batch_normalization_40[0][0]
mixed4 (Concatenate)	(None, 7, 7, 768)	0	activation_31[0][0] activation_34[0][0] activation_39[0][0] activation_40[0][0]
conv2d_45 (Conv2D)	(None, 7, 7, 160)	122880	mixed4[0][0]
batch_normalization_45 (BatchNo	(None, 7, 7, 160)	480	conv2d_45[0][0]
activation_45 (Activation)	(None, 7, 7, 160)	0	batch_normalization_45[0][0]
conv2d_46 (Conv2D)	(None, 7, 7, 160)	179200	activation_45[0][0]
batch_normalization_46 (BatchNo	(None, 7, 7, 160)	480	conv2d_46[0][0]
activation_46 (Activation)	(None, 7, 7, 160)	0	batch_normalization_46[0][0]
conv2d_42 (Conv2D)	(None, 7, 7, 160)	122880	mixed4[0][0]
conv2d_47 (Conv2D)	(None, 7, 7, 160)	179200	activation_46[0][0]
batch_normalization_42 (BatchNo	(None, 7, 7, 160)	480	conv2d_42[0][0]
batch_normalization_47 (BatchNo	(None, 7, 7, 160)	480	conv2d_47[0][0]
activation_42 (Activation)	(None, 7, 7, 160)	0	batch_normalization_42[0][0]
activation_47 (Activation)	(None, 7, 7, 160)	0	batch_normalization_47[0][0]
conv2d_43 (Conv2D)	(None, 7, 7, 160)	179200	activation_42[0][0]
conv2d_48 (Conv2D)	(None, 7, 7, 160)	179200	activation_47[0][0]
batch_normalization_43 (BatchNo	(None, 7, 7, 160)	480	conv2d_43[0][0]
batch_normalization_48 (BatchNo	(None, 7, 7, 160)	480	conv2d_48[0][0]
activation_43 (Activation)	(None, 7, 7, 160)	0	batch_normalization_43[0][0]

Appendix XI

activation_48 (Activation)	(None, 7, 7, 160)	0	batch_normalization_48[0][0]
average_pooling2d_5 (AveragePoo	(None, 7, 7, 768)	0	mixed4[0][0]
conv2d_41 (Conv2D)	(None, 7, 7, 192)	147456	mixed4[0][0]
conv2d_44 (Conv2D)	(None, 7, 7, 192)	215040	activation_43[0][0]
conv2d_49 (Conv2D)	(None, 7, 7, 192)	215040	activation_48[0][0]
conv2d_50 (Conv2D)	(None, 7, 7, 192)	147456	average_pooling2d_5[0][0]
batch_normalization_41 (BatchNo	(None, 7, 7, 192)	576	conv2d_41[0][0]
batch_normalization_44 (BatchNo	(None, 7, 7, 192)	576	conv2d_44[0][0]
batch_normalization_49 (BatchNo	(None, 7, 7, 192)	576	conv2d_49[0][0]
batch_normalization_50 (BatchNo	(None, 7, 7, 192)	576	conv2d_50[0][0]
activation_41 (Activation)	(None, 7, 7, 192)	0	batch_normalization_41[0][0]
activation_44 (Activation)	(None, 7, 7, 192)	0	batch_normalization_44[0][0]
activation_49 (Activation)	(None, 7, 7, 192)	0	batch_normalization_49[0][0]
activation_50 (Activation)	(None, 7, 7, 192)	0	batch_normalization_50[0][0]
mixed5 (Concatenate)	(None, 7, 7, 768)	0	activation_41[0][0] activation_44[0][0] activation_49[0][0] activation_50[0][0]
conv2d_55 (Conv2D)	(None, 7, 7, 160)	122880	mixed5[0][0]
batch_normalization_55 (BatchNo	(None, 7, 7, 160)	480	conv2d_55[0][0]
activation_55 (Activation)	(None, 7, 7, 160)	0	batch_normalization_55[0][0]
conv2d_56 (Conv2D)	(None, 7, 7, 160)	179200	activation_55[0][0]
batch_normalization_56 (BatchNo	(None, 7, 7, 160)	480	conv2d_56[0][0]
activation_56 (Activation)	(None, 7, 7, 160)	0	batch_normalization_56[0][0]
conv2d_52 (Conv2D)	(None, 7, 7, 160)	122880	mixed5[0][0]
conv2d_57 (Conv2D)	(None, 7, 7, 160)	179200	activation_56[0][0]
batch_normalization_52 (BatchNo	(None, 7, 7, 160)	480	conv2d_52[0][0]
batch_normalization_57 (BatchNo	(None, 7, 7, 160)	480	conv2d_57[0][0]
activation_52 (Activation)	(None, 7, 7, 160)	0	batch_normalization_52[0][0]
activation_57 (Activation)	(None, 7, 7, 160)	0	batch_normalization_57[0][0]
conv2d_53 (Conv2D)	(None, 7, 7, 160)	179200	activation_52[0][0]

Appendix XII

© The Editor(s) (if applicable) and The Author(s), under exclusive license to
Springer Nature Switzerland AG 2023
K. N. Mishra, S. C. Pandey, *Cloud-IoT Technologies in Society 5.0*,
https://doi.org/10.1007/978-3-031-28711-4

conv2d_58 (Conv2D)	(None, 7, 7, 160)	179200	activation_57[0][0]
batch_normalization_53 (BatchNo	(None, 7, 7, 160)	480	conv2d_53[0][0]
batch_normalization_58 (BatchNo	(None, 7, 7, 160)	480	conv2d_58[0][0]
activation_53 (Activation)	(None, 7, 7, 160)	0	batch_normalization_53[0][0]
activation_58 (Activation)	(None, 7, 7, 160)	0	batch_normalization_58[0][0]
average_pooling2d_6 (AveragePoo	(None, 7, 7, 768)	0	mixed5[0][0]
conv2d_51 (Conv2D)	(None, 7, 7, 192)	147456	mixed5[0][0]
conv2d_54 (Conv2D)	(None, 7, 7, 192)	215040	activation_53[0][0]
conv2d_59 (Conv2D)	(None, 7, 7, 192)	215040	activation_58[0][0]
conv2d_60 (Conv2D)	(None, 7, 7, 192)	147456	average_pooling2d_6[0][0]
batch_normalization_51 (BatchNo	(None, 7, 7, 192)	576	conv2d_51[0][0]
batch_normalization_54 (BatchNo	(None, 7, 7, 192)	576	conv2d_54[0][0]
batch_normalization_59 (BatchNo	(None, 7, 7, 192)	576	conv2d_59[0][0]
batch_normalization_60 (BatchNo	(None, 7, 7, 192)	576	conv2d_60[0][0]
activation_51 (Activation)	(None, 7, 7, 192)	0	batch_normalization_51[0][0]
activation_54 (Activation)	(None, 7, 7, 192)	0	batch_normalization_54[0][0]
activation_59 (Activation)	(None, 7, 7, 192)	0	batch_normalization_59[0][0]
activation_60 (Activation)	(None, 7, 7, 192)	0	batch_normalization_60[0][0]
mixed6 (Concatenate)	(None, 7, 7, 768)	0	activation_51[0][0]
			activation_54[0][0]
			activation_59[0][0]
			activation_60[0][0]

dropout_1 (Dropout)	(None, 3, 3, 2048)	0	mixed10[0][0]
global_average_pooling2d_1 (Glo	(None, 2048)	0	dropout_1[0][0]
dense_1 (Dense)	(None, 128)	262272	global_average_pooling2d_1[0][0]
batch_normalization_95 (BatchNo	(None, 128)	512	dense_1[0][0]
dense_2 (Dense)	(None, 2)	258	batch_normalization_95[0][0]

```
==================================================================================
Total params: 22,065,826
Trainable params: 22,031,138
Non-trainable params: 34,688
```

None

Index

Printed in the United States
by Baker & Taylor Publisher Services